THE UNDERCURRENT OF FEMININE PHILOSOPHY IN EASTERN AND WESTERN THOUGHT

Sandra A. Wawrytko

UNIVERSITY
PRESS OF
AMERICA

Copyright © 1976, 1981 by **Sandra Ann Wawrytko**

(originally titled *The Philosophical Systematization of a 'Feminine' Perspective in terms of Taoism's "Tao Te Ching" and the Works of Spinoza*)

University Press of America, Inc.
P.O. Box 19101, Washington, D.C. 20036

All rights reserved
Printed in the United States of America
ISBN: 0-8191-2068-5 (Perfect)
ISBN: 0-8191-2067-7 (Cloth)

BD
450
.W33
1981

Library of Congress Catalog Card Number: 81-40591

Dedicated to my mother,
ALYCE CIOCH WAWRYTKO
my personal archetype of
das Ewig-Weibliche.

ACKNOWLEDGEMENTS

I would like to take this opportunity to acknowledge the generous assistance given to me by numerous individuals during the preparation and composition of this text, originally written as a doctoral dissertation, and to extend my deepest gratitude to all concerned. First and foremost, I would like to thank all the members of my dissertation committee for their well-considered criticisms and recommendations of my work as it progressed: Jerome Schiller, for consenting to serve as chairperson of my committee, for his invaluable support in the face of the initial difficulties with the topic, and for his profound patience throughout our long discussions concerning the text; to Joyce Trebilcot I am similarly indebted for long and fruitful hours of discussion, which served to clairify my objectives in my own mind; Richard Popkin, for devoting his time to a careful reading and correction of the chapter on Spinoza as well as for his scholarly lectures which led me to a deep appreciation of and a new way of looking at Spinozistic philosophy; Robert Hegel for his well-appreciated and incisive suggestions for revising the treatment of Taoistic thought; Stanley Spector, for his generous offer to serve on the committee and his enthusiastic involvement during the initial stages of work on the dissertation.

I also would like to thank all the faculty members of the philosophy department of Washington University who served as exemplary models of good scholarship, both directly and indirectly, and Washington University itself for providing the fellowship which supported my early research. Outside of the University I am indebted to Dr. Mikiso Hane, of Knox College, for promoting my initial interest in Chinese philosophy and for his subsequent encouragement of my continuing studies; and to my honored friend, Chen I-Chuan, for the sympathetic reception he has always given to my ideas, and his own ideas offered during our frequent philosophical dialogues.

For support of a more personal kind I am indebted to my family and friends: to my mother, Alyce Cioch Wawrytko, a perpetual source of inspiration, for her love, encouragement, and sacrifices through the years;

to Gil Ontai, both husband and very special friend, for being a constant source of comfort, both tangible and intangible, and for his great reserves of good humor which have sustained my spirits; to my brother Stephen, who has shared the academic experience with me and has been instrumental in making my education possible. And I would like to thank JoAnn Caster for her patience and professionalism in surviving the trials of typing the final draft.

Finally, I would like to extend my gratitude to the University Press of America for the opportunity to bring this work to publication.

TABLE OF CONTENTS

	Page
ACKNOWLEDGEMENTS	v
ABBREVIATIONS	xi
INTRODUCTION	xiii

Chapter

I. THE FEMININE/MASCULINE POLARITY 1

    A. Establishing the Dichotomy of Perspectives 1

        1. Yin and Yang 3

        2. Contemporary Approaches to Polarity 7

            a. The Biological approach . . . 8
            b. The Cultural approach 11
            c. The Symbolic approach 13

    B. An Exploration of the Feminine Principle 15

        1. Manifestations of the Feminine Principle 17

            a. The Elementary character . . 19
            b. The Transformative character. 24

        2. Modes of Being Under the Feminine Principle 28

            a. Inwardness/all-is-one-ness . 29
            b. Receptivity/non-assertion . . 32
            c. The link with Nature/ materiality 35

    C. Implications of the Feminine Principle for Socio-Political Organization 38

TABLE OF CONTENTS (continued)

				Page
	Summary			46
II.	THE YIN PHILOSOPHY OF THE <u>TAO TE CHING</u> .			49
	A.	The Manifestations of Tao--Theoretical Foundation		51
		1.	Metaphysical Manifestations: The Structure of the Universe .	51
		2.	The Dual Characters of Tao . . .	52
			a. Nameless Tao--the Elementary character	55
			b. The Ten Thousand Things of Named Tao--the Transformative character	62
		3.	Epistemology: The Process of Enlightenment	69
	B.	Modes of Being Through Tao		83
		1.	Ethics: The Individual's Enlightenment Path	84
			a. Inwardness--the Tao of humanity, <u>Te</u>	86
			b. Receptivity--the sage ideal	97
			c. Materiality--the link with Nature	114
		2.	Socio-Political Implications: The Enlightened Taoist State . .	119
			a. The communal sense--all-is-oneness.	120
			b. The non-assertion of the sage/ruler	125
			c. Harmony with Nature and Tao	134
III.	SPINOZISM AS A FEMININE PHILOSOPHY . .			139
	A.	The Manifestations of Substance:		

viii

TABLE OF CONTENTS (continued)

		Page
Theoretical Foundations		141

    1. The Metaphysics of the One: The Structure of the Universe 141

    2. The Dual Characters of Substance   145

        a. <u>Natura Naturans</u>--the Elementary character 147
        b. <u>Natura Naturata</u>--the Transformative character . . 153

    3. Epistemology: The Dynamics of Blessedness 164

        a. The levels of knowledge . . . 165
        b. The dual roles of intellect . 173
        c. The knowledge/experience of blessedness 184

  B. Modes of Being: Philosophy as <u>Praxis</u>   192

    1. Ethics: Relating to the Universe   194

        a. Inwardness--the perfection of human virtue/power 195
        b. Receptivity--the philosopher ideal 209
        c. Materiality--the link with Nature 225

    2. Socio-Political Implications: The Enlightened Commonwealth 233

        a. All-is-one-ness--the single mind of the commonwealth . . 236
        b. Non-assertion--the balance of citizen and sovereign 251
        c. The commonwealth in harmony with Nature 263

IV. CONCLUSIONS CONCERNING FEMININE 269

    APPENDICES 279

TABLE OF CONTENTS (continued)

		Page
I.	Standard Interpretations of the Spinozistic System	279
II.	Individual Responsibility in a Deterministic Universe	280
	NOTES	285
	GLOSSARY	314
	LIST OF WORKS CONSULTED	319
	INDEX	325

Abbreviations

E   Ethic, trans. W. H. White, contained in John Wild's ed. Spinoza Selections (New York: Charles Scribner's Sons, 1958); references indicated by part, proposition, etc.

IU   On the Improvement of the Understanding, Elwes, Bohn trans., from Wild's Spinoza Selections; cited by page references.

PT   A Political Treatise, trans. R. H. M. Elwes in Vol. 1 of The Chief Works of Benedict de Spinoza (New York: Dover Publications, Inc., 1951); references indicated by chapter.

ST   Short Treatise on God, Man, and His Well-Being, trans. and ed. A. Wolf (New York: Russell and Russell, Inc., 1963); references made by part and chapter.

TM   Thoughts on Metaphysics, Spinoza's appendix to The Principles of the Philosophy of Renè Descartes, trans. Frank A. Hayes in Earlier Philosophical Writings (New York: Bobbs-Merrill Company, Inc., 1963); referred to by part, chapter, and paragraph.

TP   Theologico-Political Treatise, trans. Elwes and contained in Vol. 1 of Chief Works; cited by chapter.

TTC   The Lao Tzu (Tao-Te Ching), trans. Wing-tsit Chan and contained in his A Source Book in Chinese Philosophy (Princeton, New Jersey: Princeton University Press, 1963); referred to by chapter.

INTRODUCTION

Dualistic classifications of schools of thought are frequently encountered within philosophical discussions, and perhaps occur with greater frequency there than in other disciplines. The student of philosophy is quite early beset with a sequence of either/or labels; empiricist versus rationalist, idealist/materialist, nominalist/realist, and, once considered essential in the assessment of a fellow philosopher, Platonist/Aristotelian. Thus, it is with little hesitation, and with the prospect of remedying a noticeable oversight in the accepted classificatory range of philosophy, that I propose to deal with yet another, possibly the most primal, polarity--the feminine perspective set in contrast to the masculine.

The essence of the feminine Weltanschauung as foundation of an alternative philosophy of life, of ontology, of epistemology, and of ethics, is set forth in preliminary form in the following pages. Given this essence, it is feasible to infer an entire life style, encompassing intellectual, religious, and political elements, which promises to be of scholarly interest as well as offering intriguing solutions to those perennial problems which are the proper task of the philosophical enterprise: What is truth? reality? the Good? The risk involved in entering such an obscure realm of thought is more than compensated for by the prospect of revitalizing values which have tended to be neglected due to the dominance of "masculine" philosophy in our own culture.

In view of the modern movement to socially and politically equalize the sexes, this study might be interpreted as one response to Margaret Mead's warning that "removal of all legal and economic barriers against women's participating in the world on an equal footing with men may be in itself a standardizing move towards the wholesale stamping out of the diversity of attitudes that is such a dearly brought product of civilization."[1] The individual woman's demand for justice and equality cannot be ignored, but perhaps diversity can be spared. To forestall the sacrifice of social complexity once sex discriminations have been de-mythologized, as threatened by the masculine

---

[1] Margaret Mead, Sex and Temperament in Three Primitive Societies (New York: William Morrow and Company, 1963), p. 316.

attitude of many modern feminists, it is necessary to investigate the set of values which traditionally have been assigned to women in this and other societies. This task can be accomplished by means of a coherent and biologically-abstracted systematization of the gender-based principles of being.

With the pronouncement regarding the very existence of a feminine/masculine distinction in philosophy, in all its generalistic glory, I immediately anticipate, and rightly so, outbursts of protest from such deverse sources as covertly sexist academics, hiding behind claims of impersonal scholarship, and outraged feminists, in search of liberated neuters. To quell the apprehensions of both dissenting extremes, I need only insist that the terms feminine and masculine, as employed here, are intended to refer exclusively to an individual's Weltanschauung, regardless of the sex of the person. Contrasexuality, the coexistence of feminine and masculine qualities, or its potential, is assumed to be inherent in all individuals. As Buytendijk has astutely observed, "Everything that passes as genuinely feminine is human, and everything that is human is able to be genuinely feminine."[2]

I also must disclaim any concern in this study with the politicization of sexuality. The discussion of the feminine perspective is not intended to provide either a supplement or alternative to current feminist views; the feminine perspective is not being recommended here as a new basis for feminist thought. Nonetheless, the goal of both women's and men's liberation may be advanced by a clarification of the dual Weltanschauungen responsible for a culture's discriminations between groups. The recognition of the feminine perspective's status independent of the female sex may help to release women from an identification, traditionally enforced by society, with "feminine" values and modes of being.

A distinctive perspective on the universe, a veritable way of life, is indicated by the various values and archetypes espoused by a philosophy, either consciously or unconsciously, which determine what it condones, encourages, or condemns. The entire feminine/masculine issue is pervaded by a polarity

---

[2] F. J. J. Buytendijk, Women: A Contemporary View, trans. Denis J. Barrett (New York: Newman Press and Association Press, 1968), p. 219.

founded on the way in which the elements of reality are interpreted by a given philosopher, in accordance with certain predispositions of thought. In reference to Jungian theories, dominant archetypes, the "pre-existing formative elements" said to alter our perceptions of the world, play a similar role. Jung declares that concepts of both religion and metaphysics are rooted in "archetypal foundations"; metaphysics in particular is "a physics or psychology of the archetype, and its dogma (or teaching) formulates the knowledge of the essence of dominants, that is, of unconscious 'leit-motives'."[3] Hence, philosophy absorbs the polarity manifest in sex-distinguished archetypes through the duality of perspectives.

The next obvious objection will be to the use of the sex-specified terms feminine and masculine when, in fact, the biological implications of female and male "nature" per se explicitly have been disavowed. The rationale for this terminology lies in the near-universal tradition of a dualism of the sexes, a primal polarity which readily can be applied to almost any set of extremes. The complementary and encompassing polarity of Chinese thought, Yin/Yang, represents a case in point; the receptivity of Yin was identified with the feminine outlook, while Yang's creativity was attributed to the masculine forces. Despite the recent surge of radical opposition to distinctions based on sex, certain sets of characteristics and modes of behavior have been in the past and continue in the present to be assigned to groups of human beings for no other apparent reason than biological development. The present task is not to question these assignments with regard to their appropriateness or inappropriateness, but rather to study the grouping of tendencies, and most especially of "feminine" tendencies, insofar as they cohere in a unique approach to the human condition and to the universe at large. To fulfill this task, it is necessary to refer to the well-known, if dubious, fund of sexual stereotypes insofar as they reveal the fundamental elements of the feminine/masculine polarity under two distinct principles of being.

A similar dichotomy based on perspective has been

---

[3] C. G. Jung's introduction to Woman's Mysteries--Ancient and Modern: A Psychological Interpretation of the Feminine Principle as Portrayed in Myth, Story, and Dreams, by M. Esther Harding (New York: Bantam Books, 1971), p. x.

advanced by Friedrich Nietzsche in the Apollonian/Dionysian distinction elaborated in The Birth of Tragedy. Two patterns of antithetical thought and behavior are discerned by Nietzsche within the context of ancient Greek culture: the "inner world of fantasy" guided by the principium individuationis and represented by the artist-intellectual Apollo (paralleling the masculine perspective as set forth here), as distinguished from the spirit and wine intoxicated "mystical Oneness" whose patron is the Nature deity Dionysos (identifiable with the feminine perspective).[4] Human imagination, the masculine, confronts the feminine reality of Nature; egotistical self-assertion challenges the overwhelming power of the cosmos experienced as one.

Also of note by way of philosophical precedence, is the polarity of anima and animus set forth by Gaston Bachelard. Extending the initial usages of these terms in Jungian psychology, Bachelard outlines two independent lives of the human soul, the masculine "social activity" of the animus as opposed to, and complemented by the solitary "feminine repose" of the anima.[5] Although the description of the masculine pole as outer appears to conflict with the inner fantasy assigned to it in Nietzsche's scheme, the two characterizations can be reconciled by pointing out the artificiality of human creativity as external to the reality of Nature, but internal in reference to the human individual. Correspondingly, the inward-turning feminine realm is supported by a microcosmic-macrocosmic view of reality, the Dionysian urge to harmonize with Nature. The Bachelardian vision of human fulfillment requires the presence of both elements, which together regulate all aspects of our complex being.

Given a dichotomy of perspectives, that is, of ways of perceiving reality, designated as feminine and masculine, it is possible to refine the criteria for a thinker's being identified as an adherent of either perspective. Those who share a certain view of the world are predisposed to approach things in a certain manner. By organizing the assumptions and attitudes

---

[4] Friedrich Nietzsche, The Birth of Tragedy, trans. Francis Golffing (Garden City, New York: Doubleday & Company, Inc., 1956), pp. 21, 23.

[5] Gaston Bachelard, The Poetics of Reverie: Childhood, Language, and the Cosmos, trans. Daniel Russell (Boston: Beacon Press, 1971), pp. 61, 63.

regarding reality shared by the adherents of a given perspective, a principle of being can be posited which follows from that perspective, a principle which underlies the forms of thought and modes of behavior of its adherents. Just as the feminine perspective engenders a feminine principle of being, this principle in turn gives rise, through a process of rigorous systematization, to philosophies which can be termed feminine.

The ultimate goal of this study is made clear through the gradual refinement from perspective to principle of being, and thence to philosophical system. Our purpose is not merely to demonstrate that philosophies can be deemed feminine, as opposed to masculine, but further, to present existing examples of feminine philosophy and of how an adherent of the feminine perspective, living in accordance with the feminine principle of being, might function within the limitations of the discipline of philosophy. One of the benefits of a feminine perspective is that a philosopher can offer unique, although not necessarily definitive, solutions to perennial problems. Thus, at the most fundamental level, a feminine philosophy complements masculine views and contributes to a balanced approach to reality. Furthermore, reference to a feminine/masculine polarity of perspective provides the philosophical critic with an additional and also a beneficial means of evaluating philosophies. The placement of a philosophical system at one of the two poles, or the identification of its elements as a synthesis of both perspectives, helps to clarify the underlying assumptions and values of the system's basic approach to reality, as well as indicating its primary goals.

The thought of Benedict de Spinoza, a prime product of the feminine perspective, has been chosen to introduce us to the realm of feminine philosophies, illustrating the feminine perspective and principle of being by means of a coherent and encompassing system. Spinoza's is a philosophy pervaded by feminine values, one which carries those values to their culmination in various areas- metaphysics, epistemology, ethics, and political theory. Given the unorthodoxy of many of his views, this choice is supported by Spinoza's outcast status in the Western, and largely masculine, tradition of philosophy. His uncertain status often has caused him to be ranked amoung the suspect fringe elements of mysticism. The *Ethics* has been declared to be metaphysically without parallel in modern times, as it presents a world view and corresponding life style seldomed equalled with respect to comprehensiveness.[6] And yet, as this study demonstrates, the values and implications of Spinoza's philosophy can be understood fully only within a feminine context of thought.

The Spinozistic system, with its unique conception of godhead, often is dismissed as simple pantheism, a convenient, although erroneous, means of categorization, which has the effect of consigning it to an acceptable philosophic pigeonhole. However, despite the many attempted interpretations which adopt a Procrustean approach, Spinoza's thought does not "fit" the standard criteria of philosophy. Those views which are "acceptable" have been stretched almost beyond recognition; simultaneously, other elements, judged inconsequential, have been lopped off. Thus, Spinoza, the philosopher of the whole, is read selectively, with great emphasis being placed on the metaphysics and epistemology of the first two parts of his masterwork, the Ethics, while little or no attention is paid to the ultimate goal set forth in the fifth and final part, itself a veritable primer of enlightenment. In contrast to this approach, we have Spinoza's own admission that he was in substantial disagreement with his contemporaries, in whose company he is usually placed, regarding views of godhead, and preferred to align himself with the opinions of St. Paul, the ancient philosophers (presumably Hellenic), and the Hebrew thinkers of old.[7]

Furthermore, pointing up Spinoza's alienation from the Western tradition of philosophy, he has been hailed as one of the few philosophers in the West to implement his philosophical doctrines in his own life. Wolf registers a masculine objection to this feminine tendency on Spinoza's part, judging that the latter lacked the power to detach the theoretical from "practical everyday life", a power which Wolf is tempted to describe as a "gift."[8] Spinoza seemingly was

---

[6] Stuart Hampshire, Spinoza (Baltimore, Maryland: Penguin Books, 1951, rev. 1962), p. 226.

[7] Spinoza to Henry Oldenburg, November or December of 1675; letter LXXIII. As trans. A. Wolf in his ed. The Correspondence of Spinoza (London: George Allen and Unwin, Ltd., 1928), p. 341.

[8] A. Wolf, in his introduction to Spinoza's Short Theatise on God, Man & His Well-Being (New York: Russell & Russell, Inc., 1963), p. xxxv.

incapable of distinguishing philosophy from reality, or reality from philosophy. Contrastingly, this "weakness" in character is embraced by the adherent of the feminine perspective as a sign of consistency.

As confirmation of Spinoza's philosophic femininity, the marked parallels between his thought and the self-acclaimed feminine or Yin philosophy of the Tao Te Ching have been taken into account in this study. The discussion of Taoist thought serves as a bridge linking the initial outline of the feminine principle of being to the systematic philosophy of Spinoza. Motivations and metaphysics, ethics and social proposals, overlap considerably in the two philosophies, a fact ultimately explicable by reference to a shared perspective on the universe, despite certain discrepancies in the matter of culturally-influenced details. Once the superficial imposition of socially-conditioned expressions has been stripped away from the Taoist and Spinozistic texts, two mutually-sympathetic philosophies emerge. Given the wide range of frequently contradictory translations of the Tao Te Ching available to English readers, I have chosen to restrict quotations, with few exceptions, to one of these interpreted translations. Wing-Tsit Chan's version has been selected as the work of a noted Chinese scholar, as well as one widely recognized in circles of Taoist study.

The difficulties of classical Chinese are forcibly evident for any translator, unavoidably casting one in the role of interpreter as well; the Sinologue James Legge has observed, "there is not so much as [sic] interpretation of the characters employed by the writer as a participation of his thoughts--there is the seeing of mind to mind."[9] These difficulties, however, also promote a wide freedom in reconstructing Taoist philosophy. Given the necessity of supplying mood, tense, gender, etc., to Chinese characters, no interpreter can claim to possess a definitive assessment of the Taoist system of thought. However, if for Taoism less in more, in terms of its terse style, the more provided by Spinoza often appears less than enough to establish firmly what his views are, as is demonstrated in the course of our study. Hence, a comparison of the two systems is instructive.

Various sources in Western philosophic circles

---

[9] As quoted in Raymond Van Over's introduction to his book Chinese Mystics (New York: Harper and Row, 1973), p. xxviii.

support the linking of Spinozistic and Taoist thought. Kant makes reference to a "Lao-Kuin", identified by Lewis Beck White as, in all probability, Lao Tzu, the reputed author of the Tao Te Ching. Both oriental philosophy and Spinozism, Kant asserts, "are closely akin to the primeval system of the emanation of human souls from the Godhead (and their final realization into it)."[10] A direct relationship between Tao and Spinoza's one substance is mentioned by Hegel, and cited as a general opinion of the time (with which, however, he himself hesitated to concur).[11]

The above observations are not meant to imply the historical claim that Spinoza had direct knowledge of Taoism; nor is it contended that Spinoza was a Taoist, latent or otherwise, or the Tao Te Ching a precursor of Spinozism. The two philosophies merely may be said to share a common Weltanschauung with respect to many important issues. Finally, given the textual evidence to the contrary,[12] there is no attempt made to cast Spinoza in the role of an enlightened advocate of feminism in terms of the female sex per se. The masculine, i.e., Judeo-Christian, influences upon Spinoza's thought manifest themselves in the course of our study, necessitating reconstructions of certain of his doctrines along more strictly feminine lines to preserve the consistency of Spinoza's system as a whole. Nonetheless, through a process of comparisons drawn between the Yin elements of Taoism and the feminine aspects of Spinozism, plus contrasts with standard masculine philosophies, the substance of a philosophical alter-

---

[10] Immanuel Kant, in his essay "The End of All Things", included in Beck's ed. collection of Kant's essays, On History; trans. Robert E. Anchor (New York: Bobbs-Merrill Company, Inc., 1963), p. 79.

[11] G. W. F. Hegel, Reason and History: A General Introduction to the Philosophy of History, trans. Robert S. Hartmann (New York: Bobbs-Merrill Company, Inc., 1953), p. 81.

[12] For example, citing the lack of cases in which women share the ruling power with men, or of societies in which traditional sex roles are reversed, Spinoza concludes "one may assert with perfect propriety that women have not equal right with men"; Political Treatise, XI, 4, Vol. 1 of R. H. M. Elwes' trans. The Chief Works of Benedict de Spinoza (New York: Dover Publications, Inc., 1951), p. 387.

native, to be designated feminine, can be seen to emerge.

What in effect has tended to occur in the philosophies of Western culture is that the (generally male) philosopher delineates cherished masculine values as the ideal of intellect and of society at large. The corresponding negations of those values, by a "logical" process of elimination, have been assigned to the female of the species, who therefore is judged to be the "weaker" or lesser sex in all significant respects. Among those inclined to philosophize in this manner, one discovers the "genius" of Aristotle,[13] Hegel,[14] and, of course, Schopenhauer.[15] It is precisely that

---

[13] "The female is less spirited than the male . . . softer in disposition . . . more mischievous, less simple, more impulsive . . . The fact is, the nature of man is the most rounded off and complete, and consequently in man the qualities or capacities above referred to are found in their perfection. Hence, woman is . . . more jealous, more querulous, more apt to scold and to strike . . . more prone to despondency and less hopeful . . . more void of shame or self-respect, more false of speech, more deceptive . . . more shrinking, more difficult to rouse to action." Aristotle, History of Animals, book ix, chapter 1 (608b), trans. D'Arcy Wentworth Thompson and included in Vol. 9 of the Great Books of the Western World, ed. Robert Maynard Hutchins (Chicago: Encyclopedia Britannica, Inc., 1971), pp. 133-34.

[14] "Women may have happy ideas, tastes, and elegance, but cannot attain to the ideal . . . Men correspond to animals, while women correspond to plants because their development is more placid and the principle that underlies it is the rather vague unity of feeling . . . women regulate their actions not by the demands of universality but by arbitrary inclinations and opinions." G. W. F. Hegel, Philosophy of Right, addition 107 to paragraph 166, trans. T. M. Knox (New York: Oxford University Press, 1967), pp. 263-64.

[15] Schopenhauer's works contain a "wealth" of misogynous observations. To quote but one example: " . . . women are as a rule inferior to men in the virtue of justice . . . Owing to the weakness of their reasoning faculty, they are far less capable than men of understanding and sticking to universal principles, and of taking them as a guide . . . On the other hand,

set of "negative" qualities attributed to the female, woman as "other", which has evoked contempt, and simultaneously, fear, from the masculine forces as constituting a threat to the latter's aspirations toward perfection. Masculine egotism feels challenged by feminine altruism, aggression by yielding (redefined here as receptivity), rationality by intuition, and individualism by a communal outlook.

In the Tao Te Ching explicitly, and in Spinoza's writings implicitly, the highly-esteemed masculine values have been subordinated to their feminine "negations", which thereupon attain a positive significance. The feminine values and qualities are held to be true expressions of the workings of the universe within a feminine context of thought. The "weakness" of woman, symbolizing the feminine realm in general, thus is exalted by Taoism. Patience, being receptive rather than uniformly aggressive, is a virtue; power is indicative of holding to one's true nature, understood in relation to Nature as a whole, not merely an attempt to exceed personal nature or conquer Nature, as in the masculine mode of being. In short, the point of view, the perspective, of the feminine mode confronts traditional masculine notions with other means and even other ends.

It is characteristic of the feminine attitude that masculine values are not dismissed summarily but rather are incorporated into its encompassing scheme of the universe. This attitude stands in direct opposition to the practice of masculine philosophy, which denounces its imagined rival with a vehemence proportionate to its distrust; e.g., the common rejection by Western philosophers of any elements of human nature which are not controllable by reason alone, resulting in the condemnation of intuition, and the denial of the libido or treatment of it as a necessary evil. Contrastingly, the adherent of the feminine perspective, exemplified in Spinoza and the Taoist, merely counsels us against the counter-productiveness of persevering in masculine modes of behavior, even though that behavior may prove useful as an interim means to an ultimate feminine end. Masculine either/or logic is supplanted by the feminine

---

they surpass men in the virtue of philanthropy or lovingkindness, for the origin of this is in most cases intuitive" On the Basis of Morality, trans. E. F. J. Payne (New York: Bobbs-Merrill Company, Inc., 1965), p. 151.

formula of both/and. It is thus that reason prepares the path for intuition, the highest form of knowledge which is feminine, for Spinoza's philosophy. The feminine perspective shows itself to be not merely the antithesis of the masculine thesis, but, moreover, the synthesis of the primal poles. This paradox will be unraveled in the course of our discussion.

In dealing with the topic of feminine thought several stages of investigation are required, spanning the development from primal perspective to full-blown feminine philosophies. It is first necessary, in the opening chapter, to establish the existence of the proposed feminine/masculine polarity in general thought, a polarity which results in two distinct perspectives or ways of looking at the work (Weltanschauungen). To further refine the precise criteria of a feminine principle of being, we must discuss the motivating force of the feminine advocate through the feminine manifestations and modes of being which underlie every feminine philosophy. It should be emphasized that this discussion concerns the opinions, both considered and common, involved in a division of perspectives along lines of sex, without the need to defend the factual basis of said distinctions. The intent is purely descriptive; the inevitable grouping of certain characteristics under a distinct Weltanschauung and their organization into a "feminine" principle of being is of greater importance here than any claims as to its constituting, or not constituting, a faithful reflection of reality. The fact that our models of feminine philosophy are found in two individuals who are biologically male speaks for itself.

The second and third chapters lead directly into the realm of philosophical thought. The form of a feminine philosophy derived from the feminine principle, as outlined in the first chapter, is exemplified in the second chapter through the Taoism of the Tao Te Ching. The feminine roots of Spinozistic thought then are exposed in the third chapter. A thorough understanding of both philosophical systems is requisite to reveal their common feminine orientation. Spinoza's emphasis upon the masculine method of discursive reason provides a useful line of communication between feminine thought and traditional masculine philosophy, especially since masculine terminology is employed by Spinoza to express the values and assumptions of an essentially feminine perspective.

The structure of the feminine principle is compared with these two feminine philosophies. Its manifestations (under the Elementary and Transformative characters) and modes of being (inwardness, receptivity, and materiality) are applied successively to the philosophies of the Tao Te Ching and of Spinoza to demonstrate the grounding of both systems in the feminine perspective. The manifestations of the feminine principle become evident in the theoretical discussions of metaphysics, the all-encompassing reality of Tao/Substance, and epistemology, how we can know that reality and attain enlightenment/blessedness. Correspondingly, the practical application and realization of feminine values in ethics, through the cultivation of Te or personal virtue/power, and socio-political philosophy, organizing an enlightened community, take place in accordance with feminine modes of being. The high degree of correlation between Taoist and Spinozistic elements of thought, traceable to their shared feminine perspective, is made clear by this structure.

Thus, the outline of the feminine Weltanschauung is traced in the pages of this study. Beginning with the positing of a feminine perspective, which is distinct from a masculine one, its values are organized into a properly feminine principle of being. The philosophical potential of the feminine principle is made manifest in the feminine philosophies of the Tao Te Ching and Spinozism. From the metaphysical sources the path leads through our peculiar human means and modes of knowledge, and into the implementation of those combined insights for purposes of personal perfection. The practicality of a feminine philosophy is tested by the interweaving of its elements into the social fabric. The socio-political move is necessary due to the twofold recognition that the human individual is a social animal and that, by virtue of our intimate relationship with the whole of nature, harmony, of an inner (personal) as well as an outer (universal) type, is the highest goal. That goal is an eminently feminine one.

Chapter 1

THE FEMININE/MASCULINE POLARITY

A. Establishing the Dichotomy of Perspectives

The construction of polarities is possible along various lines, and has been considered by some to be an unavoidable, and even a highly productive, task. Thus, the "tragic counterplay" of inner and outer, instinctual unconscious and socialized persona, is recognized by C. G. Jung as a tension necessary for "the energetics of the life process".[1] For Lou Salomè there is the contrast between the "unappeased longing to be one with and in all" and the attempt to distinguish everything from the self or "define every single thing more precisely".[2] The polarity of values imposed by a given culture is cited by anthropologist Margaret Mead as being responsible for an enriching variation suited to the range of human temperaments, with sex as the most "striking" means of division resorted to.[3]

Significantly, the poles so drawn readily lend themselves to the designations feminine and masculine, based on socially conditioned attitudes, primal (archetypal) responses, or both. If, as Mead contends, basic human temperaments do exist, one or more of which are standardized and selectively cultivated by a given culture or for specific groups within that culture, the general conception of the feminine may be interpreted as the projection of a temperament, and corresponding Weltanschauung, upon the female sex. These projections would be the polar opposite of and complement to the masculine temperament and perspective. A study of the uniform characterizations of women among various cultures would then reveal the elements of the feminine principle of being, as distinguished from the masculine one whose values tend to dominate in our own culture.

The "experts" consulted here in clarifying the feminine/masculine polarity include representatives from the fields of philosophy, psychology, and theology, who together cover a wide range of opinions on the subject. However, following Sigmund Freud's closing advice in his 1932 lecture on "The Psychology of Women",[4] further information concerning the feminine also has been obtained through a consideration of personal experience and poetic pronouncements, from common preconceptions (misconceptions) and literary inspirations. Hence, a smattering of less than rigorous sources has been cited, focusing on the discriminations which are spontaneously made between sexes. Even data from suspect experiments relating to "factual" sex differences can be enlightening when transferred from objective reality to the plane of perspective. The values ascribed to the feminine and masculine spheres of being by these various sources are noteworthy, not as statements of fact, but as the descriptive discriminations assumed to be normative by society which have their basis in gender.

Although these sources are not always in agreement with one another, their discrepancies usually can be traced to the conflicting interpretations of certain "facts" involving manifestations of or modes of being in the feminine perspective. Underlying these interpretive approaches is a common concept, the "y" factor which remains the same whether referred to, for example, as passivity or receptivity. It is this shared root of meaning which is being pursued here, and which will be re-interpreted in the subsequent presentations of full-blown feminine philosophies.

These trans-cultural complementary designations, referred to by Salomè as "basic constituents of all life",[5] seem to encompass the universe of possibilities in regard to being. Under the archetype of the Uroborus or "great Round", symbolized by an encircled snake biting its own tail, all polar oppositions are embraced: female and male, negative and positive, unconscious and conscious, etc.[6] It is the "symbol of the united primordial parents",[6] the original undifferentiated chaos of unity which Nature and humanity has ever after sought to regain. Subsequent divisions in the Great Round are reflective of the extremes in essential elements of the life experience--being in versus transcendence of Nature, cyclical change and linear progress, harmony and conquest, feeling and fact, depth and superficiality, inner and outer, psyche and intellect, body and mind, experienced wisdom and accumulated knowledge. Corresponding to this duality is an entire set of archetypal images: moon, night, Eros, and the maternal virgin goddess in contrast with sun, day, Logos, and the son/lover hero.

The feminine/masculine polarity thus constitutes an elementary recognition of two distinct temperaments and "modes of existence", the feminine and the masculine. Buytendijk even conceives of two distinct worlds, one identifiable as feminine and another decidedly masculine. Each Weltanschauung is presented here first as a principle of being, an unsystematic collection of values and qualities organized around a set of fundamental assumptions. Our major concern in this initial chapter is to delineate the feminine principle of being and its most revealing contrasts with the masculine principle. Properly approached, one can discern in the feminine perspective a distinctive principle, "an inner law or essence, a primary source inherent in the nature of things", paralleling "laws" of Nature.[7] The feminine principle may be treated as a "symbolic form" which shapes and articulates a personal encounter with "reality", much as does Cassirer's notion of an 'organ of reality'.[8]

1. Yin and Yang

In an Eastern setting, the seeker of polarities encounters the Yin/Yang dichotomy, represented by the circle of its own Great Round, the Great Ultimate, the Primal Beginning, . The Yin/Yang polarity, which is reflected in sexuality, divides the whole universe between the control of two complementary forces: "the Receptive [Yin] does not combat the Creative [Yang] but completes it".[9] The moist, cool, dark, north, receptivity, earth, autumn of feminine Yin balance the masculine Yang which is dry, hot, bright, south, aggression, heaven, winter. The primitive roots of the Yin/Yang polarity, illustrated by its implementation in the ancient and culturally pivotal I Ching, or Book of Changes, make it an excellent source for probing the fundamental sense of the feminine/masculine distinction. The I Ching employs the complementary feminine and masculine principles as a means of interpretating events, viewing the universe as both the field and the product of their interaction.

Yin, the feminine principle, has as its primal meaning 'the cloudy' or 'the overcast', while Yang, the masculine principle, denotes 'banners waving in the sun' or what is 'shone upon' (references to the shaded and bright sides of a mountain or river).[10] Related to these characterizations are the designations for the moon and the sun, respectively t'ai-yin or 'the Great Dark' and t'ai-yang, 'the Great Light'.[11] the linear expression for the principle of rest, the yielding (- -), was naturally identified with Yin, and that for the principle of movement, the firm (—), with Yang.[12]

In various combinations these two basic lines for the yielding and the firm, "the two primal powers of nature",[13] were used to form eight trigrams, generating an entire range of temperaments under the feminine and masculine principle which were then personified in a nuclear family group. These eight trigrams are being continually transformed into one another because they are essentially "tendencies in movement" or "functions."[14] Thus, they serve to illuminate the roles assigned to feminine and masculine types in context of Yin and Yang.

    Taking three lines of the yielding (☷), one has K'un, the Receptive, to which is assigned the attributes of devotion and yielding, the image of earth, and the role of mother. Correspondingly, three line of the firm (─) represent Ch'ien (☰), characterized by the strength, heaven, and the role of father. The trigrams for the six "children" of these primal parents are formed by a combination of yielding and firm lines. Combinations of two Yang lines and one Yin in the daughters represent stages of devotion, while two Yin and a Yang produce the various stages of movement in the sons. The daughters are Sun (☴), the Gentle, penetrating, wind and wood, the eldest daughter; Li (☲), the Clinging, light-giving, fire, the second daughter; and Tui (☱), the Joyous, lake, the youngest daughter. Among the sons are Chên (☳), the Arousing, inciting movement, thunder, the eldest son; K'an (☵), the Abysmal, dangerous, water, the second son; the Kên (☶), Keeping Still, resting, mountain, the youngest son.[15]

    The links to gender in the yielding and the firm are even more explicitly drawn, however: "The way of the Creative brings about the male./The way of the Receptive brings about the female". This being the case, the former "knows the great beginnings" in terms of abstractions, and the latter materially "completes the finished things".[16] Significantly, Richard Wilhelm notes the parallels between the Creative and Logos, along with those existing between the Receptive and Eros.[17] The Creative is strong and decisive; the Receptive adheres to the path of least resistance, is yielding and spontaneous. The two principles of the Receptive and the Creative are the polarities of "nature in contrast to spirit, earth in contrast to heaven, space as against time, the female-maternal as against the male-paternal", or feminine "spatial reality" as opposed to masculine "spiritual potential".[18]

    Considered in its own right, the essence of the

Receptive emerges as a possible model for the feminine principle. True to its name the Receptive is distinguished by a devoted and accommodating manner towards the Creative, whose qualities it is said to adopt and whose laws it is said to comply with. Therefore, the Receptive has "no need of a special purpose of its own"; it is non-goal-oriented, non-egotistical (in sharp contrast to the masculine principle). Similarly, earth, as image of the Receptive, is noted for its impartiality--"in its devotion carries all things, good and evil, without exception".[19]

The nature of the Receptive is pervaded by repose. In its capacity as "germ of all spatial diversity",[20] its maternal aspect is strongly apparent. The mare is associated with the Receptive due to its blending of the perseverence and speed of a horse with the gentleness and devotion characteristic of the "maternal) cow.[21] "Perfect indeed is the sublimity of the Receptive. All things owe their birth to it."[22] It is a primal shelter and point of origin as womb, as well as the point of returning for all things upon completion of their life cycle (precisely as all life returns to the earth at death),[23] the alpha and omega of existence. Two aspects can be distinguished under this container function: the closed, all-embracing "vast womb" (Elementary character of the feminine) and the openness which "causes them [individual things] to thrive and unfold",[24] (the feminine under its Transformative character). Like the mother, the Receptive both generates and sustains life.

The "daughters" of the Receptive bring forth additional facets of the nature of the feminine or Yin principle. Sun, the Gentle first-born daughter, reflects the changeableness of the wind (the fickle female?) and the seemingly indecisive change in direction (willingness to yield). Li, the Clinging, is characterized by the sun, fire, and lightening, the quick, bright flash which is "firm without and hollow or yielding within"; even the unquenchable flame is subject to flickering movements. Tui, the Joyous, is the exuberant life force, the sorceress (in contact with the spiritual realm) associated with the peaceful lake, and thus "outwardly weak and inwardly stubborn".[25] Each of these carries out the yielding nature of the "mother", though equally possessed of a certain strength in the yielding process, just as wind, fire, and placid water prevail in their endurance.

Turning to the masculine realm of the Yang principle, the Creative "father" is a dynamic dragon, "light-giving, active, strong, and of the spirit". Its essence is one of pure energy or power.[26] Interestingly enought, however, while the maternal images applied to the maternal Receptive firmly determine its sex as feminine, the Creative as a principle has tended to be viewed as "suprapersonal" in the Chinese mind, noted only through the effects of its activity rather than through that activity itself.[27] Nonetheless, it has been associated with the "superior" social position of prince and father, whereby it is hailed for its purity, firmness, and durability.[28] Other masculine traits are distributed among the Creative's three "sons": the Arousing, Chên, the Abysmal, K'an, and Keeping Still, Kên.[29] Active roles are demonstrated in each of these three temperaments, through the masculine duties to produce, labor, and protect.

Thus, Yin and Yang, the yielding and the firm, each have their own proper sphere of influence, with certain situations requiring their special forces, and their own resulting world perspectives, which are ultimately supportive of each other. As Jung observes, masculine nature "presupposes woman", in physical as well as spiritual terms, as the balancing component of the cosmos.[30] A union of opposites is derived from the Yin/Yang polarity, the middle path identified in Taoism, where even good and evil are relative. Similarly, according to Jung, the "mana-personality" combines ideal types in the ego, e.g., "the steadfastness of a superman or the sublimity of a perfect sage", represented respectively by Napolean, under the masculine principle, and Lao Tzu, under the feminine.[31]

A closer study reveals the need for a higher aspect of the feminine principle which facilitates more than a compromised union of the sex polarities and in fact results in a transcendence of the lower level polarity. This higher development culminates in the experience of the sage or philosopher within the bounds of feminine philosophy:

> The highest phase of confrontation and individuation in both sexes is initiated by the feminine . . . The feminine, in this sense, is the completing element; it is the feminine which completes individuation of each sex. The masculine initiates the emergence of [masculine] consciousness from primary [feminine] unconsciousness: the feminine initiates the completion of consciousness by re-establishing contact with the unconscious.[32]

The transcendent feminine character transforms the
polarity of the primal feminine and the masculine into
a comprehensive perspective of reality, accommodating
reality's diversified forms. The dual characters of
the feminine principle account for the seemingly
contradictory images of woman as both seductress and
savioress, mother and virgin.

    In terms of the Yin/Yang polarity, the ultimate
transcendency by Yin is confirmed by the characterization of the Receptive as concerned thought, through
which "one attains the possibility of perfection" (the
wisdom, Weisheit, of enlightenment); the Creative,
however, is merely credited with joyousness, whereby
"one gains an over-all view of good fortune and mis-
fortune" (accumulated knowledge or Erkenntnis).33

    It has been noted by Wilhelm that one must be able
both to separate and unite to determine one's position
"in the infinity of being".34 However, after the
analytic tendencies of Logos have been fully developed
from their emergence out of the undifferentiated
feminine, the force of Eros is re-asserted and the
ultimate act is one of union. The Great Round both
begins with and culminates in the feminine principle,
having undergone the transformation of the intervening
masculine principle; the feminine/masculine polarity is
envisioned as a circle rather than as two extremes of a
line, a circle which always returns upon itself. The
movement is from primal instinct (the Elementary
feminine) to activated discursive reason (the masculine), completing its circuit in intuition (the Transformative feminine). This entire process will become
clearer as the discussion of the feminine principle
unfolds.

2. Contemporary Approaches to Polarity

    The feminine/masculine polarity is equally
evident under various expressions within the Western
culture which is now dominant. Essentially three
approaches to the feminine principle itself have been
attempted in modern intellectual circles, outlined by
Ann Belford Ulanov under the headings of the Biological, the Cultural, and the Symbolic. The first of
these is best represented by a masculine interpretation of the doctrines of Sigmund Freud. As adopted by
certain segments of the Freudian school of thought, it
proclaims members of the female sex to be victims of a
deficient biology under the banner "anatomy is
destiny". The Cultural approach, advanced by such

researchers as Karen Horney and Margaret Mead, ascribes "feminine" attitudes and modes of behavior to cultural conditioning, with a subsequent denial of any objective differences between the sexes other than biological equipment. Finally, the symbolic approach, rooted in psychology, has been undertaken by C. G. Jung and his disciples, asserting that the feminine principle is not confined to the female sex and may best be explored through symbolism, archetypes, and myths.³⁵ This last approach, with its rejection of physical distinctions for the feminine/masculine polarity, is most in sympathy with the aims of the present study, despite its somewhat conflicting handling of the implications of its data.

    a. <u>The Biological approach</u>. The most widely employed method of asserting the feminine/masculine polarity has been to cite the obvious biological differences between the sexes, and the related differences in sexual function, inferring appropriate modes of existence therefrom. In terms of traditional Freudian theories, the analysis of woman, of the feminine, proceeds on the assumption that she is merely a "negative male" and that feminine character is essentially shaped by the penis envy aroused in infancy.³⁶ Physical apparatus is held to be the determining factor in psychological development, and subsequent social expressions.

    The differences between female and male are first noticed in the cradle. A study is quoted by Buytendijk concerning movement among infants, with the 'typical' female infant evidencing quiet gestures, an inward interest in clothes and body, and a close focus of attention. The corresponding male infant, however, was observed to display outgoing gestures, with a focus on external surroundings and a tendency to grasp beyond.³⁷ Or, as Freud puts it, the young girl child is "less aggressive, less defiant, and less self-sufficient" with "a greater need for affection", and thus "more dependent and docile".³⁸ One should note the manner in which the feminine characteristics are defined in terms of their variance from the "standard" of the male child's behavior; an adherent of the masculine perspective thus judges as negative what is positively valued within the feminine perspective.

    In sum, woman is assumed to encounter the world with a different set of predispositions than those of her male counterpart. The distinction is extended to explain variations in adult movement. According to defenders of the Biological approach the male's super-

fluidity if movement, 'outgoingness', contrasts with
the female's conditions of rest and conservation. The
upward tending, time, impulse, and ability to stimulate
generation are often referred to in characterizations
of the masculine, while the down tending, space,
slowing, and the ability to conceive are identifed
with the feminine sphere. Woman interacts with her
environment; man merely reacts to his, experiencing
constant resistance to his personal force.[39]

Expressed in terms of biological clocks, John
Steinbeck and Gaston Bachelard agree that the continual
(eternal) flow of the feminine clock is opposed by the
jerky progress of the masculine one.[40] The feminine
principle is associated with and reflective of the
rhythmic lunar cycle. Moreover, it is "time felt as
individual, time experienced as a series of unique
occurrences--a conception or pregnancy of the moment"
(being-here-now), while masculine time is "a series of
equal or similar movements" (the jerks of a mechanical,
man-made, clock); the feminine is "time as kairos
rather than as chronos".[41] The masculine perspective
regiments time, as a means of subjecting it to human
control; the feminine perspective, however, merely
experiences time as an integral part of our being.

The glance of the individual, indicative of the
window which one perceives the universe through,
becomes a revealing object of study for the projected
bilogical sex differences. The mode of vision natural
to or adopted by a given individual determines her or
his perspective. The feminine mode of perception has
been described as tarrying, a non-judgmental and con-
templative communion of seer and seen. The masculine
individual, however, is credited with a penetrating
glance, consciously differentiating itself from the
object and seeking to delve beyond said object due to a
discontentment with the object's mere state of being.
Supportive experiments prompted the conclusion that
perception tends to be analytical in male subjects,
while females manifest a receptivity to whatever is
presented to their sight.[42]

The biological data of such experiments is open to
many interpretations. The varied responses in female
subjects, viewed by the experimenters as a sign of
lesser stability, may equally be interpreted as evidence of a greater spontaneity, in keeping with positive feminine values. Moreover, the masculine trend
towards analysis, its need to differentiate itself from
the viewed object, results in its remaining narrowly in

and for itself. Sympathetic mergence dominates the feminine temperament; transcendance of self yields ultimate immanence by identification with externals.

Assuming certain ideal types of female and male bodies, external appearances likewise have been taken to reflect innate tendencies of the sexes. The male stature is "restless life" made visible, "a mass of reality that is simply 'there'", and characterized by hardness. Conversely, the female body is viewed as static, conveying a restful sense of completeness and softness--"the world of woman appears in her and with her".[43] Geometrically, the male thus is associated with rigidly drawn lines and angles, the female with free-flowing curves. Although the classification of the feminine among the forces of stability and repose seems adequate in relation to the Elementary character of the feminine principle, the primal and maternal essence, it fails to do justice to the equally pervasive Transformative character, which exudes dynamism. The archetypal Venus idol has two fundamental models-- the massive and static Great Mother type and the lithe, vibrant "virgin" manifested as Amazon or love goddess. The latter represents the Transformative character, with a corresponding body type which is graceful in motion and exhilarating in appearance, rather than tranquil.

Equally relevant in clarifying the sense of biological polarity are the attitudes of female and male with respect to their sex-specified bodies. The masculine center of being, under some interpretations, has been assigned to the upper body regions, to the ribcage and chest. The functions of breath and heart beat regulated by this area connote animal vitality, expansive power, and, by extension of meaning, freedom (individual, self-assertive freedom). The power of the female rests in and derives from the lower regions of abdomen and pelvis, the conserving, digestive and reproductive space. Such vitality is linked to the vegetative sphere of being, associated with growth and endurance.[44] The same distinction between the animalistic masculine and the vegetative feminine was drawn by Hegel (see Introduction).

On a psychological plane, biological differences determine the forms of dynamism said to characterize each of the sex poles. In the masculine pole a resistance-oriented or "expansive" dynamism is generated and an "adaptive", value-oriented one in the feminine.[45] The masculine principle tends to expand in the face of resistance, whereas the feminine principle dictates an avoidance of resistance by adapting to the situation, holding to values which remain unchanged despite external transformations. Somewhat differently phrased, we have Nietzsche's pronouncement: "Volition is man's nature; the nature of woman is willingness [acceptance]".[46] The masculine principle wills something exceeding reality; the feminine principle accepts conditions as they exist.

A firm indicator of woman's "otherness" in relation to the standards of the masculine pole is the so-called feminine intuition, regarded as the exclusive and inborn privilege of the female sex. Intuitive capacity presumably compensates woman for an assumed deficiency in masculine rational capabilities. However, in giving advice to the young wife, Eva Firkel quite seriously declares that, due to the woman's intuitive sense, she will be much better equipped to understand her husband than vice versa--the man "will learn the wisdom of the heart in the mirror of her being; he will recognize the polarity of all created things". Herein lies the "mysterious power" of the female.[47]

The above observations constitute a mere sampling of the conclusions drawn by advocates of the Biological approach based on the physical differences observed between sexes. This approach is significant for reasons of its long-enduring status, with persuasive "evidence" offered by a direct comparison of female and male bodies. From here it is but a short (Freudian) leap to the supposed psychological discrepancies between the feminine and masculine types.

b. <u>The Cultural approach</u>. Not even the Freudians, however, could ignore the influences of culture upon the individual development of members of both sexes. The Cultural approach to the feminine-masculine polarity has attracted numerous advocates among present day feminists in that it interprets (or lays blame for) the differences between the sexes as the result of social conditioning. Such conditioning generally is assumed to conceal the underlying oneness of human nature, with its infinite variety of individual expressions.

It is both interesting and significant to discover that the same set of basic characteristics and the same temperament which is held to be biologically determined by the Freudians emerge under the Cultural approach as socialized into woman and eventually assumed to be innate. The masculine power structure then is credited with imposing a distorting duality upon our essentially homogeneous human nature. Women tend to live up to the expectations of masculine authority that they fulfill their nature by being "passive, modest, maternal and altogether feminine": "The psychology of the inferior, the psychology of purdah is instilled to some extent in every female born to a male-dominated society".[48]

Feminine psychological phenomena pointed to by Freud as the results of internal biological sex differentiations, such as penis envy, passivity, and masochism, have been traced to external factors by Karen Horney and others. Hence, although Horney can agree with certain of Freud's observations on feminine behavior, the biological rationale for his interpretations is replaced by a cultural one.

Following Alfred Adler, Horney draws out the cultural factors which make the male's status so desireable, that is, which account for the higher value assigned by society to masculine qualities (courage, initiative, ambition, etc.) over feminine ones. The rewards, privileges, and opportunities of men also are correspondingly greater. Underlying the placid feminine facade lurks repressed ambition, repressed due to the cultural or social expectations women are pressured into realizing which exclude the masculine values. There is also the personal sense of failure women experience in terms of their shattered self-image, an image which is both attracted to and repelled by masculine success. Correspondingly, the 'repudiation of femininity' included in masculine psychology by Freud is challenged by Horney, who views it as a rejection of inferior values rather than a rejection of the female per se.[49]

One of the major areas of psychology in which Horney counters biological interpretations with cultural ones involves the "feminine" trait of masochism. Taken as "the attempt to gain safety and satisfaction in life through inconspicuousness and dependency", masochism may be traced to existing social conditions. Thus, the general assumption that dependency, weakness, and frailty are inherent to feminine nature, the need of being supported by others and of living life through one's family, all contribute to masochistic leanings in neurotic individuals, regardless of sex.[50] Similarly, the overevaluation of love, by women, also noted by the Freudians, has its roots in the soil of culture, namely in the restriction of feminine activity to the family sphere and the assignment of love and devotion to the feminine mode of existence.[51]

Social conditioning is referred to by Margaret Mead as a "determinative" element in the phenomena of differentiations based on sex. From her studies of three primitive societies Mead concludes that the temperament assigned to each sex in a given society is defined largely by the role or roles members of that sex are supposed to fulfill. Cultural conditioning begins in childhood and shapes each individual to perform specific functions within the society.[52] The society has "chosen" certain sets of characteristics as desirable for certain groups differentiated by age, sex, social class, etc. Cultural influences are then employed to inculcate these models. However, it is just this underlying fund of characteristics, the inherent temperament or potential for such existing prior to the exertion of influences by cultural conditions, which is of interest in distinguishing the feminine and masculine perspectives and which provides the foundation of feminine and masculine philosophies. No human being could be assigned a feminine role unless a prototype for the feminine perspective existed independent of role assignments.

c. The Symbolic approach. As a reflection of "inherent structural polarities of the psyche", differences in terms of feminine and masculine principles lead us deep into the realms of psychology.[53] A division of territory is made, principally by Jung, with the sphere of the unconscious falling to the feminine and that of consciousness to the masculine. They represent "two opposing 'realities'", each of which guarantees the relativity of the other to the exclusion of some absolute reality at either extreme.[54] Properly integrated, the feminine and masculine poles can reveal reality which is absolute, by encompassing the full range of expressions. This reality emerges through feminine philosophy in its incorporation of the masculine method within a feminine Weltanschauung.

Examining these psychic zones more closely, the feminine or unconscious is further specified as collective and undifferentiated, tending to a communal and cosmic perspective appropriate to its nature. The unconscious state is one of the paradoxical "narcissistic union" of sexuality and self,[55] a union which proves crucial to the functioning of the feminine principle. Masculine consciousness, on the other hand, is independent and characterized by egotistical assertion. Oneness, mergence, and harmony contrast with a divisive sense of <u>Maya</u>. Indeed, the masculine tendency to set the self apart from, rather than participating in, an event or object results in a <u>persona</u> or mask, the need to espouse a socially-imposed role.[56] Similarly, societies dominated by a masculine perspective feel the need to impose a <u>persona</u> or role upon women as a group, so that their behavior will be recognizably "feminine".

A more straightforward psychic sex polarity is that of Jung's <u>anima</u> and <u>animus</u>, the experience and manifestation of one sex by the other which approximates a state of psychic androgyny. The feminine <u>anima</u> inherent in the male is thus responsible for his diffuse and inexplicable moods; the woman's masculine <u>animus</u> contributes egotistical opinions to her ideas. Stated in another way, unmasculine behavior in the male necessarily entails feminine association, i.e., emotional outbursts generally are considered unmanly. The female, however, is able to display elements otherwise assigned to the masculine sphere, such as ego and intellect, asexually. These elements can be inclusive of "femaleness", without having the feminine principle compromised, whereas the masculine <u>must</u> be so compromised by any feminine incursions.[57] A man can be emasculated or made effeminate, but no corresponding standard terms exist for a woman. The encompassing force of the feminine principle is demonstrated by this state of affairs.

Other aspects of the Symbolic approach, such as archetypes, are dealt with in the following discussions and thus need not be considered here. It might be added that the Jungians approach the feminine/masculine polarity through the inherited mass of symbols intrinsic to cultures, symbols which have in turn been influenced by individual experiences of female and male beings. Hence, the Symbolic approach draws upon the sources of both the Biological and the Cultural approaches, without attempting to judge which factors are ultimately responsible for the common conceptions of the feminine and masculine principles.

What, if anything, is held in common by these various approaches to the feminine/masculine polarity; what traits are recognized under the Yin/Yang distinction as well as by advocates of biological differentiation, or by proponents of cultural conditioning and those of psychological symbolism? The most fundamental distinction that can be noted is that between the receptive or yielding nature of the feminine principle and the active, firm nature of the masculine principle.

Rephrasing this distinction, Ulanov discusses the difference between the types of description provided for the feminine in contrast to those for the masculine: feminine qualities require intransitive verbs of being, whereas masculine qualities tend to be conveyed by means of verbs of action.[58]

Reinterpreting the passive/active dichotomy from the viewpoint of a feminine standard, new implications arise. The "passive" feminine principle can be given a positive characterization as an acceptance of reality, the (eternal) present, the 'is'. The universe is what it is and we must adapt ourselves to it, because we are one with it and can fulfill our existence only be recognizing that oneness. The creative initiation of the "active" masculine principle results in an indeterminate flux as it reaches for the 'ought' envisioned beyond the 'is'. It operates under a state of continual striving that seeks to refashion the world in the human image. The feminine principle, on the other hand, works with natural spontaneity, expressing its creativity in collaboration with the universe or Nature.

B. An Exploration of the Feminine Principle

Having outlined the fundamentals of the feminine/masculine polarity in its primal Eastern form and through modern Western approaches, it should be evident that there is indeed an accepted tradition of recognition for a sex-specified polarity of perspectives. It now becomes necessary to explore the feminine principle, the diffuse motivating force of feminine existence, in more detail. This discussion includes a consideration of the forms through which the feminine principle manifests itself as well as its modes of being, that is, the characteristic assumptions and patterns of behavior which identify an individual as an adherent of the feminine perspective. Feminine assumptions are revealed by the manifestations of the feminine principle, and are formulated in a feminine philosophy as metaphysical and epistemological presuppositions. Feminine patterns of behavior are structured along the lines of the feminine modes of being, which in turn may be systematized in a feminine code of ethics.

Before entering the feminine realm, however, it is useful to review the main aspects of the masculine principle which evoke its tension and complementarity with the feminine. It is unnecessary to provide a detailed characterization of the masculine principle, inasmuch as it permeates the traditional values of contemporary Western culture. This culture is a compounding of several exemplary masculine forces--the patriarchal social structure, the Greek Apollonian spirit, Judeo-Christian doctrines, the Protestant work ethic, Puritan morality, and many more influences too deeply ingrained to be readily discernible.

In the masculine perspective discursive reason is the dominant means of personal "salvation", whether conceived of in an intellectual or spiritual sense. Hence, the irrationality of Nature poses a challenge for the adherent of the masculine principle. Nature must be conquered and made subservient to human beings, so that it falls into line with the anthropocentric focus existent in society and assumed in Judeo-Christian theology. Certain primary principles are imposed upon the cosmos by the human mind, such as achievement, order, rationality, and analytical discrimination. The masculine principle embodies "the capacity to penetrate, separate, take charge, initiate, create, stand firmly and over against, to articulate and express meaning".[59]

The role of the ego can hardly be overemphasized in the masculine Weltanschauung. Extreme individualism conflicts often with an equally enthusiastic imposition of human law. The anguish and despair of the existentialist is thus a by-product of the masculine perspective--freedom is pursued not only as a means of escaping our own subjectivity (which the feminine principle glories in as a reflection of objective reality), but also "as a given task to remain free in the face of any objective and absolutely normative value."[60] Hell is other people (as Sartre puts it), precisely as other; suffering is a highly personalized experience, hence very real. The self-imposed isolation of the masculine soul is at the root of its anxiety.

These same values are reflected in the animus, compounded as it is of woman's projection of her own masculine tendencies and temperament, promptings of the collective unconscious, and her experiences of actual men. In addition to the creative and procreative thrust of the animus as fertilizing "spermatic word",[61] Jung judges its special task to be a fostering of internal associations, to establish a relation between a woman and the unconscious contents of her psyche.[62] Or, as interpreted by the psychologist, Irene de Castillejo, the animus does not constitute part of a woman's spirit, but merely helps her to focus and clarify "things she already knows innately".[63] In a similar manner, discursive reason clarifies instinctual knowledge, leading the way to its final refinement as intuition.

1. Manifestations of the Feminine Principle

The two primary manifestations of the more mysterious essence of the feminine principle require individual investigation. These are (a) the feminine principle embodied in the Great Mother archetype, the Elementary character, and (b) the power source of the feminine principle, personified as priestess, muse, Sophia, in its Transformative character. Each area of discussion serves to disclose further the subtleties of the feminine perspective. Over-all there is a spontaneity and an adherence to natural instincts, often in redefined form, which sharply contrast with the human contrivances valued by the masculine principle.

Before dealing with these dual characters some mention must be made of the point of view from which they are being approached. The feminine principle, with its values of unity and integration, cannot be responsible for the artificial divisions made of its essence, hence we must look to the masculine principle as the imposer of distinctions. The abstractness of language and its deficiency in conveying the concreteness of reality contradicts the feminine method of immediate intuition. The masculine conception of the feminine principle with which we are concerned here, that is to say, a conception which is guided by discursive reason, requires that the aspects of the feminine be categorized in a manner comprehensible to the intellect. A book about the feminine principle which espoused a purely feminine point of view would most likely be composed of enigmatic poems, pictures, or blank pages (cf. Tao Te Ching).

Within Jungian psychology the _anima_ provides the requisite intellectual categorization of the feminine principle for the male psyche. The contrasexual elements of the masculine individual are personified in the feminine _anima_ in order that they may be dealt with as an independent entity. The _anima_ encompasses the sum of man's experiences of woman in subjective relationships with real women (the models for the _anima_) as well as objective feminine archetypes. As the primal inner soul of the male, the unconscious, the _anima_ counterbalances external, masculine ego concerns.

Erich Neumann, a noted adherent of Jungian psychology, has explored the manifestations of the feminine archetype and concludes that the feminine principle can be considered under two main categories of being: the stable, conservative Elementary character, the Great Round (the closed womb of the Receptive, K'un), and its dynamic counterpart in the Transformative character (the Receptive as open, stimulating things to thrive and unfold). Vague references have already been made to these characters above in an attempt to impose some structure on the diffuse aspects of the feminine principle. Thus, Jung views the <u>anima</u> in terms of its Transformative potential to perfect the psyche through an integrating transcendence of the masculine principle. With an emphasis on the Elementary character, Bachelard attributes stability and tranquility to the <u>anima</u> as "interior principle of our repose" and "harmonious (<u>unie</u>) substance".[64] Together these characters constitute the encompassing duality, in function as well as in Nature, of the archetypal feminine principle, and justify its title as archetype of life.

    The first of these characters, the Elementary, reflects the primal dominance of the unconscious, the state in which the ego remains undifferentiated and under the benign dictatorship of matriarchal (maternal, for the young child) control: "Everything born of it belongs to it and remains subject to it".[65] This character of the feminine principle is "receptive, dark, ingoing, moist, enclosing", paralleling the impartiality of Nature's closed system, with an impersonal unchanging (within its cyclical flux) quality.[66] It is the closed womb in a state of perpetual pregnancy, containing all that exists. Most interpretations of the feminine principle are derived from the experiencing of its Elementary character, of the individual woman as mother, as is evident from the previous discussions of approaches to the feminine/masculine polarity.

    Complementing the stability of the Elementary character in the realm of the feminine principle is the transcendent development of the Transformative character. Its function as open womb is manifested in such events as birth, where the woman is "sign and instrument" of the transforming power for both her own being and that of her offspring.[67] Carried to the spiritual plane, the Transformative feminine is pregnant with salvation or enlightenment, promising transcendence of its own primal sense-related functions (the Elementary character). It is the source of inspiration, of motive power, which harmonizes the individual with the feminine principle of being in general by guiding us on the path of the feminine perspective.

Thus, the two characters of the feminine principle are not mutually exclusive, but rather interrelated and mutually supportive. The Elementary as Great Round leads the Transformative back upon itself, to its "own eternal sameness".[68] They represent diverse ways of looking at the one feminine reality. The force of the feminine principle is felt through the two intertwining planes of being, through two characters which simultaneously parallel one another and intersect as manifestations of the oscillating feminine life force.

Irrevocably linked with life in the cycle of existence is death, therefore some mention must be made of the negative aspect also intrinsic to the feminine realm. Emerging primarily from the Elementary character, a negative archetype rules over death and destruction in the form of the Devouring Mother, Kali. The maternal protectress becomes a threat; the womb is transformed into a tomb. The perversion is completed by representing the feminine archetype as auto-erotic, narcissistic (in an egotistical sense), 'ingrowing', and totally involved in ego concerns—she is then the antithesis of the benevolent Great Mother.[69] This negative feminine is given expression through the figure of Zarathustra, whose Dionysian (feminine) ideal is "to be beyond terror and pity and to be the eternal lust of becoming itself—that lust which also involves the joy of destruction".[70]

The impersonality of this destructive force effectively thwarts any summary condemnation of it. Kali is not vindictive, as the male deities tend to be, merely inherently fatal. Hers is not a self-righteous wrath, but rather the dispassionate devastation of Nature's forces. Hence, the power of Yin is symbolized by the stalking tiger, "waiting to leap upon its prey with claws and fangs, yet looking all the while sleek, gentle, catlike, making one almost forget its ferocity".[71] In conjunction with this facet of the feminine principle, and linked with the Transformative character, is woman's reputation as a heartless seductress (Circe, Carmen), the *femme* *fatale* archetype.

   a. The Elementary character. In the archetypal manifestations of the feminine principle a host of primal images and their intellectualized derivations emerge. Under the Elementary character the Great Mother archetype is all-pervasive. Its most primitive expression, according to Neumann, is in the 'maternal uroborus', in which it encompasses both male and female in the as yet undifferentiated archetypal feminine. Developed as the more defined Great Mother, the archetype reveals the universally experienced condition of utter dependence by the infant on its mother, and the domination of the unconscious. From this state a certain emotional-psychological reaction results, along with set behavior patterns, in response to the various maternal functions. The figure of the mother is hedged in universal terms--the 'eternal mother' as source of security, readily recognized as origin and destiny, bringer of life and death, for all.

The central symbol of the feminine, at the root of the primal responses it evokes, is judged by Neumann to be the vessel or container, mirroring the general human experience of the female-"woman=body=vessel". At the most rudimentary level the child is contained in the womb, remains part of the mother's body. The female body is also the source of primal nourishment and continued sustenance: "Mother *is* warmth, mother *is* food, mother *is* the euphoric state of satisfaction and security".[72]

Containment may be extended further to the woman's encompassing of the phallus during intercourse (interpreted by Freud as man's desire to return to the womb). Spiritually considered, the feminine is the source of the wisdom and/or grace able to nourish the soul in a manner paralleling the nourishing of the body. This one primal function of motherhood thus conjures up a host of related images which are the product of the universal human experience of woman as mother. Directly related to the containment function of the mother is the function of caring, of conserving and protecting humanity as a whole. As Buytendijk observes, "the activity of taking care is one that is most in accord with the feminine manner of movement and the one that best represents the meaning of woman's existence." The female is said to be morally determined to this occupation of caring, which is quite naturally carried to the extreme of self-sacrifice.[73] Similarly, Firkel tersely contends that the entire feminine nature is inclined "to care for all that is alive", while Ashley Montagu maintains that there is "not the least doubt" that the maternal (caring) instinct is innate to all women.[74]

Caring in turn matures into full-fledged love, compassion, one of the most significant contributions

of the feminine principle to human existence. As the
maternal sensitivity to the needs of others, caring incorporates "the wonder of the miracle of creation and
the miracle of love".75 This particular form of love
has appropriately been described by Milosz as "the
eternal divine-feminine of Alighieri and Goethe, the
angelic sentimentality and sensuality, the virginal
maternity".76 Love is the very modus operandi of the
feminine principle, paralleling the function of discursive reasoning in the masculine sphere.

As for the male, representative of the masculine
perspective, basking in the love unreservedly emitted
by the female, he has often been accused of a radical
interpretation, or misinterpretation, of the real
meaning of love. This is the charge made by Simon de
Beauvoir, who cites this problem in masculine love as a
major factor dividing the sexes. In extreme cases, man
has been totally denied even the potential for loving,
and has been stigmatised with an "emotional invalidism"
said to be intrinsic to the masculine character: "Men
can't love".77 The hero of myth typically seeks love
for purposes of ego-satisfaction, however well disguised that goal may be, while the archetypal heroine
gives love in an attitude of self-sacrifice (sacrificing of and for the shared Self)-Don Juan versus
Psyche.

To differentiate the precise sense of the
feminine form of love among the diverse manifestations
of that emotion, Jung and his disciples have designated feminine love Eros. However, it is Eros under a
very special definition, not a mere sensual or sexual
arousal (although it also encompasses sensuality and
sexuality in its Dionysian aspect), but rather "capacity to relate". This sense of Eros Jung sets in
opposition to masculine Logos, "discrimination, judgment, insight".78 Eros is in the Receptivity of Yin
just as Logos is in Yang's Creativity.

In association with the stable and maternal Elementary character, the Eros of the feminine principle
expresses itself in concern and caring, adapting to
the specific needs and desires of a specific individual charge and a specific situation. Flexibility is
fundamental.79 And yet, under this flexibility is included the universe of possibilities for those who need
care. Being flexible insures stability; the person who
yields to a temporarily invincible force is insured of
survival, while the resisting challenger risks doom.
Eventually yielding and flexible water can wear down

the resistance of the most unyielding stone.

The prototype of all love is maternal love. For Alain it is held to be spontaneous, the most natural of all loves, the ultimate caring which closely approximates <u>Agape</u> (by reason of its impartiality).[80] It constitutes an "infectious" love of life passed on to the infant by the mother, the 'milk' of "care and affirmation" with which the child is nurtured,[81] an affirmation arising from "great depth of feeling".[82] The wholehearted involvement of the mother in her child makes maternal love essential for proper development, while the corresponding paternal love does not share its character of indispensibility.[83] Maternal love evokes all possible superlatives in terms of purity, efficiency, compassion, and sympathy.[84]

Buytendijk adds that maternal love is unique in that it can never go unrequited; being an unchosen love it demands no payment in kind for its best efforts.[85] This altruistic bent leads Fromm to consider it the highest form of love and "the most sacred of all emotions"; it alone of all loves is unconditioned and beyond individual efforts, for it is neither earned nor deserved.[86] Fromm also does not discount the negative element in this type of love; according to him, maternal love is always beyond our control and cannot be evoked when it has not first been freely given. The importance of natural generosity in women is thus underscored.

And yet a narcissistic element has been observed by many in maternal love, specifically in the mother's identification with her child. She loves it because it is hers, has come from her, grew from her body. For Lou Salomé narcissism can be quite positive; it is creative and "the persistent accompaniment of all our deeper experience".[87] Love (<u>Eros</u>/relatedness) gives us "the gift of ourselves", a self which has been made "more actual, more encompassing, more wedded to ourselves",[88] all of which applies most especially to the case of a mother and child. The superficially paradoxical element of positive narcissism which leads one to rank it with masculine egoism reveals itself as feminine and "altruistic" when love of self involves the shared Self rather than the ego-self. This will be explained more fully in subsequent discussions of feminine modes of being.

The condition of the mother, or even of the potential mother, has other implications as well, affecting the supposed state of feminine nature. Motherliness is said to be founded on physical "defenselessness and tenderness" combined with the exuding of "youthfulness".[89] Firestone asserts, "The special tie women have with children is recognized by everyone".[90] Given a more negative interpretation, Schopenhauer concludes that women are eminently suited for child care functions in that they are "frivolous and short-sighted; in a word, they are big children all their life long".[91] However, because feminine knowledge is experiential, the feminine individual comes to understand children by experiencing the child's actual state of being. Thus it is that the woman, when true to the feminine principle, is identified with her product, and described in terms of perennial innocence, the naïveté of the chronically immature.

The power of the "weaker" sex is said to derive from the indulgence of the strong, but it can also be expressed as extortion, when that weakness (the weakness of the child) is exploited.[92] Such an explanation fits well in the masculine view, for it rationalizes the triumph of the non-obstrusive feminine force over masculine assertiveness and aggression. From a feminine focus, the power of the feminine principle is seen to be drawn from Nature, whose spontaneous dictates it emulates. Feminine "weakness", maternal tenderness, may be imitated, but properly cannot be judged nor even analyzed into oblivion by an ill-fitting masculine standard. It is only natural, as Buytendijk observes, that masculine adherents will experience the "irrestable" feminine power as a threat to their egocentric outlook. Samuel Johnson's famous remark both supports and illustrates this point: "Nature has given women so much power that the law cannot affort to give her more."

The individual woman is constantly reminded of her maternal potential, deemed by many to be her highest possible destiny. Concurrently, mothering stimulates a transcendence of narrow, personal concerns in order to function on the level of the maternal archetype, as a mother in all situations:

> The highest and most universal aim of the education of girls is to train them to be mothers. All other powers derive from this. Hence, being a mother is the basis of womanhood, whatever the actual state.[93]

Transferring this assertion to our concern with depicting the feminine perspective, it is apparent that the adherent of the feminine principle is properly feminine in the Elementary sense only when the archetype of the Great Mother is imitated, by either men or women, in the fact of motherhood or in a maternally protective and supportive mode of behavior. The mother creates her offspring, "the replica of herself", in the same manner that the artist creates a work of art.94 The artist and the mother can be equally maternal in their creativity, for in both cases what is created embodies our being in a new form.95

By extension, the Great Mother archetype manifests the feminine principle as the whole of "concrete natural existence".96 It inspires a collective sense of security, protection, and nurturing, traced to a common maternal source, a source which is the repository of encompassing primal power. Each individual woman is credited with some participation in this power, a part in the feminine mystique. The maternal figure is "the home we come from, she is nature, soil, the ocean", standing in opposition to the paternal, or masculine, realm "of man-made things, of law and order, of discipline, of travel and adventure".97

Herein lies the basis of feminine power under its Elementary character--as container, shelter, source of nourishment (material and spiritual), with humanity "dependent on it and utterly at its mercy". Woman is equivalent to the world, as Neumann puts it. The feminine principle is in sympathy with the world, is a self-contained container, the material Uroborus as self-generateing, bearing within itself the masculine principle which it likewise harbors. Plato's image of the passive Receptacle, requiring the stimulus of the Demiurge, is left far behind. In the beginning was the world, the material and creative being which had no need of an abstract Word to stimulate it.

b. The Transformative character. In its most refined state, feminine power manifests itself in the function of transformation, of salvation, under the Transformative character. This character of the feminine principle allows a development beyond the primal Elementary role, incorporating supportive elements from the masculine principle. The Transformative character is often symbolized as the daughter of a powerful father, as in the case of Athena, who thus is able to draw upon the resources of the masculine while retaining its feminine identity. As "root and origin of human reality", woman, in the image of mother, uniquely fosters the realization of all potential (of virtue in the Greek sense of Arete) by supra-rational means.[98] Birth is the "bringing forth out of one's prime matter of new reality, a new attitude or feeling."[99] If the Elementary feminine is the mother in fact, the Transformative feminine is so by potential, in a state of spiritual and/or intellectual pregnancy. Through images of birth and rebirth, of the child "emerging from the dark womb", the Transformative character becomes the inspiring muse who engenders "feelings of being caught up in a creative process".[100]

The transcendence function is fulfilled by the anima, and through the actual woman upon whom the anima is projected by men as an 'other', providing inspiration to artist and would-be saint alike. She is the compassionate spirit-guide who blazes the path of enlightenment, embodied in such figures as Beatrice, Kwan-yin, and Pallas Athena. To the Bachelardian dreamer "it seems that the world must be redeemed by the feminine being".[101] Accordingly, feminine values are strongly present in world saviors such as the Buddha, Krishna, and Jesus Christ.

The feminine's Transformative character reflects the dynamism of the psyche, the "divine madness" and ecstasy engendered by Eros.[102] In this case the love reaches from the individual to the whole, just as under the Elementary character Eros/relatedness extends down from the impersonal and encompassing Great Mother to Her universal children. Through the Transformative character one experiences the "urge of feminine relatedness" to get in the midst of things and to merge with them".[103] It is a moving out of the narrow ego-self and a union with the communal or shared Self, culminating in "full emotional involvement",[104] a "psychic urge to relate, to join, to be in-the-midst-of, to reach out, to value, to get in touch with".[105] Hence, the feminine artist is said to employ art as a vehicle of love (Eros).[106]

By this Eros involvement the feminine-oriented individual transcends personal (in the sense of egotistical) aims and ambitions. In the process, one attains a relation to a non-personal value, paralleling the non-personal truth of Logos, which results in a redemption from "the desire for personal power".[107] Feminine power has a higher purpose. The personal merges with a higher source, the whole or reality, from which it has been alienated by the illusion of separateness: "The largeness of God is found in the smallness of each personal detail, which makes each smallness into a largeness".[108] Hence, the feminine perspective emphasizes the microcosmic/macrocosmic condition of reality.

Love's "primary joy" consists in "the recollection of the totality so extravagantly attributed to the beloved as though it were itself all".[109] Feminine Eros is capable of embracing the universe which is the all as well as considering its individual love as the all. The giving of the self in love, to share in a greater Self, eliminates the I-other duality. Indeed, love of God (as of the universe) has been described as "the complete self-love"; assuming the "primal union" of lover and beloved, as in the Platonic myth (Symposium), or that of self and Nature, love (Eros) is merely a process of "rediscovery".[110] The feminine activity initiated by Eros progresses from love to loving to acting upon that love, and thence to a veritable Eros mode of being.[111] Eros/relatedness is a way of life for the adherent of the feminine perspective.

The salvation offered by the Transformative character of the feminine principle likewise expresses itself under the guise of Sophia, wisdom (in contrast to the masculine principle's accumulated knowledge). The ties to Eros are simultaneously maintained nonetheless. The dove which symbolizes the wisdom of the Christian Trinity in the Holy Spirit is identifiable as the messenger of the Goddess of Love, Aphrodite. The wisdom contained in the feminine principle is the wisdom of "ecstasy and illumination" gained through experience; it is the self-generated light added to feminine darkness.[112] Such wisdom transcends, while incorporating, the rational processes of masculine logic.

The distinctive quality of Sophia or feminine wisdom may be traced to the equally distinctive qualities of feminine consciousness and of the feminine mode of understanding. In terms of consciousness, the feminine is associated by Ulanov with matriarchal 'heart-ego' functioning, appropriate to links with the unconscious and in opposition to the patriarchal 'head-ego': the former is effective because it harmonizes with the primal inner being of the unconscious.[113] What this amounts to is an encompassing instinctual and/or intuitive approach by the feminine, rather than masculine intellectual restrictiveness. The feminine principle engenders a perceiving through the whole being, and not merely through a selected part of that being. The reality of our material being is not repudiated, nor even made subordinate to the intellect, as is common in the dualism of the masculine perspective.

The course of feminine understanding deepens these tendencies: "Unlike an act of intellect that can swiftly register facts, analyze, or classify them, . . .it conceives a content, walks around it, participates in it, and then brings it forth into the world".[114] For Neumann this type of understanding qualifies as an <u>Einfall</u>, a hunch, a transcendental message which is a 'conception' rather than an intellectual act.[115]

Most commonly, the feminine understanding has been referred to as intuition, which is characterized by the immediacy of its processes. As described by Helene Deutsch, feminine intuition arises from the unconscious: "the subjective experience of another person is made one's own by association and thus is immediately understood". Intuition is a re-experiencing of another's situation which approximates a state of <u>Einfühlung</u> (empathy).[116] The key concepts in this description are 'experience' and 'association', for they link the feminine to a personal involvement in knowledge and reflect the extension of the feminine self to other selves in accordance with the relatedness of the guiding <u>Eros</u>. The result is the shared Self. Woman, it is said, "finds her being in the intuitive knowledge of life and mind".[117] This mode of being, with its potential for transformation, is likewise open to followers of the feminine principle in general.

The success of feminine wisdom, with its unique sources in intuitive understanding, stems from its grounding in reality, its participation in real processes. The direct experience intrinsic to feminine wisdom constitutes a radical empiricism, for to know reality in the fullest sense the feminine individual participates in its oneness directly. Sophia is non-speculative, non-idealistic, preferring "what actually is to what should or might be" (the masculine 'ought'). Women are credited with being both better realists and better idealists than men by Montagu in that they live "more profoundly in the present" (being-here-now) and have the wisdom of knowing what cannot be changed (namely Nature) as well as what can (personal perspective).[118]

Feminine wisdom is also a "responsive wisdom", the product of instinct (unrefined intuition), the unconscious, and human relationships; it is "bound to the earth, to organic and psychological growth, to living reality". It can afford to be paradoxical, as paradoxical as reality is itself, substituting 'both/and' for 'either/or' logic.[119] The feminine principle displays an openness to experience as "revelatory of what already exists",[120] a fuller expression of its own inner, microcosmic reality. What is revealed by feminine wisdom is seldom acceptable to masculine reason however, for the latter demands a world confined within the limits of its human vision.

In sum, the Transformative character of the feminine principle, in its openness and fidelity to reality, expresses "a constant redemptive move"; it enlightens us as to the hidden meaning of feminine darkness, not by intellectually rationalizing these elements in human terms, but by presenting them as nothing less than the primal mystery.[121] As Goethe, the esteemed worshipper of the feminine, has declared succinctly in the closing lines of Faust, "Das Ewig-Weibliche/ Zieht uns hinan". The feminine principle is to the masculine individual a beckoning ideal hovering beyond our reach, but within the feminine sphere it is the existent reality.

2. Modes of Being Under the Feminine Principle

In citing the above predispositions among those adhering to the feminine principle as archetype, that is, as it has been psychologically conceived, as well as in their functioning and potential, we have clarified the general tendencies of feminine nature. By extension, three essential feminine modes of being are identifiable which express the ways in which the world is encountered by a feminine individual. The relative value of each is open to interpretation insofar as one's perspective is feminine or masculine, leading to judgments of their being either positive or negative.

The modes of being to be considered here are (a) inwardness or all-is-one-ness, the Eros/relatedness principle as the urge to wholeness; (b) "masochism" or receptivity, and the related quality of passivity, that is, non-assertion; and (c) the materialistic identification or link between the feminine and Nature. Each of these modes of being is held to be expected behavior in those of the feminine temperament. Although artificially differentiated for purposes of discussion, they in fact are mutually intertwined in the feminine individual, representing various facets of a single attitude towards life. Taken together, they serve as an outline of a code of conduct by which advocates of feminine philosophy may be identified, serving as the necessary, but individually insufficient, conditions for being considered an adherent of the feminine principle.

a. <u>Inwardness/all-is-one-ness</u>. In the traditional view, women have no <u>interest</u> or aptitude for the objective, extrovertive concerns of life, namely business, politics, and science, all of which have tended to be male monopolies. The masculine mind, whether inhabiting a male or female body, prevails in these areas. The feminine being, on the other hand, bestows attention on the details of personal inter-relationships--woman as the essentially social animal, the civilizing influence in society. If approached as a matter of personal concern, intimately related to our inner being, any field can be considered feminine.

Masculine progress in the "external" world (the world encountered as external), is balanced by the conserving force of the feminine principle within the realm of human activity where the feminine considers itself as one with the whole. The feminine experience involves one's whole being rather than just one part of that being, usually the mind or intellect. The masculine principle is oriented towards performance and problem-solving, the feminine towards the "human meaning" underlying a task. The feminine attitude is characterized by a turning within, addressing oneself to a specific personal need rather than concentrating on the accomplishment of a general task (as in the masculine attitude).[122] Hence, the masculine physician would treat the symptoms of a disease, dealing with the mechanics of the situation, while a feminine one would seek out its root causes, as they affect the whole person (holistic medicine).

Alternately expressed, the inner-directedness of the feminine principle produces the "realization of '<u>Dasein als Wirheit</u>' (of authentic human existence as togetherness with others)".[123] All of humanity is encompassed in a single inner space by virtue of the fact that plurality merely indicates the diverse possibilities of all human existence. The rejection of superficial institutional values, or more appropriately, of codes to control human behavior, in favor of a common humanity, which exercises self-control by the extension of the ego-self into a shared Self, yields a harmonious community under the feminine perspective.

Somewhat paradoxically, by becoming aware of our
distinctly human elements the feminine principle recognizes that humanity is one with the cosmos. To realize
the essentially human role is simultaneously to realize
the encompassing unity of reality, that all-is-one
under various manifestations and at various levels of
being. Thus, the feminine principle is characterized
by a unique sensitivity of the intricacies of human relationships: given the feminine "genius . . . for being
human", " it is the function of women to teach men how
to be human".[124] That is to say, the feminine principle stipulates the realization of our uniquely human
potential, which once attained yields our harmonization
with the universe as a whole. Fulfilling our role as
human beings is tantamount to filling our role as
members of the cosmos.

A further paradox in feminine all-is-one-ness is
that its cosmic sense not only illumines and is supported by the realization of our human essence, but
also stimulates and is stimulated by a realization of
selfhood in a positive narcissism. This feminine narcissism, noted previously in conjunction with maternal
love, serves as the link between mother and child--the
child, as an extension of the feminine self, serves as
a catalyst for the emergence of the shared Self.

On a cosmic scale, the self is extended beyond the
individual child, even beyond humanity itself, to encompass all of being. Positive narcissism provokes a
"'self'-forgetting identification with all that exists", to the exclusion of egocentric isolationism.[125]
As has been so astutely observed by Lou Salomé, the
legendary Narcissus is transfixed by his image in "the
mirror of Nature", rather than in a mirror of human
creation: "Perhaps it was not just himself that he be-
held in the mirror, but himself as if he were still
All."[126] The principle of all-is-one-ness works in the
feminine perspective precisely because that all is nar-
cissistically, and quite positively, identified with
the one self.

Such inner direction has been described, by masculine forces, as mere subjectivity and emotionalism,
suffering in comparison with masculine concerns of
"laws and principles of outer worlds".[127] However, it
also could be argued that inner direction is accompanied by inner laws, the laws of Nature and instinct.
From the feminine metaphysical perspective the outer
is the inner; the principle of the soul is identical
with the principle of Nature, follows a microcosmic-

macrocosmic pattern. The soul, our link to the source of the material sphere, has almost invariably been recognized as feminine, as in the case of the psyche and <u>anima</u>. The poles of spirit and body, soul and Nature, thus have been assigned to the feminine principle. This reflects the duality of the Transformative and Elementary characters of the feminine and provides the essential continuity between realms which only <u>seem</u> to be opposed in the context of our narrow human perspective.

To compensate for the sense of deficiency experienced in common existence, the feminine advocate consciously strives for wholeness through the completing function. Inner-directedness is slowly extended, like the ever-widening circles on the surface of a pool, from self, to humanity, to Nature, until the inner microcosm has been recognized as one with the outer macrocosm in its fullest scope. Jung describes this urge as "a longing for meaning and fulfillment, a growing disgust with senseless one-sided-ness, with unconscious instinctuality and blind contingency".[128] It follows from a primal need to see ourselves 'as' something, within some context, specifically within the context of the entire cosmos. As noted above, one expression of this urge towards wholeness is motherhood, physical or mental creativity, which fulfills the self by extending it into a shared Self.

The move towards completion, hailed by Ulanov as the pre-eminent function of the feminine principle, parallels the completion experienced or actually implemented by the mother in regard to her child; the child is both a manifestation and a fulfillment of her biological function. Completion is characterized by encompassing rather than exclusion; the feminine "does not exclude in order to purify, as does the masculine, but instead embraces all elements in order to redeem".[129] Unity results from a non-discriminating mergence of opposites--spiritual/material, religious/sensual, personal/abstract (archetypal), transformative/elemental.[130] It represents a new Gestalt, so to speak, one which does not merely draw its lines differently from those of the masculine Gestalt, but which actually eliminates lines altogether.

<u>Eros</u> has its own role to play in achieving the goal of wholeness. Feminine love aims not a relationship in the sense of an I-Thou <u>Begegnung</u> or meeting. Rather, the feminine principle entails relatedness, the fact of being related, a mergence or union which recog-

nizes no discriminations. Eros is an involvement 'for the sake of personal subjective emotional union' which is more than self awareness or awareness of another.[131] Love serves to unite us all in one being.

Maternal love is an exemplary expression of the urge to wholeness. As "the true spirit of humanity" maternal love is characterized by the mother's free and unconditional feeling for the child, her self-extended being.[132] Montagu goes so far as to hail this type of love (identified here with Eros) as "the evolutionary destiny of human beings", such that women are given the task of teaching men "to live as if to live and to love were one".[133] The wholeness of Eros, if implemented in our existence, results in both universal love and universal life.

In this sense, the feminine principle demands surrender of its adherents, a surrender based on the utter confidence that one is surrendering to the oneness of the true or shared Self. The "fruits" bestowed by a woman (feminine individual) who loves "abide in her bosom".[134] Love aims at an expansion of the self, quite apart from the masculine "pursuit of the everdesireable, because unattainable woman".[135] Hence, the feminine being is "the antithesis of the Faustian man", embracing within the (extended) self the goal of das Ewig-Weibliche.[136] The feminine principle has no external goal but is an end in itself, which accounts for the fact that the Transformative character follows a circular path of enlightenment back to the Elementary character. Both represent the same reality encountered from different foci.

b. Receptivity/non-assertion. The second mode of feminine being is derived from the common opinion which attributes masochistic tendencies to women, as one who seeks pleasure in pain. As set forth by Helene Deutsch, disciple of Freud, masochistic drives evolve from the female's passive role in sex. It is assumed that women are conditioned to experience pleasure in subjugation, the pleasure "of undergoing things, of giving herself over into the grasp of others, of accepting unfreedom, patience, and even suffering."[137] The masculine bias of the Freudian school is obvious in this assessment, for it envisions woman adjusting herself to prevailing social standards. The negativity of masochism is directly refuted by the previous discussions of narcissistic elements as central to the feminine principle; the fullest pleasure in and of the self leaves no possibility for subjugation where no hierarchy of subjector and subjected exists.

Interpretations of feminine "masochism" are available which do take into account the full situation of the feminine principle. Lou Salomé (herself a critical student of Freudianism) espoused the view that women recognize reality "as something received [in the attitude of acceptance], or even conceived [creatively], within herself [as a product of inwardness], not something which she seeks [opposed to masculine pursuit of an ever unattainable ideal]".[138] It is interesting to note Karen Horney's suggestion that masochism, a tending toward "the goal of oblivion" and an escape from the conflict-prone limitations of the self, is a "pathological modification" of Nietzsche's Dionysian (negative feminine) perspective.[139] Hence, masochism is directly relatable to the previously discussed sense of all-is-one-ness, although in perverted form.

One can assume, then, that some normal feminine mode of being corresponds to the perversion of masochism, which has been dismissed as masochistic by masculine interpreters. The positive implications of this attitude merely need to be reasserted for the negative connotations to be dispersed. Only the neurotic personality considers pain pleasurable, hence genuine masochism is possible in the feminine principle only when its values have been misplaced or destroyed.

The true case of feminine "masochism" appears to lie in the attitude of receptivity, of acceptance, of Yin yielding. The woman in natural childbirth is assuredly no masochist, at least under normal circumstances, nor is she exchanging temporary pain for a child. The latter type of exchange is indicative of the masculine barter system of relinquishing or enduring something for an ultimate gain to compensate the ego. Buytendijk mistakes this for the feminine attitude, seeing it as a means of instilling value in the pain, such that the woman deems that reinterpreted pain worthy of being suffered.[140] Instead, applying a purely feminine interpretation, the woman accepts the pain of childbirth as a natural accompaniment of the process, without either bestowing upon it a contrived value or making it an end in itself. Similarly, the generalized attitude of receptivity involves a recognition of the processes of Nature as irrevocable and ultimately the only feasible course of events in terms of the over-all context. Nature functions impersonally, without the occasional interventions of a vindictive (or even benevolent) anthropomorphic deity. Pain is therefore not inflicted directly upon an individual, as revenge or a test of worthiness imposed by the divine, but rather comes as an unavoidable and relatively insignificant by-product of events.

All events in life are accepted in the same manner in which pain is accepted. The feminine being remains receptive to "the whole spectrum of life", without the masculine dedication to the "all-or-none principle" (repeated in Aristotelian logic); the possibility for accommodating adjustment remains ever-present.[141] A sensitivity to the intermediate stages of being and perfection which occupy the space between the apex and the nadir of existence, the manifold shades of grey, is intrinsic to the feminine perspective, for these too have a share in the ultimate reality.

The advocate of the feminine principle is able to assent, not subjugated to natural forces, but living in accord with natural processes. Such positive acceptance can be considered weak only in terms of masculine assertiveness, the futile challenging of Nature which seeks to dominate rather than harmonize with the full range of natural "resources". Trite as it may sound, it is still the pliant willow which endures over the mighty, but rigid, oak in the face of Nature's raging storms. This quality of endurance has been described as the "superior resiliency" of the feminine being, its natural capacity to absorb the "shocks of life". This distinctive capacity is ample enough for the feminine personality to lend its strength to others in the form of comfort, dispensed through the mothering function.[142]

Correspondingly, the passivity attributed to the feminine principle may be reinterpreted as positive non-assertion. It is woman's capacity "for letting herself be formed".[143] Or, defined as a negation of the masculine in Freud, it is "an active pursuit of passive ends . . . suppression of aggression".[144] The significant point is that passivity or the attitude of non-assertion must be "actively" chosen; it is the decision to take into account the elements of darkness in the human condition. The result is total openness to life, "suspension of intention".[145] Ego interest is not allowed to assert itself or stimulate aggression, the sole interest being for the organic wholeness, the shared Self.

For example, the incidence of fear reactions in females may be traced to a superior sensitivity to the environment, if fear is interpreted as a positive natural drive intended to insure the fullest possible chance for survival.[146] When life is significantly valued, as it is by followers of the feminine principle, all possible accommodations will be made to sustain it. Violent solutions to problems are avoided, and suicide appropriately has been termed a "masculine type of reaction".[147] The feminine tendency is to accept, to adjust, and not to give way to desperate and ultimately futile measures. All aspects of the problem or situation, considered as a whole, are investigated so that it may be solved sub species aeternitatis.

The question of passivity is made moot by the feminine encounter of the world, not as an 'other' to be resisted, the typical masculine attitude, but as an inherently valued realm, an organic whole of which she (or he) is a functioning part. Women are more "in tune with the universe".[148] Experiments have revealed that female subjects (as representatives of the feminine principle) tend to grasp a field of perception in its entirety, without any selective focus of attention. This is indicative of an acceptance of an object or view without the imposition of value judgments, in contrast to masculine analyticity.[149]

The inescapable 'is/ought' controversy of the feminine/masculine polarity asserts itself once more: the feminine receptivity to reality versus the reconstructionist aspirations of the masculine principle. The feminine willingness to see things as they are, rather than as one would hope they would be, constitutes "clarity of vision". The feminine principle's corresponding "clarity of action" derives from its openness to reality without "endorsing or condoning or appropriating or even changing what is".[150] The feminine assumption of a deterministic universe underlies this attitude, a determinism which need not subjugate us.

c. The link with Nature/materiality. To insure that the feminine principle remains in contact with reality a certain degree of materiality is required. This is provided by the third essential mode of feminine being, its link with Nature or all that is natural and instinctual, its ability to harmonize with the universe. "The feminine style of transformation is to seek the hidden meaning of concrete happenings, to go down deep into personal events and into the dark, unknown places of our own emotions"; a change is wrought in the feminine individual by surrounding events, to a far greater extent than that individual can alter events.[151] Knowledge is assimilated by "a mixing of attentiveness and contemplation"; the process of depth psychology, which proceeds by a receptivity to and participation in psychic events, is quite similar to the working of the feminine principle.[152]

Materiality is intrinsic to the feminine essence which is so intimately related to material Nature. Woman in fact has been equated with her body (see above). Her "spiritual exercises are conjugated in the flesh", and spirit suffuses the entire feminine being—"she experiences herself both as subject and object in the mysterious process." For example, in the process of pregnancy, "woman's concrete being" is simultaneously organ and instrument of transformation.[153] Spirit manifests itself in the material. The feminine individual remains open to that aspect of being which is commonly repudiated by the masculine perspective.

The conjunction of materiality and spirituality in the feminine principle is nowhere better illustrated than in the integration of sexuality in the whole feminine being. Only within the context of the feminine principle is sexuality neither ignored nor approached as a threatening "schism"; on the contrary, it "abides in the homeland of personality, which can still include all the sublimations of the spirit without losing itself."[154] Asceticism and debauchery, the polar negations of sexuality, emerge only under the influence of the masculine principle (as it seeks to negate or pervert Nature).[155] Thus arise the persistent images of woman as _femme fatale_ which are as primal as Eve. Woman is symbol of sexuality, the goddess of the erotic, patriarchal society's "symbol of sin".[156]

This very capacity for eroticism, with its potential for the direct physical expression of being, holds great reserves of energy which may be channeled to merge with other feminine modes of being. For example, the experience of union in sexual intercourse has the potential for conveying the sense of all-is-one-ness for both women and men. This state of affairs has prompted Lou Salomé to describe the sex act as "an absolute symbol of spiritual union, particularly in the case of woman who unites opposites more completely in her own more integrated being."[157] With this intent sex has been employed for mystical purposes in lefthanded Tantrism and certain sects of Taoism, while the imagery, if not the act, of intercourse has been borrowed by otherwise "pure" religious mystics (e.g., Teresa of Avila).

In its close association with Nature and instinct, the feminine principle is also close to the animal and vegetative forces of life, with the very principle underlying all life. In this respect, woman has been described as "the fortunate animal",[158] fortunate in still being an animal, true to her nature. Even Schopenhauer, well-known for this disdain for women, admits the link between the feminine and the life force, making woman an ally of Will. It has been observed by the poet Rilke that woman participates in an "inward, impersonal, unwilled bond with nature", and possesses a "mysterious interiority".[159] The mystery of the interiority lies in its microcosmic/macrocosmic identification with external reality in Nature. Simone de Beauvoir declares: "In woman are incarnated all mysteries of nature, and man escapes her hold when he frees himself from nature"; woman is even characterized as "in bondage to life's mysterious processes".[160] In fact, however, the sense of oneness eliminates the possibility of bondage.

Nature continues to be represented by a maternal figure, Mother Nature. The archetype is the same as that embodied in Isis, the material manifestation of 'Creative Spirit'. The words of Plutarch are eminently revealing of the feminine principle in Nature symbolized by Isis, and of the human encounter with that force

> . . . which is capable of receiving the whole of genesis; in virtue of which she has been called 'Nurse' and "All-Receiving' by Plato and, by the multitude, 'She of the ten thousand Names', through her being transformed by Reason (<u>logos</u>) and perceiving all forms and ideas or shapes.[161]

Isis is the all-pervasive, the matter of the cosmos, combining the physical and the spiritual in accordance with the feminine principle.

Similarly, the moon, repository of natural fecundity, instinctual wisdom, and "the at-one-ness with natural law", has been long worshipped under the sign of the feminine principle. The very rhythm of Nature and of life has been discerned in the cyclical functions of a woman's body, a cycle reputed to be guided by the lunar phases.[162] Whether or not this is actually the case, woman remains sensitized to changes in material being, both internal and external. The world

is not subject to linear progression, but involved in a
constant ebb and flow of energy (Yin and Yang) on a
massive scale, a constant returning upon itself, a
returning to the One.

In Nature, and the naturalistic religious feeling
centered in an immanent godhead, the feminine principle
combines spirit and flesh. Feminine religion is itself
merely "an intensification and deepening" of mundane
existence.[163] The feminine religious experience is both
more impersonal, by involving the whole of reality, and
more personal, in its direct participation in that reality, than any experience possible under the anthropocentric masculine principle.

To express these materialistic, Nature-oriented
concepts, the feminine individual has recourse to an
image-laden language, relying on symbolism rather than
on purely verbal means of communication. Jung refers
to this as "feminine comprehension", a comprehension
which develops gradually and culminates in the transformation of the individual so effected.[164] The symbols or archetypes are incorporated into our very
thought processes. Each archetype, each image, is able
to conjure up a multiplicity of connotations in the receptive feminine psyche. Bachelard succinctly vali-
dates this approach on the part of the __anima__ by stating
that "everything is not said when one creates words".[165]
The foregoing outline demonstrates that in its distinctive archetypal expressions or manifestations as well
as in modes of being the feminine principle can claim a
sphere of its own. Certain images and functions are
associated exclusively with the feminine individual,
just as certain forms of behavior are indicative of a
feminine temperament. Moreover, viewed in the context
of the feminine principle, the positive implications of
these manifestations and modes of being become apparent, thereby facilitating the organization of a feminine perspective which is the prerequisite for a feminine philosophy. Manifestations of the feminine principle shape the metaphysical and epistemological assumptions of a philosophy; the modes of being are reflected in feminine ethics and socio-political philosophy.

C. Implications of the Feminine Principle for
    Socio-Political Organization

Thus far, the feminine principle has been explored
as an individual expression, whether in individual
archetypes or the modes of being peculiar to individual

persons. The feminine principle provides the framework through which one can encounter the world. However, there is another plane on which the feminine principle can be implemented, namely in an over-all social context. The feminine Weltanschauung, if shared by an entire community, would be manifested in appropriate cultural archetypes and a common social code of behavior.

In order to examine the social implications of the feminine principle, its projected society is again set in contrast to the more familiar masculine social organization. The aspects of society to be dealt with here include general spheres of activity and their intellectual representatives; views of the human condition, in terms of its essence, ideals, and problems; judgments on the universe; and theological expressions. The social implications of the feminine principle are detailed in subsequent discussions of actual instances of feminine philosophies.

When at the level of extended human interrelationships certain attitudes and presuppositions are held in common, which taken together constitute a principle of being, the members of that community may be said to share a common world view or Weltanschauung. Despite the inevitable diversity of or dissent by certain individuals in that community, that viewpoint determines the way in which society as a whole works. As indicated above, the feminine principle elicits a code of values and behavior patterns from its adherents. Loosely embodied in a matriarchal form of social order, this principle results in an appropriately feminine family orientation, in a small and communally-focused group in harmony with its environment. It stands in opposition to masculine nationalism and chauvinism, in which the family serves only as "a means to an end, one of the foundations of the state"--"cosmic mist" confronts "coordinated factors".[166] The question is really one of the purpose of the state: do we need a politically organized social unit as a loose structure designed to promote the interests of its citizens or as an end in itself, the political philosophy of assorted masculine advocates? Of course, this decision is made based on fundamental metaphysical assumptions, and especially the role of human nature within that metaphysics. The reasons for the decision here attributed to the feminine perspective become clear through the examination of specific feminine philosophies and the socio-political structure they envision.

Two entirely different worlds emerge from the feminine and masculine perspectives, that of values in the feminine (being-here-now) and the masculine pragmatism which focuses on a fully human "projected goal".[167] Each of these outlooks is either discerned to be inherent in the world as now existing or else is projected into some utopian future modeled by exclusively human efforts. Imitation of Nature is more valued in the feminine view, and the construction of a narrowly human ideal in the masculine view.

The problem of perspectives recently has been outlined by Sam Keen, a philosopher and theologian by training, under the headings of the Dionysian/Apollonian or Cosmic (sub species aeternitatis) and the Rationalistic poles.[168] Although Keen's brief presentation of these perspectives touches upon several facets of their expression, we will confine ourselves to those aspects which are most relevant to issues in feminine philosophies. Certain of his evaluations of individual types and modes of behavior conflict with the feminine/masculine poles outlined above. In the context of the whole, however, and given Keen's own tentativeness regarding his outline, the minor discrepancies can be overlooked. What is significant here are the positive contributions made by Keen's suggestions in extending the feminine perspective to social matters.

In historical terms, the patriarchal social unit of the Apollonian or Rationalistic perspective manifests male dominance, hierarchical class structure, and a generally controlled society. Its values are the distinctly human ones of rationality, logic, and the truth-embodying abstractness of the word, all of which demand the supremacy of the mind over the body and of (masculine) discursive reason over (feminine) emotion or what is non-rational. The masculine principle sketched above can readily be recognized in these values.

More ancient than this patriarchal intrusion, the supposed matriarchal structure emphasized agriculture, with the community thus being taken up by and participating in the seasonal cycles, in the rhythms of life emanating from Mother Earth. The values of such a society, Keen contends, would lie in surrender, trust, nurture, imagination, and intuition. Under the positive focus of the feminine principle, these values become receptivity and acceptance, maternal caring, creativity, and feminine intuition. The 'getting' goals of the patriarchal community are set in sharp contrast to the 'giving' harmony promoted in the matriarchal communities.

Identified with these respective viewpoints are a host of thinkers and systems of thought. Under the Rationalistic heading one discovers the dualistic Greek and Christian doctrines of mind/body and spirit/flesh, expressed by Aristotle, Aquinas, and Descartes. Western scientific method, technology, Freudianism, and Behaviorism are among its products. It might also be added that impersonal and highly organized -isms fit well in this perspective, such as facism and, in their institutionalized forms, Confucianism and Marxism. Systems of thought which seek to objectify reality and to impose an order which can be comprehended in human terms are most appealing to those of the masculine perspective.

The list of those sympathetic to the Cosmic perspective includes the adherents of animism, monism, primitive and Eastern doctrines (taken in a very general sense, since certain sects are inappropriate to the Cosmic view), and some schools of pre-Cartesian philosophy in the West. Keen's candidates for representative philosophers here are the idealists Plato, Augustine, and Hegel, although objections could well be registered against each on specific points. Proponents of the Cosmic viewpoint are held responsible for the Romantic "backlash" in Eckhart, Blake, Coleridge, and Emerson, while its values have been espoused most recently by Jung, Marcuse, Transpersonal Psychology, and the Esalen Institute. Such movements tend to have a personal emphasis, guided by a founding spirit rather than by rigid principles, and advocate the Eros/relatedness method discussed above.

In assessing the position which humanity occupies in the system of the universe, its essence, ideals, and problems, the two schools of thought differ accordingly. Considering the human animal as Homo faber, the 'fabricating' animal, the Rationalistic enthusiasts assert the need to instill reason and order into an ever-encroaching world chaos through serious and "realistic" (i.e., oriented toward narrow personal profit) thought and work. The guiding notion seems to be that Nature can always be improved upon. The potential for progress is deemed to be endless, as reflected in the masculine assumption of linear progression in history.

At the opposite pole, Cosmic thought perceives humanity as <u>Homo</u> <u>ludens</u>, the playful animal, enmeshed in an illusory veil (<u>Maya</u>) of manifestations which emanate from the divine One. Human dignity thus demands play, love, spontaneity, and a fantasy to rival that of Nature itself. In fact, human activities are an expression of Nature, for human beings <u>are</u> Nature. Every action is optimally performed after <u>the</u> manner of its own intrinsic nature, which makes that action effortless, a harmonious flow with the whole. It is perhaps best to de-emphasize the play aspect here and concentrate instead on the naturalness of the Cosmic perspective and of all actions undertaken from this perspective. As such, it can be applied more readily in a philosophical context as a sympathy with universal law and order in Nature.

The masculine ideal involves a strong ego, a bolstering of one's ability to cope with "adult" responsibilities amidst unavoidable tragedy and conflict in life. The masculine virtues of courage and perseverance can be recognized here. Contrastingly, under the Cosmic vision, one looks beyond narrow societal demands of role playing, etc., and enters a universal context of being. Life is then a divine comedy whose ideal is more appropriately the innocent child (or childlike individual, as the feminine being is reputed to be) engaged in love and play and ruled by instinct and empathic compassion. The lauded assertiveness of the masculine perspective thus can be viewed as a retreat from reality by which we construct for ourselves a series of continual crises to be met and overcome. It is a choice between the Cosmic Garden of Eden and the ever-challenging "real world" of the Rationalistic person; reality can be experienced in either way, depending upon one's perspective at a given moment.

The respective evaluations of <u>the</u> human problem reflect these ideals. The Rationalistic school of thought senses danger in the extremes of libido (sexuality) and super-ego (religion and mysticism), with reality residing in the ego, as dominated by reason (Plato's charioteer). The desire for peace, nirvana, lack of conflict, is adjudged an especially perilous death wish, indicative of the persuasive power the repudiated values exercise over even the masculine principle. The "retreat" or escapism which the goal of peaceful harmony is assumed to be always remains a live option, but is interpreted as the suicidal option by the Rationalistic individual.

Flouting the morbid suggestion of a death wish, the Cosmic perspective perceives the human problem to be centered in the illusion of separateness. This illusion yields counterproductive aggressions, while misplaced ego emphasis threatens to sicken both the society and the individual. The cure is a radical (at least in masculine terms) change of systems--a change to a system capable of upholding natural balance in life, which recognizes the so-called death wish as a series of transformations (from isolated ego or ego-self to mergence with the One in the shared Self) rather than extinction. Reason has a tendency to tyrannize the emotions (the instincts), and must be carefully monitored. The instinctual outburst of emotion is self-destructive if suppressed.

With regard to the functioning of the universe, its chaos and plurality plague proponents of the Rationalistic view, while design and unity are assumed to predominate in the Cosmic view. The Apollonian view considers unity as a mere human projection or imposition (or imposed by an anthropomorphic diety), alien to reality (the primal chaos). Consequently, it is necessary to force the ordering system of a social contract on naturally divisive humanity. Since human nature is considered to be basically evil and aggressive, individual welfare requires the sacrifice of certain rights within the state to guarantee law and order.

More optimistically, the Cosmic universe offers continuity and love in the one divine source, expressed through natural synchronicity. The ideal socio-political community likewise reflects a harmony of interdependent parts, an organic whole comprised of humanity and Nature, of the humanity which is a manifestation of Nature. A totally artificial human creation of a state is unnatural and hence ultimately unworkable. An appeal must be made to the ecological balance existing among beings. In this way the interests of the individual citizen can be identified with the interests of the state, both reflecting the natural instinct for preservation (conatus). There is no stronger bond than this positive narcissism, when true self interest becomes one with community interest, or, the interest of the shared Self. Human nature, assumed to be naturally good, has no need for the structure of a state once it has been perfected, that is, harmonized with Nature.

Finally, the theological position of the Rationalistic perspective posits a transcendent being actively interfering in history through miracles. This anthropomorphic deity also maintains a strict distinction between time and eternity, the sphere of humanity and that of God, the sacred and the profane. The Cosmic godhead, however, is immanent, the pervasive substance underlying the universe in which all participates to varying degrees. The sacred is nothing other than the real, and plurality is once more relegated to illusion (or a lesser degree of perfection and reality), to our own human deceptions or misconceptions.

A further discrepancy between these concepts of deity, unnoted by Keen, is that of the human and personal character of the Rationalistic God, his overwhelming ego, as opposed to the impartiality, or lack of specialized interests, of the Cosmic deity. Suzuki cites this impersonal love as the most remarkable aspect of Zen (with its Taoist-influenced Ch'an roots). Contrary to the personal quality of Christian mystic experience as an ego relationship (see the accounts of Saint Teresa and Saint Bernard), the Zen experience is a mergence of the self in the one reality, and is impersonal and intuitive in the highest degree. References to a definite figure, to a heavenly Father or Mother, are added only after the fact to heighten the overall effect of enlightenment.[169]

A further point of significance relating to godhead concerns the distance felt by the individual with respect to the divine. Although the Rationalistic God is a personal one, the highest state the devotee can look forward to is to be _with_ God. The proponent of the Cosmic view, however, is _able_ to actually _merge_ with the impersonal deity or being, to become one with the universe, to _be_ God, at least in part. Paradoxically, then, the impersonal godhead is able to foster a more personal experience by eliminating the distance between the individual and the divine.

The conclusion drawn by Keen in the face of his established distinctions of perspective is the need to recognize a viable alternative to the accepted Western Weltanschauung, which last has indeed proven deficient for satisfying the demands and temperament of certain individuals in our culture. This new alternative he hails as the revival of an old one, "the recovery of a perennial way of looking at the world".[170] The range of human possibilities can only be covered by taking both perspectives into account. Without its feminine complement, the masculine perspective is unbalanced.

Significantly, Keen's Dionysian perspective is substantially in agreement with the fundamentals of the feminine principle which have been outlined above. This fact is attested to by the modern reviver and advocate of the Dionysian Weltanschauung himself, Friedrich Nietzsche: "May I venture to suggest, incidentally, that I know women? This knowledge is part of my Dionysian patrimony."[171] In evaluating the extent of Nietzsche's self-avowed knowledge of women, representatives of the feminine principle, one must allow for the incursions of the negative feminine in his views, making them not entirely expressive of the positive reality of the feminine perspective. But, in any case, the link between Dionysos and the feminine is clear.

In sum, the orientation and aspirations of the feminine principle and its perspective have been clarified through their contrast with the traditional masculine principle and perspective. Interest in the material or sensual realm, as valuable in and for itself, is advocated by the feminine principle; the material universe is an expression, manifestation, or mode of the divine and replaces other-worldly (Nietzsche's 'true world') concerns. There is no need to sacrifice present desires to meet the requirements of future fulfillment in a blessed afterlife or utopian state. Rather, the positive narcissism of the shared Self prevails, integrating the individual in Nature. Both can be served simultaneously by a proper self-centeredness, one which recognizes that there is only one center for the multiple selves, just as the mother yields to the needs of her child because that child is an extension of her self.

Nor must individuality be sacrificed on the altar of the state, as envisioned in numerous science fiction fantasies (see in particular Huxley's Brave New World). Giving and receiving are the same activity in the context of a harmonious universe. Spiritual as well as material ecology yields a balanced whole. Moreover, the "feminine" state of being constitutes the standard of enlightenment or blessedness. This state of being is assumed to be natural for the feminine principle and serves as a model for others to imitate, the Ewig-Weibliche blazing the path of our ascent.

The masculine principle is not totally excluded from the feminine sphere of the enlightened, but is incorporated in the ultimate state of perfection, a transcendence of polarity in the higher evolution of the feminine principle, the Transformative character. The working out of the masculine principle spans the intermediate area of development between the primal Uroborus of the Elementary character to a refined reassertion of the feminine principle under the guidance of the Transformative character. Discursive reason propels us from static instinct in the Elementary character through the masculine perspective's intellectual understanding and into the dynamic intuition of the Transformative character. Such is the course of a feminine philosophy.

Summary

To summarize what has been learned here concerning the feminine principle on which any feminine philosophy must be based, let us review the previous topics of discussion. The polarity of the feminine and masculine principles has been considered from various points of view. In the sphere of traditional Chinese thought, the relationship between Yin and Yang, the yielding and the firm in the context of the I Ching, has been sketched as a complementarity of primal forces. These forces, as expressed under the trigrams of the Receptive and the Creative, have likewise been linked with feminine and masculine modes of being.

In modern Western terms, three main approaches to the feminine/masculine distinction have been outlined: the biological basis argued for by Freud and the Freudians; the cultural counter-proposal of Horney, Mead, and others; and the Symbolic approach followed by the Jungian school of thought. In conjuction with the Yin/Yang polarity, these three approaches, however much their various claims may conflict, offer proof of at least the subjective existence of two alternative perspectives, loosely indentified as feminine and masculine, the passive-receptive and the active-assertive.

In addition to the fact of a sex-specified distinction of perspective, certain qualities and characteristics have been assigned to the feminine pole and generally agreed upon by the polarizers. Taken together as the expressions of a feminine principle, these qualities and characteristics reveal a multi-faceted Weltanschauung. To explore these facets more carefully, separate discussions were devoted first to the manifestations of the feminine principle and then to its modes of being.

The feminine principle manifests itself in two

forms, by which we objectify its reality: we experience the surrounding world via the 'other-ness' of the <u>anima</u> and the subjective experience of the two-fold feminine archetype characterized as the Elementary (maternal, enclosed, encompassing container) and the Transformative (Sophia as source of inspiration and salvation) aspects. From this survey it was discovered that the feminine principle functions in the roles of completing the masculine (<u>anima</u>), as loving and caring mother (the Elementary character), and as intuitive guide to artistic creativity and ultimate intuitive wisdom (the Transformative character). The significant paradox of narcissistic <u>Eros</u>/relatedness, the method of the feminine principle, was noted for future reference.

As for the feminine modes of being, different facets of one feminine attitude toward life, they emerge as threefold. Inwardness or the sense of all-is-one-ness relies upon the peculiar insights of feminine <u>Eros</u> in the inner direction and communal or human concerns of the feminine adherent, as well as in the urge toward wholeness. Under the second mode of being, the assumed feminine trait of masochism has been exposed as a perversion of spontaneous receptivity, an understanding of and yielding to the irrevocable conditions of Nature. Related to this receptive attitude are the advantages of remaining sensitive to one's environment. Finally, the strong link between the feminine principle and organic Nature, its firm and uncompromised grounding in the materialistic, was noted. Entailed in this aspect of feminine being are woman's heightened sexuality, the force of instinct, and a direct participation in the realm of Nature.

A final set of contrasts is drawn between the feminine and the masculine spheres of being through a viewing of the social implications of applying their respective principles. Employing Keen's distinction between Cosmic and Rationalistic views, two distinct realms of social existence are revealed through attitudes towards the community, humanity, the universe, and the godhead. The Dionysian character of the Cosmic view provides proof of its link with the feminine principle.

For a final look at the feminine principle, we might return to the <u>I Ching</u> and an image-laden discussion of the Receptive:

>   The Receptive is the earth [Nature],
>   the mother [maternal love and caring].

> It is cloth [encompassing], a kettle
> [container, womb], frugality, it is
> level [impartial], it is a cow with
> a calf [sprirtual and material fer-
> tility], a large wagon [vehicle of
> transformation], form [opposed to
> content], the multitude [source of
> plurality], a shaft [of the tree of
> life].172

The feminine principle is expressed through all of these, and more. Confronted by it, one might be tempted to utter Lou Salomé's sentiments (in reference to psychoanalysis): "Never before have we felt as we do now that our knowledge depends so much on what we are and that our being has been released from its narrowly personal confines into the depth and breadth behind us, which is one with life itself, indistinguishable from ourselves."173

This then is the feminine principle of being organized from the diffuse feminine perspective which is systematically presented in the context of Taoism and Spinozism, exemplary feminine philosophies which demonstrate how and why one becomes an adherent of the feminine principle. The comprehensiveness of the feminine perspective, as a style of life and method of thinking, can be understood more fully through such concrete instances of the feminine principle at work, that is, in existing systems of feminine philosophy, to which we now turn our attention.

Chapter II

THE YIN PHILOSOPHY OF THE TAO TE CHING

One of the distinguishing characteristics of a feminine principle is the manner in which its elements are dependent upon the structure provided by all the other elements for support and justification. The force of the over-all system is crucial in feminine thought, as is appropriate to its urge towards wholeness in perceiving reality. For these reasons, the concepts of Taoism discussed here cannot be understood properly until the underlying feminine or Yin perspective has been understood in its entirety. In other words, the parts must be understood within the context of the whole, which is more than the mere sum of its parts.

Nonetheless, for purposes of demonstrating the feminine elements of Taoist philosophy, and facilitating a discursive understanding of these elements, artificial divisions have been drawn in the content of thought, with a view towards an ultimate feminine comprehension. A basic distinction has been made between matters of metaphysics and epistemology, on the one hand, and those of ethics and socio-political thought on the other. It is a distinction between the theoretical foundations of Taoist philosophy and their practical application in the areas of personal and societal existence; between the feminine assumptions concerning and manifestations of reality, and the effect which the knowledge, or acknowledgement, of that reality has upon the human life style/modes of being, including implications for society.

The first section of this chapter, then, deals with Taoism's philosophical theories and assumptions: (1) the metaphysical structure of Tao, (2) its dual forms, and (3) the means by which human beings, as participants in that reality, can gain knowledge of and within that structure. Tao is the primary topic of discussion--the human role is of secondary importance, noted only insofar as we relate or belong to Tao. Following the feminine principle, Tao's twofold manifestations are adopted as a guide to is theoretical framework: (a) under the Elementary character, and (b) through its Transformative aspect. Epistemology grows naturally out of metaphysics, indicating the appropriate ways in which Tao's reality is able to be known.

Turning to the specific human role in the universe, the practical applications of the revelations given by metaphysics and epistemology, the second section treats of the (1) individual and (2) collective modes of being proper to the feminine perspective of Taoism. The emphasis is upon the power or virtue (Te) of the human individual implemented to achieve personal and societal harmony with the system which is Tao, how an enlightened individual or state would function in accordance with the tenets of Tao (the feminine principle). Both ethical and socio-political considerations are examined in the contexts of the feminine modes of being: (a) inwardness/all-is-one-ness, (b) receptivity/non-assertion, and (c) the link to or harmony with Nature.

The scheme is intended both to outline the essential elements of the Taoist philosophy contained in the Tao Te Ching, and to demonstrate how those elements may be interpreted as a systematized extension of the feminine principle. The prominent position given to Yin in Taoism grants substantial justification to such a move. The justification remains valid despite the fact that the feminine standard employed here goes beyond that attributed to Yin traditionally, and actually includes a transcendence of the common level Yin/Yang polarity. Yin as positively set forth in Taoist thought implies something more than a complement to Yang, and in fact is its completing element.

Furthermore, this scheme exposes the "weaknesses" of Taoism's system, that is, its deficiencies with regard to the philosophical preciseness demanded by discursive reason. The source of these weaknesses, when judged by masculine standards, also is revealed: the burden of responsibility for verification of its doctrines is shifted from the Taoist philosopher to the student of Taoism, who is expected to attain a direct experience of Tao through intuition. After enlightenment has been attained, and given the firsthand proof of feminine radical empiricism, the Taoist assumes that all philosophical doubts will be resolved, thus compounding the frustration of the unenlightened masculine thinker. Only when approached from the feminine perspective can Taoism be properly evaluated on its own terms.

A. The Manifestations of Tao--Theoretical Foundations

Being so firmly grounded in and dependent upon reality as a sustaining source of truth, a feminine philosophy would need to place special emphasis upon metaphysics and epistemology to outline what constitutes reality and how one can legitimately expect to know that reality. Unless the foundation of reality is accessible to the adherent of the feminine principle it is not possible to formulate a philosophy. A feminine system of philosophy must be able to encompass everything that is the case, must formulate a general outline of the cosmos. The assumptions made by Taoists with respect to the underlying reality of the universe serve as the foundation upon which the remainder of their philosophy, its epistemology, ethics, and sociopolitical thought, is erected.

1. Metaphysical Manifestations: The Structure of the Universe

The Tao Te Ching places emphasis upon the metaphysical reality of Tao. The aspirations of the Taoist sage are vouchsafed by Tao itself--the individual has ready access to its truth merely by the fact of being a functioning part of the system. By focusing upon the dual manifestations of the feminine principle, the two basic approaches to reality, to Tao, are revealed. These are the Elementary character, reality encountered as primal and undifferentiated wholeness; and the Transformative character, which offers the means of transforming the multiplicity of things in the mundane world and revealing their direct contact with the ground of being Tao.

Considered discursively, through the differentiating tendency of the masculine principle, Tao is discussed in the Tao Te Ching as an external. Just as the anima reveals the quintessentially feminine facet of the otherwise masculine psyche which tends to be overshadowed by masculine consciousness, Tao represents the essence of the cosmos which tends to be overshadowed in our minds by humanistic concerns. Both anima and Tao point to a primal realm of the (collective) unconscious which we initially assume to be beyond, rather than within, ourselves. That is to say, for purposes of comprehension and discussion in human terms, Tao, like the anima, has been posited as an independent entity, an 'it', an object. Ultimately, however, Tao is not a thing, and each of us necessarily, if unknowingly, participates in Tao as a universal state of being. In this sense, the anima can be considered as a convenient personification of the feminine principle acting within the individual, and as fundamentally none other than individualized Tao.

The Taoist displays an abiding mistrust of both words and of the underlying assumptions of (masculine) discursive reason which make the abstract symbolism of words in applicable to (feminine) concrete reality. Thus, rather than being offered well-formulated theories, the reader of the Tao Te Ching is led by pregnant implications and images to an intuitive awareness of the meaning of Tao. This situation presents a problem when philosophical preciseness is sought, as in the present case, a problem which can be circumvented by discussing these metaphysical points in the context of images of the feminine principle previously outlined. The conjunction of these two streams of thought, namely the feminine principle and Taoist metaphysics, serves both to point up the feminine elements of the Taoism expressed in the Tao Te Ching and to focus attention on these elements as the building blocks of a feminine philosophy.

2. The Dual Characters of Tao

A distinction is drawn in the opening chapter of the Tao Te Ching between "Named" (yu-ming) Tao, "mother of all things", and Tao which is "Nameless" (wu-ming), "the origin of Heaven and Earth". The latter alone qualifies as absolute, for "The Tao (way) that can be told of is not the eternal Tao" (TTC,1). The direct source of the material universe is set in contrast to the further removed (intellectually speaking) ground of being. Also applied in this context are the terms Being (yu), the metaphysical entity which Fung Yu-lan identifies with the One, and Non-being (wu), as ultimate source.

Relating these distinctions to the duality of the feminine principle, it is possible to recognize the invariable and eternal Nameless Tao as the encompassing primal source designated the Elementary character. The dynamic Transformative character, so instrumental to personal enlightenment, appears in the generating function of Named Tao as origin of the material universe, mother of multiplicity. The two possible approaches to the universe are thereby covered: the vision sub species aeternitatis of Unnamed Tao as opposed to that of the individual beings engendered by Named Tao. The universe may be defined either in and for itself, or as the plurality of creation. In Jungian terminology, the undifferentiated and primordial archetype intrinsic to the unconscious is succeeded by the increasingly differentiated forms of emerging consciousness.

The dynamic aspect of Tao as cosmic force necessitates the nature of all, including its more stable aspect as the One, its "product" (TTC,42). Hence, a theoretical distinction can be made between the One as a metaphysical entity and Tao as an activating power inherent in all things, these being two aspects of reality reflected respectively in the Elementary and Transformative characters of the feminine principle. These characters manifest the inextricably intertwined dual functions stemming from a single source. Each is inconceivable without the other to complete it: the action of Tao generates the One and the One acts out Tao, in accordance with its universal law and order, thereby illustrating its power concretely.

Most importantly, these two aspects, whether considered under the feminine principle or as manifestations of Tao, are mutually supportive, even identical in essence. The unity of Tao allows it to be both unchanging (Elementary) and dynamic (Transformative), equating the changeless and the ever-changing flux, "the ground or reservoir of creativity" and its mutable concrete expressions.[1] There is the actuality of the self-contained closed womb in K'un, where creation takes place, and the actualized potential of the open womb in giving birth: the mother containing her child within, a whole in herself, and the event of having the child as an extension of herself.

In giving birth, and through its completion of "primal images", Tao is the Creative, while its imitation of such images ranks it as the Receptive.[2] Although the author of this observation had the masculine Yang in mind when referring to the Creative (Ch'ien), the statement is also applicable to the peculiar creativity of the feminine principle. This creativity paradoxically achieves wholeness or completion through its unchanging Elementary character, as Tao does through wu-wei; the receptivity of the Transformative character, however, is a dynamic transformation through the principle of Reversion (by which extremes revert to their opposite). Unlike masculine activity, feminine dynamism is contained within certain bounds, namely the natural bounds or reality represented by Tao. Hence, it is possible only to act out the 'is' of feminine reality, but not any ephemeral 'ought' posited by the masculine perspective. This point is crucial for an understanding of Taoism as a feminine philosophy; it explains the meaning of wu-wei, 'non-action', which guides Taoist ethics as natural spontaneity rather than as enforced passivity, resulting in a life-affirming determinism.

The metaphysical lines are herewith drawn for Taoist philosophy. Remaining aloof and immutable, Nameless Tao indirectly determines the state of the universe through Named Tao. The latter generates and proliferates the various levels of Being and is the source of the Ten Thousand Things. Whether envisioned as a closed or open womb, only Tao can be the source of things in the world. It is simultaneously stable (as the one) and in constant flux (as the many), hence the Taoist sage seeks to comprehend "the changeless in the ever-changing",[3] without dismissing the reality of the flux.

Each of these two aspects of Tao has its own symbols and means of expression. The block of wood (p'u) connotes the primordial state of Tao, while light (ming) holds the promise of the transformation or returning experienced through enlightenment. As the two poles of primal darkness and the light which emerges from that darkness, these may at first appear contradictory. However, beyond our limited human perspective, they are readily reconciled in the over-all context of Taoist thought.[4] Similarly, the feminine principle encompasses the depths of primal unconsciousness through the Elementary character, in addition to the intuitive heights of the Transformative character.

The modes of activity appropriate to p'u and ming are revealing with respect to Tao's dual characters, The Uncarved Block's sympathy or compassion (tz'u) (roughly equivalent to Eros) "moves from all [Tao] to one [the individual]" and is the "ground of potentiality", hence approximating the Elementary character. Tz'u is further supportive of creativity (the dynamic, Transformative character), moving "from one to all".[5] Also rendered as love or deep love, tz'u is intrinsic to Tao under its maternal and undifferentiated character. The creativity of ming serves to reveal the treasure of tz'u embodied by all things. Tao radiates tz'u compassion and we respond with individually - cultivated ming (applied to those who are 'clear-sighted', "wise, discerning"[6]).

The ensuing discussion deals first with Tao in its expression of unity or wholeness, with Nonbeing and the overt parallels with the Elementary character of the feminine principle, such as that between tz'u and Eros. Subsequently, the manifestations of Tao in material plurality are presented, in relation to universal law in Being, determinism, non-homocentric orientation, and Nature, and culminating in the interaction of opposites. This interaction is itself a concrete representation of the ongoing process of harmonization in the universe under the principle of Reversion.

    a. Nameless Tao--the Elementary character.
Nature is a closed system, the closed womb of K'un, of generation and passing away, self-contained container of the Great Ultimate. Tao's universality entails a dissolution of self in the One as merged with a communion of selves--an extension of the ego-self into the shared Self. Our task here is to deal with the oneness aspect of this equation, reserving the 'all' for a separate discussion of plurality.

    The root meaning of Tao is firmly implanted in the field of metaphysics, a metaphysics which may be considered feminine by virtue of its holistic and non-anthropocentric perspective.[7] It is notable that Tao lacks a prefacing definite article--it is not referred to as 'the Tao', but simply as 'Tao', to avoid imposing artificial differentiations upon it. First it must be shown that certain masculine projections on the concept of Tao are inadequate to sustain the holistic force of the Taoist philosophy, and secondly that a feminine interpretation is adequate for such a task. The plausibility of citing Taoism as an exemplary feminine philosophy is heightened by the successful demonstration of these points.

    The obscuring influence of masculine-oriented minds in interpreting Taoism is most evident among Western thinkers, as one naturally would expect. The common English rendering of the character for Tao has been 'the Way', which in itself appears neutral in relation to masculine or feminine perspectives. Yet, numerous Western interpreters, of whom Hegel is an admirable representative, have insisted upon extending this single concept along the lines of a purely masculine philosophy.[8] In a similar rationalist vein, Paul Carus has drawn a parallel between Tao and the Greek methodos: meta, 'according to' or 'after', plus hodos, 'path', yields intimations of 'the right path', 'truth', Urvernunft, and the quintessentially masculine

Logos.⁹

While Arthur Waley hails such similarities in the "meaning-extensions" of Tao as the Way in both Eastern and Western modes of thought as conducive to a Westerner's understanding of the Chinese concept,¹⁰ they can prove only detrimental when the perspective of feminine philosophy is being applied. Indeed, to identify Tao with Logos, which is inherently linked to the masculine principle governing Western philosophy, seems singularly inappropriate if one is committed to approaching Taoism on its own terms. At its worst, it is no more than an attempt to recast an essentially feminine expression as something acceptable to the masculine orientation of the Western mind. This judgment tacitly implies that the Taoist espouses a feminine perspective, an implication which has yet to be proven. Nonetheless, many respected interpretations of Taoism appear to support such a view.

If Tao is not to be identified with the differentiating tendencies of Logos, then it must be assigned to the sphere of feminine Eros, that is it must have the function of relatedness. Indeed, the prominence of Eros within Taoist thought can easily be shown. The entire being of Tao tends towards, or more precisely, is a symbol of, primal wholeness; it serves as the all-pervasive link underlying and conjoining the superficial multiplicity of the cosmos. Hence, Tao can more readily be associated with the feminine relatedness of Eros than with the masculine discrimination of Logos.

Above all, Tao is the symbol of cosmic harmony, standing in polar opposition to the differentiation and analysis of Logos. Tao is the means, method, or 'way' of unity as well as a concrete representation of that unity (the One) which serves as a guide for individual life. Thus, a dynamic interpretation of Tao is required which accommodates its aspects as concrete metaphysical reality and also the means of attaining or realizing that reality. The universe is the One; the One is permeated by Tao, its source. Tao conditions the state of reality, but also is itself that state. The Way or Tao must then be approached as something other than an abstract principle of Logos. Rather, it must be interpreted in terms of concrete relations. Tao is the unifying force in the universe, drawing together all of Being under its encompassing standard. Tao's own intrinsic unity is assured by the continuity of its characteristics in space (infinity, immanence) and time (eternity, immutability). Even though it has been objectified for purposes of discussion and thereby viewed as an external source and model, Tao reasserts its oneness, the oneness of the universe which includes everything within its scope.

Retaining the common rendering of Tao as the Way, it must be recognized as the Way of relating, of harmonizing, the diverse elements of the universe by means of an underlying natural principle latent in all existence. These particulars serve in turn to express Tao concretely as instances of reality, providing the even firmer ties of reciprocal relationship in the wholeness. The fact that the intellectual consideration of Tao (the Named) yields less than absolute Tao (the Nameless) demonstrates the latter's tendency to unify the cosmos, to create harmony (the keynote of Taoist philosophy), rather than to foster the distinctions of Logos.

Although, according to Taoist metaphysics, Tao is present in each thing, the remaining condition of the pantheistic formula (God is everything, and everything is God) is not fulfilled, that is, each thing is not Tao in the fullest sense. Or, as Van Over points out, unity results from all things participating in the divine and the divine participating in all things. Such participation neither constitutes, nor justifies, an equation of the individual with the overriding wholeness. In any case, the concept of a part has significance only at the human level of interpretation, being alien to undifferentiated Tao.

The unity or wholeness of Tao is a "unity in multiplicity" illustrated in the Tao Te Ching (11) by the wholeness of the wheel going beyond the conglomeration of hub and spokes.[11] Each component of the universe, as of the wheel, is essential to the support of the others; the over-all function is defined in terms of the whole. Tao completes the wholeness of the universe just as it completes the wheel itself representing that wholeness. It is the 'unity of background' underlying appearances; "the primordial source of all things, the mother of the world . . . the harmony of harmonies".[12] Tao is more than a "cosmological unity", it is the "continuous field" of reconciliation envisioned by Plotinus, Scotus Eriugena, and Nicholas of Cusa.[13]

Entailed by the unity of Tao is a total lack of (masculine) distinctions, at least at the lowest, most fundamental level of being-Non-being. In this sense we

can recognize being. Tao as being the Undifferentiated of
the Elementary character. The collapse of humanly-
imposed distinctions challenges our ordinary mental
processes and therefore generates the numerous paradoxical references to it. Discussing the elusiveness
of "The Invisible", "The Inaudible", and "The Subtle
(formless)", the Tao Te Ching states that confusing
concepts unite even more confusedly in the indefinable
One (14). It is "the unfathomable . . . which must be
revered in silence".[14] And so it is that Tao which is
absolute remains without a name, Nameless (wu-ming)
Tao.

Significantly, the chapter in the Tao Te Ching
just cited goes on to describe a reversion "to nothing-
ness", referring to the unity of Tao as ". . . shape
without shape,/Form (hsiang) without object./ . . .
Meet it and you will not see its head;/Follow it and
you will not see its back." Of course, Tao has neither
a head nor a back, no beginning nor end, but is all-
pervasive. It is incomprehensible in relativistic
human terms. To express this state of affairs, the
Taoist employs perhaps the most difficult philosophical
concept in all of Taoism, the concept of Nonbeing (wu),
Tao's ultimate state of being. It is a concept which
is un-masculine in scope and function, demanding a
radical readjustment of our human perspective.

To be understood properly, that is, from the
Taoist perspective, the concept of Nonbeing must be
placed in the positive feminine context of the metaphysical scheme of things. The term Nonbeing is
itself an indication of the poverty of language to
express an absolute lying beyond our usual relativities. The Taoist is forced to make use of a superficial negation to convey an underlying positive
meaning. Nonbeing is beyond or at the root of the
ordinary sense of Being: "What we call Being is in fact
Nonbeing and just what we call Not-being, is being in
its true sense . . . What we imagine to be real is not
real, and yet emanates from the real, for the Real is
the Whole."[15] More precisely, Being (yu) possesses a
lesser degree of reality than the Nonbeing (wu) usually
relegated to the lowest level of reality. As interpreted in Neo-Taoism, Nonbeing is identified as the
undifferentiated One, "pure being (pen-wu)", "original
substance (pen-t'i)".[16] Tao transcends both being and
nonbeing in their common usages, thereby attaining its
own uniquely positive significance.

Hence, the problem of Nonbeing involves a problem

within our inherently limited human point of view rather than a problem in the concept itself. Because we cannot perceive ultimate being, it is Nonbeing; because we cannot see Tao act, its action is termed non-action (wu-wei), that is, the action is viewed indirectly through the conditioned and concrete manifestations of Tao. In reality, however, the unperceived force of Nonbeing is the essential element; the utility of a vessel is due to its Nonbeing of hollow space, and that of a window to the open space it offers. "Therefore turn being into advantage, and turn nonbeing into utility" (TTC,11). The "advantage" referred to is the relative masculine type of profit; the "utility" the feminine or Yin receptivity characteristic of Tao.

The subjective and the objective are united in Nonbeing, which is inexpressible and unthinkable, non-discursive and non-masculine. Correspondingly, the feminine principle recognizes subjectivity as objectivity, the inner as the outer. The level of reality with which we are most familiar has its source in this encompassing ground; "All things in the world come from being./And being comes from non-being" (TTC,40). Nonbeing is thereby correctly approximated by such phrases as "the ultimate", "the supreme ultimate" (T'ai Chi),[17] or even the ultimateless.[18] Because Tao is not a specific object, it is identified with Nonbeing and stands in opposition to the Being of material objects. Fung Yu-lan distinguishes the two aspects of Tao as its essence of Nonbeing (the Elementary character) and its function of, or functioning through, Being (the Transformative character).[19] Taken together, Being and Nonbeing constitute the 'Mystery of Mysteries' referred to in the Tao Te Ching's initial chapter.

Although Nonbeing as primal Tao eludes definitive statements and cannot be grasped by the human mind qua human, its meaning can be conveyed, at least in part, through symbols and images which appeal to human experience, including the Uncarved Block, p'u, and the light, ming, previously mentioned. Inasmuch as ming relates directly to the Transformative character and the individual pursuit of enlightenment, the movement of the all to the one, our discussion here is restricted to the Uncarved Block symbol of Nonbeing.

The image of the Uncarved Block implies the primacy and simplicity of Nonbeing. As such, it is rendered by Fung Yu-lan as 'Unwrought Simplicity".[20] The Block is a solid mass, connoting stability in a totally non-artificial state; being uncarved, it retains its natural "simplicity" (TTC,28) and is "genuine (Tun)" in the sense of the thick wood of solid furniture.[21] The virtue of the Uncarved Block rests in its non-utility (as far as unenlightened activity or masculine profit is concerned). P'u does not exist for some purpose, it merely exists, in a "being-here-now" state. It has not yet been manipulated for uses alien to Tao or what is natural, and so symbolizes the primordial Tao. As such, it parallels the undifferentiated and unchanging state of the Elementary character. It is the lump sum of being which is Nonbeing.

P'u has further links to the feminine principle in that it functions by tz'u. Frequently rendered into English as sympathy or compassion, tz'u has a much more specific sense which corresponds exactly to the Eros/relatedness of the Elementary character. The is, tz'u implies the total mergence of one thing in another, the mother's identification, or merging of identity, with her child as an extension of her self. Tz'u is truly the relatedness of Jungian Eros as "capacity to relate", an encompassing and non-pejoratively narcissistic concern for the welfare of the offspring. Thus, the Uncarved Block is the Taoist version of the Madonna and child archetype in its most primal form.

Love or sympathy of the tz'u variety historically has been associated with maternal affection. This is demonstrated by its use as an epithet for mothers. It is appropriate that in characterizing the Tao (or Nonbeing), as acting by means of tz'u, it is depicted as "the great mother, the infinite, free from conditions of time and space"; a unity of "infinite possibility and potentiality . . . ontological basis for the fulfillment of the great sympathy".[22] Accordingly, tz'u cannot be presented as love per se, but as "the primordial, immediate source of love, the secret root of all love and compassion", interfusing subject and object. From the viewpoint of the individual, tz'u qualifies as "an ontological experience" culminating in an identification with the cosmos,[23] with the Great Mother image of Tao.

The maternal associations evoked by tz'u, continue in explicit references to Tao as mother throughout the Tao Te Ching. Based on the function and nature of Tao, the Taoist naturally tends to depict it through feminine, Yin, images. As simultaneously source and goal, Tao readily lends itself to being cast in a maternal role, expressed as both generating Gaia and devouring Kali. Tao is hailed as "beginning of the universe/

Which may be called the Mother of Universe" (52), or the oneness prior to differentiation which "may be considered the Mother of the Universe" (25).

Fulfilling yet another maternal function, Tao is a font of power, source of nourishment--"It is continuous, and seems to be always existing./Use it and you will never wear it out" (TTC,6). The mother "serves" her offspring in the same receptive manner. As noted in the feminine principle, Tao's willingness to care for its offspring, reflects a positively narcissistic extension of Tao to that which is a concrete expression of itself. All things depend upon it: "Heaven is eternal and Earth everlasting./They can be eternal and everlasting because they do not exist for themselves,/ And for this reason can exist forever" (TTC,7). The universe supports the Ten Thousand Things which constitute its Self, the shared Self, and flourishes in allowing those things to fourish. The power of the One has wide-ranging effects on the elements of the universe. By its means Heaven "became clear", the Earth "tranquil", "spiritual beings . . . became divine", the valleys "became full", all things "lived and grew", and rulers "obtained the One" (TTC,39).

In discussing the maternal image of Tao we have transgressed the tentative boundary between Nameless and Named Tao. One cannot expect to comprehend Tao which is absolute except through its direct relation to what can be perceived. Nameless Tao is given the name of Mother, merging it with Named Tao. Indeed, they are the same concept, viewed from different levels. Named Tao marks the end of primal Tao and the beginning of differentiation. The duality of the Elementary and Transformative characters, of the one and the many, is bridged by the device of the Named Tao which brings together elusive wholeness on the one hand and its concrete manifestations on the other. Nameless Tao, the ultimate reality, is "the origin of Heaven and Earth"; Named Tao, the name we attribute to Tao, is "mother of the universe" generating the names of the Ten Thousand Things. "I do not know its name; I call it Tao" (TTC,25).

The sage draws "sustenance from Mother (Tao)" (TTC,20), the power of Tao. "Tao is hidden and nameless./Yet it is Tao alone that skillfully provides for all and brings them to perfection" (TTC,41). Properly considered, only Named Tao expresses what we commonly consider maternal affection. Nameless Tao is impartial, purposeless, as the maternal Uroborus. It does not claim possession of anything: "It accomplishes its task, but does not claim credit for it./It clothes and feeds all things but does not claim to be master over them" (TTC,34).

To summarize, Nameless Tao, the ultimate ultimateless, parallels the Elementary character of the feminine principle by virtue of the common non-differentiation, wholeness, Eros/relatedness, closed womb character, and impartiality. As the origin of the universe which is beyond human relativistic descriptions, Nameless Tao is expressed by the concept of Nonbeing (wu) and the primal naturalness of the Uncarved Block (p'u). The sympathy of the cosmic wholeness, tz'u, is Nonbeing's mode of operation offering a suitable correspondence with Eros.

The maternal images evoked by the tz'u concept, as well as the container and caring functions referred to in the Tao Te Ching, signal the ascent from fundamental reality to Named Tao, the beginning point of differentiation (see TTC 1 and 42). The Tao which is named, assigned a place in the humanly-constructed hierarchy of the observed universe, bridges the gap between the bedrock being of Nonbeing and its mundane material manifestations in manifold Being.

b. The Ten Thousand Things of Named Tao--the Transformative character.

Tao stands at the apex of the inverted metaphysical pyramid: "Tao produced the One./The One produced the two./The two produced the three./And the three produced the ten thousand things" (TTC,42). Tao generates a chain reaction from the One as material source, to the duality of Nonbeing and Being, and then to the threefold set of Yin, Yang, and their interaction, leading finally to the individual things of the world.[24]

The order of metaphysical knowledge follows the same course as the order of generation. Of Tao it is said that latent "in it are things" (TTC,21). These objects are known through their source, through Tao in its capacity as "Mother of the Universe"--"He who has found the mother (Tao)/ . . . thereby understands her sons (things)" (TTC,52). These sons are, rightly, the offspring of Named Tao and are referred to as "its name (manifestations)" (TTC,21).

Tao, under its Transformative character, is the activity of being, the 'way', of the universe, not on the analogy of a humanly constructed or reconstructed principle (<u>Logos</u>), but as a natural order tending toward a recognition of the relatedness of the Elementary character. Metaphysically, the <u>Tao Te Ching</u> refers to this integrated system as the One, the active agent functioning in accordance with Tao and simultaneously the passive recipient (the material world) being acted upon in accordance with Tao. For, as the feminine principle reveals, there is no reality without the material expression, itself one aspect of reality.

An investigation of the material manifestations contributes to an understanding of Tao itself, giving some insight into what is inherently elusive. For example, we know the shape of Tao "Through These!", that is, through the "manifested forms".[25] Tao is most readily comprehended by the human mind through its reflective manifestations, not in itself.[26] Hence, the resorting to concrete images in the <u>Tao Te Ching</u> seems well justified. Of course, the insight provided by the forms stimulates ultimate enlightenment only once we have recognized the metaphysical framework of oneness in reality into which the additional information is placed, that is, if we have adjusted our perspective on the universe to a vision <u>sub species aeternitatis</u>. The experience of oneness results from having undergone transformation, that is, the enlightenment process.

In the realm of material things Tao functions as a creative principle. Considered in itself, Tao is fully actualized and can be said to embody potentiality only with regard to its potential for diversification in plurality by means of the Named Tao device. Our own tendency to discriminate leads to a view of the One as "creating" that which is actually intrinsic to its own being and encompassed by an all-inclusive unity. The pregnant woman holds not the mere potential for a child in her womb, but rather the child itself in a state of inseparable dependency with respect to its mother. One existence is shared by the two beings. In the same way, things in the world exist within the encompassing unity of Tao. Tao's is a "self-creativity", the basis of which consists in seeing "infinite potentiality manifested in each particularity". From the perspective of human relativity, there is a plurality of created entities; from an absolute perspective, the One creates only within itself.[27]

The dependency link between the many and the One is maintained through the nurturing and transforming power of Named Tao. Symbolically, Neumann views water in the "primordial womb of life" as the maternal fluid of life, which contains the child, supplies nourishment, and provides conditions for transformation.28 The womb is closed as Nameless Tao and opened in the event of giving birth as Named Tao. The Ten Thousand Things evolve from the primal One while remaining conjoined with it. The exact process is not explained fully in the Tao Te Ching, although it appears to follow a course of successive emanation (42). More specifically, in relation to the naturalistic bent of Taoism, the so-called created universe represents an unfolding of the "potential" of Tao, a somewhat regrettable movement toward differentiation which must be reversed in enlightenment, the Returning action of Tao.

The process of unfolding takes place in accordance with the universal order of Tao instantiated in the realm of Being (yu). Hence, the Tao Te Ching makes frequent use of illustrations of the working out of this order, as found in Nature. For example, the downward-tending movement of water is compared to the action of Tao (TTC,8). The laws governing the natural realm result in an achievement of "full realization" and the unified whole of an "integrated organism".29

As already noted, Tao is 'the Eternal Law', ch'ang, a law intimately connected with individual destiny and the sine qua non for the (feminine) goal of repose in Taoism: "All things flourish,/But each one returns to its root./This return to its root means tranquillity./It is called returning to its destiny./To return to destiny is called the eternal (Tao)" (TTC,16). The eternal Tao regulates the process of growth and decay, the "necessary alternation of opposites"; it also has been interpreted as a 'universal law of nature', and as a law inherent to human existence.30 Each of the Ten Thousand Things can be said to follow this law insofar as it conforms to its own nature, a nature which is coordinated with the metaphysical system of Tao.

From the order of Nature the natural law of Tao may be derived. Knowledge can be gained by observing and noting Tao's lawlike functioning in Nature. This is possible due to the deterministic, and feminine, orientation of Taoism. The universe is structured on the model of Tao, primal, unitary, undifferentiated, from which source all else follows in a definite order. Things are determined to act in harmony with Tao, by its laws, following Nature insofar as they adhere to their individual nature. Limitations as well as potentials are inherent in that nature (Te); the enlightened individual works within this range to achieve fulfillment by perfecting natural potential.

The only note of dissonance sounded in the natural order occurs among human beings who seek to thwart their own nature. This explains why a Taoist philosophy is needed at all, to counteract those incursions of human reasoning which inhibit our natural spontaneity. Even in that unnatural state, the law of Tao remains a constant undercurrent. The principle of Reversion stipulates that everything returns to its opposite and that the reversion process is perpetually ongoing. The dynamism of the Transformative character is allowed to function by means of this principle and is the metaphysical foundation for Taoist ethics (as discussed below).

Such a metaphysical structure leaves the bewildered masculine intellect with the problem of explaining the apparent indeterminacy of the universe, the element of change, and our sense of human freedom. Having been influenced by the philosophy contained in the I Ching, whose wisdom is itself derived from the "chance" configuration of the yarrow stalks, the Taoist is well aware of the high level determinacy of events when they are considered in a cosmic view, the wholeness which constitutes reality at the highest level. Even the most trivial events reveal their latent significance in the context of the whole. Our misinterpretations of universal determinism stem from a lack of information: if only certain pieces of the puzzle are available, it is likely that we will err in our speculations as to what the whole picture depicts. Jung explains the attitude of the Chinese sage to "chance" occurrences, expressed in the acausal principle of synchronicity, as it contrasts with Western (masculine) assumptions:

> The jumble of natural laws constituting empirical reality holds more significance for him [the Chinese sage] than a causal explanation of events that, moreover, must usually be separated from one another in order to be properly dealt with [as in Logos differentiation] . . . While the Western mind carefully sifts, weighs, selects, classifies, isolates, the Chinese picture of the moment encompasses everything down to the minutest nonsensical detail, because all of the ingredients make up the observed moment.[31]

The feminine attitude encourages an indiscriminate acceptance of the data of reality without laying stress on favored elements. Every detail of Being demands our attention by virtue of its status as a mediated expression of Nonbeing.

In order to attain the perspective of Tao, which reveals the deterministic state of reality, the Taoist abandons human criteria as being possessed of merely relative value. There is in the Tao Te Ching no homocentric deity sympathetic to human needs and petitionings, but rather the impersonal Tao, self-existing and self-operative.^{32} The human standard, typical of masculine thought, has no place as far as the structure of reality is concerned. Rather than compromising reality to make it conform to our limited human perspective, the Taoist realizes that it is our vision which must be expanded to accommodate the cosmic perspective. This is the essence of enlightenment.

The impersonal, non-anthropomorphic character of Tao extends to and actually develops the entire system of values in Tao Te Ching. The accepted values of the human community are exposed for what they are--a collection of relativities. Beauty is known only by its contrast with ugliness, the notion of the good appears only in opposition to that of evil: "When the people of the world all know beauty,/There arises the recognition of ugliness./When they all know the good as good,/There arises the recognition of evil" (TTC,2). Tao itself remains beyond good and evil in their limited senses.

The new standard replacing the egocentric human one is in fact the primal standard of Nature, itself an expression of Tao. Nature is impartial, "Jen-less", that is, it lacks the humanistic emphasis of Confucian Jen. It will "regard all things as straw-dogs" (TTC,5) temporary ritual objects, that is, honors them one moment and discards them the next. Tao deals impartially with itself, its offspring or manifestations, and cannot be judged by human standards. Nature, as the material realm of Being, holds a prominent place in Taoism's metaphysics. In fact, Lin Yutang contends that the overriding philosophical message of the Tao Te Ching is "the oneness and spirituality of the material universe".^{33} Chinese culture appears to have profoundly influenced, or been influenced by, this view, for Nature historically has held great significance for the Chinese, a significance reflected in the artistry of painting and poetry.

The importance of Nature is so great that even Tao takes it as a model: "Man models himself after Earth./Earth models itself after Heaven./Heaven models itself after Tao./And Tao models itself after Nature" (<u>Tse-jan</u>, 'self-so', 'self-formed', 'spontaneity') (TTC,25). Tao, to function optimally, must be spontaneous and natural. Re-emerging in Neo-Taoism, <u>Tse-jan</u> is posited as having an inherent principle of existence and transformation, a power or virtue also found in individual natures; in adhering to this principle, things function spontaneously, from the depths of Nonbeing.[34] Similarly, the feminine principle effects transformation under its dynamism, relating the plurality of the world by means of <u>Eros</u> as it moves from the individual to the whole.

Over and above the flux of transformations, the spontaneity of Nature must itself conform to the cosmic law: "Nature says few words./For the same reason a whirlwind does not last a whole morning./Nor does a rainstorm last a whole day./What causes them?/It is Heaven and Earth (Nature)./If even Heaven and Earth cannot make them last long,/How much less can man?" (TTC,23). This situation perhaps explains why Tao, with its quality of eternality, is more fundamental than Nature in the metaphysical hierarchy, despite the fact that the latter is a model for Tao.

Moving upward on the scale of being, we arrive at the Ten Thousand Things which issue from the womb of Nature. Their mutual function is fulfilled by means of spontaneity, as determined by individual <u>Te</u>, the nature, power, or virtue possessed by a given entity or group. Unique in the universal scheme, the natural spontaneity of human creatures has been interfered with by the distractions of civilization. Human variance from the cosmic standard, from the metaphysical system of Tao, brings into play the need to point out the path for a 'return' or reversion to Tao. The transformative process leads us down the scale of being to Nonbeing and Tao.

The prime element in the universal order, embodied in the Transformative character of Tao and exemplified in the offspring of Named Tao, involves the interaction of opposites. Such interaction is represented in the alternation between the complementary principle of Yin and Yang. This device likewise accounts for the evidence of change and flux within unchanging Tao. It is an explanation eminently in keeping with the feminine principle in that change is viewed as a cyclical process rather than as the linear progression of the masculine perspective. The Ten Thousand Things "carry" Yin and "embrace" Yang; harmony prevails "through the blending of the material force (ch'i)" (TTC,42). In this context, however, Yin (the Elementary character) is one portion of the encompassing feminine principle envisioned is a feminine philosophy.

The alternation of Yin and Yang "is called the Way, Tao" according to the Great Appendix of the I Ching.[35] This Tao, or, more accurately, this facet of Tao, belongs to the dynamic and Transformative character balancing the unchanging wholeness of the Elementary character's Nameless Tao. It is Tao as an "ever-evolving process through which all beings emerge", marking Taoism as the Chinese version of 'process' philosophy. Linguistically considered, as Alan Watts notes, some Chinese words can function as either verb or noun, leading to a view of the world as "a collection of processes".[36] This view of a "dynamic and relational" cosmos is particularly Chinese in that it emphasizes concrete situations and interactions (the material orientation of the feminine principle and Eros).[37]

The functions of Eros in the Transformative character, to foster the individual's identification with the whole, emerges in Tao's function of reconciliation. The ultimate level of Tao serves as the plane at which all opposites, Yin (the Elementary character) and Yang (the masculine principle) are reconciled. The end result is none other than the encompassing One of the transformed feminine principle. Tao "sets in motion and maintains the interplay of" Yin and Yang, thereby representing the (peculiarly feminine) power of completion.[38]

Hence, all elements of flux are in reality "merely changing phases of Tao".[39] The once paradoxical cycle of change is clarified in the light of Taoist metaphysics as a system united in the whole: "Being and non-being produce each other;/Difficult and easy complete each other;/Long and short contrast each other;/High and low distinguish each other;/Sound and voice harmonize with each other;/Front and back follow each other" (TTC,2). Neither extreme can be properly viewed in isolation from its opposite or from the wholeness of Tao.

Given a definite characterization, the state of Tao is referred to as the principle of Reversion:

"Reversion is the action of Tao" (TTC,40). This reversion (fan) or 'return' (fu) is the most pervasive of Nature's laws and rests on the contention that a movement to any extreme, positive (Yang) or negative (Yin), results in a change to the opposite state.[40] Thus, it becomes necessary, for purposes of control, to avoid extremes and practice the moderation of maintaining a constant and intermediate state. In this sense, Tao represents the Middle Path, balancing Yin (the Elementary feminine) and Yang (the masculine) by recognizing both (see TTC,28).

By the Reversion principle Tao empties what is full, i.e., prosperous, assertive, masculine, and fills what is empty, that is, unpretentious, receptive, feminine. Moreover, the positively considered and transformed values of Yin, generally assumed to be the nadir point of being, attain fundamental status while the corresponding highly esteemed Yang values revert to a subordinate position. By stating that reality, Tao, favors or acts along the lines of a feminine principle of being Taoism presents a radical perspective and brings forth an ethics founded on the metaphysical priority of the receptive Yin values.

Therefore, the metaphysics of Taoism outlines and supports a transformation in the direction of the feminine principle, espousing feminine values as the standard of the universe in that Tao or reality itself follows that standard. The structure of the universe not only recommends a return to spontaneity, but actually denies any positive alternative. There is only one reality, only one Way, with numerous lines throughout the manifest forms that culminate in one point. It is the open womb of Names Tao which brings forth these Ten Thousand Things. They in turn remain united by the underlying law and order of the universe determined by Tao. A non-homocentric view of Nature, the naturalism of Taoist philosophy, holds a prominent place in the system of material Being, and Nature is a model of spontaneity even for Tao itself. Tao reconciles the opposites of this realm through itself with the interaction and alternation of Yin and Yang. The Reversion principle, so essential to Tao, follows the feminine cyclical path and sets the stage for the espousal of a feminine perspective in imitation of the universe.

3. Epistemology: The Process of Enlightenment

Given the above metaphysical structure in the universe, of what is contained in the cosmos (fundamentally nothing more than the unity of Tao and what follows from it), it becomes possible to outline an individual program of transformation, that is, enlightenment, by adherence to the established path or "Way". Insofar as we are participants in the One, we are able to cultivate, or realize, that knowledge which constitutes enlightenment. Without first having established the fact of this peculiar and intimate relationship with the universe, the claims of Taoist epistemology would be groundless indeed.

With epistemological concerns we also move to the more familiar area of the manner in which ultimate reality appears to and is interpreted by our human minds, an area much less elusive than the metaphysical dimensions of Nameless Tao and Nonbeing. By referring to the metaphysical framework presented above, that human viewpoint can be reconciled to what is. While presupposing the previous principle of metaphysics designated Tao, the Taoist theory of knowledge remains centered in the human subject, dealing with the manner or mental apparatus by which Tao becomes manifest for us.

In view of the masculine orientation of most epistemology, it is instructive to begin a discussion of the Taoist conception of knowledge from a negative approach, indicating what Taoist knowledge is not in terms of its divergence from masculine views. The generally masculine approach to Taoism by thinkers nurtured in the Western philosophical tradition accounts for the paradoxical portrayal of Taoism as engendering an epistemology which in principle rejects all knowledge. It is of the utmost importance to understand precisely what is being rejected when the Taoist repudiates the learning process, as well as what alternative type of knowledge is implicitly being advocated by that rejection.

Corresponding to masculinely-interpreted Tao, ch'ang Tao or T'ien Tao as "eternal Reason" and the Tao of Heaven, a Tao of humanity has been posited--jen Tao, "the process of ratiocination".[41] As already demonstrated, viable interpretations of Tao as beyond either human discursive reason or Logos, and in harmony with feminine philosophy, are available. Just as Logos does not adequately express the meaning of Tao, ratiocination is not the path which leads to knowledge of Tao.

In an important sense, Taoism can be construed as

a rejection of (or, given certain historical assumptions, a reaction to) the essentially masculine approach to knowledge. Discursive reason is the tool of the analytical thinker who views the principle-pervaded universe as a "conscious entity" to be emulated by an identification "with its rational meaning".[42] This view is sharply contrasted by the Taoist's intention of reducing, rather than increasing, masculine cumulative knowledge. The humanistic focus of the masculine view encounters things in light of human nature and seeks to understand the mind by a study of externals; enlightenment is considered to be achieved when these studies have been exhausted, reducing it to a purely intellectual attainment.

The tools of consciousness are intended to facilitate the goal of ch'eng, interpreted here as "sincerity, perfection, realness" (once more, under a masculine and humanistic judgment of what is real). The I Ching refers to "exhaustive study of principles" as leading to the "utmost fulfillment of one's own nature", which the Confucian text, The Doctrine of the Mean, advances ch'eng as "the way of man".[43] By the ch'eng method we rectify our attitudes, presumably by an alteration of perspective paralleling that which takes place in Taoism. The essential difference between the Taoist and the analytical methods lies in the level at which enlightenment is achieved--whether by mere consciousness, intellectual awareness, or in a manner integrated with one's entire being, and hence transcending even intellect. The Taoist Chuang Tzu conceded that the usual means of thought, identifiable as discursive reason, has a value, but one which is "relative, limited, and subject to change"; "Tao cannot be reached by mere intellection".[44]

Before outlining the feminine Taoist alternative to discursive reason, intuition, it is useful to set the epistemological stage upon which the Taoist produces the enlightenment experience. By understanding what it is that the Taoist takes to constitute valid knowledge of Tao, the impossibility of relying upon discursive reason to attain that knowledge becomes apparent. The goal of the Taoist is liberation from "truth as 'correctness of looking', or 'the correctness of representing all beings according to ideas'."[45] In place of logical 'correctness', the Taoist has a spontaneous and natural knowledge. the active (masculine) pursuit of knowledge contrasts with a (feminine) receptivity to what is: "The further one goes, the less one knows./Therefore the sage knows without going about,/

Understands without seeing,/And accomplishes without any action" (TTC,47). Returning to Tao signals an end to discrimination (pien), to "perceive (noesis) Nature itself".[46] Knowledge is found within, and the microcosmic-macrocosmic assumption of the feminine principle assures us that inner knowledge reflects our outer reality.

The difference between the common view of knowledge and that of the Taoist is expressed by Wing-Tsit Chan as one between knowledge as "cleverness and cunning" (for purposes of ego-self interests) and a concern with "harmony and the eternal . . ., contentment . . ., where to stop . . ., and the self". The latter kind alone has value within Taoist philosophy.[47] Cumulative (masculine) knowledge of what is external to us constitutes being "learned", while (feminine) wisdom is a matter of self-knowledge (knowledge of the Shared Self) (TTC,33). The individual as a microcosm of the universal macrocosm, can experience personal, and simultaneously cosmic, revelation.

Similar expressions in opposition to the common idea of knowledge and learning may be cited from the Tao Te Ching: "A wise man has no extensive knowledge;/ He who has extensive knowledge is not a wise man" (81), or "The pursuit of learning is to increase day by day./ The pursuit of Tao is to decrease day by day" (48). The method of Taoist chih (intuition) is described by Chuang Tzu as "the knowledge of no-knowledge, or genuine knowledge".[48] This characterization of how the Taoist philosopher conceives of true knowledge parallels Bachelard's views concerning the anima: "Whoever dreams (songe) of life, of the simple life without looking for knowledge (savoir) inclines toward the feminine".[49]

A knowledge of one's own ignorance also is involved in Taoist epistemological theory. It is best to know one's limitations, to know that one does not know, rather than assuming more than is within the scope of human perception, presuming to grasp the absolute by reason. Those who make a pretence of knowing that of which they are ignorant are diseased; to recognize the disease for what it is, as does the Taoist sage, is an indication that one is not so afflicted (TTC,71). Similarly, those who understand the Tao Te Ching remain cognizant of their ignorance--"When one enters into the Tao Te Ching, one must remember that one is leaving it. In this way one will indeed attain Tao."[50] Once again we glimpse the paradoxical returning action of Tao.

Within this framework, ignorance has a positive value for the Taoist. The method of the ancients in following Tao was to keep the people ignorant (i.e., uncorrupted by futile striving); the disruption of peace results from "too much knowledge". The "complete harmony" is possible only when the imposition of rule on a nation by knowledge is supplanted by the "blessing" of not endeavoring to obtrude an artificial rule (TTC, 65). The prerequisite for harmonious living is to "Abandon learning" for then "there will be no sorrow" (TTC,20).

In addition to the ineffectiveness of intellectualizing, the Taoist encounters certain problematic aspects in common sense experience. Sense experiences engender desire, and hence are rejected as an inadequate and detrimental means to knowledge.[51] The value of sense-derived knowledge is repudiated insofar as the impingement of sense data causes us confusion (12). By its concern with some object of desire, its yielding of knowledge of such objects, or usefulness in gaining them, sense data is disruptive of Taoist contentment.[52] Once desire has corrupted our primal oneness with Tao, new measures are required for returning. Hence, although the Taoist relies heavily upon concrete sense images in presenting the philosophy of Tao, sense experience in itself is insufficient for the goal of enlightenment. Sense data merely serve as concrete illustrations of Tao at work, as points of departure, similar to the images in William Blake's "Auguries of Innocence":

>   To see the world in a grain of sand
>   And Heaven in a wild flower,
>   Hold Infinity in the palm of your hand
>   And Eternity in an hour.

Related to the Taoist's distrust of discursive reason and sense experience for gaining insight into Tao, there is a deep and abiding distrust of the linguistic conventions which have emerged under the influence of these two sources. As revealed by Ludwig Wittgenstein, the limits of our language are the limits of our world, that is, the limits of what we experience are determined by the range of available linguistic expressions. The Taoist, however, could not rest content with such humanly-imposed limitations to thought, but sought to broaden our perceived universe to the very dimensions of Tao's encompassing reality by breaking out of the linguistic prison. In most cases, this tactic results in leaving us with nothing to say, or nothing which can be coherently communicated through language: "He who knows does not speak./He who speaks does not know" (TTC,56). How well Wittgenstein understood this same problem in regard to values--"What we cannot speak about we must pass over in silence".53

The essence of the problem lies in the attempt to convey absolute reality by means of our relativistic human tools of verbal expression. The very first sentence of the Tao Te Ching warns us that "The Tao (Way) that can be told of is not the eternal Tao;/The name that can be named is not the eternal name" (1). Words impose artificial (masculine) distinctions to what is in fact undifferentiated. The name bestowed on Named Tao dooms even that concept to a non-absolute status.

In Tao, or to the enlightened Taoist sage, the subject/object distinction between the one who speaks and what is being spoken about, intrinsic to language, is lacking; "when we are in the void, in the one, there is no room for speech".54 This state of affairs contrasts sharply with the needs of discursive reason as well as with the spirit of philosophy, generally conceived, which last has been described by Suzuki as "wordiness". Fortunately for Taoism, language, by virtue of its concrete images, is capable of transmitting more than an intellectual meaning. The mention of a mere particle of dust can indeed "reveal the whole truth underlying all existences".55 Nonetheless, the Tao Te Ching cautions that a word cannot be simultaneously "true" and "fine-sounding", for these two qualities are mutually exclusive. The person of Tao does not indulge in idle argumentation, or playing with words (TTC,81): "Much talk will of course come to a dead end" (TTC,5).

Thus far we have discovered those epistemological paths which are dead-ends for the Taoist: the penetrating searches and researches of discursive reason cannot lead to knowledge of Tao, but have far different goals, while an empirical path is beset by the pitfalls of desire. Language is doubly-damned in partaking of both rational abstraction and sense data. Silence is a preferrable means of expression, just as the knowledge of one's ignorance surpasses the opinion of learnedness. Something beyond the approaches offered by common sense knowledge and human contrivances of discursive reason is required for the Taoist's purposes.

This third alternative appears in intuition

(chih), the feminine form of knowing which transcends and encompasses both sense data and discursive reason as a means to knowledge. Like sense perception, the intuition of the Taoist is immediate or spontaneous, lacking the deliberation or analytic process of discursive reason. However, chih offers more than sense experience can offer, being "a mode of apprehension which supervenes on the ordinary methods of knowledge and is supposed to reveal truth which could not be disclosed by any other method".[56]

In relation to discursive reason, Taoistic intuition likewise has definite advantages. Cast as the method of chih chu, 'confronting the crooked with the bent', intuition is an extension of Confucian theory. The Confucian interest in rational perfection is supplemented by the Taoist with the experiencing of "the dark shadow" (the darkness of the feminine or Yin principle). Early Confucians reputedly recognized the insufficiency of the rational method when left to itself, and thus also recognized the same need felt by Taoists to transcend discursive reason.[57] Like the Taoist, they emphasized the element of personal experience.

But to achieve this comprehensive knowledge, the holistic knowledge of Tao, requires as a first step a renunciation of the mind (TTC,10). Simultaneously this move provides an extreme method of transcending the human limitations of intellect. Despite this renunciation, it should be noted that the Taoist must first recognize the mind, and the trivial bypaths in which intellect can be lost, before advocating the renunciation. A rational decision is made to renounce human intellect as part of the natural progression to feminine ends. Discursive reason is not condemned in itself, but only in relation to its misuse and corruption by the types of people who equate wisdom with accumulated knowledge. The omnipresent danger is that we will become entangled in our own rational constructions and web of words.

The wisdom valued by the Taoist is both more concrete and more significant to personal life than that of the learned scholar. Wisdom comes with experience, and the knowledge of the Taoist sage, in being experiential, is a kind of wisdom. It is equivalent to a state of being, an inexplicable, indescribable state. Taoist epistemology concludes that, on a scale of the various levels of knowledge, as sensual, rational, etc., the knowledge born of direct experience, which is intuitive, carries the greatest value, and is indeed the sole means of knowledge of Tao. To know Tao is to be Tao, that is, to directly experience our participation in Tao. In the same manner, feminine knowledge is a state of being and participation in the "object" of knowledge, the feminine principle's radical empiricism.

This thesis is confirmed by the parallels between Taoism's epistemological framework and the doctrine of 'Double Truth on Three Levels' expounded by the sixth century Buddhist Chi Tsang. In the Buddhist scheme three levels of knowledge or truth are posited: 1) that of the common people, yu or Being; 2) that of the Buddhists, wu or Nonbeing; and 3) a transcendent alternative to both of these. First level 'common truth' (opinion and sense data) stands in opposition to a 'higher sense of truth' on the second level, yet both have only relative value beyond which stands the third level, the 'non-One-sided Middle Path'. On the third level one understands things as neither yu nor wu.[58] In reality, then, no one-sided assertions are made through intuition. The highest knowledge is the neti, neti ('not this, not that') of the Upanishads. "The common masses mistakenly suppose that learning is in learning; the Sage teaches that non-learning [as opposed to not-learning] constitutes learning".[59]

Under this three-leveled scheme, Tao can be considered the Middle Way, negotiating a path between, but beyond, the extremes of common and intellectual thought. The truths of sense experience, of the realm of Being, are denied at the level of discursive reason (wu). Intuition, however, neither denies nor asserts what reason offers, or, it is Chuang Tzu's denial of a denial, the 'losing and losing' method in the Tao Te Ching.[60] Significantly, this double negation points back to the level of yu, although in a transformed sense; absolute Being is beyond the simple opposition of being and nonbeing. There is no linear progression of knowledge, rather the circular path of enlightenment leads from the primal instinct of the Elementary character, through masculine discursive reason, and around to the intuition of the Transformative character.

As related to philosophical concerns, the most crucial point in the Taoist system of epistemology involves the passing from discursive reason to intuition. As the Transformative character of a feminine philosophy demands, the Taoist sage moves from primal experience and through the discursive level on the way to <u>chih</u> or intuition. The move from the second to the third level is the most challenging to traditional Western thought. The intuition of Tao is a returning to the natural state, as symbolized in the infant figure. In Western tradition many respected philosophers have made the move from sense data to rational processes; however, only "mystics" venture beyond to intuition. The reason-intuition move thus warrants a fuller treatment to satisfy the questions that might be raised either in regard to Taoism or Western thought.

The intrinsic limitations of discursive reason, with regard to the values of the Taoist, have been noted above. Nonetheless, its position as an epistemological aid, if not a necessity, for attaining the enlightenment state, of knowing/being Tao, should be recognized. Although reality lies beyond the scope of discursive reason, of human intellect <u>qua</u> human, reason nonetheless is a step away from the confounding desires of sense. What it lacks is "the wholeness of experience".[61] Intuition (<u>chih</u>), on the other hand, is "immediate, direct, primitive penetration . . . manifested by the interfusion and interpenetration between the universe and all things,"[62] a vision without discursive reason's urge to differentiation.

The epistemological framework of Taoism is directly dictated by its prior metaphysical assumptions. Given Tao as the encompassing unity of the universe in which we have a part, we are able, theoretically at least, to gain knowledge of its state. That knowledge comes to us as the direct experience which is intuition. For these same reasons both common sense data and discursive reason are insufficient for the goals of the Taoist sage; they treat Tao as an external to be perceived or studied. In a related sense, the linguistic system which we have constructed from our limited human-centered perspective is unable properly to convey the meaning of the absolute reality of Nameless Tao.

Only intuition, <u>chih</u>, remains open as a means to enlightenment for the Taoist in that it takes the correct inward-turning approach. The microcosmic self is delved to its primal roots to obtain knowledge of the macrocosm. These facts account for the Taoist's explicit repudiation of cumulative knowledge and learning, because they tend to obscure inner knowledge. Simultaneously, there is an implicit espousal of the intuitive alternative. The Taoist theory of knowledge thus involves a recognition of three levels of knowledge—common sense experience which gives way to discursive reasoning, and both culminating in the intuitive level.

Of the two intuitive enlightenment paths identified in Taoism, the 'ontological insight' of *ming* and the 'quiescence' of *ching*,[63] only the former, experiential knowledge, concerns us here in relation to epistemological interests. *Ching*, as the path of self-realization, belongs more properly to the sphere of (feminine) ethics and is handled in the context of how one becomes an enlightened Taoist sage. *Ming*, however, involves the sudden enlightenment discussed thus far, induced by the elements of sympathy (*Tz'u* or *Eros*), and creativity. These elements are revealed by means of *chih*, Taoist intuition, hence, *ming* has a marked epistemological significance and also relates to the Transformative character as the bright expression of Tao as being contrasted with the darkness of the Elementary character (symbolized by an Uncarved Block).

Ming is intuitive insight into or a direct and spontaneous experience of the undifferentiated. Previously hidden mental powers thereby are made manifest, the "unknown recesses in our minds, which lie beyond the threshold of the conceptually constructive consciousness", yielding the (feminine) powers of the unconscious.[64] With the benefit of intuition, the Taoist transcends the previous need to consult mundane sense experience, recognizing the source of knowledge within: "One may know the world without going out of doors./One may see the Way of Heaven without looking through the windows" (TTC,47). In lieu of an "external" source of sense data, the Taoist sage refers to the internal microcosmic self, the inner which is the outer represented in the shared Self.

Being in direct contact with the source of creativity, with Tao, the artist is particularly prone to manifest these Taoist tendencies, at least in Chinese culture. The universe is apprehended through artistic intuition, a sympathy with and participation in the whole. The great artist is capable of redirecting the creativity of Tao to a specific project at various levels of existence, ranging from created objects to an over-all creative life style. Thus, Chinese painting, which has been strongly influenced by Taoist (as well as Buddhist) philosophy, has been characterized as "the manifestation of an ontological experience, which emerges from the depth of the unconscious . . . revelations of Tao".[65] The spirit of Tao is communicated in the famous Sung dynasty landscapes of misty mountains and open sky, the valley of the Mystic Female and the void of Nonbeing. The direct perception of the mystical unity experienced by the artist provide the inspiration for such scenes. Taoist painting is simply "the spontaneous reflection from one's inner reality", merging subjectivity and objectivity.[66]

Similarly, the poet has the limitless inner realm of the unconscious in which to create, the product of a free, spontaneous, and intuitively non-discursive mind. This far surpasses the horizons of the "ordinary man" who remains limited by mundane sense experience, as well as exceeding the grasp of the intellect. Poetic expression is the spontaneous and immediate revelation of the "secret meaning of Tao" which stirs the poet's "primordial innocence", as a result of an intuitive experience of reality.[67] Chinese poetry is exemplary in this respect. The poet Li P'o is very much a Taoist sage when he comments of the bliss of solitude:

> You ask me why I stay in these blue mountains
> I smile but I do not answer.
> O, my mind is at ease!
> Peach blossoms and flowing streams without a trace,
> How different from the mundane world![68]

The <u>Tao Te Ching</u> is itself an extended intuitive poem, suffused with vivid, concrete imagery. The sense data of Nature are employed as suggestive devices to stir the reader's own inner and intuitive experience. Terse descriptions function, like the Zen koan, as catalysts of sudden enlightenment.

The process of recognizing reality in its wholeness involves the special sense of feminine wisdom, Sophia. Wisdom of this type is grounded in reality, as befits feminine understanding, and is responsive to its surrounding conditions, as is characteristic of feminine consciousness. The knowledge which relates the Taoist to ultimate reality is an ontological experience, just as feminine wisdom is an experiencing by the entire being. The dynamic process culminates in its practical application as enlightenment. Knowing, in the Taoist sense of intuitive or highest level knowledge, is a state of being, rather than a mere set of doctrines or a philosophical outline expounded by intellect. It is only possible as the product of the feminine principle's radical empiricism.

The transformation or enlightenment attained through feminine understanding, then, has two facets: a personal participation in the object of knowledge to eliminate its object-ness, and the immediacy of feminine intuition. Tao is known or understood by our direct identification with it, not in terms of a mental projection but as a metaphysical fact. In being more than merely a first hand observation this knowledge constitutes the feminine radical empiricism of participatory experience, of being at one with Tao. In short, to know Tao is to be Tao.

The first of these conditions, participation, is fulfilled by the Taoist through the metaphysical acknowledgement of Tao's all-encompassing force. Intuitive knowledge follows from the realization of oneness, when cosmic wholeness has been directly experienced. The individual merges with the One as the individual self, becomes one with the shared Self. This union or "ontological experience", reinstates the nondifferentiation and nondiscrimination of primal Tao.[69] The Taoist sage "returns to the state of simplicity (uncarved wood)", of undifferentiated unity (TTC,28). With the eradication of the (masculine) "ego-conscious self" one now lives "within the moving forces of the universe...[is oneself] a part of it."[70]

The Eros/relatedness discussed as the characteristic method of the adherent of the feminine principle thus also is encountered in the Taoist sage. It is significant that in both cases the force to relate, under the auspices of the Transformative character, moves from within the individual microcosm to the universal macrocosm. The sense of oneness which constitutes enlightenment is a fact, the state of reality, yet it goes unrecognized by the vast majority of people in the world. The analytic approach is ultimately useless for grasping this truth, having made no allowances for our present enlightened condition.[71] Adherents of discursive reason assume that enlightenment is something to be won or earned; they err due to the simple fact that what has never been lost also can never be bound. Accordingly, the Tao Te Ching rejects the self-deluding process of striving and holds to a practice of wu-wei, non-action or non-interference. All that is required is for our inner perspective to be made receptive ("feminized") with respect to the outer reality of oneness.

Central to this radical change in perspective is the removal of the artificial distinction between self and non-self, self and the world. Feminine wisdom then fills the void. Chuang Tzu compares the suddenness of intuitive awakening to a burst of laughter, while Hsieh Ling-yun (fifth century) employs the metaphor of a leap across a chasm.[72] Enlightenment is an all or nothing experience, lacking degrees of partial success: one either succeeds in making the leap or does not succeed. It is not possible to have a 50%, 75%, or even a 99% enlightenment experience. Furthermore, no conscious (masculine) deliberation intervenes in the flash of knowledge, rather "it is non-action which immediately gives way to actions".[73]

For Chang, the very essence of the Tao Te Ching's message is this "direct, intuitive experience of Tao".[74] Psychologically considered it is the basis of all other experiences, is the "principle of unification and co-ordination", concrete and dynamic in the fullest sense.[75] By this means, the Taoist does more than re-experience Tao, as in Deutsch's interpretation of feminine intuition as a re-living of another's experience, but actually experiences its immediacy, the being-here-now of Tao. Time and space are annihilated, "existence is reduced to a point-instant".[76] The experience takes place in the eternal present.

Also entailed here is feminine consciousness-a link to the unconscious as primal center of being, to instinctual nature (Te), and a perceiving through the mind/body/spirit complexity of one's being. Rational consciousness is transcended in order to reach into the depths of being where Tao abides. One relies upon pure inner consciousness, which is "immediate" and "primordial", and experienced "from the highest [intuitive] level of one's own nature.[77] The consciousness necessary in Taoism is as paradoxical as any other element in its philosophy. It requires that we lose hold of the "thing" of consciousness. Perfect Te is not conscious of itself, and hence is able to preserve its natural state. Conscious nature, however, is indicative of Te which has been corrupted or alienated. Perfect Te is actually non-Te in that it has reverted to Tao, and is undifferentiated from the whole.[78]

In attempting to convey the feminine sense of Taoist consciousness and Te, in its interplay with the collective unconscious of Tao, an examination of the recommendations made for attaining the experience of Tao is instructive. The dynamic process parallels the returning of the Taoist sage to Tao (discussed below), is both beyond thought, in being intuitive, and recollected, as a remembrance of a primal state. Essentially it is an incommunicable experience, meaningful to and understood by only those who have had it.[79]

The recommendations for securing enlightenment, the feminine perspective, are necessarily oblique. The creativity of the artist exemplifies the method by which we can draw upon our own inner resources of Tao. Using the experience gained by this imitation of maternal Tao, that is, by giving birth to our own "offspring", we can eventually translate personal creativity into a reflection of cosmic creativeness. The universe so created, the product of the unconscious, reflects an inner reality which is one with the outer reality of Tao. The Tao Te Ching employs the images of the material world to stimulate experience/knowledge in the reader, that is, to precipitate recognition of the shared experience of present enlightenment. The epistemology of Taoism quite simply is founded upon the assumption, drawn from metaphysics, that the knower belongs to that which is to be known, the reality of Tao. Tao is both subject and object of knowledge from our limited human perspective, while, from the absolute perspective, it is neither subject nor object, but merely a state of being that we naturally "participate" in. As in metaphysics, oneness or unity is the key to Taoist epistemology, "an acceptance of the spiritual oneness of all that exists".[80] For Chuang Tzu, this is Ta T'ung, "the grand interfusion" transcending intellection,[81] paralleling the primal and undifferentiated Great Round of the Elementary character.

One consequence of this metaphysical intimacy is the identification of transcendental or "divine" and human thought. Properly considered, our intuition is that of Tao; our nature (Te) contains the seeds of truth (Tao). The participation of the many in the one is "the great sympathy" (Eros/Tz'u); the one entering into each thing is "the great creativity".[82] These two ontological possibilities insure that the path of knowledge/experience is always accessible to us.

Symbolically, this cosmic intimacy is presented by in terms of the infant-mother relationship. Just as the human mother is identified with her child in terms of behavior and existence, so the follower of Tao adopts the ideal of the infant to represent our direct link to maternal Tao. The infant is an extension of Tao; by approximating to its state of being we can

approximate to the state of Tao, for it is at this
stage of life that the offspring is most closely
identified with its mother. In this way Tao shares
with us its experiential knowledge and power. The
infant embodies the strength in weakness associated
with the Yin principle. Through this manifestation
of its force Tao reaches down to the plurality of the
Ten Thousand Things without deviating from its
characteristic impartiality. The positive narcissistic attachment of the mother to its offspring
preserves that impartiality intact, for the infant is
not cared for by the mother as an individual, but as an
extension of her self.

Unfortunately, the experiential essence of Taoist
intuition, of knowledge through direct participation in
what is known, although crucial to the Taoist system,
also accounts for the obscurity of Taoist epistemology
for proponents of the masculine perspective. If the
ultimate appeal is to experience, those lacking that
experience cannot hope to understand reality fully. A
hiatus always will exist between the intellectual
awareness of the natural order, what is assumed in
metaphysics, and the immediate participatory experience
of that order, the promise of feminine epistemology.
This situation is entirely unsatisfactory to masculine
discursive reason, which seeks to gain its knowledge in
the role of objective observer. Subjective participation in the "object" of knowledge inevitably taints the
credibility of the Taoist in the masculine mind. Here
again the disparity between the means and ends of feminine vs. masculine philosophy is substantial and tends
toward mutual misunderstanding and repudiation.

To summarize the metaphysical and epistemological
manifestations of Tao, we can state that the individual's knowledge of Tao constitutes a direct and
participatory experience of reality referred to as
enlightenment. This experience proceeds from a grounding in feminine wisdom, an intuitive understanding of
our sympathetic participation in the "object" of
knowledge (knower=known). The responsiveness of this
wisdom under feminine consciousness is possible by
drawing upon the deep resources of the unconscious,
which are also the resources of Tao itself.

B. Modes of Being Through Tao

In any philosophy which expects to prove itself to
be a living option for human beings, and most especially in a feminine philosophy which purports to

outline an encompassing life style, the ethical code entailed by its system must be a focal point of investigation. A natural extension of this ethic, transferred to the plane of community interaction, is socio-political philosophy. Whether or not the metaphysical system of Taoism is logically consistent or even true, or its theory of knowledge feasible, it must pass the ultimate test of being able to be incorporated into the daily life of human beings. This test is rarely, if ever, administered to masculine philosophy, and we are accustomed to accepting something as true in theory but inapplicable in practice (see Kant, The Old Saw). The claims of a feminine philosophy to be grounded in reality, in the 'is' as opposed to the masculine 'ought', can only be substantiated through the success or failure of its individual and communal codes of conduct.

Appropriately, then, the Tao Te Ching devotes many passages to outlining the behavior which is proper for the Taoist as both sage and sovereign, proper in the sense of being conducive to both individual and societal harmony with Tao. The ethics of a feminine philosophy is a curious kind of ethics when viewed from the traditional Western perspective, due to its lack of an ultimately unreachable standard of perfection (an 'ought'). Non-conformance to ethics, to the reality principle embodied in Tao, is the exception rather than the rule of Nature, and occurs only when the natural "virtue" of Te has been corrupted. To be ethical, it is simply necessary to return to that "virtue", the standard of Tao, to become reconciled to reality (the "is").

The law of the universe pervades the whole, insuring a parallelism at all levels, from the apex of Tao down to the details of material existence, including human existence. The feminine modes of being are applied here to emphasize the feminine assumptions of Taoist ethics and socio-political thought and reflect the encompassing force of feminine metaphysics. Through these modes the participation of human creatures in the whole is revealed. This point is essential for understanding the feminine perspective and its philosophical expressions.

1. Ethics: The Individual's Enlightenment Path

The following survey of Taoist ethics, undertaken from the standpoint of feminine interpretation of the Tao Te Ching, proceeds according to the three modes of being previously outlined for the feminine principle, each of which illuminates one facet of integrated feminine attitude towards life. In light of Taoist metaphysics and epistemology, Taoist ethics is essentially a matter of implementing the knowledge, or fulfilling the experience, of the human role in the universe. The modes of being necessary to accomplish this task are (a) inwardness, (b) receptivity, and (c) materiality (the link with Nature).

For the purpose of assessing the cosmic human role, it is necessary to define the Tao of humanity, our inherent human virtue or power (Te) which belongs to human beings qua human. As appropriate Te corresponds to each level of being, although in essence they are all united due to their common derivation from Tao. Through inwardness, turning within, the Taoist reaches a realization of the nature or Te held in common with all human beings and is able to initiate the process of reversion to Tao. Out of this realization grows the positive narcissism based on shared Selfhood, which constitutes the fundamental assumption of Taoist ethical conduct. Underlying it all is an urge toward wholeness, to be in harmony with the only reality by realizing that the inner is the outer.

Given an understanding of human virtue or Te, the virtuous ideal person can be specified. The model sage of the Taoist ethics embodies the receptivity mode of being which reflects the "passivity" or yielding of the Yin principle. Considered from the feminine perspective this is a positive acceptance of Nature and an openness to life. Reality is accepted for what it is, without futile attempts to reform or reconstruct it in a humanistic mold. Such receptivity is not based on the fact that the Taoist relinquishes choice, but rather for the reason that our choice is restricted by the natural limitations imposed by the conditions of existence. The enlightenment path of the sage entails ching, quiescence, the gradual development of a life style in imitation of Tao. The receptivity mode of being is best represented in the Taoist concept of wu-wei, non-assertion.

Concrete examples of Taoism's ethical code are apparent in natural phenomena. The spontaneity of Nature is reflected in the processes of Tao, and material facts of life are integrated fully with the ethical aspiration of philosophy. The Taoist sage functions as a whole in the whole, in harmony with all aspects of personal being as well as with the universe at large.

Thus, images of Nature can be employed to express the principles of the ultimate reality, and even sensuality offers the potential for enlightenment, if approached from the feminine/Yin perspective.

    a. Inwardness-the Tao of humanity, Te. The mode of being designated as inwardness, or the sense of all-is-one-ness, is grounded in the fundamental assumption of a feminine philosophy that our internal reality is equivalent to the outer one. Hence, the "external" world can be understood most immediately by a return to the center of individual being. Several points are involved in this assumption. The metaphysical recognition of wholeness and the epistemological knowledge/ experience of it in the universe stimulate the urge to live an "ethical" existence in accordance with that unity. The guide in attaining this wholeness is our own nature/virtue/power of Te, the innate source of values and principles which microcosmically represents the macrocosm of Tao.

    Through our Te we also come to a realization of our common humanity, the sharing of Te with other human beings, as well as our link with the Ten Thousand Things. The proper role of the human being in the cosmos, a role far different from that specified by masculine adherents, is also revealed by our Te. From this revelation there emerges the positive narcissism whereby self-centeredness becomes ethical because the Self is shared with the world-self-interest=cosmic interest.

    Fundamental to the ethical overtones of inwardness is the primal urge to wholeness, expressed in feminine adherents as an interest in interrelationships, in inner values and principles. Once more, Chinese art provides a case in point. The mood of Ch'an Buddhist and Taoist painting communicates a sense of oneness; a "wholeness of spirit which goes out, free and unafraid, into wholeness of universe".[83] Correspondingly, the poet transforms a closed, personal experience into the open, universal experience of the shared Self, thus becoming "part of the universe" by sharing in and of its creativity.[84] As a Zen enlightenment poem declares: "When we have found the truth/There is no single man in the Great Earth."[85] On the contrary, the view from the highest reality reveals the interdependence of the universe and forbids isolationism.

    The individual bears within the very structure of the universe under the correlates of microcosm and macrocosm, which thus serve as the basis of our knowledge of Tao. The stages of contemplation along the path to wholeness correspond to the state of Tao. These are given in the Tao Te Ching (16) as Jung, "all-embracing", Kun, "selfless" (or ego-less), Wang, "all-pervading", and T'ien, "transcendent". These stages symbolize the gradual "interfusion and interpenetration of self and others, man and universe".[86] By this progression the sage imitates Tao, its spontaneity and naturalness, harmonizing with the whole. The end result is the "ontological experience" previously discussed as knowing, a fusing of subjective and objective.

The interfusion is not a new state of being, but a reversion to a primal one, a return to "inexpressible, primordial innocence".[87] There is a reversal of the common (masculine) course of mind, which has been engaged in "dividing itself externally", through a movement to "original inner unit" as 'one-thought-viewing'. The culmination point is the non-intellectual "inner awareness of ultimate reality" which is enlightenment. All of this is made possible by the presence of a fundamental innate "faculty", employed in the traditional Chinese method of realizing reality and described by Zen as "the seeing of one's own 'original Face' before one is born", that is, prior to the individuation of birth. It is the Tao Te Ching's 'Return to the Ultimateless', whereby (masculine) consciousness as the ultimate of T'ai Chi realizes (feminine) unconsciousness, Wu Chi, the ultimateless (corresponding to Nonbeing.)[88]

Here then is our guide for regaining wholeness and framing an ethical code of conduct, the "object" of inwardness referred to as Te. The intuitive knowledge experienced by the Taoist is precisely the knowledge of Te (personal reality), which leads directly to Tao (universal reality) as the inner which is the outer by participation. The enlightenment path followed here is the transformative and dynamic returning of ming.

Te itself has been equated with chih, intuitive knowledge, as an 'honest state of mind', in which the mind is straight rather than crooked, that is, corrupted by superficialities. The ancient character for Te, 德, at least under some interpretations, supports this equation: taken literally it is composed of 彳, "to move or to act"; 心, "heart" or "mind"; and 目, "eye" or "to look".[89] Taken together, these elements of Te signify a movement or action of looking into the heart/mind, into our life principle. Stressing the dynamic aspect of the character, it represents "the state when the eye is turned inward to the kernel of things, thus it discovers and follows the inner rhythm of things."[90]

To avoid what Ellen Marie Chen considers the inappropriate (for Taoism) rationalism of the Chou period, by which the concept of Te later came to be interpreted, this primitive delving of its etymology must be dissected more carefully. The Te of the Tao Te Ching is the state of "original perfection of nature", undifferentiated and unconscious, having its seat in the belly or instinct (the belly-feeling). The eye on the other hand, is a symbol of the seat of consciousness, the discriminating organ which specializes in making distinctions, in analysis. In this sense, the eye symbolizes the state of alienation in which natural balance has been disrupted, yielding a universe of multiplicity in place of the primal unity "which gives to all" (Tao).[91]

By turning the eye inward, however, the sage is able to reverse the trend towards differentiation. 'Cutting up' is avoided and return effected by the process of 'losing and losing'. What is lost are the artificialities previously imposed by the discriminating intellect in the shih state of imbalance: "For this reason the sage is concerned with the belly and not the eyes,/Therefore he rejects the one but accepts the other" (TTC,12). In governing, the sage/ruler "keeps their hearts vacuous (hsü),/Fills their bellies,/Weakens their ambition,/And strengthens their bones" (TTC,3). Provisions made to satisfy the instincts carry a higher priority than those for consciousness.

Much of the problem of interpreting Te, which makes it easy prey for masculine-oriented philosophers, centers on the second element of the ancient Te character, identified above as "heart" or "mind" (hsin). For Buddhists and Neo-Confucians, hsin represented a distinctly human capacity of mind or thought, as well as "the true nature of the universe". A continuity between mind and Nature, consciousness and instinct, was assumed. Quite the contrary view prevails in Taoism, however, as already indicated; the Tao Te Ching considers consciousness, the beginning of differentiation processes through discursive reason, as the disruption of Te.[92] The hsin element included in the Te character, Chen contends, therefore cannot be interpreted as mind (in the masculine sense), but is rather the kernel of Nature existing prior to consciousness (the feminine unconscious).

These revelations shed further light upon the problems of human Te, the common humanity entailed by the wholeness urge and its deviation from general humanistic considerations. Contrary to the interpretations of such scholars as Joseph Needham and Kuo Mo-jo, Taoism's original use of Te does not focus on the element of "the thinking power of man".[93] Aside from the obviously masculine character of thinking as rationality, which is unconducive to the assumed feminine mood of Taoism, it appears to conflict sharply with the contextual use of the Te concept in the Tao Te Ching. By examining Te's function as an ethical guide, it becomes possible to determine whether or not Te performs a unique function for human beings.

As previously noted, feminine ethics is unlike the traditional Western conception of ethics founded on 'oughts' and moral dictums. To be ethical the Taoist merely must fulfill the conditions of reality. The fact that only humans seem to have developed an ethical code, that is, that they alone among the Ten Thousand Things require one, is a matter for embarrassment rather than pride on our part. Only human creatures seem to have deviated from the primal standard of Tao, our true nature, so as to be in need of returning and a method by which to effect that return. Hence, when Te is rendered in English as 'virtue' or 'character' it involves an innate power, and not some ideal state for which we must aim. Te is not a consciously cultivated "moral perfection".[94]

Confucian influences have tended to give to Te the masculine moralistic overtones of virtue as the object of conscious cultivation, the very antithesis of Taoist thought. However, many interpreters, Arthur Waley, J. J. L. Duyvendak, and Needham among them, have chosen to translate Te as power. Along with Tao, Te serves as a major focus of the Tao Te Ching, whose title has been rendered as The Way and Its Power by Waley. Thus, the text can be said to encompass the unity as well as the multiplicity of reality. Tao is "the hidden foundation", Te "its manifestations as nature".[95] All creatures participate in and express Tao through their own individual Te. It is a power which can be exercised fully only when there is no conflict in the universal progression, yielding spontaneous development in each of the Ten Thousand Things.[96] Wing-Tsit Chan derives Te from the homophone 'to obtain', making it that which has been obtained from Tao, that is, individualized Tao.⁹⁷

The virtue/power of Te is expressed in diverse forms, but is essentially feminine or of the Yin temperament due to the fact that it is rooted in feminine Tao: "The all-embracing quality of the great virtue (te) follows alone from the Tao" (TTC,21). Te's power is shared with what is weak, yielding, tender, and small in a positive sense;⁹⁸ "All things, the grass as well as trees, are tender and supple while alive./ . . . . / The tender and weak are companions of life" (TTC, 76), "The softest things in the world overcome the hardest things in the world" (43). Feminine power is the power of the life force, of receptivity, of enduring strength, of Tao. Water, the Valley, and the Uncarved Block, are among its special symbols.

An illuminating aspect of this power emerges by a comparison with the negative or perverted feminine philosophy of Nietzsche. In Taoism there is a transcendence of moral virtue in the usual sense, as demonstrated in the adherence to the standard of Tao and symbolized by the infant; Tao's values both precede and go beyond humanistic relativities.⁹⁹ Similar to Nietzsche's philosophy, Te is beyond good and evil. It is significant that the final metamorphosis of Zarathustra after the camel (Elementary feminine) and the lion (masculine), is to a child (the Transformative feminine). Nietzsche uses the example of the bird of prey to explain nature or virtue-the predator's nature prompts it to attack weak sheep, it is an instinctual act not open to human moralistic condemnation.¹⁰⁰ Similarly, Yin is cast as a tiger, or more appropriately, tigress, stalking its prey, and thereby fulfilling its Te as impassively and impartially as Tao itself. From these observations Nietzsche fashions a glorification of the Ubermensch, and in doing so betrays the very principle underlying this thought. Working from similar data, the Taoist advances the more consistent ethical code of what may be termed the Untermensch. In both cases, there is a "going under" in the Eternal Return. However, to take credit for being natural, as does Nietzsche, is itself a sign of failure, whereas, the continued non-assertion of the Taoist assures success.

Nietzsche and the Taoist agree on the importance of unconscious instinct. To act by "superior" Te means to act unconsciously. A man of "inferior" Te, however, "never loses (sight of) his virtue,/ And in this way he loses his virtue"; they act with an ulterior motive, consciously striving for a goal, which cancels spontaneity (TTC,38). What primal Te does for the Ten Thousand Things is to encourage natural growth and development, assisting Tao in their rearing and development (51). After Tao has given birth to things, Te functions as the internal source of ongoing power needed to sustain new life: "Whatever man possesses through the strength of his own nature cannot be lost".[101]

In light of Te's function in the Tao Te Ching, the assertion of masculine thinkers that Te is "the thinking power of man" cannot be upheld. Thought is a process of consciousness, involving differentiation and abstraction. To assume that thought relates us to Tao, the undifferentiated and concrete, is clearly absurd. If Te is indeed our primal state, "when nature, having emerged from Tao, returns to and abides by Tao, and when man, as a child of nature, keeps close to and abides by nature",[102] the metaphysical structure of Tao will not allow us to maintain such harmony by means of divisive masculine discursive reason. In sum, rationality is not the nature of Te or humanity, but rather signals a disruption of that nature. The necessary reversion process takes place through Te as we move "from the male and the illustrious, which are symbols of consciousness and differentiation, to the female and the obscure, which are symbols of Tao".[103] We must be aware of Yang, but cling only to Yin (TTC,29).

For these reasons, the Tao Te Ching launches several attacks against the ultimate concept of humanistic moral virtue in Chinese philosophy, Jen, which epitomizes the view of morality as a process of intellectual attainment or cultivation. Carus' interpretation of Te's root meaning as human straightheartedness,[104] applies well to Jen, but is sorely inadequate for understanding Taoism's Te as interpreted above. Unlike Jen, Te is neither uniquely human nor does it require consciousness. In fact, the moral consciousness of the humanistic perspective is the beginning of the end for true Te.[105]

Furthermore, Jen, the foundation of Confucian and Neo-Confucian moral philosophy, is but the first in a series of increasingly divisive and degraded substitutes which are introduced following the loss of Tao:

> Therefore, only when Tao is lost does the doctrine of virtue arise.
> Only when virtue is lost does the doctrine

> of humanity arise.
> Only when humanity is lost does the
> doctrine of righteousness arise.
> Now, propriety is a superficial expression
> of loyalty and faithfulness, and the
> beginning of disorder.
> Those who are the first to know have the
> flowers (appearance) of Tao but are the
> beginning of ignorance.
> For this reason the great man dwells in
> the thick (substantial), and does not
> rest with the thin (superficial).
> He dwells in the fruit (reality), and does
> not rest with the flower (appearance).
> Therefore, he rejects the one, and accepts
> the other. (TTC,38)

Dwelling in the lowly places of Tao, the sage refuses to rise above to the increasingly precarious positions of alienation, each possessed of a correspondingly greater degree of superficiality. Tao is primal, the fruit of absolute knowledge; <u>Jen</u>, the doctrine of humanity, is merely its flowery expression and hence "the origin of folly". Eventually <u>Jen</u> reveals the stagnant artificiality which negates any of its original worth, descending first to the superficial doctrine of righteousness (justice, <u>I</u>), and thence to empty ritual, the doctrine of propriety (<u>Li</u>).

This rejected moral system seems very forced when compared with the natural ease of Taoist ethics. Positive narcissism provides a more efficient motive force than moral imperatives, and the natural inner standard of <u>Te</u> seems much more effective than an externally imposed standard. Finally, intuitive wisdom is uninterrupted by intervening judgments. Tao does not merely produce love (<u>tz'u</u>, <u>Eros</u>/relatedness), but <u>is</u> love in its functioning, binding all together under the encompassing whole.

The doctrine of <u>Jen</u> distinguishes human beings from others among the Ten Thousand Things of the universe by the emphasis upon rational capacity. Taoism's devotion to the unity of things directly contradicts this doctrine. Moreover, the <u>Tao Te Ching</u> objects to human-centered priorities: the goals of being learned by knowing others and of conquering by brute force stand in opposition to the Taoist wisdom of self-knowledge and the strength of self-conquest in the sage (TTC,33). The very fact that names, such as <u>Jen</u>, must be employed and ideals erected sounds suspicious to the

Taoist, for these names and ideals interrupt the spontaneous flow of Te. They would not be necessary if the primal (feminine) nature had not been lost already, for as previously demonstrated, language is in the province of the masculine principle.[106]

How then does Te reveal human nature within Taoist philosophy? To be consistent with the feminine principle it can do so only with reference to the whole. Te represents the individuation of Tao in its multiplicity and variation--"the many which has come from the one (yu) [Named Tao] which is born of nothing (wu) [Nameless Tao]", "the Specific Inborn Nature of Each Thing".[107] Hence, the Te concept underscores the deterministic character of Taoist metaphysics. The various expressions of Te are, as Lu Hui-ch'ing declares, the "tending forces" of things which "make them necessarily so".[108] In addition, Te assures us of metaphysical oneness, for in being derived from Tao it inherits its "all encompassing quality" (TTC,21). We are the 'here-now' reflection of Tao's eternality.[109]

Most importantly, Te is "Tao's Manifestation as Nature", of all of Nature and not specifically of human nature.[110] No privileged position is held by human beings in this feminine philosophy. A common nature, in essence at least, is possessed by all of the Ten Thousand Things. Taoist ethics urges us to examine our own Te prior to attaining Tao; the act (which is also a "non-act") of turning inward secures knowledge of external reality. Virtue is as simple, and as difficult, as adhering to the primal nature or power within, which is itself the sign of our present participation in Tao. No judgement is made as to any possible inferiority among non-human creatures vis-à-vis human beings. As noted above, returning is a peculiarly human problem, and assuredly no mark of superiority.

The consequences of these doctrines for our ethical interaction with other human beings, and with the world as a whole, are indeed great. We fulfill ourselves and our ethics simultaneously; there can be no question of a conflict of interests. The reality of universal reciprocity guides Taoist ethics. The same nature is not only shared with all other human beings, but also with all participants in Tao. No person or thing can be treated as an 'other', no action can be without consequences for our self, for everything affects the one shared Self. The sage transcends the (masculine) self/other distinction in returning to the primordial undifferentiated state of Tao.[111]

The transformation of the (masculine) ego self into the (feminine) shared Self is effected by a transformation of our perspective to correspond to the wholeness of feminine reality. This is the experience or recognition of mergence; the sage is "living within the moving forces of the universe and he is himself part of it". It is said that "The awareness of the identification and interpenetration of self and nonself is the key that unlocks the mystery of Tao.[112] The unrealistic 'ego-self' is lost while the shared Self is regained, the feminine concept of selfhood emanating from a common center. Discussing a similar psychic transformation, Jung contends that it constitutes a renunciation of "ego-bound intentions" and a submission (receptivity?) "to the supra-personal decrees of fate".[113]

In this Reversion process the (feminine) unconscious penetrates the "hard core" of the (masculine) ego and "turns it inside out" (just as water wears down a rock). Contrasting masculine striving for selfhood through discrimination and differentiation, the Taoist sage applies the unifying methods of nondiscrimination and nondifferentiation, that is, gropes towards the primal source of Te by means of "no-knowledge". There is a 'losing and losing' of the superficial artificalities accumulated through the corruption of Te.

The virtue/power of "living for others" is demonstrated by the universe itself. Heaven and Earth are everlasting because "they do not exist for themselves" (taking self in the sense of ego). The universe gives to others and thereby sustains itself indirectly. From this state of affairs the sage learns the lesson of being in the background, but simultaneously "finds himself in the foreground./ . . . . Is it not because he has no personal interests?/That is the reason why his personal interests are fulfilled" (TTC,7). In not attempting to satisfy personal and limited ego desires the sage is able to satisfy the more essential needs of the Self, shared with the whole on the highest plane of reality.

The true selfhood upon which Taoist ethics is founded thus can be recognized as the positive narcissism of the feminine principle of being. As Chang states "One of the great contradictions of Chinese philosophy is the theory that man perfects himself through the cultivation of egoless selfhood", which is indeed the basis of Taoism. The realization possible through the Self makes analytical methods unnecessary, and even counterproductive, in that they nourish the ego's tendency to make distinctions and so prevent "the emergence of the great self".[114]

Lin Yutang has stated that the practical aspect of Taoist philosophy is contained in the eight characters he has rendered as follows:

> Reveal thy simple self,
> Embrace thy original nature,
> Check thy [egotistical] selfishness,
> Curtail thy desires. (TTC,19).[115]

Self, in the sense of our primal nature, is the focal point of the sage's concern, is loved more than fame and more valuable than material wealth. The Taoist poses the rhetorical question: "Loss (of self) or possession (of goods), which is the greater evil?" (TTC,44).[116] The Self-centeredness of positive narcissism is what makes Taoist ethics work. This "true selfishness", Lau laments, is rarely found, "and when it is found in a man it makes him eminently suitable to be a ruler", inasmuch as it guards against self-destructive policies.[117] The egoism that is frightening and abhorrent in a Thrasymachus becomes enlightenment in the Taoist sage, due to the added dimension of positive narcissism. Once the inwardness mode of being has been implemented successfully through enlightenment, the behavior of the sage reveals the radical bent of the feminine perspective. The enlightened individual, in identifying with the universe, shares in the existence of all things. The Self encompasses ego knowledge, but the knowledge of the ego is experienced as non-self. Unifying self and non-self is the very function of nondifferentiation. The Taoist-tending poet relies upon the inner resources of the Self and thus works in the realm of "nonego-self"; the poet is then able to communicate with the reader of the poem, using the medium of their shared experience.[118] The same principle applies to painting (cf. Mu ch'i's (d. 1249) Six Persimmons, a "chronicle" of the enlightenment experience, through the use of light and shadow).

One final consequence of the inwardness revealed in and through all-is-one-ness relates to the promise of immortality in Taoist thought. In identifying with the whole, with eternal Tao, we too become eternal: "He who does not lose his place (with Tao) will endure./He who dies but does not really perish enjoys long life" (TTC,33). In terms of intuition, "death 'objectively' comes to the master but has no power over 'that' which makes the boy [the student] respond to the master's call". The 'that' is what F. S. C. Northrop refers to as the 'undifferentiated continuum' fathomed by intuition.[119] The enlightened Pu-liang Yi described is 'able to enter where there is no life and no death. That which kills life does not die; that which gives life to life does not live.' Or, as Burton Watson explains, "that which transcends the categories of life and death can never be said to have lived or died; only what recognizes the existence of such categories is subject to them."[120] And, of course, the feminine individual avoids all such divisive categories.

Taoist religion later erroneously interpreted the claims of immortality in a literal sense, stimulating a centuries-long search for the Elixir of Life. However, in terms of Taoist philosophy, to be in accord with Tao is to be eternal, not in the sense of personal immortality, but by virtue of one's participation in the life force: "Being in accord with Tao, he is everlasting,/And is free from danger throughout his lifetime" (TTC,16). In the sage "there is no room for death"; she or he is invulnerable to tigers or wild buffaloes or weapons of war. The principle of Reversion is active one more--death enters only where life has been, arises "because of . . . intensive striving after life" (TTC,50). An additional incentive is hereby attached to the ethical teachings of Taoism.

Thus, the mode of being known as inwardness establishes the beginning point of Taoist ethics, makes it possible at all. Stimulated by the metaphysical and epistemological knowledge/experience of wholeness or cosmic unity, the Taoist turns to the inner ethical guide, the individually manifested Tao of Te, to uncover the basis of an ethical life. The sense of Te in the Tao Te Ching not only discounts the uniqueness of human nature, expounded in the Jen concept with its emphasis on human rationality, but further seals our oneness with the universe. Te is the inherent virtue (Arete) or power which makes us participants in Tao, our inheritance from the maternal One. Implementation of Te, the sole ethical task for the Taoist, depends not on masculine consciousness and differentiation, but rather on the feminine unconscious and mergence.

From these premises arises the ethical conclusion of positive narcissism in Taoism. This ethical code is supported by the direct interest each individual has in the interests of all others, including all of the Ten Thousand Things, human and non-human. Furthermore, the restrictions of the ego-self are rejected in favor of a return to the primal shared Self. This Self is what is experienced in enlightenment. Finally, immortality is assured by virtue of our participation in what is eternal. With Tao we survive through the ongoing processes of the universe.

    b. <u>Receptivity--the sage ideal</u>. The most characteristically feminine of the modes of being also most strongly characterizes the ethical ideal of the sage in Taoism, namely receptivity or spontaneous acceptance. Recast from its pejorative masculine designation as passivity or even masochism, receptivity expresses the essence of the Yin principle, of <u>K'un</u> as the Receptive. Under this mode of being are included the sage's openness and sensitivity to reality, the tranquil life in imitation of universal Tao and based on individual <u>Te</u>. All of these elements converge in the pivotal Taoist doctrine of <u>wu-wei</u>. In the sage ideal itself we come face to face with the personification of the feminine code of ethical conduct, following directly from the revelations made by inwardness and treading the <u>ching</u> enlightenment path of quiescence.

    Receptivity is the true mark of the sage. Of Lao Tzu it is said, "Men all seek happiness. He, alone, sought completion in adaption."[121] That is, the highest priority is set upon being able to adapt to reality rather than on attaining personal, egotistical happiness. As opposed to the suddenness implied by the enlightenment path of <u>ming</u>, this approach on the part of the Taoist sage appears as the gradual adaption process of the <u>ching</u> path. By this means 'quiescence' becomes both incorporated and implemented in one's daily life. The process entails "continual losing"-- "The pursuit of Tao is to decrease day after day" (TTC, 48). One must strip away the successive layers of artificiality which have accumulated since our birth in primal innocence and which prevent us from drawing upon our <u>Te</u>. In addition to the negative rejection (transcendence) of intellectualizing, <u>ching</u> involves the positive "consciousness of the unconscious" or its equivalent in <u>Te</u> itself.[122]

    Having fathomed the primary ethical problem of liberating <u>Te</u>, the Taoist must reverse the repressive situation in order to became a sage. Tranquillity and the sense of cosmic harmony increase in proportion to the decrease in superficialities:

        To know harmony means to be in accord with

> the eternal.
> To be in accord with the eternal means
>   to be enlightened.
> To force the growth of life means ill omen.
> For the mind to employ the vital force
>   without restraint means violence.
> After things reach their prime, they begin
>   to grow old,
> Which means being contrary to Tao.
> Whatever is contrary to Tao will soon
>   perish. (TTC,55)

It is of the utmost importance, for true Self-interest, to avoid or 'lose' the artificialities of form and language, thereby achieving inner serenity and full receptivity. Hence, it is said of one who had become enlightened, "He dealt with everything and accepted everything."[123]

The artist achieves a similar state: "Things have their reality and will participate in the subjectivity of the painter when he allows them to captivate him." The tranquillity of Chinese landscapes approaches the experience of the Taoist on an aesthetic plane, leading to the cosmically shared "inexpressible ultimate."[124] Jacques Maritain has noted the "dynamic harmony" of Chinese art; the artist who succeeds in revealing the reality of things 'sets it free and, in turn, he liberates and purifies himself,' such is 'the action of Tao.'[125]

Tranquillity is a sign of the dawning of enlightenment, giving way to the "heavenly Light", then the recognition of "the Real Self" (the shared Self), and culminating in the Absolute. By this process our restrictive human elements are gradually left behind and the "Heavenly" ones (of Tao) emerge ever more strongly.[126] The path is clearly laid out:

> All things flourish,
> But each one returns to its root.
> This return to its root means tranquillity.
> It is called returning to its destiny.
> To return to destiny is called the eternal
>   (Tao)
> To know the eternal is called enlightenment.
>   (TTC,16)

Cultivating inner tranquillity the sage recognizes the role of the human individual as an intrinsic part of the order of the 'always so'.

The attainment of absolute quietude, of recognizing our <u>Te</u> and interfusing with the Ten Thousand Things, <u>is</u> non-discursive and constitutes the egoless state of Nonbeing. It is a state of total non-differentiation, described by Chuang Tzu as follows: 'Virtue will be your beauty, the Way will be your home, and, stupid as a newborn calf, you will not try to find out the reason why.'[127] The tranquillity of the sage is a complete openness to experience, being receptive to everything without interpreting data or making projections. The external world ceases to be external, and all human limiting conditions fade.

Ethically considered, the achievement of tranquillity by the <u>ching</u> path amounts to the implementation of a new/old life style, the primal existence in Tao. One's daily life is raised to a new level of cosmically-integrated consciousness (via the unconscious), while the negative superficialities of fear and anxiety are rejected. Being rooted in the "deep underlying harmony" which is ultimate reality, the peace of the Taoist sage is a lived reality of harmonization with Tao. The same daily routine of eating, sleeping, working, etc., is carried out by both the unenlightened and the enlightened, however the individuals of the latter type are able to adjust their attitude toward life in accordance with their transformed being. Only the enlightened are able to practice or live the mode of receptivity.

The sage's way of life, if it is to be productive of tranquillity and enlightenment, must focus on the elimination of disruptive elements and an adherence to tranquil ones. The ripples on the surface of the sea of reality must be stilled, the plurality of manifestations must be quieted in order to recognize the wholeness of Tao. This "Mystic Unity", also rendered as "All submerged in the One" (Lin Yutang), is attained by just such a stilling process:

>   Close the mouth.
>   Shut the doors (of cunning and desires).
>   Blunt the sharpness.
>   Untie the tangles.
>   Soften the light.
>   Become one with the dusty world. (TTC,56)

The sage calms the churning confusions which create the illusion of an ego-self, to reveal our inner nature as the shared or Real Self. Taoist painters and poets were reputed to enhance this state of oblivion by imbibing ample doses of wine prior to engaging in their work. The resulting releasing of inhibitions left them receptive to the mergence with Tao.

To realize this end, the Tao Te Ching recommends the negation of desire, wu-yu, to the sage. In the usual paradoxical manner, the object of the Taoist's desire is 'the undesired':

> Therefore the sage desires to have no desire.
> He does not value rare treasures.
> He learns to be unlearned, and returns to what the multitude has missed (Tao).
> Thus he supports all things in their natural state but does not take any action. (TTC,64)

The 'losing and losing' method employed to eliminate the accumulations of superfluous knowledge applies equally well to desires. They must be reduced to the barest minimum, although they cannot be eliminated entirely, by reducing the objects of desire. This is particularly true of those desires which violate the Taoist sense of balance: "the sage discards the extremes, the extravagant, and the excessive" (TTC,29).

The use of desire here is not meant to refer to natural instincts, which derive from the pure source of Tao. Only the impure or egotistical desires are to be eliminated.[128] Desires of this type, which emerge as passions, are self-destructive. With the development of (masculine) consciousness, the making of distinctions, the natural protective layers (the buffer of instincts) encasing "the vital principle within" are gradually removed, resulting in the exposure of the heart, hsin, which then "beats so rapidly that it goes mad."[129]

To avoid these extreme consequences, the sage begins a series of transcendences, first of mundane affairs, then of material things, and finally of personal existence (life and death). Although each is useful at a given stage of development, they are eventually superceded by the more fundamental mergence with Tao. These are the steps along the (ching) path of enlightenment. At the highest level of tranquillity one is free from superficial confusions. The sage is beyond "being and nonbeing, life and death, construction and destruction"; this constitutes the nonattachment of the enlightened, who seek to identify "completely with objectivity and yet to be entirely free from it."[130] The Uncarved Block (p'u) is the symbol of the simple life idealized by Taoist ethics, a life which follows from the serene state of mind, "not devoted to the pursuit of profit or marked by hypocritical humanity and righteousness", but rather devoted to "plainness, tranquillity, and purity".[131] The sage is "the man of P'u" who rejects "artificial efforts toward morality and intellectual distinction".[132]

Equanimity, being satisfied with contentment, that is, with what one has as opposed to what lies beyond, is thus intrinsic to the sage's life style-"He who is contented with contentment is always contented" (TTC, 46). This phrase may sound like an empty tautology, but on closer consideration it can be recognized as proposing a totally realistic outlook in life. Working under the metaphysical and epistemological assumptions of Taoism outlined above, with their deterministic cast, satisfaction with contentment is not only the most reasonable course, it is also the only feasible one. Regardless of masculine charges of defeatism, the open and receptive attitude of the feminine adherent thus can be interpreted positively. One who "does not want to fill himself to overflowing. . . . is beyond wearing out and [the need for] renewal" (TTC,15).

Contained in the ideal of contented contentment is an avoidance of conflict. Both the counterproductiveness and the divisiveness of conflict make it abhorrent to the sage. The sage's alternative response is the metaphysically-approved method of yielding, being receptive to existing conditions. The I Ching advises that the "only salvation" for an individual involved in a conflict "lies in being so clear-headed and inwardly strong that he is always ready to come to terms by meeting the opponent half-way."[133] The Taoist sage surpasses the clear-headedness and inward strength of such a compromiser by seeming to yield entirely to the opponent, that is, spontaneously following the path of least, or no, resistance. This is the Taoist virtue of non-contending, and simultaneously the means to ultimate victory. Those of "primordial innocence" and "transcendental spirituality" are devoid of conflict, "free from entanglements of artificiality."[134] Given the pervasive Yin force of the universe, our survival depends upon observing the conditions of reality and being able to flow with the whole. A definite pattern is evident in things: " . . . he who has lavish desires will spend extravagantly./He who hoards most will lose heavily./He who is contented suffers no disgrace./He who knows when to stop is free from danger" (TTC,44). Fung Yu-lan refers to this as the all-important realization that desire to live in a certain manner necessitates "living in a manner exactly the opposite".[135]

The Reversion principle determines that things be so and not otherwise. The superficial reality of a situation is directly contradicted by its latent truth; on an absolute level of being:

> To yield is to be preserved whole.
> To be bent is to become straight.
> To be empty is to be full.
> To be worn out is to be renewed.
> To have little is to possess.
> To have plenty is to be perplexed.   (TTC,22)

Unless a thing begins by being bent, it cannot be made straight; unless it is first empty, it cannot be filled, and so on. Thus runs the deceptively simple law of the universe. It consists of the dynamic interchange of the dichotomies represented by Yang and Yin. There is a complementary interdependence between Being and Nonbeing, difficult and easy, long and short, high and low, sound and voice, front and back (TTC,2). Tranquility brings the sage beyond such differentiations, to a state of highest reality unconditioned by dichotomies.[136]

The best, and only, model for proper ethical behavior, which by definition must be in accord with reality, is Tao itself, and so the sage imitates its metaphysical being (Nonbeing) at the level of individual life. In the <u>Tao Te Ching</u> a distinction is made between three types of individuals based on their reaction upon hearing the truth of Tao. The "highest" (intuitive) type "deligently practice it"; the "average" (rational) individuals "half believe in it", knowing without direct experience; the "lowest" (common sense) type "laugh heartily at it" (TTC,41). The first of these types qualifies as mystic under Van Over's criterion--"one who practices putting himself into direct relation with Deity or other unifying principles of life."[137] These philosopher/sages also belong to the category of those who act in accordance with the revelations of intuition, and hence with ultimate reality. In China such thinkers express themselves in practical, even prosaic terms, adopting a "direct and matter-of-fact" approach.[138] While the Taoist philosopher experiences intuitive knowledge, the accomplished sage lives its matured wisdom.

The sage imitates Tao on many levels. The infant ideal, incorporating simplicity in terms of both ignorance and lack of developed desires, has been mentioned above as an extension of maternal Tao, with the sage taking the role of Tao's offspring being nourished by "the Mother". Distinguishing himself from the markedly masculine tendency of the common run of humanity, who are engaged in merry-making, " . . . as though feasting on a day of sacrifice,/Or like ascending a tower at springtime", the sage remains uniquely unattached and inert:

> The multitude all possess more than enough,
> I alone seem to have lost all.
> Mine is indeed the mind of an ignorant man,
> Indiscriminate and dull!
> Common folks are indeed brilliant;
> I alone seem to be in the dark.
>
> Common folks see differences and are
>   clear-cut;
> I alone make no distinctions.
> I seem drifting as the sea;
> Like the wind blowing about, seemingly
>   without destination.
> The multitude all have a purpose;
> I alone seem to be stubborn and rustic.
> I alone differ from others,
> And value drawing sustenance from
>   Mother (Tao).   (TTC,20)

As we have learned from Taoism's philosophy of life, everything is quite opposite of how it appears from the human perspective. The sage is only "seemingly" aimless. The stress laid upon a state of being muddled, dull, confused (lacking distinctions), depressed, stubborn, etc., is merely an indication of the highest clarity, insight, and so forth. The negative judgments arise from the relativistic human perspective. Perfection in its most extreme manifestation seems to be imperfection when an encompassing (feminine) viewpoint is lacking --"greatest abundance" seems "meager", straightness crooked, the "greatest skills" clumsiness, and the "greatest eloquence" mere stuttering (TTC,45). The Reversion principle transforms things into their opposite when viewed at the non-absolute level.

When the lowest type of individuals bursts into

laughter upon hearing Tao, the Tao Te Ching explains "If they did not laugh at it, it would not be Tao." Correspondingly, if the sage were not laughed at and derided, she/he would not be acting in accordance with Tao, would not be in Tao: "The Tao which is bright appears to be dark./The Tao which goes forward appears to fall backward./The Tao which is level appears uneven./Great virtue appears like a valley (hollow). /Great purity appears like disgrace./Far-reaching virtue appears as if insufficient./Solid virtue appears as if unsteady" (TTC,41). It is hardly surprising, then, that the Taoist sage appears as "a divine fool" when measured against the humanistic masculine ideal, and that Taoist virtue seems to be amoral.[139]

The Tao Te Ching clearly recognizes the "marketing" problems of this apparently inane ideal and expends greatest efforts in outlining the appropriateness of the sage's life style: "All the world says that my Tao is great and does not seem to resemble (the ordinary)./ It is precisely because it is great that it does not resemble (the ordinary)./If it did resemble, it would have been small for a long time" (TTC,67). In essence, this ideal is the inner reality of all, inasmuch as the sage is simply and spontaneously fulfilling human Te and universal Tao. One need only embrace Tao to become enlightened; "everyone has the potentiality to become a sage".[140]

Yet the fact remains that most people do not, and in all probability never will, attain the sublime state of enlightenment to experience reality as it is. The sage declares:

> My doctrines are very easy to understand and very easy to practice.
> But none in the world can understand or practice them.
> My doctrines have a source (Nature); my deeds have a master (Tao).
> It is because people do not understand this that they do not understand me.
> Few people know me, and therefore I am highly valued.
> Therefore the Sage wears a coarse cloth on top and carries jade within his bosom.   (TTC,70)

This state of affairs accounts for the contingent elitism which emerges in the figure of the Taoist sage/ruler, an elitism which is contingent upon the fact that others have yet to realize their enlightenment potential. "The readiness is all." But the ethical ideal of the sage can neither be attained nor understood until the over-all system of reality in Tao first has been understood. Chuang Tzu defines a sage as one who "regards Heaven as the source, Teh [Te] as the foundation, and Tao as the portal, which is evidenced in all the changes of life."[141] When these conditions, which hinge upon knowledge of the metaphysical framework of ultimate reality, are fulfilled the only remaining requirement is to enter through the portal of Tao by imitation. The Tao Te Ching indicates the criteria by which one can judge of one's success or failure in this regard: "Can you keep the spirit and embrace the One without departing from them?/Can you concentrate your vital force (ch'i) and achieve the highest degree of weakness like an infant?/Can you clean and purify your profound insight so it will be spotless?" (10). The sage likewise is expected to " . . . make muddy water gradually clear through tranquillity . . . make the still gradually come to life through activity".

Among the other qualities of the sage are tolerance, which stems from knowing the Eternal Law, leading to impartiality, and then kingliness (one who is wang, 'cosmopolitan', 'regarding the world as one'[142]). Being in harmony with Nature, and in accord with (receptive to) Tao, culminates in eternality, such that the sage "is free from danger throughout his lifetime" (TTC,16). To be in accord with Tao as well with one's Te yields an identification with it, just as abandonment of Tao or Te leads to a severing of relations--"He who is identified with Tao--Tao is also happy to have him" (TTC,23), to share its essence.

Our life is what we make of it, and the ethical choice involves an identification with the inner principle along with a receptivity to the reality of our specific virtue/power (Te). The persistent masculine problem of free will undergoes a radical and distinctly feminine reinterpretation in Taoist ethics, as is appropriate to the feminine perspective in general. Given the artificialities of civilization, it is indeed possible to stray from the standard of reality, Tao, although we always remain at one with the whole by virtue of our Te. The problem is not how free will can be possible in a deterministic system, but rather how to overcome its misuse in the humanistic alienation from Tao. It is not a matter of whether we can exercise our free will, but rather that it can be exercised to create disharmony as well as harmony in the universe.

Direct parallels therefore can be drawn between how Tao functions and the functioning of the sage. "The Way of Heaven is to benefit others and not to injure./The Way of the sage is to act but not to compete" (TTC,81); the "square" character of the sage (indicating firm principles), does not pierce (is without corners, infinite as Tao), and the sage "is as acute as a knife but does not cut . . . is bright as light but does not dazzle" (TTC,58). Tao's "profound and secret virtue", by which it gives birth to and nourishes the Ten Thousand Things "without taking possession" (51), is emulated by the sage who " . . . acts, but does not rely on his own ability./He accomplishes his task, but does not claim credit for it./He has no desire to display his excellence" (77) and thus displays "profound and secret virtue (hsüan-te)" paralleling Tao's (10). In sum, the sage emulates Tao's cosmic maternity.

Nor is the sage's cosmic accomplishment totally ignored by the common masses, once the principle of Reversion takes effect. In embracing the One, the sage becomes "the model of the world"; in not revealing self-interest is "luminous", "prominent", without boasting "is given credit," and being without self-pride "can endure for long" (TTC,22). Being beyond love and hate, profit and loss, honor and disgrace, the sage is "honored by the world" (56). Under Jung's interpretation, the Taoist sage fulfills a task for the entire community (as the mother does for the offspring), by being responsible for the re-establishment of Tao in the world "by ritual meditation. In this way he brings his own heaven and earth into harmony", and restores the natural order for all.[143] This aspect of the sage's life becomes particularly significant in relation to socio-political concerns.

In imitation of Tao's impartiality, the sage refrains from making personal value judgments. Both the good and the bad are declared good; both the honest and the dishonest are believed. The mind of the sage "forms a harmonious whole with that of his people" (TTC,49). We are enjoined to profit from the experience of the good individual as "teacher of the bad" as well as from the bad as "the material from which the good may learn" (Tse, "raw-material, resources, help, something to draw upon for profit"[144])--"He who does not value the teacher,/Or greatly care for the material,/Is greatly deluded although he may be learned." This is the "essential mystery" (TTC,27).

Those things which the sage deems worthy of love reflect the over-all attitude of Tao, including dwelling in "(lowly) places", profundity of heart, kindness in human interrelationships, sincerity in speech, order in government, competence in business, and timeliness in action (TTC,8). Above all, the sage must be receptive to reality, remaining open to the world: "There is no greater guilt than discontentment./There is no greater disaster than greed" (TTC,46).

Of Tao it is said, "All things depend on it for life, and it does not turn away from them./It accomplishes its task, but does not claim credit for it./. . . . All things come to it and it does not master them; it may be called The Great" (TTC,34). The sage's greatness stems from the same lack of assertiveness. The best, like Tao, always remain inconspicuous:

> A good traveler leaves no track or trace.
> A good speech leaves no flaws.
> A good reckoner uses no counters.
> A well-shut door needs no bolts, and yet
>   it cannot be opened.
> A well-tied knot needs no rope and yet
>   none can untie it. (TTC,27)

The qualities of the sage are equally inconspicuous and natural. The sage is wise in self-knowledge, strong by self-conquest, rich in contentment, strong-willed in determination, enduring in retaining an inner center (<u>Te</u>) (TTC,33).

By holding "fast to the Tao of old/in order to manage the affairs of Now", the sage is aware of "the Primeval Beginnings", the "continuity" (<u>chi</u>, 'system' or 'discipline')[145] of Tao. This knowledge is readily applicable to the sage's life style, yielding an awareness of and receptivity to the metaphysical reality. Various useful observations follow therefrom. The principle of Reversion dictates the perils of the supposedly high-placed, and we are furnished with lists of how <u>not</u> to behave:

> He who stands on tiptoe is not steady.
> He who strides forward does not go.
> He who shows himself is not luminous.
> He who justifies himself is not prominent.
> He who boasts of himself is not given credit.

> He who brags does not endure for long.
> From the point of view of Tao, these are like
>   remnants of food and tumors of action . . .
> Which all creatures detest.
> Therefore those who possess Tao turn away
>   from them. (TTC,24)

If any of these artificial attitudes have been adopted, the alienation from Tao has already proceeded so far as to consign those involved to the very lowest type of humanity.

Successful harmonization requires that we refrain from action rather than assert ourselves futilely. Action spoils things, grasping results in a slipping away of the object of desire; the sages spoil nothing because they do not act, and nothing slips away because they do not grasp (but rather they hold fast to Tao by not holding fast). "People in their handling of affairs often fail when they are about to succeed./If one remains as careful at the end as he was at the beginning, there will be no failure" (TTC,64). Success is not taken for granted by the enlightened individual. Entailed here is a proper assessment of the situation at hand, a realistic appraisal of its difficulties. If a promise is made without careful prior consideration it will be hard to fulfill, and if one continually minimizes difficulties they will arise even more forcefully, accumulating by neglect; "For this reason even the sage regards things as difficult,/And therefore he encounters no difficulty" (TTC,63).

There is a great danger in attempting to attain excellence, the danger of over-enthusiasm which negates all possible benefits. This attitude is expressed as follows: " . . . it is often the case that things gain by losing and lose by gaining" (TTC,42). Concrete examples of this situation are presented in the <u>Tao Te Ching</u>. If a vessel is filled to overflowing, our excessive enthusiasm entails a loss, or if a sword is honed to too fine an edge, it is soon worn away. Similarly, those who have amassed an excess of wealth will be unable to protect it--"To be proud with honor and wealth/Is to cause one's own downfall" (TTC,9). For like reasons, brave soldiers are not violent nor prone to lose their temper, the great conquerer avoids minor disputes, and those who know how to command do not assert their authority. "This is called the virtue of not-competing./This is called the strength to use men./This is called matching Heaven, the highest principle of old" (TTC,68).

The Taoist virtues detailed above correspond well to the feminine mode of being, while the complementary "vices" are those associated with a masculine perspective. In short, the Te sage is essentially an adherent of the feminine principle, of Yin, this being the type of behavior required to imitate the equally feminine Tao. The supple, receptive accommodating feminine attitude is ultimately the most productive, whereas the rigid, assertive, demanding one of the masculine perspective is counterproductive in the context of the ultimate reality. The feminine and masculine perspectives share a common human concern for survival, although they differ in regard to their criteria for judging the efficacy of a method. This difference is traceable to their disparate metaphysical assumptions.

The "tender and weak" (Yin) is associated with birth or life, the "stiff and hard" with death: "Therefore if the army is strong, it will not win./If a tree is stiff, it will break./The strong and the great are inferior, while the tender and the weak are superior" (TTC,76). Survival depends on "failure", in contrast to the masculine sense of success. Taoism effectively inverts the masculine scale of values, placing the feminine at the apex of existence (which is also the primal depth) by virtue of its link to Tao. In the same manner, "the heavy", which emulates the heaviness of (feminine) Earth in being stable and honest,[146] "is the root of the light", the unstable (masculine), and "The tranquil is the ruler of the hasty". The Taoist sage displays an enduring heaviness, a "leisurely and indifferent" mode of existence (TTC,26).

The Taoist ethical ideal is founded, then, upon the manifold advantages of "weakness", that is, feminine receptivity or yielding which is redefined as ultimate strength, just as Nonbeing is ultimate being. Only the feminine mode of being fulfills inner Tao: "The supreme goal for the common man as well as for the ruler is survival, and the means to this goal is simply to hold fast to the submissive."[147] "Weakness" is a virtue because it complements and overcomes conspicuous strength (TTC,28), it is, in fact, an expression of inner strength (45). Ultimately it always overcomes superficial (masculine) strength (48).[148] Indeed, this feminine power is valued by the Taoist sage chiefly for its potential to transcend the limitations of active masculine power. "Hasty movement overcomes cold,/(But) tranquillity overcomes heat./By being greatly tranquil,/One is qualified to be the ruler of the world" (TTC,45).

The sage is encouraged to "rest in the Absolute" and avoid later "distress" by adhering to the strength of weakness and the enlightenment which is able to discern "the small".

The subtle Way (Tao) of Heaven is to conquer without strife, to reward without words, to appear without being called, to achieve without "obvious design". Nonetheless, it remains all-encompassing-"Heaven's net is indeed vast./Though its meshes are wide, it misses nothing" (TTC,73). As the bow is bent, what had been on top (the masculine) is lowered, and that which had been at the bottom (the feminine) is raised. The Way of Heaven "reduces whatever is excessive and supplements whatever is insufficient", contrasting sharply with the human way which takes from those with little or nothing to give to those who already have too much. "Who is able to have excess to offer to the world?/Only the man of Tao" (TTC,77).

It is only natural, then, that the well-informed and Tao-tending sage affects the lowest position which guarantees the greatest natural compensation from Tao. The "three treasures" of the Taoist reflect this realization: the deep love of tz'u (Eros), "frugality", and "not to dare to be ahead of the world". The first of these yields courage, integration in the wholeness of the universe; the second, indicates generosity; while the third entails a movement to the leadership of the world. These may be related to the three facets of feminine behavior expressed by the modes of being: the integration of inwardness, the power of receptivity, and the recognition of our role in Nature. Tz'u in particular is singled out as invincible: "When Heaven is to save a person/Heaven will protect him through deep love" (67).

Given this extended explanation of the foundations for the ethical principles personified by the Taoist sage, it now becomes possible to understand the pivotal concept of wu-wei used to describe the sage's action by 'non-action'. As might be expected, wu-wei follows in the paradoxical vein of Nonbeing (wu) and the negation of language by silence, both of which convey the otherwise inexplicable meaning of the ultimate reality. Unfortunately, "Few in the world can understand teaching without words and the advantage of taking no action" (TTC,43). Translated by itself, wu (無) indicates a negation-'lacking in, nonexistent, without'. Added to the term wei (為), 'to do something', 'to act', 'to make a show, to show off, to pose, to parade oneself', it means 'to do without ado', 'to act without acting', 'non-assertion'.[149] Wu-wei is a receptivity to the universe, "an action of [feminine] creative intuition" standing in opposition to (masculine) assertiveness; it is the free and limitless product of the inner light which contrasts with the "limited and finite" character of rationality.[150]

The non-assertion of wu-wei causes us to relate to the universe in a positive manner, The Buddhist master Tao-an has declared: "By non-action we come into accord with things. By non-desire harmony comes to our affairs. By being in accord with things we can see into their nature. Through harmony in our affairs we can accomplish our missions. . . . This is to achieve integration into the One."[151]

The ultimate simplicity corresponds to what is natural or spontaneous. In this sense, wu-wei consists in "letting things take their own course",[152] non-interference in Nature. Otherwise expressed, as appropriate to the yielding and receptivity of the feminine principle, it consists of "following the line of least resistance".[153] The non-action of wu-wei is in fact a "natural from-Tao-emanating movement".[154] Not surprisingly, then, Tao itself functions in this manner:

> Tao invariably takes no action, and yet
>   there is nothing left undone.
> If kings and barons can keep it, all
>   things will transform spontaneously.
> If, after transformation, they should
>   desire to be active, I would restrain
>   them with simplicity, which has no
>   name.
> Simplicity, which has no name, is free
>   of desires.
> Being free of desires, it is tranquil.
> And the world will be at peace of its
>   own accord. (TTC,37)

Through the practice of wu-wei, then, Tao stimulates cosmic harmony by allowing things to follow their natural course. The value of "taking no action" is apparent in the case of "Non-being" penetrating "that in which there is no space"; only the most yielding of substances can effect such penetration, and they can do so only through recourse to wu-wei (TTC,43).

In imitating Tao the sage follows the same non-assertive practice and is advised, "Act without action.

/Do without ado./Taste without tasting." By tackling difficult problems in their minor emergent stages, extreme action is indeed unnecessary: "Therefore the sage never strives for the great,/And thereby the great is achieved" (TTC,63). A similar theory underlies the 'losing and losing' process of the student of Tao. "The pursuit of Tao is to decrease day after day./It is to decrease and further decrease until one reaches the point of taking no action./No action is undertaken, and yet nothing is left undone." The establishment of an empire can be accomplished "by having no activity (laissez-faire)', that is, not interfering in natural processes; "If one (likes to) undertake activity, he is not qualified to govern the empire" (TTC,48).

Clearly, then, the feminine mode of being designated as receptivity, which encompasses the openness, Yin yielding, or "passivity" attributed to the feminine perspective, is fully present in the person of the Taoist sage as moral role model of that philosophy. Progressing on the enlightenment path of ching or quiescence, the aspiring sage gradually implements the principles of Tao, indicated by metaphysics and revealed by intuition, in her/his daily life style. This constitutes a quieting of superfluous, human-oriented, elements which tend to alienate our primal nature, Te, from its harmony with the ultimate reality of Tao by the method of 'losing and losing'.

Imitation of Tao is necessary to become a sage; Tao is lived through our individual lives, in order that we may live ethically. From the common viewpoint, the sage seems to be like a dull infant, a divine fool, just as the teachings of Tao appear to be folly. Consequently, the sage is distinguished from the rest of humanity, in a contingent, theoretically unnecessary, elitism. Within, in terms of their primal Te, everyone is already enlightened, at one with Tao. Under its human-centered interpretations appearances are deceiving, and the Taoist thus looks beneath to the root of Tao, of truth, ignores the flower in favor of the fruit.

The sage embraces the One, is tolerant, impartial, non-possessive, inconspicuous, just as is Tao. By taking the lowly position the sage is exalted, in accordance with the universal principle of Reversion. the enlightened awareness or experience of this principle motivates us to go down in order to be exalted, to suspend masculine striving in order to achieve true success. The sage takes everything seriously, and so nothing serious or difficult matures to block the course of Nature.

These very values of lowliness, yielding, receptivity, acceptance, prompt a direct identification of the sage character with the feminine principle or Yin. The virtues of quiescence, solidity, and weakness are pointed to in the Tao Te Ching as possessing ultimate strength for over-coming masculine activity, lightness, and force. Love, as tz'u or Eros/relatedness, is especially associated with the path of the Taoist sage as the ultimate means of conquest. Moreover, explicit references to the superiority of the feminine over the masculine principle within the context of the Taoist's ultimate reality are contained in the symbols of the valley or ravine, the primally dark Yin, and the "weakness" of water. Together, they promise the sage special power in the mold of the infant, Uncarved Block, and Nonbeing. All of these elements coalesce in chapter 28 of the Tao Te Ching:

> He who knows the male (active force) and keeps
>   to the female (the passive or receptive
>   element)
> Becomes the ravine of the world.
> Being the ravine of the world,
> He will never depart from eternal virtue,
> But returns to the state of infancy.
> He who knows the white (glory) and yet keeps
>   to the black (humility),
> Becomes the model for the world.
> Being the model for the world,
> He will never deviate from eternal virtue,
> But returns to the state of the Ultimate
>   Non-being.
> He who knows glory but keeps to humility,
> Becomes the valley of the world.
> Being the valley of the world,
> He will be proficient in eternal virtue,
> And returns to the state of simplicity
>   (uncarved wood).

The paradoxical concept of wu-wei, the standard of the sage's action in 'non-action', is explained by the underlying conditions of the Taoist ethical ideal. Wu-wei is revealed as a quintessentially feminine mode of action by non-assertion, non-attachment, and non-interference in the natural course of things. The artificialities of the humanistic masculine perspective are avoided. Tao itself acts by the spontaneity of wu-wei and thereby accomplishes its ends without effort; the sage is encouraged to do likewise. The wu-wei method parallels the natural flow of Tao and seals the Yin significance chosen by the Taoist to accomplish the ethical ends of this philosophy.

  c. Materiality--the link with Nature. Having surveyed the essence of Taoist virtue in the inwardness of Te, and the ethical ideal of the receptive sage, we progress to the ethical state of harmony with Nature. In terms of logical priority, one might well argue that materiality precedes the other two modes of being. Both inwardness and receptivity presuppose such a link to the material realm. However, it would also seem that only the enlightened sage, who has followed out the promptings of individual Te and is living in imitation of Tao, is adequately prepared to appreciate the significance of the link and to benefit from the lessons of the natural order.

  The sage draws upon the realm of Nature to supply knowledge of the state of Tao. Disavowing any suggestion of a masculine mind/body dualism, there is a total integration of the Self with instinct and the life force. These conditions are reflected in the imagistic language of the Tao Te Ching. Much of what is involved here has been evident in previous facets of the feminine attitude, such as the underlying oneness of the universe, with the result that our survey of this facet of Taoism's feminine attitude can be brief.

  If it were to be pigeon-holed in accordance with accepted philosophical categories, Taoism would be included under the heading of naturalism, the identity of Nature and reality. Tao is held to be immanent in Nature and even takes Nature (tse-jan), the 'self-so', as its model with respect to spontaneity (TTC,25). Self-so-ness is the key to attaining Tao; as the Neo-Taoist Kuo Hsiang remarks, "what is spontaneously so, and not made to be so, is naturalness."[155] It is under this characterization that the Taoist deals with Nature.

  In imitation of Tao, the Taoist sage also takes Nature as a model and experiences a profound sympathy with it. Nature is eminently worthy of imitation, being characterized by the same feminine qualities found in Tao:

> Nature creates all beings without erring: this is straightness. It is calm and still: this is its foursquareness. It tolerates all creatures equally: this is its greatness. Therefore it attains what is right

for all without artifice or special intentions. Man achieves the height of wisdom when all that he does is as self-evident as what nature does.[156]

Through Nature, the sage is able to grasp "the truth of Tao" which "lies in the concrete realities of or daily activities."[157] This is only possible because the metaphysical truths of Tao are reflected in the processes of the material world, as is Tao itself. "All things come into being./And I see thereby their return. /All things flourish,/But each one returns to its root" (TTC,16).

The individual possesses the inner guide of nature, Te, discussed at length above. Te is described as "the original perfection of Nature, when Nature is yet closed within itself and unconscious of distinctions."[158] The nondifferentiation of the sage stems from the Te-Tao continuum and gives rise to the ethical code of non-interference in Nature, embracing spontaneity and avoiding artificiality. The sage " . . . learns to be unlearned, and returns to what the multitude has missed (Tao)./Thus he supports all things in their natural state but does not take any action" (TTC,64). Hence, the virtuous individual is sympathetic to Nature, due to the promptings of individual nature, and is so not consciously, but spontaneously.[159] Appropriately, then, the Tao Te Ching is very much concerned with inculcating a cosmically productive interaction with the world.

Appearances, the concrete manifestations of Tao, can and do reveal much about the inner working of reality. What are significant are not the superficial appearances by which the unenlightened are deceived into positing a masculine perspective in the universe, but rather the appearances interpreted in the context of feminine Tao. Both the "subtlety" (miao) and the "outcome" of things are referred to as "deep and profound (hsüan)":

> Therefore let there always be non-being so we may see their subtlety,
> And let there always be being so we may see their outcome.
> The two are the same,
> But after they are produced, they have different names. (TTC,1)

Lin Yutang translates miao as "the Secret of Life",

which we see by stripping ourselves of passion, while its "manifest forms", are seen when "one regards life with passion".

This assumption of parallelism existing between Tao and Nature is implemented in the <u>Tao Te Ching</u> as part of its program of indirectly suggesting, rather than directly expounding, philosophical theory. Burtt views the constant references to natural phenomena as indicative of a "Reasoning" method grounded in the material world. Given the "obvious facts" observed in Nature, the Taoist concludes that certain metaphysical and ethical principles can be deduced. For example, the pull of gravity which causes water to flow downward, seeking the lowest point, prompts the sage to emulate this action by adopting a yielding attitude.[160] This approach seems to partake of that "utterly Chinese" form of mental training whose intent was similarly conceived "to broaden a person's vision, sharpen his imagination, and sensitize his mind so that he can see and grasp truth instantly at any time and anywhere."[161] The radical empiricism of the feminine principle, which dictates a direct experiencing of what is known, is exemplified here as the sage implements concrete knowledge in life.

Not only do the concrete manifestations of Tao reflect their source, allowing the principles of Tao to be grasped through a careful observation of natural phenomena, but moreover the indirect method of employing images from Nature to suggest the character of Tao has proven most successful. The impossibility of finding adequate linguistic expressions of Tao in ordinary terms has already been cited as justification for the Taoist's appeal to imagistic language. The images so employed have the advantage of being open to experience in a way that is not possible when dealing with comparatively sterile intellectual concepts. The vivid imagery of the Taoist poet communicates to us on several levels, as do the misty valleys and empty voids of Taoist paintings. The effect is an evocation of primal archetypes. The paintings in particular convey a subtle, but quite forceful, reminder of the human role in Nature, for the human presence, although always included, is reduced to the smallest possible scale in the overwhelming field of the expansive landscapes.

Included under the link with Nature for the adherent of the feminine principle is the integration of sensuality in the total being of an individual. Although such a view is barely hinted at within the

Tao Te Ching, it does fit into the over-all system of a feminine philosophy. It is said that 'What we value and what we fear are within our Self', or "We have fears because we have a self./When we do not regard that self as self,/What have we to fear?" (TTC,13). Under this rendering by Lin Yutang, these statements may be interpreted as an argument for the holistic point of view, or a rejection of the ego-self in favor of the shared Self. However, some translators, such as Waley and Wing-Tsit Chan, have rendered the word "Self" (shen) as body. This interpretation could conceivably lead one to conclude that these statements are an indictment of our physical being for entangling us in unnecessary fears. However, the Taoist would seem to have too great a reverence for Nature to reject any of its expressions. The body, like the self or ego, is a hindrance only insofar as it is not considered as an integral part of the universe, when it is considered to be merely my body, in an artificial and human-centered alienation from the whole.

To be consistent, then, the Taoist like the adherent of the feminine principle, cannot be alienated from the body. No mention is made in the Tao Te Ching of a mind/body dualism. Barring an abhorred divisiveness body and mind must be equally expressive of Tao. Chang cites as "the central principle of Taoist meditative practice" the unification of "conscious spirit" (hsing) and "substantial ether" (ming); both substance and spirit participate in the oneness of Tao, are dissolved with the self (ego) in the One.[162]

The apparent rejection of the senses in the Taoist text also can be misleading if not interpreted in the over-all feminine context. When the Taoist declares "The five colors cause one's eyes to be blind./The five tones cause one's ears to be deaf./The flavors cause one's palate to be spoiled" (TTC,12), or "Close the mouth./Shut the doors (of cunning and desire)./And to the end of life there will be (peace) without toil" (52), what is being rejected are not the senses per se, but rather the unnatural sensuality which is disruptive of our primal Te. The opening of the doors referred to results in an over-involvement in mundane affairs, such that "to the end of life there will be no salvation" (52). These affairs include the striving for personal fame and advancement. A complete rejection of the senses, our means of access to Nature, would be inconsistent with the Taoist's use of Nature as a model.

As noted, the Taoist does refer to the observations of the senses in obtaining and communicating information about the functioning of Tao, and trusts the data of downward-tending water and supple vegetation. Ranking above these externals, however, is the inner sense of the primal feminine unconscious, the 'belly': "For this reason the sage is concerned with the belly and not the eyes,/Therefore he rejects the one but accepts the other' (TTC,12). Furthermore, the belly is the seat of instinct, of the most primal urges. As indicated above, the center of feminine being similarly has been assigned to the "belly" region.

A case also may be made for the function of sexuality, one specific expression of sensuality, in Taoism, reflecting the feminine principle's use of sexual functions for purposes of mystic revelation and oneness. There has been some speculation that the question "Can you play the role of the female in the opening and closing of the gates of Heaven?" (TTC,10), refers to a ritual use of sexual intercourse among Taoists. A vague reference to this situation may appear in the lines translated by Lin Yutang as "Oftentimes one regards life with passion/In order to see its manifest forms" (TTC,1). In any case, passion seems to be a legitimate means for increasing our understanding of the universe, if approached properly. And certainly Taoism as a religion availed itself of sexual resources, the interaction of Yin and Yang, to stimulate the life force.[163]

It is clear that the Taoist establishes a firm link with Nature, expressed as a contact with the ultimate reality, regardless of what specific forms the latter may manifest itself under. Spontaneity and naturalness are intrinsic to the life style of the sage. Te constitutes the individual's personal Tao, as an individualized manifestation of Tao, and is innate to all of the Ten Thousand Things. Moreover, natural phenomena, appearances, provide a concrete expression of the functioning of Tao from which valuable lessons can be drawn. Hence, the imagistic language of the Tao Te Ching is quite appropriate for the content of its philosophy.

Thus, one may argue that sense data, instinct or unconsciousness, and sexual experience, the facets of materiality, may all serve to advance our knowledge/ experience of Tao. No distinction is drawn between mind and body, and none between the inner reality of

instinct and the outer reality of the universe. The
obvious injunctions against the confusion resulting
from the senses refer more specifically to an ego-
centered over-indulgence in desire, which corrupts the
natural instincts of life. Attainment of Tao means to
"be free from the confusions of external conditions, to
be rid of the perplexities of life, to be fully charged
with primordial creativity."164 Such a state excludes
neither external conditions, life, nor creativity, but
merely their respective confusions, perplexities, and
artificialities.

    In sum, the ethical modes of being which follow
from the tenets of Taoism as a philosophical system are
of the same nature as those identified under the feminine principle. Inwardness is expressed through the
urge to wholeness and the guide of T̲e̲, itself a power
or virtue, yields a recognition of all-is-one-ness
exceeding the humanistic concept of J̲e̲n̲. As an ethical
code of conduct, the revelations of T̲e̲ culminate in the
positive narcissism by which the satisfaction of the
Real or shared Self entails the satisfaction of all
beings based on the assumption of our interdependence.

    The mode of being known as receptivity is the
keynote of the ethical ideal embodied in the Taoist
sage. Taking the c̲h̲i̲n̲g̲, quiescence, path of enlightenment, the sage effects a gradual quieting of superficial and artificial disturbances in her/his life
style. Being tranquil, the sage is totally open to
reality and lives a life in imitation of Tao itself.
The w̲u̲-w̲e̲i̲ concept epitomizes such a life; it is the
non-assertion which allows the spontaneous and natural
development of the universe, of the community, and of
the Self.

    Being intimately linked with what is natural, the
sage also recognizes a kinship with the whole of Nature.
Appearances serve as a guide to the ultimate reality,
sense data are indicative of the functioning of the
cosmos, and even sexuality has a possible role to play
in the enlightenment process. The Taoist is not only
integrated with the apparent externals of Nature, with
animal and vegetative life, but is also integrated
within, in terms of the unconscious and individual
instinct.

    2. <u>Socio-Political Implications: The Enlightened
        Taoist State</u>

    Having dealt with enlightenment under the form of

an individual code of ethics, we now turn to the application of that code to stimulate the collective enlightenment of a community. The importance of establishing such a state is evident in the Tao Te Ching, which devotes a proportionately large amount of discussion to socio-political management and philosophy. Wing-Tsit Chan estimates that approximately 80% of the text concerns the function of Tao places special emphasis upon its societal context.[165]

Typical of the feminine perspective, the Taoist recognizes the influence of external surroundings upon the individual and the resulting necessity to provide an environment in which the sage can fully implement a life style in imitation of Tao, living in and through the shared Self, as a member of society as well as of the universe. The Taoist does not advocate the escapism often associated with mystics who live a life of solitude. Indeed, if unity underlies the universe, the self-contradiction of attaining enlightenment in isolation from others becomes clear.

The same feminine modes of being which have been applied above to the individual may be observed in the ideal society. However, these are given a slightly different emphasis where social and political matters are concerned. The inwardness expressed by Te becomes the communal attitude of all-is-one-ness; receptivity is reinterpreted as the non-assertion and anarchistic tendencies of the Taoist sovereign; and the link to Nature emerges as the harmony established between the organized human community and the cosmos.

    a. The communal sense -- All-is-one. The ethical code of Taoism, revealed by inner and primal Te, is founded on positive narcissism. It is this code of the shared or Real Self which provides the basic support for the harmonious society envisioned by the Taoist. The promptings of interdependent self-interest lead to an organized and ecologically sensitive community in which the individual identifies with the whole. In the oneness of the "universal great self", the ego-self is expanded to encompass the Self of the all. The Taoist social organization is analogous to water in its functioning:

> Water flows to unite with water, because all parts of it are subject to the same laws. So too should human society be held together through a community of interests that

allows each individual to feel himself a
member of a whole. The central power of
a social organization must see to it that
every member finds that his true interest
lies in holding together with it.[166]

One expression of this oneness involves the
Taoist's rejection of capital punishment; the sage
questions the effectiveness of the death penalty as a
deterrent to crime. Since no fear of death is observed
in the masses, it presents no real threat to them, and
thus is useless as a means of controlling criminals.
Even assuming that the threat of death did arouse the
expected fear, there is the persistent problem of
deciding who would dare presume to carry out the
sentence:

> There is always the master executioner
> (Heaven) who kills.
> To undertake executions for the master
> executioner is like hewing wood for
> the master carpenter.
> Whoever undertakes to hew wood for the
> master carpenter rarely escapes injuring
> his own hands. (TTC,74)

The harmony of the universe, of social relations, can
only be disturbed or shattered by the policy of capital
punishment, but never strengthened; its positive
benefits are outweighed by its inherent dangers.

The surest guide, for the state as well as for the
individual, is Te: "Who is firmly established [in Te]
is not easily shaken./Who has a firm grasp does not
easily let go." This same firmness is attainable by
both the state and the individual. Virtue or power can
be passed down through the generations, permeating
larger and larger spheres, starting with the individual
(the sage in particular) and ultimately encompassing
the universe. In this way, the Te cultivated by the
individual becomes "genuine", that of the family
"abundant", in the village cultivated Te "will
multiply", in the state it "will prosper", and in the
world it "will become universal". Each group is to be
judged in accordance with its level of Te (TTC,54).

The social organization which is most likely to
succeed in cultivating its communal Te to the fullest
extent is specifically described in the Tao Te Ching
(80). Its territory must be limited, with an equally
limited population (cf. E. F. Schumacher, Small is

Beautiful: Economics as if People Mattered). The bonds of unity and interdependence therefore will be forged all the more strongly. Just as the individual becomes a person of p'u the Uncarved Block representing utter simplicity, the perfect society constitutes 'Unwrought Simplicity', the original nameless state of existence.[167] As such it approaches the ultimate reality of Nameless Tao. In addition, the ideal Taoist society is characterized by the following conditions:

> Let there be ten times and a hundred times
>   as many utensils
> But let them not be used.
> Let the people value their lives[168] highly
>   and not migrate far.
> Even if there are ships and carriages,
>   none will ride them.
> Even if there are arrows and weapons,
>   none will display them.
> Let the people again knot cords and use
>   them (in place of writing).
> Let them relish their food, beautify their
>   clothing, be content with their homes,
>   and delight in their customs.
> Though neighboring communities overlook
>   one another and the crowing of cocks
>   and barking of dogs can be heard,
> Yet the people there may grow old and die
>   without ever visiting one another. (TTC,80)

Thus, the Taoist state does not lack technological advancements, but merely the desire or need to resort to them. Aesthetic enjoyment and primal sensuality are encouraged. As indicated, the ideal state is one of abundant material goods, but also one in which the people are not possessed by these goods through the ego-centered attitude of possession. An abiding contentment, a satisfaction with existing conditions, suffuses the entire community and stifles the curiosity or ambition of masculine "progress". The refinements of culture and civilization are not excluded entirely, but only those which tend to the disruption of our primal nature. Paraphrasing the Tao Te Ching's manner of expression, Fung Yu-lan states 'Great civilization looks like primitiveness.'[169] The appearance of primitiveness is actually deceiving and conceals an underlying sophistication; the Taoist state is sophisticated enough to dispense with the outer trappings of sophistication. Appearances are less valued than reality.

Implicit in the espousal of a feminine community

ideal, which is simple and limited, is a rejection of the masculine society contrived by human efforts and guided by the imposed ethical system based on <u>Jen</u>. The essence of this conflict between Taoist and masculine doctrines is discussed by Jung in terms of the social ideal embodied in the <u>persona</u>. The latter, a "complicated system of relations between individual consciousness and society", constitutes the code of behavior to which the individual must conform within an artificial and humanly-structured society. In response to these external pressures, the inner being of the feminine unconscious attempts to express itself. Recognizing this process, Jung argues, Lao Tzu, reputed author of the <u>Tao Te Ching</u>, propounded the theory of inner ascendency and the value of "weakness".[170] More precisely, the text advises us to put away the masks of social roles by returning to the primal unconscious from which we have been alienated by social conventions. This alienation is disruptive in society as a whole as it is in the individual.

Civilization, which is fashioned of human constructions, is the beginning of differentiation, the cutting up of Tao represented by instituting names: "As soon as there were regulations and institutions, there were names (differentiation of things)./As soon as there are names, know that it is time to stop./It is by knowing when to stop that one can be free from danger" (TTC,32). Once names have been applied, as in our present circumstance, it is too late to revoke them and their wide-ranging effects. At that point one only can guard against the added complications of filling in their categories, that is, of observing their forced distinctions in life. Underneath it all, the recognition of nondifferentiation is to be nurtured.

Among these dangerous names are the tenets of Confucian thought, "humanity" (<u>Jen</u>) and "righteousness" (<u>I</u>):

> When the great Tao declined,
> The doctrines of humanity (<u>jen</u>) and righteousness (<u>i</u>) arose.
> When knowledge and wisdom appeared,
> There emerged great hypocrisy.
> When the six family relationships are not in harmony,
> There will be the advocacy of filial piety and deep love to children.
> When a country is in disorder,
> There will be praise of loyal ministers.(TTC,18)

It only becomes necessary for society to extol these virtues when they already have been lost or are in the process of being lost; if they indeed are present, then they are unconscious and hence remain unexpressed, even unnoticed, due to their commonness. The ideal society will "return" to the primal condition of a lived reality as being more productive than empty moral phrases. Again, the Taoist wants the fruit rather than the flower, the action rather than the word. Although some institutions are required to sustain a social organization with any semblance of structure, these are to be carefully monitored to avoid extremism as well as the contrary effects of the principle of Reversion.[171] As the tenets of Taoism warn, excessive organization breeds anarchism, while too little organization gives way to over-organization (bureaucracy). Reversion is irrevocable, and it is we who must change our perspective to accommodate it.

The people as a whole stand to profit enormously from the policy of adhering to the fruit of reality, rather than pursuing the flowery words lavished on lost virtues. This is the reason that the Taoist enjoins us to abandon the superficialities which are deceptively precious:

> Abandon sagliness and discard wisdom;
> Then the people will benefit a hundredfold.
> Abandon humanity and discard righteousness;
> Then the people will return to filial piety
>   and deep love.
> Abandon skill and discard profit;
> Then there will be no thieves or robbers.
> However, these three things are ornament
>   (<u>wen</u>) and not adequate. (TTC,19)

What the people can depend upon as adequate is <u>Te</u>, whether of an individual or a communal extent, as a manifestation of Tao.

The all-is-one-ness mode of being in Taoism's socio-political thought thus fosters the communal attitude so essential for the survival and practical functioning of the ideal state. Having a shared Self, the people work together from a sense of shared interests. The rejection of capital punishment, as both difficult to pronounce and ultimately ineffective, reflects the experience of wholeness. It is dangerous to presume to interfere in the workings of the cosmos, to make decisions which will effect the delicate balance of life and death.

As in the case of personal ethics, the Te of the state establishes a code of conduct which is both simple and harmonius, standing in sharp contrast to the humanistic, but artificial, Jen-centered ethics of the masculine. The population as a whole reaps great benefits from the elimination of ethical constructs and a returning to the unconscious flow of relationships. The pervasive contentment of the population within the limitations of natural boundaries physical and philosophical, supports its continuance.

b. The non-assertion of the sage/ruler. Corresponding to the ethical ideal embodied in the sage, the political ideal of Taoism is embodied in the sovereign, who is also a sage. Despite superficial resemblances to the philosopher-king/queen of Plato's Republic, the Taoist sage sovereign differs considerably from the Platonic ideal. No provisions are made for maintaining a ruling elite, nor is an extensive course of education required. The Taoist head of state avoids the overt exercise of power and prepares for her/his position by the 'losing and losing' method previously cited as being the feminine counterpart of the masculine accumulation of knowledge. In this way, a balance of power is struck between sovereign and subjects, a balance reflective of cosmic harmony itself.

The tranquillity sought by the sage as a condition of ethical life reappears in the sage-sovereign's receptivity to the needs of the masses and the rejection of violence as a means to any end (except self-defense). The sovereign imitates Tao by a positive narcissistic with the interests of the populace and accomplishes political tasks, including inter-government relations, by feminine yielding. Finally, paralleling ethical action by non-action, the concept of wu-wei is essential to the sovereign's rule by not ruling. Non-interference in the affairs of the populace is required, allowing them to live with the spontaneous flow of Nature.

More than any single individual, the sage-sovereign is responsible for applying the 'losing and losing' method to reduce the artificialities of a human society, thus producing the simplified and purified environment conducive to enlightenment. The sovereign belongs to the hierarchy of universal forces corresponding to the levels of reality: "Therefore Tao is Great,/The Heaven is great,/The Earth is great,/The King is also great./These are four great things in the universe, and the king is one of them" (TTC,25).

Corruption of Te (alienation from Tao) is reversed by a removal of artificial law, statutes, and punishments.[172] Traditional approaches, moral and legalistic codes, no longer apply, but may be actually "sources of disorder".[173]

These steps are all part of the gradual movement to a tranquillity carried out on a social scale. The sovereign, as sage, works from the point of having already stilled or quieted personal desires and disturbances, and hence is able to guide the state effortlessly along the same path by a personal identification with the interests of the state. The sage-sovereign "has no set mind (ch'ang hsin) of his own", but rather adopts the mind of the masses ("regards the people's ideas as his own" TTC,49). In a state of men, the "mind is enclosed within and protected by the door (men)."[174] A synthesis of knowledge and ignorance takes place in the sovereign, who has gone through the cycle from primal simplicity (the Elementary feminine) through (masculine) discursive reason to the enlightened state of being which duplicates, yet transcends, the "primeval ignorance" of the masses (at the level of the Transformative character).[175]

The contentment of the population, its tranquillity, is the appropriate responsibility of the sage-sovereign, one who is both simple and able to understand the simplicity, the Te, of the masses. To preserve or reinstate their blissful ignorance requires the implementation of a politics of men; conscious pursuit of knowledge must be given up if the people are to be restored to the original goodness of their nature", where the heart (hsin) "is yet enclosed and protected by nature".[176] Again, the knowledge rejected here is accumulated knowledge of the masculine perspective, as opposed to the experiential knowledge-wisdom of enlightenment. Therefore in the government of the Sage:

> He keeps their hearts vacuous (hsü),
> Fills their bellies,
> Weakens their ambitions,
> And strengthens their bones,
> He always causes his people to be without
> knowledge (cunning) or desire,
> And the crafty to be afraid to act. (TTC,3)

The people thereby can reap the benefits of enlightenment even if they themselves never experience that state as the sage does.

From our own social perspective, which encourages the individual ambition and accumulated knowledge of the masculine perspective, these injunctions may sound incredibly crude and even may appear as the basis of despotism. However, a more positive view is possible from the feminine perspective. If one accepts the metaphysical assumptions of Taoism, this is the best possible policy for both sovereign and people. The knowledge of which the masses are to remain ignorant is judged superficial within this system, and the desires self-destructive. Certainly, it cannot be detrimental to keep the people satisfied, with full bellies signifying the satisfaction of instincts, nor to keep them physically strong, with strengthened frames. The "democratic" aspect of this type of state is revealed in the sovereign's pledge of non-interference, to be discussed further on.

Moreover, the sage-sovereign is best equipped to resolve the difficulties because of their point of origin. Tao is corrupted when artificialities are allowed to slip into society, and almost invariably, they originate in the highest strata--when the court is well-ordered while the fields go untilled, or when the people have insufficient grain resources while officials wallow in material goods. "This is to lead the world toward brigandage./Is it not the corruption of Tao?" (TTC,53). Reform starts at the top and filters down. The sage-sovereign's method of leadership fosters the expectation that everyone perform the simplest and easiest tasks, that is, those which are most natural; "the result is that energy is accumulated, and the simple develops quite naturally into the manifold. Thus, it grows, and the sage's mission to lead the multitude to the performance of great work is fulfilled."[177]

The attainment of tranquillity in the Taoist state is greatly assisted by the general policy of non-violence. Characteristic of the Taoist's practical attitude, the basis of the rejection of violence lies in its counterproductiveness: "What others have taught, I teach also:/'Violent and fierce people do not die a natural death'" (TTC,42). When it is impossible to avoid the use of military force, the enlightened individual "regards calm restraint as the best principle" (TTC,31). A knowledge of metaphysical principles qualifies the sage-sovereign to make such judgements.

Those who attempt to conquer the world, to form it after their own egotistical desires, will never be successful: "The empire is a spiritual thing, and should not be acted on./He who acts on it harms it./He who holds on to it loses it" (TTC,29). Those who seek to promote Tao in the state will advise the sovereign against the use of force; "The use of force usually brings requital./Wherever armies are stationed, briars and thorns grow./Great wars are always followed by famines" (TTC,30). The principle of Reversion is firmly in evidence even in the political sphere.

Tao's own model of non-assertion, taking seriously the value of not-contending, is followed by the sage-sovereign in these policies as political wu-wei. Military strategy consists entirely of defensive warfare: the Taoist ruler waits to be invaded, rather than seizing the initiative, favors retreat over advancing, and never underestimates the enemy force. The fundamental principles (amazingly similar to guerilla warfare) are:

> To march without formation,
> To stretch one's arm without showing it,
> To confront enemies without seeming to meet them,
> To hold weapons without seeming to have them.

In the confrontation of two forces of equal strength, "The man who is sorry over the fact will win" (TTC,69), i.e., the one who is opposed to killing or, in a corrected text, 'The man who yields wins'.[178]

The enlightened general is also a sage, fulfilling the military mission in imitation of Tao:

> A good (general) achieves his purpose and stops,
> But dares not seek to dominate the world.
> He achieves his purpose but does not brag about it.
> He achieves his purpose but does not boast about it.
> He achieves his purpose but is not proud of it.
> He achieves his purpose but only as an unavoidable step.
> He achieves his purpose but does not aim to dominate.
> (For) after things reach their prime they begin to grow old,
> Which means being contrary to Tao. (TTC,30)

There is a low esteem for ping, rendered as either 'soldiers' or 'fine weapons',[179] which are "instruments of evil", "Therefore those who possess Tao turn away from them." In a ritual, the general is placed on the right hand side, the side of ill-omen. Even in the midst of victorious celebrations, the mourning of a funeral ceremony is appropriate. Presumably, only the sage-sovereign is capable of the depth of receptivity required in such cases.

After the fact of victory, the sage is careful to attempt a complete reconciliation of the conflict. "To patch up great hatred is surely to leave some hatred behind", which is an unsatisfactory solution when cosmic harmony is the goal. For this reason, the sage avoids the human tendency to assign guilt, preferring to defuse potential opposition, and so voluntarily takes the inferior (guilty) position. Tao, despite its impartiality, " . . . is always with the good man", that is, provides natural support for those who imitate its functioning (TTC,79).

As evidenced by the sage-sovereign's willingness to adopt the viewpoint of the masses and to sacrifice pride to resolve conflicts, it is clear that the model of Tao is being imitated. The sage-sovereign represents the interests of the entire community, even if the community members themselves are ignorant of their true interests. Thus she/he is able to promote these interests by taking the lowly position: "He who suffers disgrace for his country/Is called the lord of the land./He who takes upon himself the country's misfortunes/Becomes the king of the empire." As is common in Taoist thought, the paradox of these statements is traceable to the deceptions of the limited human perspective—"Straight words seem to be their opposite" (TTC,78).

The positive narcissism of the feminine principle also figures prominently in the sovereign's imitation of Tao. By not living for the ego-self, the shared or Real Self of the community is fulfilled by the sovereign. The sage "does not accumulate for himself./The more he uses for others, the more he has himself./The more he gives to others, the more he possesses of his own" (TTC,81). Hence, the sage-sovereign does not slight physical well-being, but takes it seriously as a manifestation of the universe. The body politic is an extension of that personal body. Only the sovereign "who values the world as his body" is worthy to be entrusted with world government, and one who "loves the world as his body" can be trusted to care for it (TTC,13). The materiality mode of being is evident in these statements.

Further imitating Tao, the sage-sovereign is "absolute", and is nameless; despite the seeming insignificance of the Uncarved Block, it cannot be falsely manipulated and "If kings and barons would hold on to it, all things would submit to them spontaneously". The natural power of Tao underwrites their own power. Nature functions quite well, and democratically, without the need for human control: "Heaven and earth unite to drip sweet dew./Without the command of men, it drips evenly over all" (TTC,32). The wise ruler avoids cutting up the primal simplicity symbolized by the Uncarved Block (TTC,28). Moderation characterizes the entire attitude of the sage-sovereign; "To rule people and to serve Heaven there is nothing better than to be frugal", meaning to "recover quickly", "accumulate virtue heavily", "overcome everything", and acquire a capacity the limit of which is beyond anyone's knowledge", all of which qualify one for ruling (TTC,59).

The lowest position is best suited to the ends of the sage-sovereign. Traditionally in China the ruler was described as 'the orphaned', 'the lowly one', 'the unworthy'. The Tao Te Ching is quick to draw upon the paradox of these titles and explain them in terms of Taoist philosophy, i.e., as stemming from the fact that the sovereign is actually dependent upon the masses for support. The power of the subjects effectively balances the sovereign's otherwise absolute power. The people represent the parts of the chariot in which the ruler is borne along, but without the chariot, no movement is possible for anyone. He is then advised, "Rather than jingle like the jade,/rumble like the rocks" (TTC,39). Or, the high position of precious jade (Yang) is not as advantageous as the "lowly" one (Yin) of common rocks.

Moreover, the people should be oblivious both to their position and to the key role played by the sage. To be truly superior, the sovereign then must keep low, talk like inferiors, be foremost by walking behind. This lesson is learned from the rivers and seas, who have attained their high positions "Because they skillfully stay below" the mountain streams. Similarly, the sage, though above others, exerts no weight upon the people below (does not assert authority) and walks ahead without incurring hatred, "Therefore the world rejoices in praising him without getting tired of it' (TTC,66). Above all, the ruler should not be a burden to the ruled.

The wu-wei concept encapsulates the attitude of the sage-sovereign and the manner of rule imitative of Tao. Non-assertion, or non-interference in the natural course of events, is of primary importance in governing a country. If the people are hungry and therefore unruly, this is the fault of the sovereign, who has disrupted the delicate economic balance by demanding excessive amounts of tax grain. As already indicated, the threat of capital punishment is not an effective deterrent to revolution since the people "are anxious to make a living" and do not fear death. "It is only those who do not seek after life that excel in making life valuable" (TTC,75).

The evils of government interference are catalogued in the Tao Te Ching. It is best to do nothing, to act by wu-wei:

> The more taboos and prohibitions there are in the world, The poorer the people will be.
> The more sharp weapons the people have, The more troubled the state will be.
> The more cunning and skill man possesses The more vicious things will appear.
> The more laws and orders are made prominent, The more thieves and robbers there will be. (TTC,57)

Excess breeds excess. Admittedly, the situation is being over-simplified here, however, in essence, it does reveal some truths. The increasing sophistication of military hardware outruns any attempts at non-proliferation treaties; technology produces increasingly "cunning", and inane, products; laws create criminals in cases of victimless crimes.

Realistically, then, the proper rule of a state is compared to the frying of small fish by the Taoists; if the fish are attended too closely, if they are constantly turned and interfered with, they will soon be in pieces, and so will the state (TTC,60). The sage-sovereign's capacity for self-restraint must be impressive. If the government is to interfere at all, it can only be to institute preventive measures aiming at "the establishment of public security and peace."[180]

By following the practice of wu-wei, multiple benefits accrue for the society as a whole. Under a non-discriminative government the populace remains "contented and generous"; under one which is "searching and discriminative" (in masculine terms) they are full of discontent (TTC,58). Naturally, the Taoist system puts a high priority on the value of contentment, such that one cannot but choose the "inefficient" government over the well-ordered one. This latter type we can well imagine to be a firmly structured bureaucracy, wound in red tape and buried in meticulous records. The Taoist state borders on anarchy with its disregard for state-dominated projects. The power and the responsibility is dispersed among the people, and they are forced to develop and rely upon their own resources, their Te. However, Te is also assumed to be their best possible resource:

> I take no action and the people of themselves are transformed.
> I love tranquillity and the people of themselves become correct.
> I engage in no activity and the people of themselves become prosperous.
> I have no desires and the people of themselves become simple. (TTC,57)

The quality of the ruler is inversely proportional to the degree of exposure she/he receives among the people. The best are only known to exist, the second best are known enough to be loved and praised, the next level are feared, and the worst are reviled. Obscurity is beneficial, as it is for Tao's subtle workings. The sovereigns who have failed most completely are correspondingly the most vocal. Having lost the faith of the people they are desperate enough to "resort to oaths" to regain that faith. This extreme measure is, of course, doomed to failure, and resembles the extreme praise heaped upon absent virtues. "[The great rulers] value their words highly./They accomplish their task; they complete their work./Nevertheless their people say that they simply follow Nature (Tzu-jan)" (TTC,17). This is the ultimate in being inconspicuous, when the masses can take credit for the hidden accomplishments of the sage-sovereign.

Undeniably, this is an optimistic outlook, placing great faith in the goodness of human nature, which is Tao. Yet it does follow quite consistently from Taoism's metaphysical and ethical assumptions. The application of wu-wei in the governing of a state follows the reversion process of Tao and then "there is nothing that is not done (wu pu wei . . .)", while by non-rule "there is nothing that is not ruled".[181]

Given the historical conditions under which it was formulated, the Taoist injunction against interference by the sovereign may be viewed as a sincere attempt to allow participation by individual subjects in governmental processes. By minimizing the activity at the higher, more exclusive, levels of society, the power of the few over the many likewise would be weakened. The resulting power vacuum could then be filled spontaneously by the people themselves, or so the Taoist assumes (leaving out the possibility that another elite group might attempt to seize control in such a situation). If the people did gain that power for themselves, the state authority would be decentralized effectively and, in addition, individual communities would have the power of self-determination. The same results could be expected in forms of government other than that nominally dominated by a single ruler like the sage-sovereign; decentralized aristocracies and democracies readily can be envisioned. In more contemporary terms, a socialist or communist state could be structured to function in this way.

The distinguishing factor in the Taoist monarchy sketched in the Tao Te Ching lies in the great importance bestowed upon the sage-sovereign as a model for the state as a whole, while she or he lives in imitation of Tao itself. The very necessity of having such an individual tends to weaken the social structure in view of the manifold difficulties involved in maintaining this high standard of leadership indefinitely, or at least until such time as enlightenment becomes universal. A heavy burden of responsibility is delegated to the sovereign, first to attain personal enlightenment, and then to exercise a non-interfering controlling influence over the community.

If this can be accomplished, however, the non-assertion of the receptivity mode of being results in an enlightened environment for all. The tranquillity of the sage re-emerges as a protection of, or return to, the primordial innocence of the population and a policy of non-violence. Warfare, with the exception of defensive tactics, is rejected as constituting a disruption of the harmony which is the aim of the state. Emphasis is placed not on victory, but on the lives lost in pursuit of victory.

In imitating Tao, the sage-sovereign practices a positive narcissism whereby she/he represents and fulfills the interests of the state in the shared Self. Feminine yielding is recommended to accomplish these tasks, and the lowly position is necessary to take advantage of the principle of Reversion. By this means, a balance of Tao-inspired harmony is struck between the explicit power of the sovereign and the implicit power of the subjects.

Through <u>wu-wei</u> the sage-sovereign rules the state by not-ruling, practices the non-interference which insures the natural flow of social events, and permits the highest Taoist ends to be realized. Bordering on anarchy, the inefficient (by masculine criteria) Taoist government structure saves the people from discontentment and promotes the primal innocence of <u>Te</u>, the self-reliance of the people on their own <u>Te</u>. The overwhelming faith of the Taoist in the people is founded on the metaphysical assumptions concerning our inherent virtue/power and our participation in the power of the universe.

    c. <u>Harmony with Nature and Tao</u>. The purpose of both the communal all-is-one-ness mode of being and the non-assertion of the sage-sovereign is essentially contained within this last mode of being, namely, to attain or return to the primal harmony between the human community and the universe or Nature. After recognizing the common Self of a society and securing a non-interfering political leader, the Taoist state attains the enlightened position of harmonizing with other states and with Tao. This is the "<u>Primordial State of Society</u>" which harks back to a <u>golden age</u>, what Chuang Tzu calls the 'Age of Perfect <u>Te</u>', paralleling the state of the infant ideal. Like <u>Te</u>, this utopia represents "a vision of the original state of nature, a state when all is in all, when the whole universe is a continuous process of a single life process."[182] In addition to the ethical assumption that human nature (<u>Te</u>) is inherently good, the Taoist assumes that the state of Nature, from which we have become alienated by civilization, is positive. Hence, the Taoist could well understand Rousseau's declaration: "Man was born free, and everywhere he is in chains" (<u>The Social Contract</u>). The chains, of course, represent masculine values in terms of the artificialities of civilization. Intuition is the vehicle of liberation.

    For society, this return to a primal state of

Nature involves essentially the same path that is trod by the ethical individual in becoming an enlightened sage. The guide of inner Te is enhanced by the sage-sovereign, who inconspicuously leads the community towards enlightenment. The microcosm presented by the sage as sovereign reflects the macrocosm of Tao. Once these conditions have been fulfilled within a receptive society (made receptive by the sage's policy of wu-wei), enlightenment, with its double-edged inner/outer harmony, develops spontaneously.

The underlying harmony is none other than the wholeness of the universe, manifesting the unique ability of Nature to interpenetrate and interfuse. Interpreted as heavenly music, this harmony is composed of "the self-assertion of each aperture of music of Earth and each instrument of the music of man; self-assertion is indicative of diversity encompassed by unity."[183] For those living in China more than two thousand years ago, this harmony was assuredly much closer and more easily envisioned than it can be for us in the present. For the Taoist this fact signals that we are that much more in need of Tao, and the feminine perspective.

In the realm of inter-government relations, harmony also is desired, and is attainable through the feminine attitude of yielding. The aim of a large country, the Tao Te Ching concludes, is merely to "annex and herd"; that of small countries "to join and serve others". Both conditions, being mutually supportive, can be satisfied when the large country keeps itself low. In modern terminology, this may be interpreted as keeping a low profile. Adopting the method of the female, the large country, "the converging point of the world" is able to absorb small ones--"the female always overcomes the male by tranquillity,/And by tranquillity she is underneath". This same tactic is effective for the small country, due to its naturally low position (TTC,61).

As a result of the universal "harmony and tranquillity", ho p'ing, the (feminine) peace of contentment arises.[184] The highest peace parallels Whitehead's sense of 'the deep underlying Harmony of Nature', inherent in the cosmos as well as in humanity. Without it, nothing positive can be accomplished, and there is "on its surface the ripples of social efforts, harmonizing and clashing in their aims at ways of satisfaction.[185] Certainly ecology would be foremost among the concerns of this society.

Hence, in the consummate Taoist state all social clashes will have been eliminated by a total integration in Nature, in what is natural. This tranquillity is accomplished under the auspices of the sage-sovereign, whose practice of <u>wu-wei</u> or non-interference results in the spontaneous emergence of human virtue (<u>Te</u>). As noted, the same effect may be achieved under various forms of government, provided feminine assumptions and principles are adhered to. The chain of being runs from Tao to Nature to the individual, and back through Nature to Tao.[186] "Being in accord with Tao, he [the sage] is everlasting" (TTC,16). This is certainly also true of the Taoist state. Nature, "the great form (Tao)", attracts the following of the entire world, which thus "They come and will encounter no harm; /But enjoy comfort, peace, and health" (TTC,35).

Contrary to many mystic philosophies, the feminine perspective expressed by Taoism is not satisfied with an individual's isolated experience of Tao, but seeks further to enlighten the surrounding community, in accordance with the metaphysical assumptions of underlying oneness. The inner harmony of ethics thus can be successfully extended by the enlightened sage-sovereign to encompass the whole of a society and political organization, in which the population lives at the primal level of innocence. Such a state is that most conducive to the fulfillment of the natural ends outlined by Taoist philosophy. It insures human survival without simultaneously disrupting the environment upon which we are ultimately dependent, through both its pacifism and its ecological orientation.

If this socio-political philosophy appears naive and unworkable under present conditions, it yet contributes a few points worthy of note. The hazards of excessive government interference, bureaucratic superstructures, and of living in a society which is founded on ultimately self-destructive principles which threaten its natural environment as well as its inner harmony, are self-evident. If the Taoist utopia cannot be realized <u>in toto</u>, it nonetheless serves to indicate areas of social and political relationships which are in need of reform. There is a positive value in contemporary attempts by the ecologically-minded to reapproach Nature as our source, in de-centralizing the growing power of modern states, and in emphasizing our similarities as human beings rather than our differences as distinct individuals, nationalities, or races. All of these attempts are symptoms of a feminine attitude towards life, and an outgrowth of the feminine modes of being in both ethics and socio-political philosophy.

Chapter III

SPINOZISM AS A FEMININE PHILOSOPHY

Spinoza's system of philosophy has remarkable parallels with the perspective of reality set forth in the Tao Te Ching, and thus Spinozism would seem to qualify, with Taoism, as a feminine philosophy. Although the differences between the two systems of thought are undeniable, it is more important for our present purposes that their similarities are equally undeniable. The obvious differences may be attributed to a greater intellectual sophistication in the Spinozistic system, as a more complex and carefully argued plan of philosophy. Spinoza's collected works cover many more topics, with more pages of explication, than the five thousand characters of the Tao Te Ching. A discussion of these added elements is appropriate to complete our presentation of the feminine perspective in philosophy.

The intellectual "sophistication" separating Taoism and Spinozism is more properly a hiatus of several hundred years time, filled with the counter-proposals of masculine philosophy, the compounded philosophical traditions of the West which Spinoza had to take into account when expounding his own philosophy. The environment in which Spinoza philosophized was saturated with the predispositions and assumptions of the masculine perspective. Spinoza not only challenged this perspective with his original ideas, but further attempted to rationalize his alternative views through the masculine method of discursive reason. Consequently, his system encompasses both masculine and feminine elements, although, as argued here, the feminine ones hold the ultimate significance for him. By contrast, the Tao Te Ching was produced in an environment which was generally receptive to the feminine perspective, and its author felt no compulsion to present its views in a manner acceptable to masculine discursive reason. On the contrary, masculine conventions are flaunted openly. Spinoza could not afford this luxery himself if he expected to be taken seriously by his contemporaries.

The advantages of turning to Spinozism in order to

illustrate the inner workings of a feminine philosophy are obvious due to Spinoza's intellectual rigor and mindfulness of masculine objections. Having grasped the feminine (Yin) character and main components of such a philosophy through the unassuming simplicity of Taoism, it now becomes possible to examine the masculinely-framed form of argumentation advanced in its defense by Spinoza. Nonetheless we should be aware that the very necessity of Spinozism's extended explanations and intellectualizing would be taken as a sign of increased alienation by the Taoist. This trend toward alienation could be reversed only by a mind such as Spinoza's, feminine by natural inclination and masculine by training, making a dialogue between the two extremes of thought possible.

The common denominators of feminine philosophy in Spinozism and Taoism, as well as their variances, emerge clearly by following out the structure of the feminine principle. In the first section, the theoretical foundations of Spinozism, embodied in metaphysics, are discussed through the dual manifestations of the feminine principle: (a) the Elementary character of Natura Naturans, and (b) Natura Naturata's Transformative character. The levels of knowledge in epistemology follow naturally from the metaphysical degrees of reality. Under the practical implementation of theory in human life in the second section, as personal ethics and communal socio-political implications, the three modes of being apply once more: (a) the inwardness of human nature/power/virtue, (b) the receptivity and non-assertion of the philosopher, citizen, and sovereign, and (c) the materialism or reestablished harmony with Nature.

Also included are discussions of certain problematic aspects of Spinoza's philosophy with respect to its reputed feminine perspective. Many apparent problems in the Spinozistic system can be resolved by interpreting the whole within the context of feminine thought. On the other hand, the irredeemably masculine elements of Spinoza's assumptions are reconstructed along feminine lines. Not only does this reconstruction yield an exemplary feminine philosophy, but furthermore it imparts a new sense of consistency to the system. Spinoza himself may well have revised his thought along these same lines had he lived in a cultural context supportive of the feminine perspective.

A. The Manifestations of Substance:
   Theoretical Foundations

The feminine principle of being manifests itself under two forms, that is, that there are two possible approaches to reality. These manifestations are equally evident in Spinoza's system of philosophy. Hence, the reality embodied in Spinozistic Substance can be analyzed under two categories of being. The Elementary character conveys the undifferentiated aspect of reality, as the one (God or Substance) relates to the many (the modes). Through the Transformative character the individual as mode becomes aware of its link with this oneness and initiates the transformative process which culminates in "blessedness," the experience of "participation" in the absolute.

1. The Metaphysics of the One: The Structure of the Universe

The point of entry for Spinoza's main work, the Ethics, is identical to that of the Tao Te Ching, namely, the ground of being. The first part of the Ethics is entitled "Of God", just as the opening lines of the Taoist text introduce Nameless Tao. For Spinoza Substance or God is the ontological basis of the universe, the encompassing source and sustaining presence of all that exists. The metaphysical state of the universe is determined by the nature of the One Substance, and from it Spinoza derives the remainder of his philosophical system, expressed in terms of epistemology, ethics, and socio-political philosophy.

Thus, a knowledge of what is meant by the terms Substance and God is a sine qua non of understanding Spinozism and, by extension, contributes to our understanding of the structure of a feminine philosophy. Spinoza declares that ethics "as everyone knows, must be based on Metaphysics and Physics".[1] Accordingly, his philosophy aims at "understanding the necessity of things". Metaphysics is the key which unlocks the mysteries of the various other aspects of reality, the light which simultaneously illumines and creates the shadows cast by the contents of the universe.

The complexity of the Substance concept is augmented by a certain ineffability, also evident in Tao, which hinders a full expression of its essence. Although this essence may be known to us rationally, and even experienced intuitively, problems inevitably arise when one attempts to communicate it to others. This state of affairs prompted the Taoist to resort to suggestive images, as noted above, while Spinoza hoped to minimize the problem by treading the narrow path of logic (as he understood it in the geometrical method) and by fashioning a metaphysics comprehensible to human reason.

In pursuing his self-appointed task, Spinoza outlines the logically necessary qualities and characteristics of the ground of being. Under the headings of the Elementary and Transformative characters are treated here, respectively, the primal wholeness of the source (Substance as undifferentiated) and the dynamic process of "emanation" which links the One to things of the world (the modes of Substance). The link between these two characters or aspects of Substance is made possible by the conceptual device of the divine Attributes. They function as an aid in the rational reconstruction of an essentially trans-rational reality. In terms of philosophical cogency, they represent a decided advance over the inherent obscurity of Taoist metaphysics.

If then, Substance is to be scrutinized and categorized it must be treated as an external. Hence, to further this introductory approach, Spinoza temporarily adopts the masculine analytical method of discursive reasoning. Underlying this pose, however, is the ultimate revelation of wholeness by means of feminine intuition, a conclusion to which the reader of the Ethics is subtly but firmly guided. Once the fundamental concept of reality as Substance has been established, it is a simple step to add the experiential to the intellectual recognition of the encompassing force of that reality, by means of radical empiricism.

As a philosopher influenced by the Western tradition of thought, and specifically by the Cartesian school thriving during his lifetime, Spinoza was dedicated to a rationalistic methodology for the general exposition of his system. For this reason, his presentation of Substance in the first part of the Ethics is primarily a logical one, built upon fundamental definitions and the conclusions deductively extracted from them. The single concept of Substance serves as the foundation of his carefully explicated systematization of philosophy. As such it stands in sharp contrast to the revelatory insights which comprise the Tao Te Ching, a series of cryptic remarks lacking even a definitive compilation or division into chapters.

Spinoza, a philosopher and logician of the geometrical method, was meticulous in the choice of terminology employed to convey the precise sense in which a given term was to be interpreted. Each of the key concepts in the Ethics is provided with a succinct but consummate definition, fully comprehended once its meaning has been examined in the context of the Spinozistic vocabulary. Spinoza's deceptively simplistic and theologically impeccable (in his day) definition of God as "Being absolutely infinite, that is to say, substance consisting of infinite attributes, each one of which expresses eternal and inifinite essence" (E1,4), is in fact an encapsulated version of Spinozistic metaphysics. Through an elaboration of the underlying meaning of the concepts involved here, unpacking being, infinity, substance, attribute, eternality, and essence, Spinoza logically deduces the structure of reality. Despite attempts to link Spinozistic Substance to established philosophical traditions (see Appendix I), when the concept has been unpacked we discover that it is essentially feminine in nature.

Justifying these claims requires a close examination of the first fourteen propositions of the first part of the Ethics which deal with the divine per se. In the carefully plotted path of his geometrical demonstrations on divine nature, Spinoza first establishes the independence of a substance in general (propositions one through six), then determines the essence of a substance to be existence compounded with such divine properties as infinitude (propositions seven through ten), and recognizes the concurrent identification of God with substance, adding arguments for God's necessary existence (proposition eleven). Finally, in propositions twelve through fourteen, the indivisibility of God as sole substance and encompassing unity is set forth. The proofs for each of these propositions are either directly or indirectly related to the pivotal definition of God. Therefore, only one substance can be maintained within Spinoza's metaphysical scheme, unique in its kind when logically considered.

Here is a ground of being, an ultimate cause, worthy of Spinoza's aspirations--the focal point of the universe, encompassing explanation of the universal order, and that to which all else is related. Having assessed the requirements for universal functioning, the geometrical demonstration method leads irrevocably (at least in Spinoza's mind) to a deity indentifiable with unique, self-caused substance. As Forsyth expresses the situation, there is only one substance, which is God, "or God can only be this.[2] In view of the traditional connotations of the term 'God', Spinoza's deity is more appropriately and less confusingly referred to as Substance. Spinoza's rigorous deductions from the essence of Substance reveals its logically necessary functions and characteristics. Essence≡Existence (Reality)≡Truth≡Universal Cause≡Life Force≡Absolute Perfection≡Infinite, Immanent, Eternal Immutable Being. If Substance is to qualify as the ultimate ground of being it must fulfill all of these roles within the Spinozistic system. These are the categories through which human intellect is able to conceive the universe, categories previously encountered in discussions of feminine reality. Perhaps the best summary of how Substance or God is conceived has been provided by Spinoza himself, listing the "properties" of divine nature as follows:

> He necessarily exists; that He is one God; that from the necessity alone of His own nature He is and acts; that He is . . . the free cause of all things; that all things are in and so depend upon Him, that without Him they can neither be nor be conceived, and, finally, that all things have been predetermined by Him, not indeed from freedom of will or from absolute good pleasure, but from His absolute nature of infinite Power. (E1, Appendix)

Beyond the well-established divine Attributes of Thought and Extension, whatever has been ascribed to the nature of God is either an 'extraneous denomination', such as "that he exists through himself, is Eternal, One, Immutable, &c", or refers merely to divine activity, "that he is a cause, predestines, and rules all things". These are properties of God which yield no additional information about divine essence (ST,1,ii). They are attributed to God from the perspective of the sum total of attributes (in their non-Spinozistic sense), as eternal, self-subsisting, infinite, cause of all, immutable, or from the perspective of a single Attribute--for Thought, omniscient and for Extension, omnipresent (ST,1,vii). Hence, by the manner in which God or Substance has been defined above, its functions and characteristics constitute a way of intellectually conceiving what it is, with no guarantee that its essence has been penetrated or communicated. Spinoza ultimately overcomes the deficiency of this masculine method of intellectual conceptualization by resorting of feminine intuition, the direct experiencing of reality.

2. The Dual Characters of Substance

To pursue an intellectual discussion of Substance as encompassing reality, eliminating the inevitable contradictions of our limited human perspective, Spinoza found it advisable to observe a distinction with respect to the two possible viewpoints from which the universe may be considered insofar as we are related to it. Reason distinguishes between God as immanent cause of dependent ideas, "with reference to his works or creatures", and as these ideas are taken as "a whole" (ST, dialogue 1). The division follows from the fact that in Spinoza's system "besides substances and modes nothing is assumed" (El, xv, Demonst): the universe must be approached either from the standpoint of the all-inclusive one Substance or from that of the manifold modes.

This same distinction already has been discerned in the feminine principle under the Elementary and Transformative characters, the undifferentiated Substance holistically considered and its manifestations expressed under various individual foci. As Elementary, Substance qualifies as an eternal, infinite, and immutable reality, the all-encompassing primal source; the dynamic Transformative character, however, involves our personal existence and makes possible the experience of blessedness, our reconciliation with reality. Both aspects are necessary to account for our relationship to the universe and also the manner in which we, as human individuals, can fully grasp reality.

Spinoza applies the terms Natura Naturans and Natura Naturata to express these dual characters of reality, adopted from the Scholastic distinction between Creating Nature of Unconditioned substance and conditioned Created Nature.³ Such a duality emulates the anthropomorphic model of active agent and passive material, without destroying the underlying oneness of the two personae. Natura Naturans, under Spinoza's usage of the term, is being conceived "through itself", without reference to externals (ST,1,viii). In other words, it is the primal oneness, reality prior to differentiation or the imposition of human distinctions. Opposed to the "free cause" of Natura Naturans, Natura Naturata or Generated Nature consists of the all which follows from and is dependent upon the necessisty of divine nature (El,29,Schol), namely the modes of Substance. Thus we have God per se, and everything that follows from God or the divine Attributes, which are themselves in God.

The Attributes are responsible for the continuity conceived between Substance and modes, between Nature as creating and created. Without this device, Spinoza would have been hard pressed to explain the underlying unity and the way in which the one flows into and is the many. These Attributes, the basis of our conceptualization of Substance, are infinite. However only two are known to us through human (discursive) reason, namely Extension and Thought, which explains why things are known to us as either extended (physical) or mental. Properly speaking, the Attributes belong to the sphere of Natura Naturans, are expressions of God without being modes or modifications. Intellectually at least, they mediate the distance between God or Substance as the whole at the apex of being, and the modes, reality as it is filtered down through the lower levels of the pyramid of existence with its ever-broadening base. It is solely through the divine Attributes that we are able to discuss Substance at all, because, unlike Substance, they conform precisely to the limitations of human intellect, or rather are themselves responsible for those limitations.

As in the case of the feminine principle, both aspects of Spinozistic Substance, the Elementary Natura Naturans and the Transformative Natura Naturata, demand seperate attention if an adequate understanding of the over-all system is to be attained. Metaphysics is compounded of seeing objects of the real world, and also seeing the framework through which they are apprehended. The universe is viewed from a shifting Gestalt, as we focus now on the foreground of the individual part, and at another time on the background of the whole. The parts of the whole are evident from a consideration of things "in so far as their natures are mutually adopted so that they are in accord among themselves". When the differences between things are emphasized, however, "each produces an idea in our mind, which is distinct from the others", and hence qualifies as a whole in its own right.[4] To ignore either element diminishes the depth of our understanding and violates the openness of the feminine perspective.

In discussing Substance, the background of reality, under the Elementary character several topics are entailed. The unity and wholeness of the undifferentiated <u>Natura Naturans</u> are related to the closed womb of the feminine principle. With regard to the inherent problems of conveying the meaning of primal Substance, Spinoza's approach to language and the bridging device of the divine Attributes are pivotal elements. Finally, the maternal aspects of <u>Natura Naturans</u>, as originating, impartial, and positively narcissistic, are examined as a means of linking the Spinozistic ultimate reality directly to the feminine principle.

Moving into the diversified modes of Substance, the foreground of <u>Natura Naturata</u>, the Transformative character explains the process of "creation", of how the modes are derived from and related to Substance. These modes are governed by the universal system of law and order in Nature, which is deterministic in a uniquely feminine sense. The modes fall into several categories, including the infinite modes of Extension, Motion and Rest, which provide the dynamic interaction of opposites that make change possible within the harmonious unity of Substance.

    a.   Natura Naturans--the Elementary character. Throughout Spinoza's writings he displays no hesitancy to explicitly identify God, Substance, and Nature. J. Martineau has attempted to differentiate the members of this trinity with a view to the specific functions emphasized under each heading; hence, God is "universal cause of things", Substance "the permanent reality behind phenomena", and Nature "continuous Source of birth".[5] Each of these functions is intrinsic to the Elementary character of the feminine principle, the closed womb or closed system of Nature. Under this manifestation, the unity which is God/Substance/Nature performs the tasks of origination, underlying support, and sustaining force, in relation to individual things/modes.

The Spinozistic system, being feminine, lays great stress upon the fact of unity, of the primal oneness or wholeness which characterizes the ultimate reality. Nature is the unifying force--"all things are united through Nature, and they are united into one [being], namely God" (ST,II,xxii). The "faithful image" of Nature can only be reproduced by deducing its ideas "from the idea which represents the origin and source of the whole of nature" (namely, God) (IU,15). God or Substance is the sum total of being, what is necessary to uphold the universe, while Nature, as revealed in what follows, goes beyond base materiality, and yet encompasses it.

The precise meaning of the unity of God and Nature, as well as the manner in which it can account for the multiplicity observed in the world, has long perplexed interpreters of Spinoza's philosophy. In many cases, this has led to gross misinterpretations which leave one questioning Spinoza's powers of intellect (e.g., Pierre Bayle's discussion in his Dictionary). Confusion arises from Spinoza's tendency to identify apparent distinctions as essentially expressive of one and the same reality, especially where the divine characteristics are concerned; hence, divine will is equivalent to divine power, and that to divine intellect (TM,II,viii,2). He himself traces the problem to the fact that we, as modes of Substance, lack an encompassing point of view: "because we are parts of a thinking being, whose thoughts—some in their entirety, others in fragments only—constitute our mind" (IU,29).

Unfortunately, Spinoza's language is often less than precise, and even inconsistent, throughout his writings, providing an actual basis for the accusations of his critics. For example, Spinoza logically determines that a being whose existence is necessary also is single, that the nature of the divine includes the conclusion "that he is one [quod sit unicus]" (E1, Appendix). But elsewhere he contends that no general idea can be formed of the divine essence, and it is clear "that he who calls God one or single [unum vel unicum] has no true idea of God, or is speaking of Him inappropriately."[6] Now, as Spinoza repeatedly claims to have a true idea of God (see epistemology discussion), it can only be the case that his references to oneness, or single nature, in God are inappropriate in an absolute sense, or true only at the level of discursive reason, insofar as they can be logically deduced from our conception of the divine essence.

The source of the problem seems to lie in the fact that, while attempting to convey to us a reality which is essentially feminine, Spinoza falls prey to the pitfalls of distinction inherent in language, and flounders in the linguistic morass characteristic of the masculine mind's analytic emphasis. The result is a series of self-contradictions which has induced Spinoza's interpreters to reform his thought along a single masculine line of thought, without any attempt to reconcile the contradictions themselves in a multi-leveled (and essentially feminine) system. Spinoza only intensifies the philosophical dilemma by ignoring the incidence of these contradictions and not making an explicit appeal to the saving grace of the levels of knowledge.

In one theory put forth to explain this situation, A. Wolf refers to the 'Negative Theology' employed by Philo Judaeus of Alexandria (Neoplationism), as well as by Arabic and Jewish Medieval philosophers. By this method, the absolute unity of God was maintained while avoiding a comparison with human (masculine) terms.[7] In Maimonides, the Negative Theology is essentially a delineation of what God is not, using "One in reference to God to express that there is nothing similar to Him, but we do not mean to say that an attribute Unity is added to his essence."[8] This tactic is typical of feminine thought, in that it circumvents the limited homocentric associations of terms.

It is indeed true that Spinoza regarded language with great suspicion. Words are relegated to the lowest level of reality, that of imagination. He recognized that their use can be erroneous, allowing a linguistic affirmation or negation where none exists in (absolute) reality. A case in point is the term "infinity", which we can only conceive of as a negation of the finitude of our own experience (IU,35). A feminine philosophy is doomed to adopt the negative approach when attempting to communicate with masculine tools, such as language, due to the necessity of providing a contrast to the "positive" assertions of the masculine perspective.

Rather than developing an independent, though superficially contradictory, form of linguistic expression, (as did the Taoist), Spinoza chose to work with the philosophical jargon of his time, redefining terms to be more conducive to his feminine perspective. It seems sufficient that we as users of words be made aware of the inherent dangers of language and "keep strictly on our guard" (IU,35). Spinoza seems determined to surmount the manifest difficulties by designating very specific applications of terms in his meticulously-wrought definitions.

Metaphorically speaking, the human condition parallels the state of a worm in the bloodstream--the worm views particles of blood as entities in their own right and, given its limited viewpoint, is unable to fathom the integration of these parts in "the universal nature of blood" mutually interacting and harmonizing in one organic system. Taken as a closed system, the blood (like the one Substance) is "considered always to be a whole and not a part", with any changes attributable to the motion of the assumed parts acting in conjunction with one another.[9] From a universal point of view, Spinoza observes that every body is related to an interconnected whole of infinite scale, with the "infinite ways" of an "infinite power" yielding "infinite changes": "all bodies are surrounded by others, and are mutually determined to exist and to act in a definite and deterministic manner."[10]

The continuity in Substance is emphasized in all of these points, overshadowing the apparent divisions. However, it is equally unacceptable to take Joachim's position that Substance is devoid of all "real" distinctions, implying that any attempted distinctions are purely illusory.[11] Spinoza never denies the existence of the finite world as if it were some sort of illusory state of *Maya*. The actual Spinozistic doctrine of unity appears to lie between the two extreme interpretations which either denounce the philosophical possibility of eliminating all distinctions (as does Bayle), or assert that Spinoza judges distinctions to be illusory in all instances (e.g. Joachim). Although absolute distinctions are rejected by the Spinozistic system, it remains legitimate to implement certain "real" distinctions on the lower levels of reality. The degrees of reality recognized by Spinoza (and reflected in his levels of knowledge under epistemology) insure that the distinctions made by human reason are excluded only from the highest or absolute level of being. Unless they are taken seriously, Spinoza's philosophy is doomed to inconsistency.

The issue of the unity of Substance is crucial for understanding Spinoza's references to the whole and the parts of the encompassing reality. The concept of the whole as compounded of connected individuals or parts which can be either the same or different is admitted to be a "thing of Reason" (ST, 1,2nd Dialogue). Strictly speaking, then, God or Substance is not a whole, that is to say, is not something composed of parts. Rather, it is "an entirely simple being" (TM,II,v,3). Logic demands, Spinoza says, that a being that exists necessarily have no parts, inasmuch as the parts would have to exist prior to the whole in order to compose it. Obviously, nothing exists prior to a necessarily existent being, and we therefore can not conceive of it as having parts.[12]

The case of Substance parallels that of matter, which "is everywhere the same"; parts are distinguisable in matter only "as we regard it as affected in different ways . . . with regard to mode, but not with regard to [absolute] reality" (E1,15,Schol.). Clearly, a mode of Substance is not equivalent to a part of Substance, and one properly cannot be said to participate in Substance (even though Spinoza occasionally slips into talk of participation) but merely to be a modification of its Attributes of Thought (as mind) and Extension (as body). There is no whole of Substance which is composed of the sum of its parts. There is only Substance and the manifold ways in which it is modified, as seen from the point of view of a level of reality lesser that the absolute reality, the reality of modes.

Within his self-imposed linguistic and conceptual restrictions, Spinoza presents a primal Substance which corresponds to the Elementary character--an encompassing container, the womb of existence. Moreover, the impartiality of the Elementary character, with respect to human interests, as well as its positive narcissism, by which it promotes its own interests, are equally identifiable in Substance.

The manner in which Substance contains all things already has been made clear, and is summarized in the statement that "What is, is in God" (E1,15). Things can be said to exist only insofar as they share in the one absolute reality and occupy a position at some level of lesser reality. There is nothing else for them to be, Substance or God is the sum total or the ground of being. This is again a logical conclusion, founded on the role Substance performs vis-à-vis the modes and its function as originating cause, from which things draw their existence, their life force.

The impartiality of Substance, or the Spinozistic deity, confounds the anthropomorphic masculine presuppositions about the divine. No intimate personal interest in human kind is exhibited by Spinoza's God (EV,17,Corol). Human emotions or passions are not reciprocated by the deity. In following out the divine nature, God cannot allow any personal whims or prejudices to interfere.

A further indication of divine impartiality is the fact that no teleological orientation can be ascribed to God. Spinoza dismisses as superstition the common "prejudice", typical of the masculine perspective's human focus, that the world has been fashioned specifically for human use. The result of this immodest assumption has been the development of religions founded on purely egotistical motives: "each man has devised for himself, out of his own brain, a different mode of worshipping God, so that God might love him above others, and direct all nature to the service of his blind cupidity and insatiable avarice" (EI, Appendix). These human-centered views have no place in the feminine universe of impartial Substance. God shows the same impersonal concern for the human individual and the lowest rock.

If anything can be said to motivate the Spinozistic deity, it can only be a positive narcissism, the effect of universal conatus. The love of God for humanity is not an affect which would require something external to God, "since all form only one thing, which is God himself" (ST,II,xxiv). Rather, there is a narcissistic divine love in the mold of feminine Eros which extends from the one of Substance to the many of its manifestations. The mysterious intellectual love of God (Amor Dei intellectualis) can be understood in this sense. It is equated with God's self-love despite the fact that the emotion or affect of love is denied to God: "God loves Himself with an infinite intellectual love" (EV,55). The love which God bears us is the same as the intellectual love we have for God (EV,36, Corol), or, by loving us, God, in fact expresses self-love. The implications of the Spinozistic form of love (Eros) are further revealed in the context of blessedness.

To summarize, Spinoza's Substance as the activating force of Natura Naturans, Nature naturing, reflects the Elementary character of the feminine principle in several respects. Both are primal and undifferentiated, the self-contained system of natural force. They are both "one", or fully unified. In asserting this unity, Spinoza neither concedes that distinctions cannot be eliminated nor denounces all distinctions as illusory. Instead, he accommodates both the logically demanded oneness of Substance itself and the observed distinctions within the lower levels of reality. Substance undifferentiated is absolute reality, but when conceived by human intellect, utilitarian distinctions are observed.

The linguistic difficulties which accrue from Spinoza's attempt to convey this accommodation through the masculine tool of language are not directly confronted by him, and thus contribute to the perplexities of his interpreters. To be consistent, Spinoza must abandon talk of part and whole, except as clearly-labeled conceptual aids, and discuss the relationship between Substance and its modes as that of reality and the ways in which that reality is made manifest. The degrees of reality concept must be made explicit.

Finally, the similarities between Substance and the Elementary character extend to their common containing function, impartiality, and positive narcissism. Substance encompasses the things of the world, bears them in its womb, and nothing can be said to exist outside of it. Yet, it remains aloof from human petitions, and has no special interest in human affairs. One expression of this impartiality is its non-teleological orientation. The only love which is attributable to God differs from the human emotion entirely, following the pattern of narcissistic Eros. God's love is self-love, which also is identical to the intellectual love the blessed bear towards God, an Eros/relatedness which links all in the one unity of Substance. God/Substance is, indeed, the only possible object, or subject, of love.

     b. Natura Naturata--the Transformative character. Although Spinoza contends that our knowledge must begin with "the first principle . . . a being single and infinite . . . the sum total of being" (IU,30), as embodied in the Elementary character, it is also necessary to continue the descent down the scale of being to the realm of the modes, the plurality of Substance's manifestations. These constitute Natura Naturata, Nature natured, as generated by Natura Naturans. Herein lies the Transformative character of the feminine principle, setting the metaphysical stage for the dynamic move to blessedness. Although lacking the perfection of absolute reality, the individual mode undertakes to perfect its nature as far as is possible to reassert its share in existence.

Knowledge of God yields knowledge of its effects (modes) (El,axiom 4). God "contains eminently what is found in created things formally" (TM,II,i). Out of the one Substance are derived the two known Attributes of Thought and Extension, which yield the three infinite modes--Understanding, under Thought, and Motion and Rest, under Extension--and the multiplicity of finite modes as minds and bodies. By this framework of reality, the Transformative character allows the individual mode of the human being to rationally realize its universal status as related to Substance, and then to retrace its steps back to the experience of undifferentiated unity.

To understand the chain of transformation back to eternal Substance, one must consider the function of Substance as Creative Principle, how it generates the modes, and hence how this process can be reversed to reaffirm our share in the absolute reality. This is a very unusual creation, for Substance cannot actually create what follows naturally and necessarily from its own nature. All degrees of reality are actualized through God: "the laws of His nature were so ample that they sufficed for the production of everything which can be conceived by an infinite intellect" (El, Appendix). It cannot be creation of the ex nihilo variety, inasmuch as no time prior to creation, the existence of what is or of Substance itself, can be posited; the creation and sustaining of the universe occur simultaneously (TM,II,x,1-6). Substance is only logically prior to its modes, for when there was Substance, the eternal, its modes were also present. Or, "there is in Nature no creation but only generation". Creation, in the sense of imparting both essence and existence, "can really not be said ever to have taken place" (ST,I,ii, note). Human beings "are not created but only begotten . . . their bodies existed already before, although in another form."[13] In modern terms, this amounts to a kind of eternal recycling process.

The universe is "self-generating and self-sustaining".[14] The divine will by means of which things are "created" is the same as the understanding by which these things are known.[15] That is to say, the state of the universe is reflective of and determined by the nature of God. Whether or not this can be equated with emanation is a matter of continuing dispute. The relationship between Substance and its modes, although similar to emanation in certain respects, is rather unique. Most essentially, things cannot be said to actually participate in Substance or its reality because Spinoza denies that there can be any parts to the absolute.

A pivotal role in this relationship is played by Natura Naturata, Nature which has been "natured" by Substance and, thus is directly responsible for the transformation and sustenance of the modes. Natura Naturata is not active per se, only insofar as it is related to God or Substance--"everything which follows from the necessity of the nature of God, or of any of God's attributes" (E1,29,Schol). There is no direct emanation, but a filtering of Substance's absolute reality, first through the Attributes (to be considered at the end of this section), and then into the various levels of natured Nature. As conceived by human intellect, the process takes place by means of a graduated series of degrees of reality.

The relationship between Substance and its modes differs from both that of subject and its predicates, as in Lockeian substance, and the Aristotelian model of genus and species. Neither a predicate nor a species presents us with a microcosm of the respective subject or genus macrocosm. Yet the feminine microcosmic-macrocosmic patterns seems to be required in Spinoza's standard, for an individual or thing merely expresses absolute reality at a lower degree of being. Full actualization has been hindered by a certain impotence, that is, non-being. Insofar as we are or act, we are identified with the absolute reality of Substance, but insofar as we lack being or are acted upon, we are alienated from reality. An analogy has been drawn between the substance/mode relationship and "the logical relation between ground and consequent", the divine nature and that which logically follows therefrom.[16] Certainly, for Spinoza, the logical arrangement would appear the method, or level, at which discursive reason is able to conceive of the relationship. Being both human and creatures of reason, we must accept such an explanation as adequate to our intellect, *qua* human.

There ensues from the logical and necessary relationship of Substance and mode the positing of universal law and order, the (logical) necessity by which the cosmos or Nature functions. While Natura Naturans is the source of this necessity, it becomes most fully evident to us in the concrete reality of Natura Naturata, the level of our common experience. Due to the oneness of reality in Substance, the universe of modes cannot be derived from it directly, but must be mediated by the Attributes. The differentiated modes represent the necessary unfolding of undifferentiated Substance, Natura Naturata as the open womb of Nature with the Attributes serving as midwives.

Spinoza's peculiar use of the term necessity paradoxically involves a corresponding level of freedom. By definition, a free being "exists from the necessity of its own nature, and is determined to action by itself alone." This logical and self-determined necessity is opposed to that compulsion originating from some external cause (El,def 6). Given the previous discussions of the nature of Substance, it is clear that this being alone is free in the fullest sense, that is, acts by its own necessity, while modes generally act under the compulsion of the reality external to them.

As a manifestation of Substance and considered as something more than "a certain mass, or corporeal matter,"[17] Nature also manifests no contingency, only necessity. Everything in Nature follows from the nature of the divine "not only to exist, but to exist and act in a certain manner" (El,24 and Demonst). Things exist and function out of this same necessity, and are free to the degree in which their actions follow from their own natures.

The natural divine law is innate or "ingrained" in the human intellect (TP,IV), insofar as the mind is a mode of Substance via the Attribute of Thought. However, unlike human law, which requires vigilant enforcement, divine law is self-enforced. It is impossible for these laws to be transgressed "because whatsoever happens, is not contrary to, but in accordance with, his [God's] own decision" (ST,II,xxiv). Each species is governed by natural laws "to exist and operate in a given fixed, and definite manner" (Te), appropriate to the nature of that group (TP,IV). In human beings, these are the laws of discursive reason, discussed in depth under epistemology. Natural divine law also encompasses non-historical (eternal) relations, is non-ceremonial, and is its own reward--"the highest reward of the Divine law is the law itself, to know God and to love Him of our free choice" (TP,IV). In other words, our relationship to the law of Nature is a natural one--to act on free choice is to act by necessity, to emulate the very action of God.

This state of affairs forbids the possibility of 'unnatural' miraculous intervention by God, such as claimed in orthodox religious texts (specifically the Bible). Any seeming confusion or contradiction in Nature is due merely to the gaps in our own knowledge and judgement regarding causality (ST,cf. I,vi; also TP). From Substance's viewpoint, sub species aeternitatis, harmony reigns supreme; the "parts" are interconnected and "the laws or nature, of one part adapt themselves to the laws, or nature, of another part in such a way as to produce the least possible opposition."[18] However, the "actual co-ordination and concatenation of things" exceeds our limited human resources, and so it is both necessary and utilitarian for us to view things as contingent on the level of common life (TP,IV).

Nature, considered under any of the Attributes of Substance, exhibits the identical order of "connection of causes" (Ell,7,Schol), and the same insight is perceived. Hence, a strict correspondence is posited between ideas and their referents: "The order and connection of ideas is the same as the order and connection of things" (Ell,7). Of the Attributes of Thought and Extension, either may, and does for Spinoza, serve as introduction and guide to the other. Knowledge of Nature yields knowledge of Substance, and conversely, the "faithful image of nature" (Natura Naturata) is deducible from "the origin and source of the whole of nature"(Natura Naturans) (IU,15).

Given this metaphysical foundation, the types of things in Nature are readily reducible to but two, namely the necessary, whose non-existence would imply some contradiction, and the impossible, whose existence would be self-contradictory. No intermediate realm of the merely possible can be conceived, except insofar as our knowledge of the causes of a thing is deficient (IU,19). Hence, strict determinism reigns in the Spinozistic universe, and is indeed the best possible and only possible system of reality based upon the utterly determined necessity of its ground of being, Substance.

It is the human predilection for centering the universe upon itself, its own interests, characteristic of the masculine perspective, which prevents the realization of the multi-leveled metaphysical reality encompassed by Substance. The humanistic approach is self-deceptive, when the universe at large is being considered. As ego-centered human beings we consciously and/or unconsciously desire what is assumed to be within our own narrowly-conceived interests. There is always some end towards which things are imagined to be progressing, and those final causes (such as God) which are beyond our scope are fabricated along anthropomorphic lines. It is as if the cells in the bloodstream were to assert their independence from the whole and assume the existence of a concerned God in their own image. These self-serving assumptions are exposed as delusions and only necessity reigns supreme. Reality is distorted, replaced by mere imagination (the lowest level of knowledge), resulting in unending controversy where individuals are satisfied only with their personal views (E1,Appendix). The cure comes in the form of the transcendent feminine perspective.

Natura Naturata is early described by Spinoza as "one single idea" in the divine mind (TM,II,vii,7), stressing both its unity and intimate relation with Substance. One can also deduce that Natura Naturata is related to the Attributes of Thought and Extension; Thought, in that it is an idea, and Extension, in that an ideatum corresponds to every true idea (and God, being perfect, can have nothing but true ideas). Moreover, Spinoza implies that the natural realm is perfect. God has produced all things (or all things have followed from Substance) "in the highest degree of perfection" necessarily entailed by the essence of the divine (E1,33,Schol 2).

As noted above, the concept of natural law and order (logical necessity) is strongly present in Spinoza's system of philosophy. The two "main tenets of Spinozism," according to one commentator, are the inviolability and inevitability of natural laws, and the natural setting of humanity as subject to the laws of Nature.[19] These laws are revealed by the "Natural Light". A contradiction of reason is equally a contradiction of Nature, and vice versa, and both are equally absurd. (TP,VI).

Significantly, however, the laws of Nature are not restricted to those of human or discursive reason; the latter "aims only at man's true benefit and preservation", as more or less tailored to our specific human needs. The limiting laws of Nature, however, have a far greater range, are "infinitely wider, and refer to the eternal order of Nature, wherein man is but a speck". The extent of this order exceeds the grasp of human intellect (TP,XVI). We mistakenly assign to Nature, as to God, a goal orientation, specifically with a human-centered goal. In fact, however, no such end exists and "all final causes are nothing but human fictions." Natural order is contradicted by the very speculation of teleological aspirations, for under such an assumption the cause (Nature or God) becomes the effect, and the effect (some future good) the cause. Realistically, the most perfect effect is that which is closest, most immediate, to God, and not one lying at some distant future stage of evolution (E1,Appendix). Here we have a further example of the importance of the feminine 'is' over the masculine 'ought'.

The equation of God and Nature does not endow God with purely material aspects, as has been feared by some interpreters. Instead it grants to Nature a new (and radically unmasculine) significance, in which God is an immanent, and not transient, cause.[20] God is no mere spiritual being, but is also highly concrete as Substance. Nothing contained in the finite understanding of God does not also exist formally, that is objectively, in Nature (ST,I,ii). From the traditional conception of God as absolutely infinite being, Spinoza progressed to the conception of Nature as likewise absolutely infinite. That is, the essence of Nature is infinite, and through it arises a union of all things (modes), "united into [being], namely, God" (ST,II,xxii). The power of Nature is nothing less than God's power (TP,XVI), or "the power of God under another name" (TP,I). With decrees of the divine, those of Nature "always involve eternal truth and necessity" (TP,II). The order of Nature is "fixed and immutable" (TP,VI), as is God or Substance. The "first principle" of Nature forbids its conception as either abstract or universal; it can have no greater extension in understanding than in reality, and "no likeness to mutable things" (IU,30).

The modes which populate the realm of Natura Naturata depend upon God for their existence, essence, and individual nature (TM,I,iii,5). Taken together, the modes constitute the world as we know it, a realm of being which is not an illusory Maya, but rather a view of Substance from an interimly useful, but ultimately deficient, level of reality. The only possible illusion lies in our misconstruing it as the highest reality. If a metaphorical flight of fancy may be allowed here, the universe is a theatre (in the round) where God commands the stage as sole actor, while the modes are scattered throughout the farthest reaches of the audience. Our view of the action can be distorted if we have bad seats, are unduly distracted from the performance by surrounding disturbances, etc. Following a similar line of thought, Spinoza outlined the two ways of conceiving quantity, "abstractly or superficially" through imagination via the senses, or as Substance,"through the intellect alone". Under the first conception quantity is "divisible, finite, composed of parts, and one of many" (just as the modes are); the second approach yields quantity which is "infinite, indivisible and unique".[21] One's location in the cosmic theatre determines what is seen, or, what we see it as.

Viewed as a unity in Nature, the modes are "the face of the whole Universe" (facies totius Universi); the infinite flux of these modes does not exclude the overriding oneness.[22] Such changes are comparable to the changing gestures of a face, although it remains the same face throughout. Ultimately, "we may easily conceive the whole of nature to be one individual, whose parts, that is to say, all bodies, differ in infinite ways without any change of the whole individual" (EII,13, Demonst to Lemma 7). In a similar manner, the actor adopts different masks or personae to play various roles, but remains the same beneath the mask. The modes are then "states of substance", lacking existence (reality) except insofar as they are defined through the one Substance.[23] Or, they are the "affections" of Substance (of a substance), which are dependent upon Substance for their conception (EI, def 5). God is considered to be the cause of a given mode by virtue of the specific Attribute under which that mode falls (EII, 6). Matter is strongly uniform and its "parts" are distinguishable solely in terms of its being differently affected (EI,15,Schol). The same may be said of the ideas which fall under Thought.

Spinoza divides Natura Naturata into the "general", or modes immediately dependent upon God (the immediate infinite modes), and the "particular", modes produced by general modes directly. The former category includes the infinite modes of Understanding (under the Attribute of Thought), and Motion and Rest (under Extension) (cf. ST, I, ix). The category of particular modes encompasses all those individual expressions of the divine nature/essence, particular minds and bodies.

The infinite immediate modes of Motion and Rest, under the Attribute of Extension, must be understood in interaction with one another, even as a single mode. Motion and Rest are mutually defining: Spinoza notes (ST,I,ii), that Motion only occurs in conjunction with Rest. The two are essential as a means of accounting for change within the unitary Spinozistic system, especially crucial in view of the professed immutability of Substance per se. Motion and Rest are governed by certain specific laws, and are considered "pure" notions "which explain Nature as it is in itself".[24] To each body in Nature there corresponds a degree or proportion between rest and motion, and this alone serves to distinguish it from all other bodies (EII, 13,Lemma 1). Hence, Motion and Rest are like positive and negative poles or charges, and to each individual an identifying number may be assigned. However, this proportion may itself be altered due to external influences, resulting in body types appropriate to various ages or states of being, and even one appropriate to physical death (ST,II,Preface,note). Anything conducive to maintaining the balance between the two opposing forces, Motion and Rest, contributes to the over-all harmony, the perfect immutability, of the universe. The analogy to the complementary forces of Yang and Yin, active and passive, is obvious, particularly with regard to the emphasis on ultimate balance.

The finite modes consist of individual minds, from the Attribute of Thought, and bodies, from the Attribute of Extension. Just as the mind is "part of the infinite intellect of God" (Ell,11,Corol), the body can be said to be "part" of infinite material Nature as a manifestation of Substance. Together mind and body are "one and the same thing conceived at one time under the attribute of thought, and at another under that of extension" (Ell1,2,Schol). In the same way, Substance is seen as God and Nature, both of which are essentially the same.

In sum, within the "created Nature" of Natura Naturata Spinoza has established an intricate metaphysical framework stretching from the whole of Nature through the infinite modes and into the particulars of the finite modes. This framework explains the manner in which the mode, as modification, is related to and derived from Substance. Simultaneously, the path of transformation, whereby the individual mode can accommodate itself to reality, is revealed for future ethical reference. No creation in the true sense of the word takes place, but rather, an unfolding of the natural necessity of the essence of Substance (existence) in an open-ended system of Nature, manifested in the modes.

The realm of Natura Naturata is guided by the same universal law and order which God freely embraces in the absolute freedom of necessity. Determinism reigns in a non-compulsory necessity with which we harmonize ourselves by first realizing and then fulfilling our individual nature. Required here is a rejection of human-centered prejudices, with their attendant relativistic value judgements upon the universe. The ultimate link between Nature and Substance supports the power inherent in Natura Naturata, going beyond the scope of human limitations.

The modes themselves are relegated to the dual

authority of the Attributes of Thought and Extension, and may be infinite and immediate (as Understanding, Motion and Rest), infinite but mediate ('the face of the whole Universe'), or finite (minds and bodies).[25] Understanding is essential for the improvement which can culminate in blessedness; Motion and Rest, expressed as a proportion for each individual, are responsible for the distinctions drawn between things, as well as accounting for the change within the changeless. Finally, the finite modes of bodies and minds are dual expressions of the same individual, leading to the rejection of a mind/body dualism by Spinoza.

Thus far, Spinoza's metaphysical scheme closely parallels that of Taoism, positing the oneness of the Elementary character on the one hand and the multiplicity of the Transformative character on the other. However, a significant element is lacking in the Tao Te Ching, specifically an element which is able to bridge the gap between the infinite and absolute reality of Substance and the lesser degrees of reality embodied in the modes. Spinoza's divine Attributes perform this crucial role, contributing to the greater coherency of his metaphysical system as compared to that of Taoism. Although ranked with Natura Naturans, the Attributes can be said to occupy the lowest fringes of that absolute reality, from which point they establish the necessary continuity between Substance, from which they are derived directly, and the modes, individual expressions of Substance mediated through the Attributes.

Considered from the point of view of Substance, the absolute, the Attributes are "wholly identical", a reflection of its own oneness; for human intellect, however, they are "wholly diverse", as is proper to its lesser degree of reality/perfection.[26] Like a crystal prism, the Attributes take the single ray of white light which is Substance and refract it into the rainbow-hued light spectrums of the modes, and in so doing neither add nor subtract from the sum total of reality. Also, due to our inherent human limitations, although infinite Attributes are predicated of God, only two are accessible to human comprehension, those of Thought and Extension. They are the pair of lenses through which we perceive the universe. Through these two Attributes we are able to discern the microcosmic-macrocosmic pattern of the universe, relating our individual minds and bodies through Thought and Extension to the common source of Substance itself.

Having divided the universe into substances (ultimately reducible to the one Substance) and modes (E1, 15,Demonst), Spinoza appears to have excluded the Attributes from the realm of existing things. They occupy a limbo of merely intellectual awareness, and serve to support the human conception of the divine essence (see E1,def.4). Within the Spinozistic system the Attributes are "so many 'lines of forces' in which God manifests or reveals Himself."^{27} Each of the Attributes is 'infinite', which in Spinoza's specialized vocabulary connotes something complete and perfect,^{28} and hence contains a complete and perfect expression of divine essence from a given point of view, whether as thinking being or extended being. These last are "one and the same substance", differing only in focus (E11,vii,Schol). Extension and Thought are "the two all-pervasive characteristics of the self-creating Universe . . . conceived either as a system of extended bodies, an infinite spatial system, or as a system of thought", they are alternate ways of describing the all-inclusiveness of Substance.^{29} In other words, they do not exist independently of Substance, but rather, the existence of Substance is expressed through them; they are instruments of its manifestations.

Given the intimate connection between thought and extension in ourselves through our mental and physical functioning, Spinoza dismisses the Cartesian assessment of the Attributes of Thought and Extension as two independent substances, and explains their conjunction in terms of a common center of being (ST,I,ii,note). Absolute reality encompasses, or is manifested through, both the mental and the material. Neither is denied, and neither is subordinated to the other, a sign of the feminine perspective's openness to all aspects of reality. The extent to which Spinoza is able to carry through the equality of the mental and physical aspects of our being, demanded by feminine metaphysics, is revealed in his ethics.

Nevertheless, each of the humanly-accessible Attributes reveals a specific facet of Substance, Thought is properly a divine Attribute because "<u>God is a thinking being</u>" (E11,1); "by attending to thought alone" (in isolation from extension) it is possible to "conceive an infinite Being" (Schol). The Attribute of Thought may be viewed as "a concrete universal . . . the whole system of ideas", from which particular ideas are abstracted.^{30} Existent in Nature is "an infinite power of thought", subjectively containing "the whole of Nature", its <u>ideatum</u>. This same power is inherent in the human mind, though finite and confined to the perception of the human body.³¹ Individual thoughts are modes expressive of the divine nature "in a certain determinate manner" (EII,1,Demonst). The Attribute of Thought provides the metaphysical assurance that our adequate ideas are indeed true.

Extension expresses Extended Substance ("<u>God is an extended thing</u>" EII,2), as an organic unity, not a whole composed of parts, that is, of distinct bodies. In fact, paralleling the law of the conservation of matter, the destruction of any "part" of matter would entail the destruction of the whole—"all Extension would vanish at the same time".³² As in the case of the Attribute of Thought, it is possible to conceive an infinite being by attending solely to Extension (EII,2, Demonst). The Attribute of Extension has been characterized as "a set of facts" which are described by basic natural laws.³³ From this interpretation one might conclude that a body, as a mode expressing, "in a certain and determinate manner", the divine essence, "in so far as He [God] is considered as the thing extended" (EII,def.1), concretizes the factual (real) data.

What Extension is <u>not</u> is localized, finite, composed of distinct pa<u>rts</u>, "the primary and single foundation of all things", or able to occupy more space at one time than at another (IU,35). Nor does conceiving of God as extended entail an end to simplicity and a proliferation of parts, nor a reduction to "the condition of matter, the lowest of all beings".³⁴ Substance exalts extended matter to its own heights. In line with the feminine perspective, matter is not summarily dismissed by Spinoza as incompatible with the highest reality, but is credited with being a legitimate expression of that reality.

As they point to the integration of mind and body, the Attributes also link the highest level of being with the lowest of the modes. Substance reaches through its Attributes, what we attribute to it under the dual expressions of our existence, and into the plurality of manifested forms, the modes. In this dynamic flow each mode finds a vindication of its claim to a share in the one reality.

3. Epistemology: The Dynamics of Blessedness

Thus far we have seen what the Spinozistic universe looks like, how its metaphysical elements are interrelated and what their underlying principles are. By extending those principles into the human sphere of existence, it is possible to determine first, what approaches we can take to knowledge, and which of these is the most significant; secondly, how our knowledge is possible, and the extent of its reliability; and thirdly, what the ultimate form of knowledge consists of. Following out these three lines of questioning, our epistemological discussion deals with: (a) the dynamics of the Spinozistic levels of knowledge, (b) the movement of knowledge from God as truth to individual intellects, and (c) the knowledge/experience of blessedness as the culmination of the philosophical enterprise.

a. <u>The levels of knowledge</u>. Although concerned with a knowledge of Substance, Spinozistic epistemology is tailored specifically to the needs of human intellect. In the opening remarks to the second part of the <u>Ethics</u>, "Of the Nature and Origin of the Mind", Spinoza explicitly restricts his exposition to the human sphere. By detailing what necessarily follows from God's essence, Spinoza aims to consider "those things only which may conduct us as it were by the hand to a knowledge of the human mind and its highest happiness." No claims are made for the applicability of his statements to non-human creatures, nor does he dismiss the possibility that similar investigations could be made of non-human intellect.

One of the major factors hindering a feminine interpretation of Spinozism as a philosophy is Spinoza's own widespread reputation as a rationalist par excellence and disciple of Cartesianism, which last must be ranked as masculine within our proposed duality of perspectives. Having identified discursive reason as the typically masculine method, the frequent references to reason in the works of Spinoza would seem to demand a recognition of his masculine affinities. However, as is argued in what follows, Spinoza's reliance upon discursive reason need not be interpreted as proof of a masculine philosophical objective. On the contrary, the insights of reason are employed as a means to the higher ends of feminine intuition, to attain a type of knowledge accessible, and of value, only to a feminine philosophy. Under this feminine re-interpretation of Spinozism, the levels of knowledge outlined by Spinoza are indicative of an epistemological progression, and correspond to the levels of reality in his metaphysical scheme. A greater share in reality becomes apparent at each successive level.

The base level of imagination, the mundane experience of sense and accepted convention, refers only to the lowest reality of the finite modes. Discursive reason, at the second and intermediate level, advances our knowledge to the infinite modes and the higher realm of reality occupied by the divine Attributes as ways of conceiving God. Ultimately, however, the absolute reality of Substance is accessible only through third level knowledge of the intuitive type, which is feminine in character. By placing intuition at the very apex of his scale of knowledge, Spinoza confirms the feminine motivations which have been assigned to him.

The differences between the three levels of knowledge may be compared to the phases of the moon: while the moon, as a whole, like reality, is always present, its actual shape is revealed to us by stages in terms of a gradual increase in its luminosity. Out of the total ignorance of the new moon emerge the first glimmerings of truth, which hint at its actual shape, in its first quarter. This represents the level of imagination or opinion, characterized by superficial sense data and conventions which depict the moon as a crescent. At the second quarter of the half moon, more light/truth is revealed, and the over-all shape of the heavenly body can be surmised upon close observation. Such are the deductions appropriate to discursive reason, which draws knowledge of Substance from the Attributes, without having a direct contact with the ground of being itself. Finally, full and encompassing truth is reflected in the full moon, where reality is known at a single glance, with the immediacy characteristic of intuition.[35]

Although there can be no denial of Spinoza's rationalist leanings, a re-assessment of the priorities of the Spinozistic system reveals that intuition is *the* goal of its strenuous philosophical exercises and applications. Thus, while Spinoza's language, influenced by the intellectual environment of the seventeeth century, tends toward a glorification of discursive reason, his underlying motivations can be best interpreted within the context of a feminine perspective. Discursive reason is indeed essential in the Spinozistic system, but is to be encompassed and transcended by intuitive means on the path to the highest knowledge.

The reason why most interpreters have failed to note the overriding significance of intuition for

Spinoza, is that they have failed to observe a firm distinction between the levels of discursive reason and intuition. Admittedly, this neglect is due as much to Spinoza's own presentation of the subject, which at times appears neither clear nor consistent, as to the hesitancy among scholars to take the distinction seriously. Perhaps most misleading of all is Spinoza's use of the terms reason, mind, and intellect interchangeably. As a result of these and other bits of linguistic carelessness, foreshadowed by Spinoza's inherent distrust of language, the rational and intuitive levels have been confounded and even merged, rather than approached as a distinguishable set of steps in the over-all continuity of thought. The feminine perspective demonstrates its usefulness here by offering an alternative focus of attention to that of masculine discursive reason.

Even those who admit the existence of the distinction in question tend to interpret intuition as a mere extension of reason. When Alasdair MacIntyre declares that Spinoza can entertain "no ultimate distinction between the natural scientist, the philosopher, and the theologian,"[36] he has obviously overlooked the fact that, despite the common subject matter of God or Substance, Spinoza does not consider the three roles to be indistinguishable. Rather, he takes great pains in the Theologico-Political Treatise to separate theology's concern with piety and obedience from that of philosophy, which is truth and wisdom (xv). Science, corresponding to the level of discursive reason, can be said to occupy a realm intermediate between theological imagination and philosophical intuition. Its realm of truth is an essentially human and non-absolute truth, as is demonstrated in what follows.

Given the fact that the pivotal element of Spinoza's system, Substance, fits the pattern of feminine thought (as discussed above), we can hardly content ourselves with the general assumption that some sort of "rational mysticism" (with an emphasis on the "rational" aspect), guided his thought. Interpreters of this persuasion have always been somewhat embarrassed by the content of the fifth part of the Ethics, and have found it necessary to minimize its importance (which is in fact great) in order to support their emphasis on reason. Spinoza has been characterized more often as the logician of the geometrical method (adopted by necessity, as noted above), in the tradition of Descartes, than as an original ethical philosopher drawing upon the sources of metaphysics and epistemology. To insist upon either extreme of logician or ethicist does an injustice to Spinoza's encompassing philosophical concerns.

These and related misconstruals, derived from the rather sketchy comments Spinoza himself contributes on the subject of reason and intuition, can be corrected by delving more deeply into the significance of the levels of knowledge. Unless discursive reason and intuition are differentiated, Spinoza will remain vulnerable to charges of inconsistency and even blatant contradictions in his works. By recognizing the distinction, however, it becomes possible to unravel such Spinozistic mysteries as the co-existence of freedom and necessity in human life (see Appendix II). In sum, it is extremely difficult, if not impossible, to take Spinoza's philosophy seriously without admitting his underlying metaphysical presupposition of levels of knowledge.

Spinoza's commitment to the dynamics of levels is shown by his frequent references to degrees of perfection, reality, or power. It seems only reasonable to conclude that the reader is meant to take quite literally the distinction between the three (originally four) Spinozistic levels of knowledge. Most commentators agree that imagination is indeed set off from reason, but the upward ascent does not suddenly abate, nor does reason shade imperceptibly into intuition. Rather, there is a definite movement and increase of perfection to be attained on the third level of knowledge.

Spinoza himself implements these levels of knowledge in his writings. Each of his works is more or less expressive of a certain epistemological slant, corresponding to one of the three levels, although statements couched in terms of the remaining levels are invariably interwoven into the fabric of the text. Hence, the Theologico-Political Treatise has a high concentration of imagination, relating to Spinoza's discussion of religion, interspersed with pronouncements from the perspective of reason and intuition. A rational focus is evident in Principles of the Philosophy of Rene Descartes. In the Ethics also reason predominates, until its culmination is part five with the introduction of intuitive knowledge and the intellectual love of God. Unfortunately, Spinoza has not seen fit, or perhaps considered it superfluous, to forewarn the reader as to which particular level he is speaking from in a given passage, leaving us to infer this information solely on the basis of his previous exposition of the levels of knowledge. The linguistic hazards of which Spinoza was already suspicious were only aggravated by this policy. It remains for the philosophical reader to redraw the lines for the epistemological levels and to abide by their inherent rules.

Strange as this thesis may sound initially, in that it conjures up an image of the philosopher executing mental leaps from one level to another is his discourse, it proves crucial for an adequate understanding of the Spinozistic system. Nor is such a method entirely without precedent in philosophy. Given the reported discrepancies between the content of the Platonic dialogues and Plato's esoteric teachings, one can only lament the fact that Plato did not elaborate upon the relative values of his statements even to the limited extent that Spinoza does.[37]

A few comments from the correspondence should serve to disillusion those who insist upon seeing Spinoza as reason-possessed. For example, he explicitly states that reason is a mere means to a higher end:

> Even if I were once to find untrue the fruits of my natural understanding, they would make me happy since I enjoy them, and I endeavor to pass my life not in sorrow and sighing but in peace, joy and cheerfulness, and thereby I ascend a step higher.[38]

It is not difficult to discern here what Spinoza's actual priorities are-peace and joy take precedence over "truths" or understanding in terms of his over-all value system. Nor does he seem hesitant to entertain the possibility of error in the human process of reasoning, although one must assume that the experience of joyfulness, etc., is indisputable in its immediacy. These highly esteemed goals of peace and joy are products of intuition, with peace of mind being its exclusive product (EIV,Appendix iv). It is the level lying beyond discursive reason in degree of perfection as well as of reality.

Just ten years later, and less than two years before his death, Spinoza made the following intriguing statement: "I do not presume that I have found the best Philosophy, but I know that I think the true one" (*ego* non praesume, me optimam invenisse Philosophiam, sed veram me intelligere scio).39 One possible interpretation of the above remark is that Spinoza is disclaiming that he has the "best" system, that is, one able to satisfy the demands of reality in the various details elaborated by discursive reasoning. At the same time, Spinoza does claim to "think" a true philosophy, to have fathomed the truth in some inexpressible way, imparting certainty in his own mind. When the final goal is peace and bliss the adequacy of the means by which that goal is attained, in this case Spinoza's philosophical system, can be judged in terms of its ability to produce the desired ends. Such knowledge/experience can only derive from intuition: "As each person therefore becomes stronger in this kind of knowledge, the more he is conscious of himself and of God; that is to say, the more perfect and happier he is" (EV,3I,Schol).

The levels of knowledge or "modes of perception" are outlined in The Improvement of Understanding (7):

I. "hearsay", vicarious knowledge and convention
II. "mere experience" of a sensory sort
III. inference of one essence from another (discursive reasoning), or from cause to effect
IV. perception through an essence itself or knowledge of the proximate cause

Each level constitutes a distinct way of looking at the one Substance at various levels of reality (modes, Attributes, or essences), and therefore has some claim to truth, depending upon how clear and unprejudiced its vision is. The first two, later combined under the heading of opinion or imagination, are judged uncertain, yielding merely passions or affectations (ST,II,ii), while discursive reason and intuition yield knowledge which is "necessarily true" (El1,41), or, more precisely, true by the necessity of their levels of reality.

The problems of opinion or imagination, our most primal type of perception, are manifold, and Spinoza tends to ignore it in his philosophy as unworthy of extended attention. The senses can provide us with only a "mutilated and confused" presentation of individual things or modes (which themselves occupy the very nadir of the scale of existence). Since they must manifest themselves as signs or symbols, the linguistic conventions involved in imagination are dismissed as inadequate. They exhaust their usefulness in serving as aids for recollecting and imagining things as ideas (Ell,40,Schol 2). First level knowledge also has the dubious distinction of being the only cause of falsity, inasmuch as its ideas are naturally "inadequate and confused" (Ell,41 and Demonst). Nonetheless, even mundane experience has its indispensible role to play within Spinoza's scheme of things. He concedes that experience (<u>experientia</u>) is necessary for the knowledge of the existence of modes, for such knowledge cannot be deduced from their definitions (as is possible in the case of Substance).[40] There are even advantages to 'trifles and fancies',[41] presumably when applied with an attitude appropriate to their lesser degree of reality.

To determine the character of the two remaining levels of knowledge, we must consult Spinoza's earliest discussions concerning them. Second level knowledge is not confined to the "experience of a few particulars", as is sense knowledge, but examines things "in the light of true Reason" (ST,II,i). Variously referred to as reason and belief, it boasts the "good desires" as its products (ST,II,ii) while it "gives us the idea of the thing sought and enables us to draw conclusions without risk of error" (IU,8). Despite this ranking of certainty in the company of intuition, reason remains insufficient for cultivating the highest perfection (IU,10). It eventually must yield its place to third level knowledge, for the latter "alone apprehends the adequate essence of a thing without danger of error", hence sealing its position as foremost method (IU,9). Intuition's product is "true and sincere love" (finally crystallized in the <u>Eros</u>-like intellectual love of God) (ST,II,ii), which extends well beyond the faith of a "believer".

In further elucidating Spinoza's levels of knowledge, one can take Spinoza's example of our varying perceptions of the sun. To imagination or mere sense experience the sun is nothing more than a small bright disk moving through the sky. Discursive reason draws far different conclusions, namely that this object is in reality a burning mass several million miles distant and of immense size, with its observed motion being due to the earth's rotation. Our point of view gradually is broadened as we ascend from the first or primal to the second or reflective level of knowledge.

The scientist could rest content with such an

observation, couched in the language of logically-wrought laws of natural phenomena, having fulfilled the duties of reasonableness. The Spinozistic philosopher, however, is compelled to pursue knowledge further, into the level of intuition. There we encounter a view of a unified and universal system, within whose cosmic context the sun is viewed. This vision lies beyond our logical or theoretical construction of what the universe 'ought' to be like, based on the presuppositions of discursive reason; it is the vision <u>sub species aeternitatis</u> elevating us to the encompassing viewpoint of God, the 'is' of absolute reality. The scientist is to the philosopher as the map-maker is to the explorer--the map-maker's product is essential to the explorer, but pales beside the firsthand experience of the territory being depicted.

Similarly, there is the case of finding a number, d, in proportion to another, c, as b is to a. Working through imagination or opinion, an individual would merely recall some previously learned rule or even construct a "universal axiom" (a convention) based on personal experience (IU,8-9). Correspondingly, the trained mathematician, guided by reason, would apply the appropriate Euclidean proof to obtain the desired solution. In resorting to intuition, the solution can be grasped directly and entails no process, discursive or otherwise. Hence, the final and most decisive appeal must be to a method transcending both common sense and strict logic. By knowing God or Substance, we know everything that is, simply because there is nothing else to know.

From these examples it is clear that "adequate" knowledge arises only from a turning within, drawing upon the inner sources of human reason or universal intuition, as opposed to the superficial disunity of external sense data. In accordance with the microcosmic-macrocosmic feminine principle, our inner reality reveals the outer absolute reality. When the mind perceives things "in the common order of nature", or by contemplating them as external, in accordance with "chance coincidence", it has an inadequate knowledge of itself, its body, and external bodies. Contrastingly, an internal contemplation, where several things are simultaneously considered with regard to difference, agreement, or opposition, is clear and distinct (Ell,29,Schol). In the latter case, things are placed within one context and are understood in accordance with the position they occupy within that context. When placed within the ultimate and encompassing context of Substance, the contrived distinction between inner and outer is obliterated due to the fact that nothing can be eternal to God; this unity intellectually recognized at the second level of knowledge, is actually experienced in intuition.

The problem of Spinoza's designating both discursive reason and intuition as adequate is resolved in terms of the science/philosophy distinction underlying his thought. The criteria of adequacy is nothing more than being able to place ideas in the context of an encompassing system, encountered when an idea "stands in a certain logical relation to other ideas and . . . we see the necessity that it should be thus and not otherwise."[42] Inadequate ideas arise due to the fact that as "parts of a thinking being" our mind consists of its often fragmentary thoughts (IU,29). Taken in this sense, a scientific theory advanced by human reason may be viewed as adequate in terms of the coherency of its assumptions. It parallels the adequacy of the intuitive divine knowledge of reality insofar as both present us with a comprehensive and internally consistent system of ideas. The difference between the two lies in the encompassing viewpoint offered by intuition, Substance's view of the universe, of itself, as opposed to the view of the whole open to a mere mode, even if that mode is naturally endowed with discursive reason.

b. <u>The dual roles of intellect</u>. To grasp fully the importance of the reason-intuition distinction, it is necessary to investigate their common source in or working through intellect and human thought, the simultaneous progression of blessedness and understanding (EV,42,Demonst). The limits of our mental power are determined by the limits of our knowledge (EV,20,Schol), hence there is a power appropriate to each of the levels of knowledge. The higher the knowledge, or object of knowledge, the greater the power of intellect. Intuition instills the greatest possible power and perfection because its "object" is God. The highest perfection is the direct experience of reality, lying beyond the mere theoretical certainty of discursive reason.

Nonetheless, the human mind is subject to certain limitations insofar as it is human. It exists "only as thought specifically determined through ideas according to the laws of thinking nature".[43] Our thought is often subordinated to the passions and "limited by the nature of things" (TM,II,x,8). It is through reason that we are first able to reverse this situation, revealing the ethical task of subordinating the passions to the dictates of reason (as outlined in the fourth part of the Ethics). Reason emerges, then, as the functioning of human intellect qua human, with an emphasis throughout on human nature, human inter-relationships, and human goods.

Properly speaking, however, the individual intellect can be traced back to God's infinite intellect-- the divine ideas constitute our perception "in so far as He forms the essence of the human mind" (Ell,ll, Corol). These infinite ideas express the divine understanding, not as "one and the same kind of an individual thing, but an infinity of minds."[44] Insofar as we are individuals, the intellectual wealth and potential for knowledge is distributed among many. As a mode of the infinite Attribute of Thought human intellect has a set task to be fulfilled through discursive reason, namely to comprehend the divine modes and Attributes "and nothing else" (El,30), that is, not Substance directly.

Once knowledge has been attained "under the form of eternity", the mind advances to knowledge of God and "knows that it is in God and through Him" (EV,30). Intuition reveals itself as the functioning of intellect qua modification of the one Substance, being enlightened to its actual status within Substance. Thus, third level of knowledge can be truly characterized as "that of the divine mind",[45] in which intellect sheds its human limitations and experiences a mergence or oneness with the totality of the universe (EV,36). The knower/known distinction vanishes; intuition emerges as pure experience, knowledge without an object to be known. This is indeed a paradoxical state of being, and Spinoza seems justified to some extent for his reluctance to set forth more explicitly what is entailed here. This state of being is discussed further below in relation to blessedness.

Attaining such knowledge requires the assistance of the understanding, which presumably draws upon Understanding as the infinite immediate mode of the Attribute of Thought. The use of understanding is peculiar to the second and third levels of knowledge, and involves clear and distinct ideas. After his goal of "supreme human perfection" has been set, Spinoza decides that his first step towards the fulfillment of that goal is to amend human understanding (in line with infinite Understanding), "rendering it capable of understanding things in the manner necessary for attaining our end" (IU,6). But the goal of perfection, if carried beyond human character, demands more than discursive reason has to give, precisely that more encompassed by intuition. Reason is but a step in the right direction, that is, away from imagination. Intuition yields blessedness of the highest sort, is able to nullify the limiting effects of human understanding.

The dynamics of the desired advance of knowledge become evident in the gradual ascent through the three levels of knowledge. The individual intellect must uncover the intervening layers which obscure the sole and encompassing reality of Substance. Beginning with the experience of finite modes alone, the mind enlarges its field through memory and signs derived from sense experience. Discursive reason then objectifies previously subjective responses to its environment by turning its attention to mediate and immediate infinite modes, the 'fixed and eternal things' such as Motion and Rest, and the divine Attributes of Thought and Extension. Thus are formed the 'common notions', consistencies or laws of Nature reconstructed by scientific investigation: "elementary spatial and physical properties of bodies".[46] Finally, the properly amended intellect progresses to a direct contemplation of Substance via intuition.

In moving from the passive acceptance exhibited by imagination, being acted upon by modes, the intellect begins to exert its own power. Through discursive reason it "makes for itself intellectual instruments" with which to pursue its tasks (IU,11). The Attributes appear to be among these instruments. Reasoning is employed to bolster what is self-evident, validating each step in the chain. However, this chain of reasoning is not required for a person who acquires new ideas "in the proper order according to the standard of the original true idea" (that is, by intuition) for truth "makes itself manifest, and all things would flow, as it were, spontaneously toward him" (IU,15-16). In the absence of this optimum situation, the chain of reasoning must be laboriously set forth. From the known, the unknown is deduced and proved; from premises, logical conclusions are drawn (TP,VII). The mind actively conceives, rather than passively perceiving, its ideas (EII,def 3 and explanation).

A new realm of being presents itself on the level of discursive reason to aid us in gaining knowledge--

the logical beings or things of reason (entia rationis) function as aids for the reconstruction of reality in a way conducive to the human mind. Many intriguing references to the things of reason are found in Spinoza's little-discussed appendix to Principles of the Philosophy of René Descartes, giving support to the attempt to identify second order knowledge with the realm of intellectual constructions. The logical entities are termed "modes of thinking", modes of a mode. They fail to live up to the criteria of true ideas due to a lack of corresponding ideata, falling into the category of unvalidated, but not necessarily invalid, ideas. Thus, they can be judged neither true nor false, or are true only insofar as they are not hypostatized. Adequacy is possible for the things of reason if they present a coherent view of reality.

Unfortunately, human intellect exhibits a marked tendency to confuse logical beings with actual ideas. It is essential that we distinguish between an investigation of "the nature of things", and one of "the modes through which we perceive them" (TM,I,i,9), or between the way the world is and the conceptual framework through which we comprehend it. Things of reason are known by God (in absolute reality) not as modes of divine Thought, or objectively, but only as God "conceives and creates the human mind exactly as it is constituted" (TM,II,vii,4). And our mind is so constituted that we do work with logical entities and indeed must work with them on the secondary level of knowledge.

There are those who might object that the things of reason border dangerously close to the realm of imagination, tending to blur the distinctions between the first and second levels of knowledge. However, it does seem legitimate for Spinoza to build upon the insights of a lower level when these have been transformed to function within the framework of a higher order of knowledge. Correspondingly, intuition builds upon the basic insights developed in the second level of knowledge (EV,28), and even appears to be unthinkable without such prior knowledge. The three levels naturally flow into one another as water in a canal, however each level is separated from the others by locks which must be firmly sealed before the level of water, as of knowledge, can be raised or lowered.

Listed among the things of reason is the human ideal of a perfect individual (ST,II,iv), as well as the interaction of good and evil where these are relative terms of comparison (ST,I,x). None of these exist in Nature per se, but serve a function similar to that of Kant's regulative ideas in directing our, ultimately ethical, aspirations. While well aware of these restrictions, Spinoza does not hesitate to employ potentially deceptive terms, such as good and evil, nor to outline the course of human perfection. These inconsistencies can be successfully explained only by referring the dubious discussions to the level of second order knowledge, or discursive reason. The suspect terms are useful for the construction of an intellectual model conducive to the advance of human understanding, up to a certain point, that point being intuition. The latter, as the "clearest knowledge", has no need of "the art of reasoning" (my italics) (ST,II,i). As a mode of Substance's Attributes of Thought, thinking pertains to the nature of human intellect (E11,axiom 2), a situation which demands a certain amount of intellectual satisfaction en route to the perfected state of knowledge. Unlike Kant, Spinoza does not believe that our striving is based on the "als ob", but rather that blessedness is an unrealized reality for all, requiring only the proper adjustment of viewpoint to be revealed (see EV,33 and Schol). Yet both Spinoza and Kant do agree on the "as if" status of reason and its products.

Through the Attributes open to our perception, Thought and Extension, we are able to develop our knowledge further. Significantly, however, as observed previously, the term Attribute is defined by Spinoza as something perceived by intellect "as if constituting its [Substance's] essence" (my italics) (E1,def 4). Moreover, Spinoza states that "besides substances and modes nothing is assumed" (E1,15,Demonst), based on axiom one--"Everything which is, is either in itself or in another." An Attribute fits in neither category-- it is not "in itself" but derived from Substance, nor "in another" inasmuch as God is not "other" than its Attributes. In sum, it has utility rather than clear cut reality for Spinoza, appropriate to its use in second order knowledge.

Also of note is the fact that true ideas are judged possible arising from "non-existent modifications" when "comprehended in something else" through which they can be conceived (E1,8,Schol). In effect, then, a fragmentary and even questionable existence of Attributes and some modes applied in the advance of knowledge is justified if taken in the context of the real, Substance, as overriding conception. The characterizations of Nature as "naturing" (<u>Naturans</u>) and "natured" (<u>Naturata</u>) likewise may be interpreted as things of reason, imposed by the human intellect to facilitate its understanding through the categories of producer and product. Reason is permitted, and often compelled, to elaborate on its bits and pieces of reality for, ultimately, the "<u>order and connection of ideas is the same as the order and connection of things</u>" (EII,7).

Second order knowledge originally was characterized by Spinoza as a firm belief in the external reality of things as they are perceived, engendered by some proof (ST,II,iv,note). Belief is opposed to knowledge or "immediate union with the thing"; the former "can only tell me what the things <u>ought</u> to be and not what it really <u>is</u>, [my italics] otherwise it would not be different from <u>Knowing</u>". But belief is different. It is merely an intellectual awareness of the things external to us, "a clearer [not clearest] understanding" fostering the direct experience of the love of God (ST,II,iv). The recognizably logical "ought" applied to belief by Spinoza signifies a certain limitation at the second level of knowledge which, while rationally persuasive, does not allow a direct confrontation with reality. There remains in belief or discursive reason an inability "to unite us with the object of our belief", and thereby eliminate the subject-object distinction. When the object in question is God, such union and its attendant peace is <u>the</u> goal. As Spinoza assures us "between these two [second and third level knowledge] there is a great difference" (ST,II,iv).

Belief, nonetheless, does engender the initial stages of the love of God in terms of the gradual perfection of intellect. Knowledge of a moral sort results as well, "the knowledge of good and evil" (again, taken in a relative sense, relative to the "ideal" of the perfect human being). It likewise becomes possible to suppress the passions, an operation prefacing talk of salvation in the <u>Ethics</u>, as is discussed in conjunction with the human ideal of virtue/power.

If additional proof is required, Spinoza has graciously provided us with an unequivocal statement of his views:

> reasoning is not the principal thing in us,

> but only like a staircase by which we can climb up to the desired place, or like a good genius which, without any falsity or deception, brings us tidings of the highest good [intuition and its subsequent peace] in order thereby to stimulate us to pursue it, and to become united with it; which union is our supreme happiness and bliss. (ST,II,xxvi)

The case can hardly be stated more clearly than this. Reason is a means to a higher end, indispensible in its own right but more important in its being finally transcended. Its certainty is shown to be compatible with an intermediary status. The philosopher must not to dally on the staircase when fulfillment awaits in the rooms above.

In the Ethics, Spinoza questions the ultimate validity of discursive reason and clarifies his previous strategy. While the demonstration in part one of the Ethics, the dependence of all things on God, including the human mind, is "legitimate and placed beyond the possibility of doubt", it is not as strong as "a proof from the essence itself of any individual object which we say depends upon God" (EV,36,Schol). Only the particularity through which intuition grasps its knowledge, penetrating to essences, serves our highest ends. The logic which deals with the "ought" cannot be as convincing as the "is" derived from individual existence, especially when that individual is dependent upon God, the encompassing particular.

What remains for discursive reason is the irreplaceable task of directing intellect to the proper path. Scientific or second level knowledge is charged with instilling logical coherence into our system of ideas, arranging them in "the order of the intellect."[47] One function of philosophy is "to effect theoretical ordering of the available fund of knowledge."[48] Of course, this fund does not yet include the encompassing reality given by intuition, but a close approximation by discursive reason through the infinite modes and the Attributes.

The virtue of logic epistemologically for Spinoza, as Hampshire sees it, is in providing an explanation for "the imbecility of our reason and the relative inadequacy of our knowledge."[49] Being rule-oriented, discursive reason indeed can point to what is "better" or more useful for human nature, without granting enjoyment in the process (the conjunction of the necessary and the desired being reserved for intuition) (ST,II,xxi). The confusing and inadequate "common order of nature" (EII,29,Corol) can be submitted to the systematizing influence of human reason, making it more conducive to our understanding, if not allowing us to experience it immediately.

Spinoza considered logic, the science of reason, as a means for the perfection of intellect, a process of identifying true and adequate ideas as set forth in The Improvement of the Understanding. The characteristic example of certainty cited by Spinoza is a comparison of knowledge of the nature of a triangle engendering the knowledge that its three angles are equal to two right angles, with the logical inference of God's existence from knowledge of the divine nature. This is a discursive, if-then, type of "proof", appropriate only to second order knowledge. The immediacy of intuition is lacking, even though we might consider these conclusions ingrained truths.

If, as has been assumed, the greater part of the Ethics is written from the viewpoint of second order knowledge as a preparation for the briefly-discussed intuitive knowledge/experience of blessedness, what effect does this have upon our consideration of its "logical" propositions? A good, and perhaps the only, case in point concerns Spinoza's characterization of God, of what God "ought" to be like in order to fulfill the role of encompassing reality. This question has already been covered in terms of metaphysical 'otherness'. Given an adequate definition of godhead the divine properties can be derived by a process of logical deduction. God must be the starting point of our discussions simply because all else follows from the one reality. Of course, some of these logically necessitated properties, such as oneness, have been exposed as ultimately indefensible.[50]

Spinoza's correspondence confirms that he did not pretend to have a knowledge of the actual interconnection of the "parts" of Nature (which is God): "for to know this it would be necessary to know the whole of Nature and all its Parts", which obviously exceeds the grasp of our intellects insofar as they are human and finite (as opposed to our capacity for infinitude through intuition).[51] Granting a knowledge of the "parts" (modes) of the systematic unity of the universe, the integration of these eludes discursive reason, except as reflected in logical constructions.

Nor does an anthropomorphic approach help matters.
When we endow our idea of God with the traits of human
intellect, such as willing, we are treating it improp-
erly; a triangle would no less certainly attempt to
argue for God's triangularity or a circle for divine
circularity.[52]

How then can Spinoza presume to delineate the
essence of Substance for us in the first part of the
<u>Ethics</u> and yet maintain a philosophically pure con-
science? Only by distinguishing between pronouncements at the different levels of discursive reason and
intuition can Spinoza's credibility be spared. He
himself professes an inability to imagine (as at the
first level) God, although he can well (rationally)
conceive God:

> I do not say that I know God entirely, but
> only that I understand some of His attri-
> butes, though not all, not even the greater
> part of them, and it is certain that our
> ignorance of the majority of them does not
> hinder our having a knowledge of some of
> them.[53]

The fact that the Attributes of Thought and Extension
are nothing more than certain points of view which we,
as thinking and extended beings, have of the one
Substance, each relating back to the same reality,
allows us to entertain the confidence expressed by
Spinoza, while remaining aware that there is something
more. We possess "the true idea of God which is
within",[54] the basis of the a posteriori proof of
God's existence (TM,II,i,1). An a priori proof of the
existence of God is possible in terms of the divine
essence, or more specifically, the "true definition of
His essence" (TM,II,i,1). Reason simply follows out
the logical conclusions of this essence.

Discursive reason does have an essential role to
play in the Spinozistic system. The "<u>effort or desire
to know things</u>" intuitively springs from human reason,
but not from opinion (EV,28). Spinoza himself blazes a
trail directly through the realm of discursive reason.
The value of true belief lies in its being "the way to
true knowledge . . . the final end" (ST,II,iv). Once we
have perfected our reason, the virtue/power appropriate
to human nature <u>qua</u> human, a microcosm corresponding to
the universal macrocosm, exists also; the next step
involves the recognition that this inner state corresponds to, and duplicates the necessity of, absolute

reality in God or Substance. In short, the essence is expressed directly, intuitively, because all-is-one. As in Taoism, the unity of reality precludes the need for an object in intuitive knowledge, except insofar as intuition is the experience of the universal shared Self.

As for the specifics of the third level of knowledge, the intuitive, <u>scientia</u> <u>intuitiva</u>, besides being the "<u>highest effort</u>" of intellect, its means of understanding yields the "<u>highest virtue</u>" (EV,25). The term 'intuitive science' is borrowed from Descartes, and indicates something in opposition to both 'inductio' and 'deductio'.[55] Taking up where discursive reason leaves off, intuition works from "an adequate idea of certain attributes of God" to the "adequate knowledge of the essence of things" (Ell,40,Schol 2). The "absolutely true and adequate idea of the single comprehensive system" is revealed reflecting the universe.[56] Intellect proceeds from the logical "ought" of the Attributes to the "is" of the divine essence.

The underpinning of Spinoza's epistemology, which makes our second and third level knowledge adequate or possible at all, is, not surprisingly, metaphysical. The fact that everything is <u>in</u> God, that our thought derives from the divine Attribute of Thought and our understanding from the infinite immediate mode of Understanding, assures us, not only that we can have knowledge of reality, but, furthermore, that that knowledge can be clear and distinct, a direct insight into the absolute reality. As modes, we have an open, if often unobserved, line to the ground of being. This situation facilitates the move from the second to the third level of knowledge, and actually makes it possible. When we learn we do not recollect what had been known previously, as Plato would have it; rather, knowledge is a revelation of our nature and position in the universe, in the one Substance under its all-containing Elementary character.

It has previously been noted that the human mind shares in the infinite intellect of God. Hence, to say that a human mind has a perception is equivalent to saying that God has a certain idea, "not indeed in so far as He is infinite, but in so far as He forms the essence of the human mind" (El,11,Corol).

The fact that the essence of the human mind is divine allows us to attain knowledge. All ideas of existent things "necessarily" involve God's eternal and infinite essence (II,45), and this knowledge cannot be anything but adequate and perfect (46), being common to "part" as well as "whole" (38). And so it is that "the infinite essence and the eternity of God are known to all" (EII,47,Schol).

Alternately expressed, Spinoza refers to the "light of natural reason" or "light of Nature" (lux naturae), a power by which we are able to grasp truth without having recourse to a supernatural revelation disruptive of the law and order of Nature. God communicates knowledge to the human individual, not by "external signs" or direct intercourse, as asserted in the Old Testament, but through "the mere essence of God and the understanding of man" as we stand "in immediate union with" God (ST,II,xxiv). Both the divine mind and its "eternal thoughts" are "impressed" upon all human minds (TP,I). Spinoza refers to "the eternal wisdom of God" as manifest in everything but "more especially in the human mind".[57] To the extent that an idea is related to God, that is to say, the extent to which that idea is in God and hence agrees with its ideatum, that idea is true (EII,32 and Demonst).

We already have had occasion to mention the function of adequate ideas in Spinoza's epistemology. When traced to their source in the ultimate reality of God, the reason for their adequacy is made clear. In applying the term adequate to an idea, Spinoza explains, one is referring to "the nature of the idea itself",[58] a nature that is useful in grasping the way in which its "facts" are interconnected.[59] When contributed by discursive reason, these ideas, then, are the foundation for the intellectual reconstruction of the universe, paralleling the system of God. The adequate ideas, also designated 'common notions' (notiones communes), are held in common by all things, present in the part as well as in the whole, and must entail an adequate conception (EII,38). Being adequate, they can be distinguished from notions "derived from popular usage", inasmuch as the latter provide an explanation of Nature "not as it is in itself [by "motion, rest, and their laws"], but as it appears to human sense."[60] Popular notions are relativistic, and hence inadequate; common notions, whose scope extends to all things (modes), human and non-human alike, are absolute, reflecting the "logically necessary constitution of the universe".[61]

From this state of affairs follows Spinoza's firm conviction in the truth of his philosophy. Beyond the necessity of human logic, there is the assurance that our mind, the source of the logical constructions, is linked to the ultimate reality. Among the properties of a true (as opposed to merely adequate) idea is its certainty, of which we can harbor no doubt, along with its clarity and distinctness (TM,I,vi,6). The highest truth is intuitive. The person who knows what is true can never doubt that knowledge, just as a person who is awake cannot conceive that she/he is dreaming; the deceived individual, on the other hand, is like the dreamer who believes herself/himself to be awake (ST, II,xv). Cartesian doubts, and even the common questionings of reality, are totally alien to Spinoza and his system of thought. We always have some grasp on reality, however tenuous it may be.

Spinoza displays an utter faith in the logical certainty which displaces human prejudice, the necessity which leads irrevocably from clear and distinct ideas or definitions to impeccable conclusions.[62] Certitude and truth are not found in things themselves (TM,I,vi,6), rather they are found in that of which those things are modifications. Truth is to a true idea as whiteness is to a white body; whiteness is logically prior to the instance of a white body, just as truth (God) is logically prior to the true idea, and the truth value of the latter, its coherence with reality, is dependent upon the ultimate reality (TM,I, vi,5).

      c. The knowledge/experience of blessedness. Having determined that it is the path of intuition, leading through and beyond the realm of discursive reason, which is essential for the highest ends of Spinozistic philosophy and, moreover, that the truth and adequacy of our knowledge is assured by our intimate relationship with Substance, there remains the question of what exactly is the nature of intuitively-engendered blessedness. As the Transformative manifestation of the feminine principle, blessedness may be translated as feminine wisdom, under which heading are included feminine understanding and feminine consciousness. The first of these involves a personal participation in the one reality, with intuition's immediacy engendered by a lack of a subject/object or knower/known distinction. Feminine consciousness is dependent upon the flow of intuition from the center of one's being and involving that entire being.

A possible problem of the transformation to blessedness emerges in certain of Spinoza's statements which suggest that the human mind has inherent limitations. These would seem to preclude the possibility of attaining of blessedness. The mind is capable of knowing only those things which involve the idea of "an actually existing body" and what can be inferred from such an idea; "Therefore the mind's power of understanding only extends to those things which this idea of the Body contains in itself, or which follows from the same."[63] So it would seem that the range of our thought is restricted to the range of the body, of which the mind is an idea. The upward ascent of knowledge is thus stagnated at the level of discursive reason, the level most conducive to human nature, the nature of our bodies (EIV,35,Demonst).

However, any such problems of inherent human limitations easily can be circumvented by resorting to the dynamics of the threefold levels of reality. Blessedness, by its very nature, transcends the secondary level appropriate to human power by adhering to the level of intuition and transforms our being qua human or modal reality into being qua absolute reality, the reality of Substance. If the second and third levels of knowledge were not differentiated, blessedness would not be possible at all. Along with the expansion of being comes an expansion of our epistemological horizons; indeed, it is difficult to determine which of these occurs first, for they are intimately interconnected.

The body itself undergoes a change in status in light of intuitive knowledge. Prior to his discussion of blessedness, and immediately following an assessment of reason's role, Spinoza declares that he is passing "to the consideration of those matters which appertain to the duration of the mind without relation to the body" (EV,20,Schol). From the tone of Spinoza's remarks, he makes it quite clear that herein lies the culmination of the perfected intellect beyond the human condition, to be mentioned later in relation to the question of immortality.

The "participation" aspect of intuition occurs through a gradual shedding of human finitude. The mind must conceive of itself "under the form of eternity", sub species aeternitatis; "in so far as the mind is eternal it has a knowledge of God, which is necessarily adequate" (EV,31,Demonst). With regard to its own eternality (its share in reality, in Substance, as a mode), the mind "is fitted to know all those things which follow from the knowledge of God". Such knowledge is of the third, intuitive level (EV,31,Demonst). In other words, intuition belongs to the mind "by virtue of its being a part of the infinite intellect of God."[64]

The individual body attached to such a mind is not entirely excluded from consideration at this level. One must "conceive the essence of the body under the form of eternity" (EV,29,Demonst). This means conceiving the body under the Attributes of Extension, as modification of eternal Substance, resulting in a knowledge of God and of our being in and conceived through God (EV,30). Intuition is defined as "knowledge of individual objects" (EV,36,Schol), the particulars which have God for their cause and which are the only things that rightfully can claim God as their cause (ST,I,vi).

The radical extent of "participation" required for intuitive knowledge has been a cause for concern among interpreters of Spinoza's thought, many of whom question the feasibility of the perfection for which discursive reason strives--"there is a very good reason why one can never hope to attain it with any completeness", namely, that we ourselves would have to become God.[65] Perhaps this objectionable conclusion is not as absurd as it might seem, for, in the context of the Spinozistic system, although we ourselves do not become God, blessedness does constitute a union with God. The mergence of mode with Substance, or revelation of non-differentiation, is quite similar to the Taoist's experience--to know Tao is to be Tao. The ultimate perfection of the intellect is none other than the attainment of the highest possible state of reality (Substance) because Spinoza recognizes no distinction between reality and perfection (EII,def 6).

More precisely, our mental apparatus reaches the point at which it is able to experience the state of absolute reality directly. This reality is no longer obscured by intervening elements of human relativities, nor must it be mediated by the logical reconstruction of discursive reason. Intuition reflects the process of divine understanding which cannot be characterized in terms of "discursive reason" (TM,II,vii,1). Hence, intuitive knowledge is the actual means by which the divine may be said to understand its own being.

This mysterious mergence of God and mode which is the essence of the blessedness experience is referred to by Spinoza as the intellectual love of God. By love of the Eros/relatedness type the subject/object distinction of knower and known, lover and beloved, is eliminated. Discursive reason requires such distinctions in order to comprehend the situation abstractly, to categorize reality and bring it within the scope of our human limitations. The true state of affairs is one of nondifferentiation: "the love of God towards men and the intellectual love of the mind towards God are one and the same thing" (EV,36,Demonst). The use of the term "intellectual" is somewhat deceptive here, for it refers to the role of intellect in the Eros experience, a role not confined to the use of discursive reason, although it has been interpreted often as purely rational. Reason prepares the path for intellect, but the love of God itself can only be embraced intuitively.

The God-mode union rests upon the fact that we already are united to God in terms of being (metaphysically) as well as being known (epistemologically), demanding a knowledge as direct as that union is itself (ST,II,xxii). Engendered by this 'immediate union' is 'intellectual enjoyment' of the known. The enjoyment follows from Spinoza's definition of love as joy attended by the idea of an external cause (Elll,def 6). Intellect rejoices at having realized its position in the ultimate reality. God likewise experiences bliss in self-love, without an external cause: "the nature of God delights in infinite perfection accompanied . . . with the idea of Himself" (EV,35,Demonst).

And from intuition alone arises the "peace of mind" which is such a strong motive force behind Spinoza's philosophical enterprise, culminating in the "highest human perfection" (that is, the highest human reality) (EV,27 and Demonst). Our consciousness of self and God (reality) increases as we strengthen our intuitive knowledge, and "the more perfect and happier" we become (Ev,31,Schol). Here indeed lies the ground for the realization of Spinoza's goal of "continuous, supreme, and unending happiness". By emphasizing that in us which is eternal, which both underlies and transcends the world of merely human perceptions (by sense data) and conceptions (by discursive reason), one cannot but reach contentment and a sense of secure belonging.

The Eros/relatedness characterizing blessedness is unique in the human experience. Sense knowledge is too fragmentary to allow for a vision of the encompassing reality, while discursive reason provides the logical framework of the unity but is unable to impart the experience of this "whole". In other words, reason "has no power to lead us to the <u>attainment</u> of our well-being" (my italics) (ST,II, xxii), even though it may well be able to indicate in what that well-being consists. It does not allow us directly to experience the ultimate reality, and is "only known to us through the conviction of our understanding"; judged far superior to this is the "<u>clear knowledge</u>" which employs no reasons to convince us, but rather, the actual "feeling and enjoying the thing itself" (ST,II,ii). In this respect, Spinoza's thought obviously conforms to the radical empiricism of the feminine perspective, whereby the highest knowledge or wisdom is experiential.

    To return to our earlier analogy of the Spinozistic universe as a theatre in the round, the three levels of knowledge can be represented by three kinds of patrons. The devotees of imagination, the majority of people, occupy the outer reaches of the theatre and their view of the action (reality) is obstructed. Thus, they only have a vague idea of the substance of the play, and are continually distracted by surrounding events. Those at the level of reason are seated much closer to the stage. Moreover, their understanding of the action is enhanced by the fact that they have prepared themselves by reading the script beforehand. Thus reason makes the order of the universe palatable to the human mind. However, in both these cases the individuals remain mere spectators of the action on the stage. Intuitive knowledge alone, which entitles us to a front row seat, also brings with it the revelation that the play involves audience participation, that each of us plays a role in the cosmic spectacle. Although all of us are indeed actors and actresses, those endowed with intuition are unique in possessing experiential knowledge of reality--they share in the drama of reality. Reality does not, cannot, change, but our point of view can.

    Discursive reason confirms, through its own deductions, that the intellectual love of God is our highest good (EV,20,Demonst), and that it should be uppermost in our minds (EV,16). Thus, it points beyond itself to a higher experiential knowledge. The virtue of intuition lies in its having an "object" of love which is both eternal and immutable, in contrast to the inconstant objects by which we are commonly affected (EV,20,Schol). Properly speaking, of course, God cannot be an external object for us, that is, cannot be considered totally transcendent. Our own being is favorably augmented by embracing such a love: we are positively affected by it and our power is increased. The important difference separating human love from the intellectual love of God is that the latter "has no beginning", is always in our possession, although generally unrealized. In the same way, the perfections which we imagine to develop from the intellectual love of God are constant in us; while joy consists in "the passage to a greater perfection", blessedness signifies "that the mind is endowed with perfection itself" (EV, 33,Schol).

Hinging upon "participation" is a further distinguishing aspect of intuition, immediacy. Intuition is 'immediate apprehension',[66] a direct insight into the ground of being. No discursive process of deduction or inference intervenes between the encounter with God or reality and knowledge thereof. However indispensible discursive reason may be, it only can hope to instill the order preparatory to intuition. We cannot rationalize our way to direct knowledge-experience of reality. Nothing can contradict the joyful experience of blessedness, which is immediately known. The flash of intuition dawns upon the perfected intellect after manner of enlightenment; we become enlightened to the state of reality sub species aeternitatis, we see reality as God sees it.

Spinoza's intellectual love of God also qualifies as feminine consciousness, in that our knowledge is drawn from the center of our being. This Eros is an "eternal truth", following necessarily from the nature of our mind. The intellectual love of God has nothing contrary to it in Nature, and there is nothing by which it can be negated (EV,37,Demonst). The feminine consciousness of intuition flows from our entire being, as indicated by the intimate integration of body and mind in Spinozistic thought. These two are merely the physical and mental manifestations of one essence. Based on the human body's fitness "for many things", its ability to escape the agitation of evil affects, Spinoza concludes that such a body may possess a mind with an extensive knowledge of itself and of God. This mind also would be eternal in its "greatest or principle part" (EV,39,Schol and Demonst). More specifically, that part of the mind which is eternal is the intellect (EV,40,Corol). The contradictory, and unfeminine, separation of mind and body by Spinoza to insure immortality is discussed below under ethics, with suggestions for a reconstruction in accordance with the feminine perspective.

In sum, the evolution of human knowledge has been carefully laid out by Spinoza through his three levels of knowledge-common sense experience of an unreflective sort, mere being, stagnated at the level of finite modes, yields to the logical analysis and systematizing of discursive reason through infinite modes and the divine Attributes, being through human nature. Building upon these revelations, the intellect sheds its finitude and narrowly-human orientation, approaching the true reality of Substance through a knowledge which is pre-eminently a state of eternal being. The "ought" (the rational reconstruction of the universe) finally reveals itself as the immediately known "is" (the all-encompassing oneness of reality). Spinoza can thus be considered a rationalist by virtue of intermediate methodology, but not in terms of ultimate intentions.

Spinoza's decision to relegate reason, and with it science, to the level of second order knowledge is indeed prophetic. He realized that our human theories are merely mental reconstructions of the absolute reality, even before Western thought had succumbed to Newtonian physics and its claim to have unveiled the rational principles of the universe. Only recently has the 'cracked paradigm' of a mechanistic universe been challenged by the often paradoxical pronouncements of quantum mechanics.[67] We are just beginning to rediscover Spinoza's realization that the conception of cosmic order which is able to satisfy human intellect does not necesarily do justice to reality. The Spinozistic scheme of knowledge demonstrates its feminine roots as it tends towards a culmination in what is arational and amasculine, transcendent of both rationality and typical masculine values of assertion and ego-centeredness. The scheme allows us to perfect the highest aspect of human nature, namely discursive reason, while leaving open the ultimate perfection of the intuitive level through the infinite intellect, insofar as it shares in absolute reality. The move to intuition is supported by the metaphysical revelation of a unified Substance. The philosopher who has constructed a rational system reflective of the universal system of things remains receptive to a higher knowledge which both incorporates and transcends human efforts. The externals of sense perception and linguistic convention are inadequate and confused, and one must turn inward instead. The adequacy of our innate human discursive reason comes from its being a precisely scaled model of the ultimate reality. Yet we must turn inward even further, to the very source of our existence, for the intuitive truth which is identical with the absolute reality and absolute existence of Substance.

The cornerstone of Spinozistic epistemology is none other than the metaphysical assumption of Substance constituting human intellect qua mode. Hence, knowledge which results from the inward-turning of the second level of knowledge and is identified with the outer reality in the third level can be adjudged adequate. Within is the "light of natural reason", which insures the flow of knowledge from Substance or God to modes or individual intellects, in accordance with the structure of Nature.

Adequate ideas, or common notions, represent the fund of knowledge accessible to us, the knowledge which penetrates all aspects of existence due to the very fact that they do exist. Given these assumptions, Spinoza cannot entertain the least doubt as to the truth of his ideas and denies the possiblity of a deceitful deity, àla Descartes (see IU,30-31). Although this faith may seem excessive to those of us who are able to doubt even our own reality, it does follow from the acceptance of a universe pervaded with varying degrees of being and reality.

The highest knowledge of Spinozistic epistemology, that of intuition, has the effect of transforming our being as well as enriching our intellect. The mind and body are conceived sub species aeternitatis, as manifestations of eternal Substance. In this way the limitations of human existence are transcended, and our being is revealed in its primal configuration with the ground of being. In the knowledge/experience of the intellectual love of God, the subject-object distinction is eliminated, encompassing the loving/loved status of both mode and ground of being within the net of Eros/relatedness. From this love springs the ultimate joy or bliss experienced simultaneously by the individual mind and God, the blessedness or profound 'peace of mind' sought by Spinoza as the proper goal of philosophy.

The superiority of intuitive knowledge over both mundane sense experience and discursive reason, is manifest in the former's radical empiricism, feminine knowledge which is experience. The feeling of joy in the intellectual love of God imparts conviction far greater than the fragmented sense data of first level knowledge or even the logical deductions of the secondary level. Discursive reason itself points the way to this ultimate experience. Herein is revealed the truth of our ever-present perfection, and the realization that the intellectual love of God is eternal, what always has been and always will be the case. Thus emerges the immediacy of intuition which demands, not the developmental process of discursive reason, but the immediate recognition of reality as such.

Finally, feminine consciousness establishes the source of the intellectual love of God as inherent in our very nature, and upheld by the system of Nature. Intuitive knowledge concerns our entire being, reflecting the lack of a mind/body distinction in Spinozism. The fitness of the body for multiple functionings determines the fitness of the mind for attaining the knowledge required for perfection of the intellect.

B. Modes of Being: Philosophy as Praxis

The dual manifestations of Substance, under the Elementary and Transformative characters, has been examined in order to outline the structural aspects of the Spinozistic universe which qualify it as feminine in perspective. In passing to the equally feminine modes of being we become aware of the pattern of behavior, the rules of life, appropriate for an individual who embraces the foregoing metaphysical and epistemological scheme. To complete the cycle of the Transformative character, Spinoza includes the masculine method of discursive reason for perfecting the human intellect, that is, of making it real. Again this perfection culminates in feminine intuitive knowledge, the blessedness of the intellectual love of God as an experience of our highest state of being in the one Substance--the ultimate mode of being for the human individual as a mode of absolute Being.

The three modes of being recognized under the feminine principle--(a) inwardness or all-is-one-ness, (b) receptivity, and (c) materiality, a harmonious link with Nature--represent alternate expressions of a single movement towards the wholeness of reality. Each is given consideration here with regard first to ethics, and then to socio-political thought. In other words, what is presented are the practical applications and implications of Spinoza's theoretical framework of philosophy on both an individual and a communal scale.

Spinoza displayed an abiding interest and concern for both ethical and social-political questions within the context of philosophy. It is significant that his major work bears the title of the Ethics (Ethices). Widespread dispute has erupted over the appropriateness of that title in relation to the contents of the text. However, is seems inappropriate only when the term ethics is taken in its common, and much-restricted, usage, a usage at variance with the basic tenets of Spinozism and its intimately interconnected universe of oneness. Correspondingly, a considerable proportion of Spinoza's intellectual energies, particularly at the end of his life, were devoted to the development of a political philosophy which was a logical extension of, and pragmatic support for, his thought. Few philosophers have attempted such an encompassing philosophical scheme, founded on the premise that, if a theory is true it must apply to all areas of life. Substance serves as a model in this respect, for its reality permeates all levels of existence.

The most convincing proof of this intention in Spinoza's philosophy is framed in his own words "to show what service to our own lives a knowledge of this doctrine is":

1. "it teaches us that we do everything by the will of God alone, and that we are partakers of the divine nature in proportion as our actions become more and more perfect and we more and more understand God . . . it teaches us in what our highest happiness or blessedness consists, namely, in the knowledge of God alone"
2. "it teaches us how we ought to behave with regard to the things of fortune, or those which are not in our power . . . which do not follow from our own nature"
3. "contributes to the welfare of our social existence, since it teaches us to hate no one, to despise no one, to mock no one, to be angry with no one, and to envy no one . . . to be content with his own and to be helpful to his neighbor . . . by the guidelines of reason alone"
4. "contributes not a little to the advantage of common society, in so far as it teaches us by what means citizens are to be governed and led; not in order that they may be slaves, but that they may freely do those things which are best (Ell,49).

These points cover metaphysics and epistemology (1),

personal (2) and interpersonal (3) morality, and sociopolitical philosophy (4), and all with an end to practical applications. With a few modifications in terminology, they could serve as an outline for any feminine philosophy.

The inwardness mode of being emerges in ethics as the movement toward perfection of our inherent human nature, toward what constitutes virtue, while in the socio-political realm, it is expressed as the all-in-one-ness of communal commitments. Receptivity to reality is essential for the ethical ideal of the philosopher, the individual who acts under the guidance of reason (perfected human nature), as well as for the sovereign(s) and citizens of a commonwealth. The individual relies upon Nature for support in developing the virtue/power of her or his specific nature. Similarly, the successful civil state, although well-advanced beyond the primal state of Nature, remains in harmony with natural law and order (reality), following from the communal observance of the dictates of reason.

1. Ethics: Relating to the Universe

Ethics, as conceived by Spinoza and others in feminine philosophy, encompasses an area far broader than that associated with contemporary ethical philosophy. The notion of ethics as being concerned solely with human interrelationships, although well-suited to the limitations of the masculine perspective, which possesses a Weltanschauung that embraces the universe as a whole, without discriminations. Appropriately, then, Spinoza's feminine code of ethics outlines the conduct recommended for those who seek to live in harmonious interaction with reality, in terms of both Substance or Nature and their own human nature.

These far-ranging feminine parameters of thought must be kept firmly in mind when considering Spinozistic ethics. It is equally significant that Spinoza does not indulge in idle theorizing to impose a code of conduct, the 'ought', exceeding human capacities, the 'is'; it is only necessary to live up to our inherent nature to be ethical in a feminine philosophy. Ways are proposed by which to implement our knowledge of the structure of the universe, including our own human nature, ways which derive their concreteness and realism from feminine metaphysics and epistemology. The result is a life of peace and happiness, judged by Spinoza's feminine standards of what constitutes happiness. As an adherent of feminine philosophy,

Spinoza, like the Taoist, places great faith in human
nature, assuming it to be intrinsically good and the
underlying support of society once inhibiting factors
are eradicated.

    a. <u>Inwardness-the perfection of human virtue/power.</u>
As indicated by the epistemological levels, the ascent
of knowledge requires that we turn increasingly inward,
leaving the superficial externalities of sense data for
the constructions of discursive reason, and these for
a microcosmic/macrocosmic insight into the ground of
being via intuition. By turning from the external
impingements productive of the passions to the self-
reliance of actions through a cultivation of intellect,
the process of perfection proceeds. In this process
virtue is revealed as none other than power, the power
of acting rather than being acted upon, which follows
from our individual nature. To follow that nature,
it is necessary first to know what it consists of, thus
ignorance of the self is equated with ignorance "of the
foundation of all the virtues" (ElV,56,Demonst).

    The result of the inward-turning mode of being,
then, is a determination of what constitutes virtue,
and specifically, human virtue, within the context of a
feminine universe. The urge towards wholeness becomes
for Spinoza an urge towards perfection. Although we
must pass through masculine second level perfection of
our human essence, the ultimate feminine goal is
intuitive integration with reality or, more precisely,
a realization of an already existing integration.
Discursive reason is our guide in this process insofar
as it embodies the power of human beings <u>qua</u> human,
and has pragmatic rather than absolute <u>value</u>.

    Demonstrating his masculine inclinations,Spinoza
employs these assumptions concerning virtue to rationalize his position on the natural superiority of human
beings in relation to other living things. Yet the
rational enlightened egoism emerging from the sense of
common humanity, of all human individuals sharing a
like nature, yields to the feminine positive narcissism
characterizing Spinozistic ethics and, most especially,
its code of human interrelationships. Sustaining this
ethical code is the universal motivation of self-
preservation, <u>conatus</u>, combined with the underlying
realization that other human beings can be supportive
of our survival. Feminine ethics thereby protects self-
interest in terms of the shared Self.

    In its most fundamental form, the inwardness mode

mode of being of the feminine principle aims at wholeness. The perfection or fulfillment of the self, of one's nature, entails the fullest possible integration into reality by playing out one's appointed role in the cosmic action. This seems to have been the main focus of Spinoza's attention from a very early period. In an uncharacteristically personal passage of the Improvement of the Understanding, Spinoza documents his "conversion" from the ephemeral relativities of a superficial existence to the eternal verities of a meaningful life. Having been struck by the vanity and futility of life styles centered around sensual pleasure, material goods, and fame, he resolved "to inquire whether there might be some real good having power to communicate itself, which would affect the mind singly, to the exclusion of all else", and yielding the enjoyment of "continuous, supreme, and unending happiness" (IU,1-2). By this resolution, Spinoza made the leap from the "certain evils" of misguided sensuality, wealth, and fame, to the "certain good" of some new end which would be superior by virtue of its very constancy (3). This "certain good", later crystallized as blessedness, forms the focal point of the philosopher's strivings toward perfection.

The means to this ultimate end are twofold: the first, the fullest possible understanding of Nature, particularly our own human nature, encompasses ethics as well as the metaphysical and epistemological views discussed above. The second, a supportive social order, is considered under socio-political philosophy (IU,5). Reiterated in the Ethics, the goal is to "consider things only which may conduct us as it were by the hand to a knowledge of the human mind and its highest happiness" (11). In Spinoza's system knowledge is inseparable from the good, happiness, virtue, power, etc. It follows that knowledge of the highest good, the knowledge and love of God, is our "highest happiness and blessedness, and the ultimate end and aim of all human actions" (TP,IV). Epistemology blends into ethics; the knowledge of God (reality) holds the greatest promise of realizing self-interest (to satisfy conatus) and qualifies as the highest virtue of the mind. The mind can act only insofar as it understands, and understanding is "the absolute virtue of the mind", which reaches its apex in the understanding of God (EIV,28,Demonst). From this knowledge the love of God "necessarily flows", a love which, as we have seen above, constitutes the state of blessedness itself.[68]

Spinoza's goal also is identified with the perfection of human nature, assuming levels of perfection to parallel those of knowledge which lead to the intellectual love of God in intuition or perfected blessedness. The levels of perfection represent the degree to which things "participate" in God or being, or the degree to which they adequately express divine perfection.[69] Equating perfection and reality (EI1,def.6), our degree of either indicates the extent to which we 'participate' in the ground of being. Or, the degree of perfection attained is dependent upon the degree of our "special desire": "hence, the most perfect and the chief sharer in the highest blessedness is he who prizes above all else and takes special delight in the intellectual knowledge of God, the most perfect Being" (TP,IV). This person is also the most ethical.

A chain of being embraces all individuals in Nature. Their relative degrees of perfection and imperfection can be determined comparatively, depending on how much reality each possesses in relation to others, or what negating limitations each suffers under (EIV,Preface). Power is merely "ability to exist", and impotence the lack of said ability (E1,11,proof 3). Even the lowest of beings possess some perfection, insofar as it is a being. Its degree of perfection is derived from its essence, while its imperfection becomes manifest only by comparison with things of greater essence (greater reality).[70] In other words, a being's degree of perfection is determined by its own nature and the power appropriate to that nature (its potential for acting rather than being acted upon) (E1, App). Most simply stated, human perfection "consists in this--that we must at all times endeavour to advance further and further" (ST,11,xviii). This advancement proceeds on several levels simultaneously: moral perfection is not merely a preparation for the final intellectual perfection, but the two are identical.

Perfection, the urge toward wholeness by means of individual nature, is thus for Spinoza inextricably linked with the innate power revealed by the inward-turning of each thing, the inwardness mode of being. A "sovereign right" is bestowed upon us by Nature to act as we have been conditioned (by our essence) to act, "determined, not by sound reason, but by desire and power", inasmuch as our powers are the "individual components" of Nature's own power (TP,XVI). Nature remains the ultimate power source from which we draw our own power by turning within to individual nature.

The nature to which we turn, our essence, is human

virtue, our nature "in so far as it has the power of affecting certain things which can be understood through the laws of its own nature alone" (EIV,def.8). In agreement with the feminine perspective, Spinoza's use of the term virtue encompasses the power aspect found both in Greek <u>Arete</u> and the Taoist <u>Te</u>. In seeming agreement with the masculine perspective, Spinoza concentrates upon the intellectual essence of the human individual, "the power of the mind" (EIII,44, Demonst), also is identified as discursive reason (EV,Preface).

Without denying the masculine elements of Spinoza's philosophy, it is necessary to clairfy their position with respect to the entire context of thought. As indicated in the discussion of Spinozistic epistemology, discursive reason is pre-eminently a means to the end of (feminine) intuition. Within ethics discursive reason again plays a mediating role, as a means to the ethical goal of blessedness, as a tool in the process of perfection for the individual <u>qua</u> human. Nature as a whole is impartial to narrowly human affairs, so it is the task of human reason, expressive of a nature which is fully human, to safeguard our special human interests. The "laws of human reason" are limited to "the true interest and preservation of mankind". Natural law and order "forbids nothing"; it is discursive reason which must impose the limitations and restrictions promotive of human existence, while avoiding any contradiction of Nature <u>per se</u> (PT,11,8). The use of discursive reason to determine and then preserve our actual interests as human beings is feminine by virtue of its concrete and pragmatic method of approach. Reason thereby is employed, not to subdue or conquer Nature, but rather to actualize it on an individual plane of being as human nature.

Furthermore, the simple assertion that discursive reason is considered the essence of human nature by Spinoza does not adequately take into account his entire philosophical system. If he is to be consistent with his own tenets, Spinoza cannot exclude the material aspects of our being, for these likewise are an expression of our essence (and ultimately, of the essence of Substance) along with the mind and its power. The main problem lies in inherent complications involved with discussing modes of the Attribute of Extension; of dealing, intellectually, with things. In the case of ideas, and of the mind as the idea of the body, such discussions are quite natural; with regard to bodies, they can only be artificial and forced.

Thus, the superior position accorded intellect and its trappings in the Spinozistic system need not be interpreted as a masculine decision in favor of that aspect of our being. Instead, we may view it, with H. F. Hallett, as a purely pragmatic move:

> The primacy of Thought reflects only the relativity of the Attributes to intellect so far as the philosophic quest for understanding is concerned. It is because we are thinking beings that we philosophize, and philosophy must thus find the intellect standpoint unique.[71]

Such an interpretation considerably diminishes the much-vaunted position of Thought and intellect in Spinozism by viewing that position as an unavoidable consequence of the human condition. Human intellect *qua* human, that is, as it functions through its characteristic discursive reason, although described as a gift from the divine, is not itself divine (except insofar as its highest form of intuitive knowledge can be said to be the product of perfected intellect).

For Spinoza, then, it is not necessarily true that the essence of the human individual is discursive reason, even though this is certainly identified as the essence of the mind. In fact, our essence is more appropriately *conatus*, the desire for self-preservation. Discursive reason merely expresses the mind's desire for that same goal, our intellectual means as human beings of achieving a goal shared with all living beings. Spinoza's own prejudice in favor of intellect or the power of the mind as "the best part of our being" (TP,IV), was undoubtedly influenced by the rationalistic temperament of his times. However, it does not necessarily follow from his own philosophy, and is inconsistent with a strict feminine interpretation of that philosophy.

What is significant, in terms of the feminine perspective, is that Spinoza advises us to turn within to a personal microcosm, in order to comprehend the universal macrocosm. This is a capacity we possess not as rational human beings, but as "citizens" of the universe, "shareholders" in Substance. Each of us carries within an innate source of knowledge; referred to as "the light of nature". This natural inner essence allows a clear understanding of God, from which we can know (intuitively) and/or deduce (by means of discursive reason) what should be sought and what avoided in our lives (TP,IV).

Although Spinoza explicitly identifies this "light" with reason in the Theologico-Political Treatise, there are several compelling factors to indicate that this designation shoud not be taken too literally. Among these is Spinoza's demonstrated tendency to use language very loosely, combined with the early date of the work in question, prior to a more careful working our of a three-leveled epistemology. Moreover, the key point in the treatise in question is to distinguish the methods of religion from those of philosophy. As the latter has been shown to rely mainly upon intuition (developed from the insights of discursive reation in science), Spinoza's "light of nature" likewise can be identified as intuitive in character, "the true handwriting of God's Word" (TP, XV). He criticises the Jewish position which judges "the natural light of reason" insufficient for salvation, and needing to be supplemented by piety (TP,V). But of course, salvation or blessedness is possible only through the auspices of intuition, not discursive reason--philosophy saves, not science.

The possible perfection of humanity (ethics) requires several preparatory stages of development firmly rooted in metaphysical and epistemological insights--first, knowledge of our nature, of what is to be perfected, and of that in Nature which is necessary for attaining said perfection; secondly, a determination of the way in which the elements of reality are interrelated; thirdly, the knowledge of which modifications are possible, or our natural limitations; and, finally, a comparison of these findings with human nature and power as we know it (IU,9). Knowledge (revealed by discursive reason) is power, and that power constitutes human virtue. Reason itself is "the power of the mind" (EV,Preface), intellectual virtue. In writing to Oldenburg, Spinoza declares, "I believe that the doctrines which seem to be in accord with reason are also most useful to virtue."[72] Note that it is reason's utility which makes it valuable in an ethical sense, not as an end in itself.

Discursive reason, as a level of knowledge, has already been discussed as the scientific method, the realm of rational constructions or reconstructions of reality. Reason conceives of things in a manner befitting our human capacity and limitations. Significantly, the task of discursive reason with respect to ethical conduct is somewhat mundane. Certain limitations exist with reference to the actual control discursive reason can exercise over humanity. Virtue, the knowledge of our power and actualization of it, must be cultivated; as Spinoza states, "all men are born ignorant" (TP,XVI). More precisely, virtue is developed using the intellectual "instruments" of discursive reason to attain "the summit of wisdom" (intuition) (IU,11). The much-heralded "guidance of reason" (<u>Rationis ductu</u>) simply leads us to the greater of two goods or lesser of two evils on several scales, judging things by the relativities intrinsic to human existence (EIV,65,67).

Our possession of discursive reason serves to distinguish us from the "brutes", presumably stagnated at the level of sense data along with the unelightened human masses who have never or seldom exercised their rational potential. This assumption of a human monopoly over reason was undeniably influenced by the attitudes of Spinoza's contemporaries, both Jewish and Christian, who adhered to the accepted Western religious notion that the world was created by God specifically for human use. Such a notion allowed Spinoza to assert the unfeminine opinion of the natural superiority of human beings. In fact, Spinoza's principles, e.g., the body as <u>ideatum</u> and the mind as its idea, apply to all beings, but in varying degrees (Ell,13, Schol). Still salvation (<u>salus</u>), while a positive good for human individuals, is a matter of indifference to "brutes" and plant life, "since it does not concern them" (TM,1,vi,7). This state of affairs follows from the essentially intellectual character of salvation or blessedness as expressed through the intellectual love of God.

More forcefully, Spinoza rejects injunctions against the destruction of animals for human use as "based upon an empty superstition and womanish tenderness, rather than upon sound reason" (<u>my italics</u>) (EIV, 36,Schol). The natural right (power) of human beings over "brutes", he argues, is greater than theirs over humans, corresponding to their greater degree of perfection or greater share in reality. Notwithstanding his metaphysical tenets of oneness in the universe, Spinoza was unwilling or unable to admit the kinship of all creatures so essential to the feminine principle. His position is not the least surprising however, given his historical context, a period in which all voices were raised in praise of "man's" glories and pre-eminence in creation. Darwin's theory of the common ancestry of humans and apes, which has the effect of classifying us among the "brutes", was at that time nothing more than a bad dream two hundred years in the future.[73]

While contrary to the encompassing spirit of feminine thought, which unifies all things under the one reality, Spinoza's masculinely-tinged opinions concerning human superiority do have the effect of firmly uniting all human individuals through their share in a common humanity distinguished by the virtue/power of the intellect. Discursive reason is the most peculiarly human aspect of intellect; intuition is firmly tied to the divine itself in that it transcends human conditions and yields eternality. With this goal in mind, Spinoza recommends a course for perfecting the intellect in general. Inasmuch as our virtue is equated with our natural power, a discussion of human virtue necessarily entails a discussion of what constitutes human nature, its necessary and sufficient conditions.

Characteristic of Spinozistic thought, the human condition may be approached from two points of view, paralleling the two possibilities of existence as either Substance or the modes. Taken in itself, human nature is made manifest in the exercise of a specific virtue/power; as one of many in the whole of Nature, from which its power is ultimately derived, the human individual is dependent. In both cases we are dealing with the same human nature, although the emphasis alternates between our independent action and our cosmic dependency, from what we can hope to accomplish to what must be endured, from our freedom to our bondage. The two aspects are inextricably interwoven. Employing a common feminine tactic, Spinoza reconciles these two apparent opposites--our freedom requires a recognition of cosmic dependency. Each demands consideration if the inward-turning path to human perfection is to be understood.

As "<u>part of the whole of Nature</u>", the human individual is dependent upon and governed by natural law and order. Our perfection then lies in willingly fulfilling a role which is "necessarily" subservient (from the inner depths of our essence or nature) (ST,ll, xviii). Even those things which are within our power are so due to our position within the scheme of Nature (ST,ll,v). In general, however, human power, the power of persevering in our existence, is limited and surpassed by the power of external causes (EIV,3). This power, as a direct manifestation of our essence, is "part" of God's infinite power, the power of Nature

(EIV,4,Demonst). Human beings are "necessarily always subject to passions", following and obeying the "common order of nature" to which we must accommodate (yield) ourselves (EIV,4,Corol). It is precisely this subjugation to the passions that leads to human bondage.

From the focus of human power, following out the specific laws of human nature which delineate the human mode as a unique manifestation of natural law and order, a more autonomous view emerges. Self-preservation is the key to our action in accordance with the laws of our nature, and is reflected in the life guided by discursive reason (EIII,def. 2). We are conditioned to seek what is deemed good and to avoid what is deemed evil (EIV,19), despite the fact that our judgments of good and evil may be confused or erroneous. The value of reason lies in its ability to discern true good and true evil with respect to human interests, as noted. Through the mediating force of discursive reason individual intellect transcends to the vision <u>sub species aeternitatis</u>, the knowledge of God or of the whole and our role therein. Following this absolute vision of reality comes, first, the intellectual realization, and then the intuitive experience of the microcosmic-macrocosmic structure of the universe.

Despite the individual opportunity for transcendence, discursive reason remains the main tool by which Spinoza hopes to bring us to a recognition of our common humanity. Building on this insight he can persuade us by logical argumentation that our survival is directly related to the survival of other human beings. This assumption forms the basis of his code of ethics as positive narcissism. Although a centering of concern on the ego-self is very masculine, self-interest can be enlightened, if it shares in the interests of a community, or interprets self-interest in relation to a shared Self. Such a doctrine is one expression of the extended Self operating by <u>Eros</u>/relatedness in the feminine perspective. What is best for the individual is also best for the extended Self, and for the universe as determined by the microcosmic-macrocosmic pattern of Nature. In Spinozistic terminology, this ethical stance is derived from the overriding principle of <u>conatus</u>, the instinct for self-preservation intrinsic to each thing as its essence. Being denied necessary existence, the individual mode compensates by containing nothing self-destructive and standing "opposed to everything which could negate its existence" (EIII,6,and Demonst). Or at least it attempts to act in this manner, to the extent that its knowledge of reality allows. The support of others is required to accomplish this purpose, based on the oneness of reality.

For Spinoza this natural instinct or law of conatus is virtue itself: "The primary and sole foundation of virtue or proper conduct of life . . . is to seek our own profit", best determined by discursive reason when the mind is viewed in its human context and apart from its eternality (in intuition) (EV,41, Demonst). The greater our striving for (true) personal profit, the greater our virtue/power, while the neglect of the profit is correspondingly indicative of a proportionate degree of impotence (EIV,20). A prime case of un-virtue or impotence consists in being motivated, not by the necessity of our own self-preserving nature, but by some oppressive external cause whose power surpasses our own (Schol). Furthermore, conatus (like virtue) has no other end or object, but is an end in itself (EIV,25). Our desires for a good life, for happiness, (Spinoza's own brand of happiness that is "continuous, supreme, and unending"), presuppose the desire for self-preservation (EIV,21). There can be no question of any indifference to our own interests, for that is merely a sign of "ignorance or doubt".[74]

Discursive reason is fully qualified to guide our interests in that its demands do not conflict with what is natural, namely:

> that every person should love himself, should seek his own profit,--what is profitable for him,--should desire everything that really leads man to greater perfection, and absolutely, that every one should endeavor, as far as in him lies, to preserve his own being. This is all true as necessarily as that the whole is greater than its part. (EIV,18,Schol)

In this passage Spinoza's narcissistic feminine ethics reveals itself as simultaneously positive or enlightened, by extending the pursuit of self-interest, in its true sense, to all people. Implicit in this view is the assumption that there can be no conflict of self-interests which have been rightly assessed, an assumption made valid only within the context of the integrated wholeness of a feminine universe. Realizing the superficial paradox of such an ethics for those of the masculine persuasion, Spinoza notes his own attempt to "win the attention" of those who dismiss self-interest as impiety by means of rational argumentation, the compelling force of right reason (EIV,18,Schol).

Beyond extending the pursuit of self-interest to his fellow human beings, by virtue of a shared human nature revealed by inwardness, Spinoza's positive narcissism provides for their well-being. That is, it is in our own self-interest to promote that which brings us joy and destroy what brings sorrow (Elll,28). But, because, as Spinoza demonstrates, human individuals are a source of joy and support, it is also in our best interests to promote their existence and pursuit of perfection. In a similar way the mother identifies with the interests of the child as contingent upon and intimately related to her own being. There can be no stronger motive for ethical behavior than this. The masculine focus on the ego has been incorporated and then transcended by the feminine perspective, preserving its positive motive force while communalizing that force by means of the extended Self.

Thus, Spinoza contends that when each individual is properly engaged in seeking her or his own profit those individuals "are most profitable to one another". Through the common motivation force of <u>conatus</u> each becomes more virtuous, more powerful in acting by the laws of human nature and as discursive reason dictates, such that all agree in nature (EIV,35). The optimum state of affairs would be to have all individuals acting by the inwardness mode of being. This follows from the Spinozistic proposition that an object is profitable to us in direct proportion to its agreement with our nature (EIV,31,Corol). However, when subject to passions, human individuals do not agree in nature (EIV,32). Hence, restraint of the passions is required of those who follow the ethical ideal to be discussed next. The mutually beneficial agreement among human beings can arise only under the common aegis of reason, their shared human essence. Spinoza declares that only other human beings present the possibility of pleasure or union through friendship (EIV,App). These conclusions significantly shape the Spinozistic society.

Conversely, a thing is evil for us in respect to that in its nature which is opposed to human nature (EIV,30). Presumably, then, human beings can be evil or a threat to our self-preservation only insofar as they do not agree with our (human) nature, that is to say, insofar as they are not fully human (or are not acting under the guidance of reason).. This conclusion coincides with Spinoza's definition of inhumanity, applied to a person who does not identify with a fellow human being, "who is moved neither by reason nor pity to be of any service to others" (EIV,50,Schol). Reason and pity represent the revelations provided by philosophy and faith or religion respectively. Humanity reacts as a single organism or integrated whole insofar as its nature is concerned. The "imitation of affects" includes those of sorrow in commiseration or compassion (misericordia) and of desire in emulation (EIII,27, Schol).

Yet in terms of the inner law, "fellowship with the modes of Nature", this sense of common humanity is not necessary, unlike the necessity of one's knowledge of God. Discussions of the human condition occupy the second (masculine) level of knowledge and reality; the feminine reality of intuition transcends to the cosmic. Spinoza's discussion of human interrelationships in general applies merely to our everyday in-the-world existence, are practical given the conditions of human society, but contribute only indirectly to the ultimate goal of blessedness. Indeed, it is quite possible to live out one's perfected life in isolation from other human beings (ST,11,xxiv). However, Spinoza deduced from his metaphysics that a group of like-natured individuals would be able to increase their power (virtue) beyond what would be possible for a single person (EIV,App.7). The nature of reason demands that the highest good be held in common "as deduced from the human essence itself" (EIV,36,Schol).

As a further incentive, we naturally desire others to enjoy the good we follow as promotive of our self-interest , given the optimum situation of all individuals being guided by reason alone (EIV,37 and Demonst). In addition, it is natural for us to persuade others to love the good which we ourselves love, for the knowledge of their love increases our love and joy in the beloved object (Demonst 2). The final end is to have all human beings acting "with humanity and kindness", with perfect self-consistency (EIV,36,Schol). Hence, the worldly goal of the Spinozist as expressed in socio-political theories demands attention from those interested in the philosophical system as a whole.

In short, the spirit of common humanity reigns, in Spinoza's universe, allowing each individual to pursue true personal interest (promoted by masculine rational self-interest) with the assurance that it will contribute to the over-all interests of the community (satisfying positive narcissism). It is necessary for a philosopher to appeal to individuals at the appropriate level of knowledge, whether opinion, reason, or intuition. The most essential elements of the traditional ethical system, mutual assistance and concern, are thereby retained, but with a much higher expectation of being upheld, in that they are supported by more than one group.

What is discussed in the context of discursive reason, as promotive of human interrelationships and mutual support, is but a step on the path to the ultimate blessedness offered by intuition. While a rightly ordered communal environment can insure the conditions most conducive to individual salvation or blessedness, granting perfection to us qua human, the final step of perfection as one with reality must be taken by the individual alone. The preparatory conditions are needed at the intermediate level of striving for perfection, but the culminating experience of perfection transcends those very conditions, transcends our own human nature and discursive reason in the intellectual love of God and intuition. Hence, the knowledge of God is a necessity, while "fellowship with the modes of Nature" is helpful but not necessary (ST,ll,xxiv).

The intellectual love of God or blessedness, equated with God's love for us, is love "not in so far as He is infinite, but in so far as He can be manifested through the essence of the human mind, considered under the form of eternity" (EV,36). As such it has already been treated under the heading of epistemology. In terms of ethics, however, blessedness is considered by Spinoza to be a virtue "which necessarily exists in a man who knows God rightly" (TP,XVI,note 28). Blessedness is the highest knowledge (of Substance or God) and also the highest of virtues and of powers (the fullest expression of our power as dictated by our very nature). It is the culmination of the microcosmic-macrocosmic relationship attesting to the feminine assumption that the inner is indeed the outer.

Based upon these conditions, where inwardness reflects and expands into wholeness, the enlightened individual is assured of immortality, of continued existence. Just as division exists only in modes, but not in Substance itself, human death applies to the individual "only in so far as he is such a composite being, and not the substance on which he depends" (ST,l,ii). When we die, Substance remains unaffected. Correspondingly, to the extent that our essence is real, it continues to exist through Substance. When the mind remains united to the body alone, judging the body to be the "foundation of its love", it perishes with the body. However, if the mind is united with what is eternal and unchangeable (namely God or Substance) it too continues unchanged (is, in effect, immortal) (ST,11,xxiii). In God there is an idea expressing the essence of our body "under the form of eternity" (EV,22), an idea which is "necessarily something which pertains to the essence of the human mind" constituting that "something" of our mental essence deemed eternal "necessarily" (23,Demonst). And so it is that when the actor puts down the mask (persona) of the play, something still remains of the role in the individual, something which had been projected into the role.

But what then has become of the intimate interaction Spinoza posits between mind and body, as modes of the one Substance? Assuming that the immortality or eternal quality of mind is dependent upon God's idea of our body, how can the mind continue once our body has ceased to exist (unless it is an idea of the matter which composed that body, in which case the matter involved continues to exist after death, but in a new form)? Moreover, such eternality would seem to belong to all, philosopher and non-philosopher alike, leaving the question of why blessedness is so important. In the absence of a direct reply to those problems by Spinoza, we must frame our own under the guidance of the feminine perspective. As already noted, blessedness is not actually attained, but rather is an existing state of being which we can come to realize by gaining knowledge of reality and perfecting our human nature or intellect. The value of these efforts is purely practical and improves the quality of our present life. The advantage which can be expected by the philosopher in the pursuit of her or his goals is the present enjoyment of blessedness, by experiencing the oneness of reality usually reserved for the after-death state.

It is precisely this immortalizing union which is the goal of intellectual love of God. Immortality (or the recognition of our potential for it) is "acquired by leading a life not only of moral uprightness [in the traditional sense of ethics], but also of strenuous effort after the highest kind of knowledge [the intuitive form]."[75] The movement towards self-perfection, also expressed as the urge towards wholeness, thus culminates in immortality, as the mere mode comes to experience its gounding in Substance or reality, which previously only had been realized intellectually (through masculine or human reason).

Thus, the inwardness mode of being, Spinozistically represented, entails the perfection of human virtue, which last is none other than our power as human individuals. The urge towards wholeness stimulates the desire to perfect our human essence, identified as discursive reason. The guidance of reason facilitates human perfection per se. This is what is encountered by turning inward, a move which reveals the human microcosm as the universal macrocosm and vindicates our claims to knowledge.

The recognition of discursive reason as a distinctly human capacity, our essence insofar as we are intellects or under the Attribute of Thought, also leads to the sense of a common humanity. From the latter arises the ethics of positive narcissism, which harnesses the powerful motivating force of conatus for the highest ethical ends in interrelationships to mature into a transcendence of human concerns. Spinoza narrows the scope of feminine/relatedness by restricting his ethical code to a human context, undoubtedly under the influence of the cultural conditions prevailing in his time. Nonetheless, the underlying principle is identical to that which characterized the feminine perspective-the metaphysical support of the unified universe remains crucial in either the broad or the narrow version of the principle.

Beyond these human concerns lies the ultimate state of blessedness, attained through the third kind of knowledge, the intuitive, as developed from the perfected discursive reason. At this point, narrowly-human interests cease, transcended by virtue of intuition's grounding in the one reality. Such a state is equally beyond this-worldly concerns of human fellowship, being instead oriented toward the intellectual love of God most fully realized for Spinoza when the individual mind has achieved its immortality by realizing its identity with the whole.

b. Receptivity-the philosopher ideal. If, for Spinoza, virtue is power perfected through the guidance of discursive reason, and culminating in the blessedness of third level knowledge, then the ethical ideal is embodied in the individual who is devoted to the intellect as both rational and intuitive. Such a person would be engaged in the search for personal perfection, following the metaphysical and epistemological doctrines set forth in Spinoza's system of philosophy, hence qualifying as a Spinozistic philosopher.

In order to adhere to the philosopher ideal of Spinoza's ethics, it is necessary to live in accordance with the second feminine mode of being, that of receptivity. The latter is characterized by an openness to the reality of both human nature and Nature as a whole. A receptive individual would also imitate essential qualities of Substance or God, approximating as far as is humanly possible its impartiality, freedom and peace. A prerequisite for that life style is the mastering, if not entire elimination, of disruptive affects or emotions intrinsic to our existence as modes. The end result is a cordial relationship with other human beings based on the ethcis of positive narcissism, and a contingent elitism which is metaphysically grounded and ethically realized.

A certain path is prescribed for the Spinozistic philosophers who seek to lead a virtuous and simultaneously intellectually pure existence. "True virtue", Spinoza tells us, consists in "living according to the guidance of reason alone" (EIV,36,Schol 1). It is significant that Spinoza specifies "living" rather than merely "thinking", for this emphasizes the positive and practical tone of his entire philosophy. Philosophical knowledge, in the feminine sense, is readily integrated into one's daily life style. Furthermore, virtue is "nothing but acting according to the laws of our own nature", as founded upon the spontaneous endeavor toward self-preservation (EIV,18,Schol).

Above all, the philosopher's life style imitates the action of Substance, that is, ultimate reality, reflected in a tranquil, accepting, and peaceful demeanor. To achieve the peak of activity, it is necessary to overcome the "bondage" of the affects (explained in EIV) in the form of the passions, as far as possible. This program is laid out in the fifth part of the Ethics, "Of the Power of the Intellect, or of Human Liberty". A certain sense of elitism is engendered by the philosopher ideal, due to the fact that, despite the universal human potential for this high state of being, most individuals remain unenlightened, that is, unawakened to their own power of mind: "all noble things are as difficult as they are rare" (EV,42,Schol).

The philosopher's openness to reality, to the bare facts of existence, is founded upon a profound understanding of metaphysics and epistemology, of how the universe and the human mind are constructed (EI and II). The Spinozistic scheme asserts the deterministic character of the universe, from which various useful conclusions may be drawn concerning human behavior. If our independent attempts to make changes in the determined order of existence are indeed futile, it is to our advantage to accept the circumstances of reality and to work within our given limitations. The conditions of the universe are understood in relation to our specific human nature. We may employ what little virtue/power we have to harmonize ourselves with the whole, wherein lies our best possibility for survival: "the brave man will consider above everything that all things follow from the necessity of the divine nature" (EIV,73,Schol).

The limitations intrinsic to human power are well recognized by Spinoza. We obviously lack absolute control over externals. However, "equanimity" can be maintained even in the face of adversity "if we are conscious that we have performed our duty, that the power we have could not reach so far as to enable us to avoid those things, and that we are a part of the whole of nature." Such a realization suffices to satisfy us intellectually, and engenders the desire to persevere-"for, in so far as we understand, we cannot desire anything excepting what is necessary, nor abosolutely, can we be satisfied with anything but the truth." Understanding brings an effort "of the better part of us" to harmonize with Nature as a whole (EIV,App.,32). The aim of the free individual is not to avoid danger, but to overcome it, even if such overcoming can only be accomplished by yeilding: "Flight at the proper time, just as well as fighting, is to be reckoned, therefore, as showing strength of mind" (EIV,69,and Carol).

Spinoza makes frequent mention of an ethical ideal, referred to as "the free man" (<u>homo liber</u>), who is knowledgeable in the ways of reality, as revealed by Spinozistic philosophy, and who acts accordingly. Following Spinoza's definition of freedom as acting by necessity, the free individual is called so "only in so far as he preserves the power of existing and operating according to the laws of human nature" (PT,11,7). We act by human necessity as God, the perfectly free being, acts by cosmic necessity. Virtue is described as none other than "the highest liberty" (Ell,conclusion). Comparisons are also made between the wise and the ignorant, between those who have been able to grasp and harmonize with reality through discursive reason and intuition, as opposed to those who are mere slaves to their passions and to external conditions.

As noted previously, the concept of a human ideal is indispensible to Spinoza for asserting value judgments, even though such an ideal has the dubious status of a thing of reason. Hence, it is not legitimate to describe a specific individual as perfect, for this would confuse the ideal and the real (ST,11,iv). This same pitfall must be avoided in our own discussion of the ethical ideal by keeping in mind that the free individual or Spinozistic philosopher is merely an intellectual standard of perfection, a moral blueprint. The degree to which one has achieved, or failed to achieve, perfection is gauged by a comparison with the established model or "idea of man" (idea hominis), to be taken as "a model of human nature" (EIV,Preface) which serves to focus our striving. The link between perfection and the guidance of discursive reason makes it clear that this ideal individual is also a philosopher in the Spinozistic mold.

Adherence to the ethics of positive narcissism is one of the criteria for being classified under the ideal of the "righteous" individual. This type of individual "<u>firmly</u> desires that each shall possess his own", a conviction arising "<u>necessarily</u>" from the clear knowledge we have of our own nature as well as of the nature of God.[76] Knowledge is a prime aspect of this ideal person, whose "chief effort is to conceive things as they are in themselves [in the context of reality], and to remove the hindrances to true knowledge" (EIV,73,Schol). Death is the farthest thing from the mind of such an individual who is free, that is, "led by reason alone" (EIV,68,Demonst). Instead, the wisdom appropriate here is "a meditation of life", with a desire for action, life, and self-preservation (EIV,67,Demonst).

In contrast to this search for perfect knowledge lie the superficialities pursued by the ignorant--honor or fame, wealth, and sensual pleasures. These, Spinoza declares, "have no reality whatever!" (ST,11,v). Each is examined and found wanting in terms of Spinoza's ultimate goal of "continuous, supreme, and unending happiness". The difference between the enlightened or wise and the unenlightened or ignorant is precisely the difference between one who understands the state of reality and one who does not. The ignorant individual continually is agitated by externals, has no "true peace of soul", being ignorant of both God (Substance) and things (its modes), "and as soon as he ceases to suffer, ceases to be". The wise individual, on the other hand, suffers little or no mental agitation, and possess a sense of the "eternal necessity of himself, of God, and of things". In effect, that knowledgeable individual becomes immortal, "never ceases to be, and always enjoys true peace of soul" (EV,42,Schol). To know Substance is to share in its immortality.

Equally significant is the code of conduct entailed by Spinoza's doctrines, calling for a life style distinctly paralleling the feminine mode of being known as receptivity. A proper attitude must be instilled with regard to the inevitabilities of fate which lie beyond our control, that is, "which do not follow from our own nature". We are instructed "with equal mind to wait for and bear each form of fortune", as necessarily following from natural law and order, "the eternal decree of God" (Ell,conclusion,2). The philosopher is actively perceptive, not merely a passive recipient. What is involved is not merely a matter of acting or being passive, the usual masculine-feminine polarity, but rather of two alternate ways of acting, either through the ultimately futile assertion of imposing one's self upon events or the realistic non-assertion of dealing with conditions as they exist. To be ethical is to first know how reality works and then work with, not against, it. In this way we can supplement our power from Nature rather than expending it in resistance.

The pragmatic necessity of formulating specific rules or a plan of life is mentioned by Spinoza in various places. In the absence of a comprehensive knowledge of human affects (lacking for the finite mind of the human being), it is best "to conceive a right rule of life, or sure maxims (dogmata) of life" which yield "the highest peace of mind" (EV,10,Schol). Such a "mode and plan of life" is also indispensible for acquiring the mental stability and sense of purpose necessary for following the "true Method" of clear and distinct ideas in philosophy.[77]

Along these lines, some provisional rules of conduct are listed in The Improvement of the Understanding. Although one would expect certain modifications in these rules in accordance with the later maturing of Spinoza's thought, they nonetheless shed light on his ethical ideal. The first rule concerns the individual's relationship with the masses--one should endeavor to communicate on a level commensurate with the abilities of the general populace and to adopt those common customs which present no hindrance to the ultimate goal. Both are to be done for the purpose of gaining "a friendly audience for the reception of the truth". The necessity of cultivating this cordial attitude towards the masses relates to the survival of the philosopher as well as to the advantages of living in an enlightened community (as noted further on). Secondly, moderation in pleasure is advised, restricting such pleasures as are indulged in to those essential for the perservation of health. The advantages of a sound body able to function in concert with a sound mind are elaborated in conjunction with the link with Nature. Finally, Spinoza inserts a most practical stipulation, namely that the seeker of truth should be economically independent, self-supporting in terms of maintaining one's life, state of health, and persevering in the path of knowledge (IU,6). The Spinozistic philosopher is not a burden to the community, but a positive asset.

Each point is directed towards promoting the final goal of truth by rectifying those aspects of existence which might possibly threaten that pursuit. These may be identified as the fear and prejudice aroused in others, mainly the masses; the temptations of superficialities decreasing one's own virtue/power; and the weakness and/or uncertainty of one's continued existence. Thus we cultivate a receptive environment in others and also within ourselves. Underlying it all is an encompassing faith in the verity of Spinoza's own philosophical method--"in ordinary life we must follow what is most probable, but in philosophical speculations, the truth."[78] Hence, while his code of conduct may be provisional, his faith in a supportive reality is absolute.

Intrinsic to this ethical ideal is an imitation of Substance, as one moves ever nearer to its state of absolute reality through personal perfection. The highest type of individual is free in the same sense that Substance is considered free, while the slave, or ignorant individual, is held in bondage by a failure to realize that intrinsic potential for freedom. The "slave" functions only by the lowest type of knowledge, that of imagination or opinion, and "whether he wills it or not, does those things of which he is entirely ignorant". The free individual, however, "does the will of no one but himself, and does those things only which he knows are of greatest importance in life, and which he therefore desires above all things" (EIV,66, Schol).

The definition of the free individual is obviously patterned after the definition of a free thing in the first part of the Ethics, "Of God" (def. 7), namely, what is determined to act by the necessity of its own nature and is not compelled to action by externals. Although absolute freedom is found in Substance alone, it appears possible for the human being to approach Substance's condition on the lesser scale of human reality, by acting "not in free decision but in free necessity".[79]

Reason reveals many ways by which we can exercise this "free necessity" to the benefit of our virtue/power. Given the assumption that our degree of happiness or unhappiness is dependent upon the object of our love, unmitigated joy is guaranteed by directing our love to an object which is eternal and infinite (IU,3). Only God or Substance qualifies for that position. Joy being a positive good, it increases human power in relation to both mind and body (EIV,App.). Indeed, joy or self-satisfaction is a product of our contemplating ourselves and our power of action, "the highest thing for which we can hope" (EIV,52,Demonst and Schol). Absolute joy, or blessedness, the intellectual love of God, is none other than "the love of God towards men" (homines) (EV,36,Corol). Our final goal, then, as manifested in the ideal of the free individual, lies in the successful imitation of God via love, thereby increasing our virtue/power to the greatest extent, ultimately eliminating the propaedeutic second level distinction between lover (individual intelligence) and beloved (God). The intellectual love of God is also termed "repose of mind" (EV,36,Schol), or simply the peace which is enjoyed by the free or enlightened person.

The suitability of human beings for imitating Substance refers back to their assumed superiority over "brutes" and mere objects. As a highly complex organism, the human individual has the advantage of being affected by the environment in various ways. Hence, we are capable of a broader range of reflections of Nature, of reality, as determined by the correspondence between the increase of bodily and mental experiences and powers. The human condition thus, of all existence, most closely approximates the condition of Substance in the extent of its power. We experience this intellectual fact when the last remnants of human reason are shed via intuition, when we have ascended the staircase of reason and become oblivious to it due to our total preoccupation with the bliss in the rooms above (the knowledge/experience of intuition).

But before we reach these heights, we must mount the steps one at a time, getting closer and closer to the power of God as we remove ourselves farther and farther from human weaknesses. One essential step involves a cleansing of inhibiting affects. Most conspicuous here are those emotions or affects which betray a misunderstanding of universal law and order, such as pity, hatred, and contempt. Given a "proper" understanding of the metaphysical structure of the universe, of the necessity by which things follow from the divine nature, in accordance with "the eternal laws and rules of nature", the individual guided by reason will deem nothing worthy of these emotions. Moreover, because they entail sorrow they are counterproductive, actually decreasing our power/virtue . Like Substance, which is free of passions and affects of either joy or sorrow (EV,17), the individual who is made free by the exercise of reason displays an impartiality occasioned by a deterministic outlook, following the model of the non-anthropomorphic deity of Spinozistic philosophy who remains unmoved by the special pleadings of religious worshippers.

Since this is a feminine philosophy, the emotions, as a product of our natural desire (conatus) cannot be summarily condemned. We cannot impose our relative value judgements on reality. Desire is quite properly the "end for the sake of which we do anything" (EIV,def 7.). The crucial issue, as in all of Spinozistic philosophy, is the point of view from which these desires or efforts are understood. Since reality is fully determined, our perspective on that reality alone is open to revision. We cannot change the world, but we can change the way we react to it, at least intellectually. The intimate connection between mind and body insures us that a change in the mind is reflected in the body, that is, in our actions. When our nature is seen as the proximate cause of our desires, the latter are actions following from our nature and understood in terms of that nature alone, related to the mind as it conceives adequate ideas and indicative of our power. However, when we are considered as "part" of Nature as a whole, and hence only the partial cause of things, such desires are expressed as passions.

The essential difference between the actions (of

the enlightened free individual) and the passions (of the ignorant, who are in bondage) lies in the degree of philosophical knowledge attained, perfect in the former case and imperfect in the latter. The movement toward the perfection of intellect via discursive reason, stimulated by the inwardness mode of being and the urge towards wholeness, in the sine qua non for the ethical ideal of the Spinozistic philosopher. The "final aim" of the reason-dominated person, "by which he strives to govern all his other desires", is the desire for an adequate conception of self and everything conceivable to "intelligence" (EIV,App. 4).

By realizing the necessity of the affects in our existence, a greater power over them is gained and a lessening of their power over us (EV,6). The inescapable affects, when understood clearly and distinctly, and when images and affections of the body are referred to the idea of God (14), can be made to yield the love of God, that is, pleasure accompanied by the idea of God (15). By this means, intuition gains power over the passions. We can learn to manipulate them to achieve our own ends, "if not actually to destroy them . . ., at least to make them constitute the smallest part of the mind" (EV,21,Schol). The mission of the free individual is outlined here.

For these reasons, Spinoza devotes a large proportion of the Ethics to the potential problems of the affects, their tendency to degenerate into passions. The origin, nature, and strength of the affects, are discussed in the third part, while the entire fourth part of the Ethics is concerned with an investigation of how the individual falls into bondage to them. After covering the causes of human weakness and lack of stability, of why reason is ever rejected, Spinoza passes on to the dictates of reason of themselves, determining which of the affects promote the rules or code of conduct imposed by discursive reason and which hinder it (EIV,18,Schol). The fifth and final part outlines the path of freedom from the bondage of the affects, implementing the knowledge gained, putting metaphysical and epistemological theory into "ethical" practice.

The general method applied previously for understanding God or Substance (part one) and the human mind (part two), the reference to "the universal law and rules of nature", is employed once again in the case of the affects (E111,intro). The only possible means of restraining or removing an affect lies in counter-

acting it by an affect which is opposite and stronger
(7). We suffer from passions when the emotion we are
operating under involves the nature of our own body as
well as that of some external body (EIII,56,Demonst).
The mind attempts to imagine only such things as attest
to its power, its capacity for action, rather than its
being acted upon, the impotence of the passions (EIII,
44). When the mind is active, the affects of thinking
(desire and joy) indicate 'fortitude' under two forms--
'strength of mind' (<u>animositas</u>), the reason-engendered
desire for self-preservation, and 'generosity', by
which reason extends assistance to others and unites
with them in friendship (EIII,49,Schol). Spinoza's
ethics binds these two elements together, maximizing
the action of both personal self-interest (rational
enlightened egoism) and that of the shared Self (positive narcissism).

   As already demonstrated, emotions of joy, imitative of Substance or God, are pivotal for blessedness,
and hence would be manipulated by the philosopher to
restrain the affects in general. It is joy which
signifies an increase of perfection, while sorrow shows
a decrease by limiting our power of action (EIII,def 2
and 3). In the case of the intellectual love of God,
the joy of blessedness, God is the object of love, and
the joy involved exceeds human limitations and
stretches into the farthest reaches of reality.

   Bondage results, not from the emotion <u>per se</u>, but
from our being determined to action by the inadequate
ideas which engender passive suffering, being acted
upon. The action of feminine receptivity, by which we
become intellectually receptive to or understanding of
reality, is recommended, to implement our knowledge in
our actual style of life. This amounts to "<u>acting</u>,
<u>living</u>, <u>and</u> <u>preserving</u> <u>our</u> <u>being</u>"; these three are
synonymous for Spinoza (EIV,23 and Demonst). Action
based on "true knowledge and love of right" yields
"freedom and constancy", while acting "from the fear of
evil", constrained by evil, takes place in a state of
bondage (TP,IV). The "true knowledge of good and evil"
may serve as an emotional restraint, not because it is
a true knowledge, but as itself an affect (opposite to
and of greater power than the affect to be counteracted) (EIV,14). Of course, good and evil are conceived here as the relative terms proper to human
reason, and have no existence on the level of impartial
Substance.

   Those actions by which we can be determined by a

passion can readily be replaced by the determination of "reason alone". In acting under the guidance of reason we are acting naturally, spontaneously. We are powerless to alter the program of the universe, but we can employ its elements to the best advantage, producing a situation more conducive to our survival and thriving. The philosopher uses knowledge of Substance the way the sage uses Tao. An action may be prompted by either passions (through an external cause) or by the dictates of reason (as internally caused) (EIV,59,Demonst). In Spinoza's system, the motivation for the action often outweighs the act itself. The task of the philosopher is to make a free choice in favor of necessity, and to make that choice dependent upon the exercise of human reason. While the desire of an affect which is a passion is "blind" (EIV,59,Schol), the individual who is guided by reason may be said to have unfailing sight (or insight).

The final part of the Ethics details "the power of the mind" (of intellect through both discursive reason and intuition), and the exact manner in which and extent to which it can restrain the affects. Knowledge is the sole means of overcoming our emotions, and "from this knowledge of the mind alone shall we deduce everything which relates to its blessedness" (EV, Preface). In addition, we must separate the affects from external causes (2), relate them to objects clearly understood rather than conceived confusedly (3), and arrange them according to the order of the intellect (so that they may be more easily grasped) (5) (EV,20,Demonst). The paragon of Spinozistic virtue is led by a desire "to govern his affects and appetites from a love of liberty alone", seeks to become aware of virtues along with their causes, "and to fill his mind with that [power-increasing] joy which springs from a true knowledge of them" (EV,10,Schol).

The constancy of the idea of our ultimate object of love, namely God, is maximized by relating all other emotions to it (EV,11 and 14). When our mind is filled with the joy of blessedness it "delights" in the divine love, and becomes capable of restraining, if not entirely eradicating, desires. This pure love counteracts the debilitating passions. However, the blessedness precedes the power of restraint; that is to say, that power is not the cause of our rejoicing, but merely its product (EV,42,Demonst).

The alternative to such simultaneously ethical and intellectual restraint is indeed bleak. As Spinoza states in the correspondence, weakness does not diminish our inherent responsibility:

> he who is unable to control his desires, and to restrain them through fear of the law, [a last resort], although he must be excused for his weakness, is nevertheless unable to enjoy peace of mind, and the knowledge and love of God [blessedness]; but necessarily perishes.[80]

The masses tend to exhibit a faulty scale of values. The objects of their desire do not contribute to self-preservation, but hinder that goal--"causing the death not seldom of those who possess them, and always of those who are possessed by them" (IU,3).

In Spinoza's estimation, unperfected human nature, the material which the would-be free individual has to work with, falls quite short of the ideal, making it necessary to conscientiously strive beyond the common level of life in this world. With pity for those judged inferior to ourselves, and envy for those who are seen as superior, human nature has an urge to prevent others from possessing what is only able to be possessed by one person (Ell1,32 and Schol). The feeling is, that if I cannot possess it, others should be denied from possessing it also. This is egoism in its most unenlightened form, found in those who do not understand their true nature and its laws. Humility and despondency are alien to our character as human beings, "hence those who have the most credit for being abject and humble are generally the most ambitious and envious" (Ell1,29,Expl). None of these qualities is conducive to the ethical ideal which Spinoza has in mind nor to the perfect commonwealth. Only knowledge of reality can cure these anti-social symptoms, by revealing the interdependency of individuals, and the value of universal enlightenment.

The optimum environment for attaining the ethical ideal is one in which the community of individuals surrounding the free individual shares in the state of enlightenment or blessedness (which explains the need for an enlightened commonwealth). The end of perfection is therefore composite--"to be able to taste of union with God, and to bring forth true ideas, and to make these things known also to my neighbours." The resulting union of wills, "constituting one and the same nature", is a sign of increased perfection on a communal scale (ST,11,xxvi). Moreover, only free individuals are able to interact at the same high level. They alone possess the true capacity for gratitude, for example, because they alone are mutually profitable and closely related by friendship of a common striving motivated by love of the good realistically conceived (EIV,71 and Demonst).

A prime factor contributing to positive human interactions is love, or generosity. Within the Spinozistic system interpersonal love (<u>Amor</u>) achieves a significance approaching that of feminine <u>Eros</u>/relatedness in terms of its potential for ultimate conquest. While envy and hatred emphasize the differences between individuals, it is love that brings them together, establishes concord in place of discord (EIV,App. 9 and 11). Love is more effective than the force of arms and is capable of destroying divisive hatred, which last merely breeds more hatred (EIll,43), while replacing it with a depth of emotion exceeding that of the original hatred (44). Thus, the individual who is guided by reason bears love as a basic weapon, employing it to counteract hatred, anger, and contempt. Through its use the Spinozistic philosopher avoids agitation in both self and others, and is assured of invincibility-- "Those whom he conquers [with love] yield gladly, not from defect of strength, but from an increase of it" (EIV,46,Demonst and Schol). Love increases our power, but does not feed upon the power of the other, who also is strengthened. Properly speaking, it is <u>rapprochement</u>, not conquest. The Taoist would agree completely.

Despite Spinoza's optimism, the fact remains that many people do not possess such knowledge. The problem then arises of the proper relationship between the enlightened, or knowledgeable, free individual, and the unenlightened, passion-enslaved masses. Once again, the ethics of positive narcissism requires an extension of a receptive mode of being to fellow humans. Thus, the free individual living among the unfree seeks to form a bond of friendship with others, as noted by Spinoza in his list of the "moral advantages" of his doctrines (Ell,49). The underlying motivation here is one of Spinozistically virtuous self-interest, the interest of the shared Self--"For although men are ignorant, they are nevertheless men, who, when we are in straits, are able to afford us human assistance--the best assistance which man can receive" (EIV,70,Demonst and Schol). The attempt to turn others to the guidance of reason is done "with humanity and kindness", rather than "from impulse" (EIV,37,Schol 1).

In order to maintain a receptive attitude towards our less than perfect fellow human beings, the Spinozistic philosopher must maintain the most positive climate of thought. On a personal level, this is done by consciously concentrating upon the good (virtue/ power increasing) qualities of others in our minds, "so that we may be determined to action by an affect of joy" (EV,10,Schol). Spinoza seems to be describing his own low-key approach in the Ethics when he outlines the proper way to assist others--one should strive "above all things, to win their love, and not to draw them into admiration, so that a doctrine may be named after him, nor absolutely to give any occasion for envy". References to human vices are to be avoided and those to human weaknesses minimized, while emphasizing instead the human virtue/power which culminates in perfection, "so that men being moved not by fear or aversion, but solely by the affect of joy, may endeavour as much as they can to live under the rule of reason" (EIV,App.). It is a classic case of the use of positive reinforcement as a means of conditioning desired responses, rejecting the inefficiency of negative reinforcement.

These remarks seem to signal that an undercurrent of elitism mars the feminine holism of Spinozistic thought. Although, theoretically, the path through discursive reason to intuition and blessedness is open to all human individuals, can it be rationally expected that many will ever attain that high level of perfection? Spinoza himself declares that salvation or blessedness is extremely difficult to attain, as attested to by the fact that "it is so seldom discovered". If it were easy of attainment, he asks, "how could it be possible that it should be neglected almost by everybody?" (EV,42,Schol).

Elitist references to the masses as steeped in superstition and ready to condemn serious philosophical efforts can be found in Spinoza's writings. In the preface to the Theologico-Political Treatise Spinoza addresses his work to the "Philosophical Reader" alone:

> To the rest of mankind I care not to commend my treatise, for I cannot expect that it contains anything to please them: I know how deeply rooted are the prejudices embraced under the name of religion; I am aware that in the mind of the masses superstition is no less deeply rooted than fear;

I recognize that their constancy is mere
obstinancy, and that they are led to
praise or blame by impulses rather than
reason.

Such an attitude seems to have grown, rather than
diminished, as influenced by the negative reception to
this and subsequent texts, culminating in Spinoza's
guarded discussion of the Ethics only with trusted
friends.

Elitism may even be demanded by Spinoza's deterministic view of the universe. Each individual is
determined to a certain level of intellect and physical
ability, and of these only certain ones are capable of
attaining blessedness. Hence, it is said that "a man
ignorant and weak of mind, is no more bound by natural
law to order his life wisely, than a sick man is bound
to be sound of body" (PT,11,18). From the "common man"
Spinoza expects very little, and judges him incapable
of producing a work of "excellent thought" except by
copying from another.[81] The "creed of the multitude"
stands in direct contrast to that of the enlightened
Spinozistic philosopher. Freedom is viewed by most as
the opportunity to follow the dictates of lust over
those of reason, with a motivation to do the good
resulting from negative fear of punishment as opposed
to a positive love of the good. A reward beyond death
is anticipated to compensate for the enforced obedience
in the present life, and without that assurance "they
would prefer to let everything be controlled by their
own passions, and to obey fortune rather than themselves" (EV,41,Schol).[82]

These observations seem to indicate that, regardless of theoretical considerations, the ethical ideal
is in practice accessible only to an intellectual
elite. Perhaps this accounts for the classification of
the ideal of the perfect individual as a thing of
reason. True knowledge of God, Spinoza states, cannot
be commanded (religiously), but is a "Divine gift" (TP,
Xlll), and while pious obedience is possible for all
"there are but a few, compared with the aggregate of
humanity, who can acquire the habit of virtue under the
unaided guidance of reason" (XV). Individuals differ
from one another with respect to their affects or
emotions (desire, joy, and sorrow), just as they differ
with respect to their essences (Elll,57 and Demonst).
This is true of the differences between species of
beings, as well as that between various classes of
human beings: "the joy by which the drunkard is

enslaved is altogether different from the joy which is the portion of the philosopher" (Schol). A qualitative difference separates the joy experienced by the ignorant and that of the blessed.

Balancing this latent elitism are Spinoza's assurances that the ethical ideal in theory is attainable by all human beings: "The highest good of those who follow after virtue is common to all, and all may enjoy it" (EIV,36). This possibility must remain open if Spinoza's philosophy is to qualify as feminine. Given the common bond of our humanity, human nature which distinguishes us by the possession of or potential for discursive reason, blessedness is the goal of all. The individual "could not be nor be conceived if he had not the power of rejoicing in [experiencing] this highest good" (Demonst and Schol). The perfections of the mind are eternal, only our realization of them is lacking (EV,33,Schol). If the mass of common people have failed to come to the realization enjoyed by the Spinozistic philospher, the elitist position of the latter is nonetheless not self-imposed. The path remains open to all, insofar as they are human beings, or exercise their discursive reason. As Spinoza has stated, "the reward of virtue is virtue itself, and the punishment of folly and weakness is the folly itself."[83] Even so, Spinoza will not abandon his ignorant fellow human beings to their fate, but tries to integrate them into an enlightened system via the commonwealth. His is a contingent elitism, contingent on the present lack of realization in the majority concerning universal blessedness.

To summarize, Spinozism's ethical ideal of the free individual is mostly fully exemplified in the philosopher who acts under the guidance of reason alone en route to intuition and blessedness. The outstanding characteristic of such an individual is receptivity, an openness to and active acceptance of the reality of a universe which has been found to be deterministic. This attitude is both recommended by Spinoza and displayed in his own life style, as a true assessment of one's situation and an acting upon that knowledge to harmonize with what is.

Spinoza consciously established a human ideal, generally discussed under the heading of the free individual, as a model for the perfection of our virtue. The person guided by discursive reason is made free by knowledge of the state of the universe in metaphysics and epistemology. The superficialities of life, to

which the ignorant cling, are rejected by the free
individual as unworthy. Certain moral advantages also
accrue from the adoption of the ideal, including a
practical code of conduct which is deemed essential for
self-preservation in society.

   Equally important here are the ways in which the
ideal Spinozistic philosopher or free individual
imitates Substance or God. Freedom results from maximizing one's actions (which follow from one's own
nature), rather than being held in bondage by external
causes and passions. Spontaneity is the keynote to
activity. The intellectual love of God enjoyed by the
perfected philosopher signifies a direct equation with
God--our love for God is the same as God's love for us.
The assumed superiority of human beings over other
forms of existence, our natural proximity to God due
to intellect, insures the success of our imitative
attempts.

   The impartiality appropriate to the determinism of
the universe and Spinoza's deity is duplicated in the
enlightened individual who remains aloof from distrac-
ting emotions. The free individual is able to restrain,
if not entirely eliminate, the affects as a means of
increasing inner power. Our knowledge of the structure
of the mind allows us to implement certain devices for
that end, such as counteracting one emotion by another
and manipulating them for positive purposes (e.g., the
intellectual love of God).

   Finally, a certain code for promoting positive
human interrelationships is indicated by Spinoza's
ethical ideal, of how the free individual should behave
towards those who remain in bondage to the passions.
The values of positive narcissism are recommended here,
a receptivity to the needs of others. Love, in the
form of <u>Eros</u>/relatedness, is considered very effective
as a means of benign "conquest" in such circumstances.
The problem of whether Spinoza's ethics tends to a
doctrine of elitism also arises in this context. The
actual situation seems to be that, while blessedness
and perfection are theoretically accessible to all in
accordance with feminine oneness, only the philosophi-
cally-minded persevere on the path of knowledge, to be
rewarded with their own virtue. Those who are successful have taken as a model the ethical ideal of Spinoza's
free individual, the enlightened philosopher, but need
not be an elite.

   c. <u>Materiality--the link with Nature</u>. In discussing both the perfection of humanity through the inwardness mode of being and the ethical ideal of the receptive Spinozistic philosopher, it has become evident that the ability to follow the dictates of one's nature is essential for blessedness. However, this personal nature is merely one expression of the whole of Nature; our individual power is drawn from the power of the whole, and our individual nature from Nature itself. It is necessary that the aspiring individual gain knowledge of natural laws and natural order to understand either inwardness or the ethical ideal fully.

A strong link therefore exists between the human being and Nature, as is characteristic of the feminine perspective. Physical experiences and the affects are valid sources of knowledge for the Spinozistic philosopher. Moreover, references to empirical sources result in the integration of our physical being, the body of which the mind is the idea, into the philosophical life. The properly sensuous philosopher thereby is assured of ethical fulfillment, by means of increased power/virtue.

As emphasized throughout, the knowledge of the state of the universe is the key to salvation/blessedness within the Spinozistic system. The goal is for the intellect to acquire clear and distinct ideas, fathoming the unity of the latter by associations and arrangements, "that our mind may, as far as possible, reflect subjectively the reality of nature" (IU,36). The identification of God or Substance with Nature, under the forms of Natura Naturans ("God . . . considered as a free cause") and Natura Naturata (what follows from the necessity of the divine nature or Attributes (E1,29,Schol), is highly significant. Knowledge of God is none other than the knowledge of Nature, and vice versa; both are concerned with the way things are in the universe.

The laws of Nature thus correspond to divine law, in which context the human being is a mere instrument: "in so far as he is also a part and tool of the whole Nature, this end of man cannot be the final end of Nature, because she is infinite, and must make use of him, together also with all other things" (ST,11,xxiv). Referring to natural laws as the "right and ordinance of nature", Spinoza views all things as conditioned by them "so as to live and act in a given way" (TP,XVI). Regardless of one's state of intellectual perfection, all human beings are subject to Nature as parts of a whole (metaphorically speaking, that is, since Substance in reality has no parts). The human being "whether guided by reason or mere desire [that is, whether enlightened or unenlightened], does nothing save in accordance with the laws and rules of nature" (PT,11,5).

Such information is indispensible for the philosopher, for "the less men know of nature the more easily can they coin fictitious ideas" (IU,21). Without knowing this, a stable character, "the knowledge of the union existing between the mind and the whole of nature", is impossible (IU,5). Our agreement "with the order of the whole of nature" is proportionate to our understanding of our human limitations (EIV,App.). The resulting harmony parallels that in Nature itself, in which "the laws, or nature, of one part adapt themselves to the laws, or nature, of another part in such a way as to produce the least possible opposition."[84]

Following from Spinoza's denial of the Cartesian (and masculine) mind/body dualism, physical experience is granted great significance as an alternate means of attaining knowledge. Empiricism blends subtly into rationalism, due to the intimate relationship existing between the experiencing body and the intellectualizing mind, both of which are expressions of the one reality under two Attributes. Knowledge is experience and experience knowledge, thus we must remain open to experience on the various levels of reality--sense data, intellectual conceptions, and the joy of union in blessedness (the radical empiricism of the feminine principle in which reality is confronted directly). The mind is the idea of the body, reflected under the Attribute of Thought, just as the body forms the mind's *ideatum* in terms of the Attribute of Extension. The mind's knowledge of itself is derived from perceptions of the ideas of bodily affections (E11,23). The idea of an affection, as related merely to the human mind and without relation to the body, is deficient--"like conclusions without premises" (E11,28,Demonst).

Our problems begin in the mind-body complex and thus must be solved within the same context. Correspondingly, the mind also increases its self-understanding in proportion to its understanding of "natural objects", culminating in its absolute perfection through a knowledge of "the absolutely perfect being" (Substance or God). Such a knowledge of Nature increasingly allows the mind to avoid "what is useless"

(IU,14). Alternately expressed, by perceiving the affections of the body, the mind is adapted to perceive many things, an adaptation which increases in proportion to the ways in which the body can be disposed (El1,12 and 14). Essentially, then, the body, and our use of it, exerts a decisive influence upon the state of the mind.

Nature is hailed as the source of axioms--"philosophy is based on axioms which must be sought from nature alone." This sharply contrasts with the knowledge source of faith, restricted to Scripture and revelation (TP,XIV). As has already been pointed out, the empirical appeal to Nature must be mediated by Spinoza's own brand of rationalism. It is intellect which protects us against falling prey to the ever-present delusions of sense experience. And yet attention to Nature equally prevents us from becoming overly-dependent upon mere mental constructions (things of reason). Only in this way, then, can we interpret with any degree of consistency Spinoza's references to physical entities as that from which our ideas are necessarily to be deduced. While avoiding universals and abstractions, the Spinozistic method clings to "real entities", transversing the series of causes "from one real entity to another real entity." Significantly, however, the "series of causes and real entities" is the same as the "series of fixed and eternal things" (IU,39). Sense experience and reason, body and mind, provide mutual confirmation in the pursuit of knowledge of Substance.

Furthermore, Spinoza mentions two possible means by which to persuade others of self-evident truths, one involving the use of discursive reason and the other having recourse to direct experience. Although he obviously prefers the former, as attested to in his devotion to the geometrical method, the latter remains a living option. In terms of empirical evidence, an appeal is made to "facts of natural experience", actually an appeal based on our everyday encounter with Nature. While Spinoza favors deduction due to its reliance upon "the mere power of the understanding", he fully realizes that it is a more involved process, demanding on the part of the practitioner "a great caution, acuteness, and self-restraint". Hence, most people prefer references to experience (TP,V). Presumably, Spinoza's own frequent use of examples from nature in his texts is due to his realization that the greater part of his audience would be persuaded more readily by empirical evidence.

In addition to an appeal to experience, the integration of one's material being into one's system of philosophy, a prime mark of the feminine perspective in remaining open to all aspects of reality, is intrinsic to the Spinozistic system. Beyond the over-all intimacy existing between mind and body, there is the fact that mental decrees under the Attribute of Thought "are nothing but the appetites themselves", also known under the Attribute of Extension as bodily determinations (based on the laws of Motion and Rest) (EIII,2,Schol). Spinoza has no philosophical compulsion to vouchsafe a privileged position for the mind (although he seems to have a personal compulsion to do so). The perfect mind strictly requires and engenders a perfect body, totally integrating our spiritual and physical aspects.

From this state of affairs, one could conclude that the ideal philosopher, in being possessed of the most highly perfected active intellect, also is possessed of the most highly perfected active body. Such a body would function through the dictates of its own nature, that is, spontaneously. Spinoza does mention that the body must be kept fit for all that follows from its nature in order that the mind be fit to understand many things simultaneously--"This mode of living best of all agrees without principles and with common practice; therefore this mode of living is best of all, and is to be universally commended" (EIV,45, Schol to Corol 2).

Although Spinoza makes only passing reference to a perfect body as an attribute of the enlightended philosopher, its necessity cannot be ignored without violating the logical tenets of his thought. The idea (mind) is nourished and modified in accordance with the changes in its <u>ideatum</u> (body), both positively, by increasing power, and negatively, by decreasing power. If reality is not dualistic, but a unified whole, then our being must also be treated as a whole, and no one aspect subordinated to another. Both expressions of our being, the physical as well as the mental, must be treated equally as sources of enlightenment. This is a very feminine approach to the human condition.

But what would such a body look like? Spinoza has almost nothing to contribute on this point. One way to approach this question is to speculate on the evolution of a race of <u>Ubermenschen</u>, mentally and physically superior to the common run of humanity by virtue of their applied knowledge; these would be the philosophers. Note that the self-avowedly inferior Taoist sage (Untermensch) presents a certain contrast to the Spinozistic ideal, illustrating the influence exerted by masculine thought upon Spinoza's philosophy. Yet even the Spinozistic philosopher is advised to keep a low profile among the unenlightened (see above). In an important sense, Mary Wollstonecraft Shelley's fictional Doctor Frankenstein was a Spinozist at heart--his was a project to artificially create a being combining the highest mental and physical abilities, while Spinoza assumed that this high degree of perfection could be achieved by individuals themselves through developing innate capacities.

One possible reason why Spinoza did not pursue this idea of a fully developed and integrated human existence is that a contradictory prejudice in favor of intellect hindered his deductions. His doctrines were not pursued to their logical conclusion. Thus, he refers to "the better part of us", presumably the intellect, which can be made to agree with the natural order (EIV,App. 32). It is the power of the mind alone which is discussed in relation to blessedness, inasmuch as only the mind is judged eternal. That is to say, the intellectual love of God is related to both our mental and physical being and is an affect--"the most constant of all the affects". That most noble of emotions is intimately connected with the body, as shown by the fact that it is incapable of destruction "unless with the body itself" (EV,20,Schol). However, Spinoza also contends that the body can be destroyed, and he deems most of his discussions relevant only "to the present life". Because Spinoza refuses to posit the destruction of our love of God, which would frustrate the goal of "continuous, supreme, and unending happiness", he passes "to the consideration of those matters which appertain to the duration of the mind without relation to the body" (EV,20,Schol). Ignoring the obvious problems of having the mind survive without the body, its ideatum, Spinoza proceeds to declare that the human mind is not entirely destroyed along with the body (at death), but that it contains an unspecified "something" which is eternal (EV,23); "we feel and know by experience that we are eternal" (Schol).

Spinoza's logic seems to be obscured here by a desire for personal immortality, Platonically-tinged with a faith in the eternality of the mind as the highest aspect of our being. A reconstructed, and consistently feminine, version of this conviction concerning the eternal state of the mind would require that the body likewise be eternal in some sense.

Bodily immortality is indeed possible in a rather impersonal sense as the body is a mode or modification of divine Extension. Borrowing from contemporary physics (already seen to be sympathetic of the feminine perspective) one can claim that the atoms of which our body is composed are eternal, can neither be created nor destroyed. Under this revised interpretation, founded on the Law of the Conservation of Matter and Energy, the eternality of the mind becomes problematic unless identified with energy. Death would then constitute not destruction, but the point at which the individuation of these mental and physical elements of the universe, temporarily designated as a person x, are returned to the oneness of reality. Underlying all the changes, the elements remain in the unity of Substance, and cannot be properly termed parts of the whole. Whether or not Spinoza himself would have accepted this type of modified and impersonal immortality is questionable, though it seems to be more consistent with his over-all system of thought, as well as unavoidable as a conclusion for a feminine philosophy. Even he must admit that without the body, no memories are possible (EV,23,Note); yet an eternity of amnesia leaves little hope for a personal immortality.

Regardless of how Spinoza would react to this reconstruction of his philosophy, the philosopher cannot afford to neglect his/her body due to its intimate connection with and effect upon the state of mind. Desire, self-conscious appetite, cannot be dismissed lightly, for it is none other than the essence of the human individual, "in so far as it is conceived as determined to any action by any one of his affections" (EIII,def 1). The result of these conditions is that the life of the philosopher takes on a sensuous dimension, appropriately tempered by moderation. The incorporation of sensuality into the philosophical life is indeed alien to the generally ascetic conceptions of Western philosophy. Its presence in Spinozistic thought confirms the link with the feminine perspective. Any opportunity we have to increase our joy (as related to a positive good) simultaneously yields an increase in our power or perfection, and "the more do we necessarily partake [<u>participare</u>] of the divine nature." Hence, it is in our best interests, in the best interests of our virtue/power, to take advantage of all available sources of joy:

> It is the part of a wise man, I say, to refresh and invigorate himself with moderate and pleasant eating, with sweet

scents and the beauty of green plants,
with ornament, with music, with sports,
with the theatre, and with all things of
this kind which one man can enjoy without
hurting another. (EIV,45,Schol to Corol 2)

Behold the sensuous philosopher!

Even certain areas of activity previously discouraged as tending to immerse one in superficiality become open to the free and philosophical individual, due to a revised perspective. The life styles centering around wealth, sensual pleasure and fame, although rejected by Spinoza as unconductive to his final goal of a constant state of blessedness, can yet offer some assistance in the pursuit of that goal. Their acquisition becomes an obstacle only "so long as they are sought as ends not as means; if they are sought as means they will be under restraint, and, far from being hindrances, will further not a little the end for which they are sought" (IU,4). Indulgence in sex is also sanctioned within marriage for purposes of procreation, contributing both in terms of the education of children (potential philosophers) and in fostering a mutual love in the couple dependent upon "liberty of mind" (EIV, App). This too is a natural expression of our being and follows from human nature. Asceticism is unnecessarily restrictive, and is contrary to the integration sought by a feminine philosophy.

And so we see that, as a self-integrated being composed of both body and mind, the Spinozistic philosopher is inextricably linked to Nature. Nature is none other than God or Substance, and experiences of it yield valuable knowledge in our search for perfection. The body no less than the mind requires perfecting and thereby contributes to our ultimate success. Sense data contribute significantly to our goal. Although Spinoza himself strays somewhat in his prejudice in favor of the mind's eternality, it is possible to reinterpret his thought more consistently, such that both mind and body are equally considered eternal within a cosmic context. A unique view of the philosopher as a sensuous being emerges in Spinozism, as one increases perfection along with the joy of pure pleasures.

Spinoza's system of philosophy, in its pronouncements concerning ethics (in the feminine sense of personal perfection), thus reveals all three of the modes of being which follow from the feminine principle. The evidence of a masculine tinge to certain of

Spinoza's doctrines weakens his feminine focus to some extent: the identification of discursive reason as our human essence and the appeal to rational self interest (enlightened egoism) contrast with the transcendence of narrowly human concerns, including reason, in Taoism's Yin philosophy. Nevertheless, Spinoza employs the masculine elements within a framework which is essentially feminine to serve as means to the ends shared with Taoism and all feminine philosophies. Reason gives way to intuition and enlightened egoism to positive narcissism.

Assuming a metaphysics of oneness and an epistemology of "participation", both of which attest to a feminine orientation, Spinoza derives an appropriate code of conduct for the individual. This code fosters a harmony with the universe and therefore maximizes one's chances of attaining the enlightenment goal referred to as intuition-engendered blessedness. If we live in accordance with these modes of being, we will have a life style conducive to the attainment of that goal, the intellectual love of God, the direct experience of our share in reality.

The path of personal development laid out by the feminine modes of being, Spinozistically expressed, begins with an inward-turning concentration of our natural power, and leads to an actively-implemented receptivity towards one's environment and one's fellow human beings. Finally, there is the recognition of the significance of Nature, manifested in our own nature qua human. Being possessed of a body as well as a mind, both empirical experience and sensuality can be profitably incorporated into an ethical life.

2. Socio-Political Implications: The Enlightened Commonwealth

With the consistency possible only in a unified system of thought, and in the undifferentiated feminine universe, Spinoza pursues an investigation of socio-political problems using the method previously applied to metaphysics, epistemology, and ethics. The insights gained in these areas are extended to a communal context. Given the oneness of reality, there can be but one way to approach it, that is, realistically (taking reality in the Spinozistic sense). Our aim is not to elaborate upon Spinoza's theories of politics, but rather to use his comments to illustrate what a commonwealth and society incorporating feminine modes of being might look like in practice. We are concerned with isolating those elements which qualify the enlightened commonwealth envisioned by Spinoza to be designated feminine in perspective.

The justification for presenting this fundamentally masculine system of society, guided by discursive reason, as a product of the feminine perspective lies in the assumptions which underlie its structure. These assumptions are threefold and are derived from our previous discussions: (i) that reality is metaphysically one, but approachable on several epistemological levels, and (ii) human beings, modes of Substance, possess a specific nature/virtue which, (iii) when perfected, allows them to achieve blessedness, the ethical experience of universal oneness. Interpreted in a socio-political context, these assumptions lead the proponent of feminine philosophy to promote communal blessedness by establishing a unified and enlightened commonwealth, capable of offering benefits to all of its citizens commensurate with their level of knowledge and development.

The common motivating force of conatus is harnessed by the philosopher to forge a natural bond between the citizens, despite the fact that their self-interest is variously considered in terms of the narrow ego-self (at the lowest level of imagination), the enlightened egoism of the reason-dominated individual, or with respect to the shared Self revealed by intuition. In each case the positive narcissism of the feminine perspective is active, allowing both individual and community to flourish when harmonized, either consciously or unconsciously, within the oneness of reality. Individuals dominated by imagination adhere to the feminine state insofar as it satisfies their basic survival needs, while those guided by reason judge the state to be a necessity for protecting the interests of humanity, or even as an end in itself. Recognizing these attitudes in others, the Spinozistic philosopher is willing to benignly manipulate them as a means to the highest feminine end, in the same manner that her/his own human nature was manipulated to achieve personal ethical perfection. Only the intuitively-enlightened individual can fully appreciate the state as an expression of the oneness of the universe and as a vehicle for establishing the peace and harmony intrinsic to Nature in the human community.

As human beings, we turn to the essence of human nature, discursive reason, to guide us to our true human good. Until such time as that nature, or reason, has been perfected, the intuition which transcends to absolute reality remains out of reach. Insofar as we are in the interim state of being citizens of a human commonwealth, we do well to follow the guidance of masculine human reason; but insofar as we are sharers in the one reality at the highest level of being, we follow feminine intuition. The essential difference between the individual guided by reason and one who is intuitively-oriented lies in the fact that, although both share a knowledge of the oneness of reality, only the individual versed in intuition possesses knowledge which is direct experience. The integration of the masculine perspective within the encompassing character of the Transformative feminine is illustrated by this state of affairs.

The feminine modes of being referred to above find appropriate social and political expression in this commonwealth. The inwardness mode of being emerges in the communal all-is-one-ness attitude; the commonwealth is "guided as if by one mind", the mind of a citizenry united by a commitment to uphold the state. It is here that positive narcissism plays a major role in representing and promoting the interests of the community at large, as well as satisfying all levels of self-interest. The commonwealth itself is a necessary improvement upon the dangerous and chaotic state of Nature. It is a rational extension of the perfection of human nature, which in turn prepares the way for the ultimate perfection in Substance.

The receptivity mode of being applies to both the citizens of the commonwealth and its sovereign(s). In its communally modified form of non-assertion, this feminine mode of being is revealed as a virtue/power in cases where masculine assertion would be counterproductive. Each group remains open to reality as embodied in the necessity of the state's existence, insuring their personal survival along with that of the whole. A delicate balance thereby is secured between individual freedom and acquiescence to the demands of the commonwealth; between the absolute power granted the sovereign(s) and the natural limitations required to maintain that power intact. The state, which is guided by discursive reason, particularly when it takes a democratic form, has the support of its enlightened, reason-guided citizens while offering the conditions most conducive for the attainment of that state of being in the masses, a further example of the contingent elitism entailed by Spinoza's system.

In relation to Nature, the commonwealth has the status of an organism, and must strive to work in harmony with the laws of natural right and power for purposes of self-preservation. These same principles guide its policy with regard to international relations, as an unhypocritical protection of its own interests. If successful, the commonwealth can establish itself as eternal, matching the eternality of Nature and God/ Substance on a lesser scale. This requires a harmonization with the natural order, a working with, rather than against, the course of Nature, of reality.

a. <u>All-is-one-ness--the single mind of the commonwealth.</u> If the universe, or Substance, as well as human nature conform to Spinoza's conceptions, then a characteristically Spinozistic response is demanded in the sphere of social and political affairs. The commonwealth is a single being, a microcosm ruled by the same natural law and order that governs the universal macrocosm. Its perfection proceeds along the same path as that of the individual in ethics, with the same determination to make the best of the human condition and to gather the greatest support for that end from all aspects of its being, that is to say, from all segments of society. Being guided by reason, the Spinozistic commonwealth is a practical means to, or foundation for, the feminine end of communal blessedness, just as the life style of discursive reason has been shown to be the means to that end on an individual scale. The state is not an end in itself, nor could it be such in a feminine universe (although this certainly may be possible in a masculine one). In fact, a planned obsolescence is built into the system. As the citizens increase in perfection they outgrow the second level constructions of the state and tend toward the highest level of reality, reflected in productive (Self-regulated) anarchy.

To begin his investigation of political thought, Spinoza both denounces the general (masculine) method of philosophers and proposes his own (feminine) alternative. The method generally employed by political philosophers has been entirely theoretical, and even idealistic, both anathema to the practical feminine mind. Working under the unrealistic assumption that human beings in the ideal state far surpass the level of ordinary individuals,

> they conceive of men, not as they are, but as they themselves would like them to be. Whence it has come to pass that,

instead of ethics, they have generally written satire, and that they have never conceived a theory of politics which could be turned to use, but such as might be taken for a chimera, or might have been formed in Utopia, or in that golden age of the poets, when, to be sure, there was least need of it. (PT,I,1)

In sharp contrast with this masculine approach to the problem of politics, Spinoza's own chosen method is founded upon solid reality and the empirical evidence offered by actual practice. Above all, Spinoza is concerned with the practical application of his theories, contrary to the general opinion of his time which asserted that theory and practice are diametrically opposed. Under the latter view philosophers are deemed the most unfit candidates for managing public business, because they are too theoretical in their approach. Correspondingly, politicians (the day-to-day practitioners of political science), despite their obvious advantages in terms of experience, have gained a bad reputation for being "more crafty than learned" (PT,I,1-2).

To remedy this confusing and counterproductive state of affairs, Spinoza proposes that we "deduce from the very condition of human nature, not what is new and unheard of, but only such things as agree best with practice . . . I have laboured carefully, not to mock, lament, or execrate, but to understand human actions" (PT,I,4). This attitude provides an excellent example of the feminine perspective in action, concentrating as it does on the 'is', a realistic assessment of human limitations, rather than speculating on some ephemeral 'ought' of unattainable ideals, as the masculine perspective is prone to do. There is an openness to and acceptance of the facts of reality as they stand, without futile (at least in a deterministic universe) attempts at reforming either human nature of Nature as a whole to conform to our narrow human conceptions. Rather than vainly waiting for the ideal of universal blessedness to be realized, Spinoza is content to devise a political system which offers an environment conducive to the attainment of the highest knowledge while simultaneously making it unnecessary for all citizens to be enlightened. In the case of Spinozistic philosophy, Hamlet's statement that "there are more things in heaven and earth, than are dreamt of in your philosophy" is not an accusation, but an accepted fact of life.

The material with which we have to work in devising a practical and functional commonwealth includes the intrinsic virtue/power of human nature, as outlined above. Hence, initially there is a great emphasis upon masculine elements, elements which later are integrated into and transcended by the intuitive approach to our role in the universe as a whole. Since it is from the so-called state of Nature that the commonwealth emerges, one must be aware of the conditions of that state of being, its elements of natural right and natural law, in order that the transition to a civil state be successfully effected. This would not be possible without our previous knowledge of metaphysics and epistemology, which now must be extended to the society.

But is Spinoza's system unique enought to merit a feminine reconsideration, or is it merely a reiteration of standard seventeenth century theorizing? Both the similarities and the differences between the assumptions and conclusions of Spinozistic and Hobbesian thought have been treated at length by other interpreters, and need only be mentioned here in passing. Spinoza begins his political discussions with sweeping Hobbesian pronouncements, only to temper them later by references to (feminine) reality as Spinoza himself encountered it.[85] The very fact that Spinoza does not exempt Hobbes from the general condemnation of his predecessors in the field of political philosophy (PT, 1), can be cited as evidence that Spinoza considered Hobbes to be equally guilty of theoretical web-spinning.[86]

One concept which Spinoza did share with Hobbes was that the state of Nature, the primal condition of human interrelationships prior to formal social institutions. In his treatment of this concept Spinoza demonstrates his distinctive (feminine) perspective. The question has been raised as to whether Spinoza believed the state of Nature could be assigned to an actual period of time in human history. It has been suggested that he actually was referring to "natural propensities in men and the results which they would produce if given free rein."[87] This interpretation agrees with Spinoza's ahistorical, eternal outlook, and is in keeping with the static Elementary character of the feminine principle. A precedent for the usage of the state of Nature in this sense may be found in Spinoza's references to an ideal individual, an ethical model, as a thing of reason. In other words, it is philosophically useful to talk about a state of Nature as an intellectual construction and aid in the clarification of our ideas.

What are the conditions of this state of Nature which make it so pivotal in the discussion of a femininely-oriented politics? Under such a completely natural state of being the powerful force of conatus is revealed as our prime motivation force. Conatus, the instinct for self-preservation, leads us to avoid what is deemed detrimental to self-interest (as that self-interest is perceived, and not necessarily identical with our true self-interest). The utmost that the commonwealth can attempt is to make use of, benignly manipulate if you will, the "natural propensities" for purposes of domestic tranquillity and mutual security. The passions, to whose domination most individuals are naturally subject, must be recognized first and then manipulated to achieve the desired results: "A commonwealth ruled in this way continues, in a sense, to remain in the state of nature which, in another sense, it surmounts."[88] The same subtle manipulation is practiced by the Taoist sage-sovereign when she or he adopts the wu-wei policy. By ostensibly leaving things undone, the government encourages the people to exert their own power. For both Spinoza and the Taoist the inherent capabilities of the people are never in doubt.

So, unlike Hobbes, Spinoza does not summarily condemn the state of Nature, but accepts it as a condition of reality within whose restrictions we must learn to function. More importantly, it is for this reason that Spinoza is unwilling to accept the Hobbesian solution of totalitarian government, which Hobbes conceives of as the lesser of two evils. True to the feminine perspective, Spinoza chooses to work with and through Nature, rather than to try to usurp its power by means of an artificial human paradigm (the Leviathan).

Within the Spinozistic system, knowledge of the state of Nature gives us the power to establish a sound commonwealth, at least until such time as the passions are replaced by the guidance of reason and the latter by intuition. (At that point of course, the structure of the state would no longer be necessary). If the passions cannot be eliminated entirely, and the ideal of citizens ruled solely by human reason cannot be fully realized, the state can continue to guarantee that the results of these inevitable passions are subject to rational control. All of this assumes that the sovereign authority is to some extent enlightened and rational, or at the very least, has incorporated into its structure Spinozistically adequate knowledge of human nature.

One of the most important natural elements to be understood and manipulated by the sovereign is natural right. This right is directly related to one's degree of power,[89] that is, Spinozistic virtue. If Spinoza's perspective were not feminine and communally-oriented the doctrine of natural right would deteriorate into the simplistic formula that might (power) makes right. However, the feminine attitude forbids such deterioration by distributing both right and power among all beings in accordance with natural necessity. The instinctive drive towards self-preservation cannot be condemned by narrowly human morality, in the same sense that the workings of impartial Substance cannot be judged by human standards. We cannot contend that things 'ought' to be another way (our way), even within the confines of human society, for the fact remains that this 'is' the way things are. The limits of perfection, power, and virtue already have been determined. Our highest moral aspirations cannot alter reality. Therefore, it is in our best interests to accept that reality, to learn what our limitations and potentials realistically are, and to attempt to work within those limits. To succeed in this amounts to the attainment of blessedness, for a society as well as for an individual.

But why do individuals ever agree to relinquish their natural right when in the state of Nature (considered as either an historical period or as a thing of reason) in exchange for an inhibited existence within the civil state? This Hobbesian phrasing of the question betrays the either/or logic of the masculine perspective--either we have our rights or we have the state. In fact, the Spinozistic state does not deprive us of our natural rights at all (see note 89). However, as Spinoza himself admits, it is also a fact that the human being is the natural enemy of other human beings when stagnated at the lowest level of reality/ knowledge and operating through conflict-yielding passions of anger, envy, and hatred (PT,11,4). This much has been demonstrated in his ethics. Because this form of life in the state of Nature is singularly unsuitable for the active pursuit of intellectual perfection, with respect to both reason and intuition, it is objectionable to the Spinozistic philosopher or free individual. This is our motivation for establishing a more fertile environment in the commonwealth.

The solution offered by the commonwealth rests upon an extension of Spinoza's ethics of positive narcissism. A rechanneling of natural right is required in a manner conducive to communal interests, but which also is linked intimately to the interests of the individual. To prevent a relapse into the low level state of Nature, once it has been overcome, it is necessary for a transfer of power to be effected from the citizens to the civil authority, as vested in the sovereign(s). Insofar as that transfer is defective, or unstable, which is generally the case, the commonwealth lives under the threat of plummeting once more into chaos. The means of maintaining the proper balance are discussed further on.

The commonwealth can grant us the personal security unattainable when individuals remain in counterproductive competition with one another--"not to rule, or restrain by fear, not to exact obedience, but contrariwise, to free every man from fear, that he may live in all possible security; in other words, to strengthen his natural right and to work without injury to himself or others"(TP,XX). The positive expressions of natural right, those which are communally-oriented, are allowed free reign, while only those which are misguided and detrimental to the good of others are suppressed. The natural right appropriate to human beings is inconceivable to Spinoza, or considered unrealizable, "except where men have general rights, and combine to defend the possession of the lands they inhabit and cultivate, to protect themselves, to repel all violence, and to live according to the general judgment of all" (PT,11,15). None of these things would be possible in a pure state of Nature, unless blessedness had been attained universally. Thus, neither is the fullest expression of natural right for the greatest number possible in that state of being. In a practical sense, mutual support among human beings is required to obtain the very necessities of life (EIV,App.). The communal approach likewise provides for an essential "division of labour", allowing individuals to specialize in skills vital to insure the preservation of all (TP,V).

But nonetheless the commonwealth structure does result in certain restrictions upon its citizens, such as are required to promote communal interests. Due to the admitted lack of "truth and judgment" in the masses, a real need for a governmental authority exists (PT, VII,27). Both laws and government force are needed "to restrain and repress men's desires and immoderate impulses" (TP,V). The two requirements for a successful commonwealth plan are identified by Spinoza as first being promotive of "living in unity", and secondly, having a means "by which the multitude may be guided or kept within fixed bounds" (PT,1,3). If, for Spinoza "ignorance [is] . . . the source of all wickedness",[90] it is essential for the preservation of the common good and maintenance of peace to impose some checks on the human passions which ignorance allows to run rampant. But once again it is all a matter of perspective. The philosophers or free individuals would not experience any restrictions in their life style inasmuch as they have already liberated themselves from the passions.

Following the pattern of Spinozistic ethics, the necessity of establishing a formal commonwealth is derived from our imperfect, but perfectible, nature qua human. Political anarchy could reign in a community whose members have perfected their reason; under such conditions formal laws would be replaced by the inner law of intellect (TP,V), and intuition would emerge as the guiding force, expressed as feminine Eros/relatedness. If all our desires were aimed at what is truly most useful (that is, if all individuals were enlightened as to their true good, which is identical with the good of all) "no art would be needed to produce unity and confidence" (PT,lll,3).

Unfortunately, this is not the case. As a realist in the feminine mold, Spinoza understands that a superficial unity must be substituted when conditions do not allow community oneness to develop through a general internal movement to a higher level of knowledge. The Taoist seems more optimistic about achieving the desired conditions through natural processes and does not elaborate upon any interim structure as a substitute for the ultimate form of government. The reconstructions of reason serve the same function as a means to the end of personal blessedness.

Spinoza's scheme demands that safeguards be built into any social and political system, so that all involved, "whether they will or no", outwardly act in a manner conducive to the general welfare, creating an enforced semblance of a community living under the guidance of reason (PT,VI,3). The most desireable citizens are those whose lives are subject to the dictates of reason, and hence are candidates for the experience of blessedness. A framework is required to insure the proper order, "as if" all indeed were enlightened, regardless of the underlying fact that many minds are bound by passions. Due to the general lack of individuals who conform to rational guidance, and the influence of envy and vengeance, a great deal of "skill and watchfulness" is demanded for the establishment of communities (EIV,App.).

In analyses of Spinoza's political philosophy, much has been made of the prominence of the personal profit among its many other "amoral" elements (see Hampshire). This interpretation may well be valid insofar as Hobbes' similar statements on self-interest are concerned, but seems too simplistic to account for Spinoza's views when treated as a whole. In expressing this viewpoint, Hampshire is representative of the majority of interpreters who attempt to evaluate Spinoza's thoughts within the context of the masculine perspective. Placed in what we have argued to be its proper feminine perspective, Spinoza's philosophy emerges with its own peculiarly feminine code of ethics, a positive narcissism founded on the principle of an enlightened self-interest in a shared Self. The motivations of fear, greed, etc., are appropriate only for the unenlightened, even though an appeal to these motivations can be beneficial when more refined methods have failed. The commonwealth is "established by a free multitude", which tends to be guided by hope rather than by fear in its pursuits. Consequently, the population "aims at living for its own ends", as opposed to the aims of the enslaved negatively engaged in "escaping death" (PT,V,5).

Without the feminine metaphysics which postulates a holistic and intimately integrated universe, Spinoza's political recommendations would indeed qualify as blatant egotism. But his appeal to self-interest cannot be understood simply as personal in the sense of the ego-centered masculine perspective. Approached from the second level of reason, self-interest is universal among human beings, while at the level of intuition it has cosmic applicability. The inner is always the outer for the feminine philosopher, the individual microcosm reflects the universal macrocosm, and neither can be fully comprehended in isolation.

Specific appeals are made to positive narcissism in securing an obedient citizenry. Spinoza mentions several ways in which the commonwealth can convince the citizens of its merits with respect to self-preservation. To begin with, the alternative to communal life is solitude, which all individuals fear due to the inability of any one person to guarantee their own defense and even basic survival. Hence, we possess a "natural" aspiration for a civil state (PT,VI,1). Moreover, our union with other individuals of a like, or human, nature has been shown, on ethical grounds, to increase both our power and right over Nature beyond what is possible singly. The greater the number of individuals involved, the greater our collective power (PT,II,13). The validity of any compact is judged by Spinoza in terms of its utility "without which it becomes null and void" (TP,XVI), and our highest advantage is insured by being a member of a human community. As demonstrated in the Ethics, what agrees with our nature is most useful to us, namely, other human beings: "Nothing, therefore, is more useful to man than man [homine]. Men can desire, I say, nothing more excellent for the preservation of their being than that all should so agree at every point that the minds and bodies of all should form, as it were, one mind and one body" (EIV,18,Schol).

Thus banded together, the citizens seek the preservation of the communal being, the body politic, as a reflection of "the common good of all". This provides excellent training for the lifestyle of reason-guided individuals, who live the ethics of positive narcissism. It accustoms people, in pursuit of personal advantage, to "desire nothing for themselves which they do not desire for other men" (EIV,18,Schol). The identification of the commonwealth as a single-minded individual also is supported by Spinoza's definition of an individual thing as the union of several things in action, "all simultaneously the cause of one effect" (EII,def,7). The right of the supreme authorities in the state rests on the assumption "that they are, as it were, the mind of the dominion" (PT,IV,1).

By contrast, Spinoza provides us with some hints of what constitutes or contributes to an unsuccessful state. Such a commonwealth is unable to maintain peace and harmony, harboring dissident elements, social viruses, in its own being. It lives under the constant threat of war from external elements, and suffers internally from widespread disobedience to its laws (PT,V,2). The "unsatiable desire" for wealth and fame are cited as common contributing factors in the downfall of a commonwealth,[91] and are symptomatic of discontent among the citizenry. In effect, the unsuccessful commonwealth fails to convince its citizens that their interests are bound intimately to those of the state.

As for the actual means by which the state successfully accomplishes its tasks, they too are centered in positive narcissism. As mentioned previously, certain safeguards must be built into the system. A state which depends upon "good faith" and the honesty of its administrators will inevitably be unstable due to the inherent instability of unperfected human nature. If a state is to be successful it must, in a sense, be foolproof, or proof against the manifold folly of mankind. Its system must be so constructed that it will work regardless of the motives of its administrators, who, "whether guided by reason or passion, cannot be led to act treacherously or basely." The state cannot be dependent upon the tenuous virtue of its movers (PT,I,6). Unlike Plato's Republic, the sovereigns of Spinoza's commonwealth need not be enlightened philosophers (although this certainly would be an advantage).

The underlying power of this self-supportive system derives primarily from the benign manipulation of human passions, noted earlier. Fear and reverence insure obedience in those cases where reason is lacking sufficient force, in accordance with the encompassing law of Nature (PT,IV,4). Spinoza declares that the "multitude becomes a thing to be feared if it has nothing to fear" (EIV,54,Schol). As revealed by Spinozistic ethics, affects can be restrained only by greater and opposite affects--

> every one abstains from doing an injury through fear of a greater injury. By this law, therefore, can society be strengthened, if only it claims for itself the right which every individual possesses of revenging himself and deciding what is good and what is evil, and provided, therefore, that it possesses the power of prescribing a common rule of life, or promulgating laws and supporting them.

The Spinozistic commonwealth does make this claim (EIV,36,Schol 2).

To defend the constitution of the state, "common human passion" must supplement the resources of reason--"otherwise, if it relies only on the help of reason, it is certainly weak and easily overcome" (PT,X,9). Spinoza details the causes of crime in terms of the internal disruptions of domestic peace, "disgust at the present--desire for change, headlong anger, and contempt for poverty" (PT,XVII). The solution to the problem lies in making change both unnecessary and undesireable within his society. If the state is perfect, or sufficiently perfect to run efficiently, no one will be motivated to act against it in a criminal manner. Hence, the safety of a society is dependent upon the condition that the greater power rests with the upholders of the laws and conventions, rather than with those "having an interest in overthrowing them".[92] Spinoza's personal motivation for avoiding a life of crime is appropriately philosophical--it is "expressly repugnant to my special nature, and would make me stray from the love and the knowledge of God."[93] The state should strive to duplicate this attitude in all its citizens.

Underlying all of these practical reasons for giving allegiance to a commonwealth, one can sense Spinoza's true objective in promoting domestic order and tranquillity, namely, the securing of an environment conducive to the philosophic pursuit of blessedness. The commonwealth's "ultimate aim" is "to enable them [the citizens] to develope [sic] their minds and bodies in security, and to employ their reason unshackled" (TP,XX). That commonwealth is judged best which allows the fullest expression of human life, "defined not by mere circulation of the blood, and other qualities common to all animals, but above all by reason, the true excellence and life of the mind" (PT,V,5). Discursive reason is the culmination of human nature qua human, and yet merely the means to a universal goal, union with God or reality, transcending the human level of existence. Ethics, educational theory, medicine, and technology are all elements instrumental in such a society, but the most important element is "improving the understanding and purifying it" (IU,5). And unless we ultimately purify ourselves of all human elements, the intellectual love of God sub species aeternitatis will remain beyond us.

There are a few points under this aspect of Spinoza's political philosophy which warrant further clarification in order to avoid seeming contradiction in his thought. On the one hand, the best or ideal commonwealth functions under the dictates of reason and is referred to as a necessary condition of attaining the Spinozistically good life. But where is the source of reason in the state? Who or what insures that the laws of the commonwealth will conform to the dictates of reason if the guidance of reason can only be realized within the confines of the commonwealth?

On the other hand, Spinoza states that our inherently developed reason prompts our obedience to the state and demonstrates that such an environment contributes to our self-interest. This arrangement solves the problem of the source of the state's rationality as coming from those whose own rationality pre-dates the formation of the commonwealth. However, if the acquisition of the guidance of reason is possible prior to the existence of the state, and yet constitutes the prime motivation for the establishment of such a state, then the latter obviously is not as essential as we have been led to believe. Thus the founding of a state both presupposes the existence of reason-dominated individuals and makes possible the cultivation of our rational nature.

This apparent contradiction can be dealt with in several ways. Let us first examine some of the remarks made by Spinoza concerning this issue. The state which has the greatest freedom has laws "founded on sound reason", with the result that every citizen has the opportunity to be free, "that is, live with full consent under the entire guidance of reason" (TP,XVI). The best state supplies the environment for attaining freedom in the Spinozistic sense of acting by natural necessity. The rule of the multitude "by one mind" is judged impossible unless the laws of the dominion conform "to the dictate of reason" (PT,11,21).

The criterion for a dominion's agreeing with the dictate of reason is the degree to which it possesses "the right of the supreme authority" (PT,VIII,7). In other words, the dominion is rational in proportion to its absolute right, insofar as it represents the citizens or "the will of all" (PT,111,5). Hallett describes this as a very practical form of reason, "accommodated to the prevalent level of human nature among the individuals subjected thereto".[94] The dynamics of Spinoza's levels of reality and knowledge are once again crucial. Discursive reason, the essence of human nature, both reveals and acts upon the knowledge of our true self-interest, being directed toward the "true good" of humanity as a whole (TP,XVI). It facilitates the move up the scale of being.

The value of the all-is-one-ness mode of being which leads us to combine our powers within a state lies not only in the strengthening of self-preservation but also in the opportunity to "cultivate the mind" (PT,II,15). The benign manipulation of the affects within the state with regard to the multitude has similar results-"at last, they come to live according to the guidance of reason, that is to say, become free men, and enjoy the life of the blessed" (EIV,54,Schol). The state "opens the way to positive moral and cultural development" without being the actual "organ" of enlightenment (the intellect alone being such an organ).[95] The same situation is represented in the classroom: by being in that room, individuals are offered the opportunity to learn, are exposed to a potential learning experience. However, from their mere presence in that room, it does not necessarily follow that they will learn anything, or even learn what they were intended to be taught.

References have already been made to the various passages in which Spinoza admits that discursive reason is a weak force among humanity in general. Reason is not our sole motivation, and rarely the prime one; "blind desire" has many more devotees (PT,II,5). Moreover, no one individual of any type can claim to act unfailingly under the guidance of reason or "be at the highest pitch of human liberty" (TP,II,8). While well aware of these realistic hindrances, Spinoza adopts a positive view; our attention must be focused on our highest potential. Because the essence of human life involves discursive reason, our positive meditations center around the human individual *qua* human, that is, under the guidance of reason.

It is the ever-present possibility of forming perfected human individuals, who conform to the ideal type of the Spinozistic philosopher or free individual and can live a life under the guidance of reason exclusive of the state, that accounts for the foundation of the state itself guided by reason. Spinoza does refer to the existence of such individuals in the pre-commonwealth state of Nature; being led by reason, they are "most powerful and most independent" (PT,III,7). The irrational state would be created by individuals "destitute of reason", just as the rational state is the creation of those guided by reason (PT, III,6).

The contingent elitism recognized in Spinoza's ethics disperses the apparent contradictions in his commonwealth which is both founded by rational individuals and provides the environment for becoming rational. The enlightened elite (at the levels of reason and intuition) are responsible for instilling the dictate of reason into the system of the state, while the unenlightened masses (at the level of imagination) reap the advantages of having an environment conducive to their own attainment of blessedness. Both groups benefit from this arrangement-the philosopher has the peace and security necessary for intuitive contemplation, and the scientist for the continued constructions of reason, while the multitude has the opportunity to become equally blessed. Reason rules against the solitary life "so long as men are liable to passions" (i.e., so long as we hold the potential of being contrary to our own human nature): "reason altogether teaches to seek peace, and peace cannot be maintained, unless the commonwealth's general laws be kept unbroken" (PT,III,6). It is in our own best interests, as advocates of reason, to teach others to live by reason also (EIV,App.9). As an enlightened philosopher, Spinoza's assertion with regard to his earliest text (The Principles of Descartes' Philosophy) applies equally well to all of his works-"I should like all men to be able easily to persuade themselves that these [matters] are published for the good of all men."96

The all-is-one-ness mode of being in the feminine perspective therefore achieves expression in Spinoza's idea of a commonwealth guided by a single mind, a mind which functions as if it were rational, and is able to act as a springboard to the intuitive experience of oneness. Through the mediation of reason's enlightened egoism, a primal state of Nature, with the supports of natural law and natural right, evolves into a commonwealth which rests upon the extension of conatus in the ethics of positive narcissism. The necessity for such a commonwealth becomes manifest on several levels, including its advantages over solitude, the greater power and right exerted by a community of individuals, as compared with a single person, and the usefulness of associating with individuals of a like nature. The good state is organized in such a way as to promote harmony and peace, which is accomplished by means of a benign manipulation of human passions.

Most especially, and most persuasively for Spinoza himself, the necessity of the commonwealth is made clear in relation to the ideal human life in accordance with discursive reason. A rational state both promotes the continuance of such a life for the enlightened and provides the conditions for attaining it (or at least superficial trappings) among the unenlightened masses. An appeal to Spinoza's contingent elitism is required to locate the source of the state's rationality in the type of the free individual who is motivated by a narcissism that become a positive under the feminine perspective.

b. Non-assertion--the balance of citizen and sovereign. The receptivity mode of being maifiests itself politically as feminine non-assertion. In relating this mode to the Spinozistic system one may also refer to the delicate balance of power between the naturally powerful citizen and the contingently empowered sovereign(s). According to Spinoza's own metaphysics, a system of checks and balances exists naturally, and it is necessary to remain open or receptive to this reality in order to survive as either an individual or a commonwealth. The individual citizen avoids a direct confrontation with the laws of the commonwealth, inasmuch as it is the seat of an overwhelming authority, while the sovereign remains aware of the inherent dangers of alienating the multitude, the ultimate source of power which could be revoked at any time. Viewed in this context, feminine non-assertion is a virtue for both the citizen and the sovereign(s).

The significance of the balancing factor in Spinoza's political system has not escaped the notice of interpreters. Speaking from a fundamentally masculine orientation, Hampshire prefers to describe the balance as one "between forces of self-assertion",[97] emphasizing the "positive" or masculine assertiveness, rather than the "negative", feminine yielding of non-assertion. Both are equally essential here. Spinoza can be said to introduce a feminine element into politics, for the feminine recommendation to encourage spontaneity or naturalness transcends the balance of assertion and non-assertion in the anarchistic community of the blessed, where intuition reigns supreme. Spinoza's pessimistic (realistic?) assessment as to the likelihood of achieving such a community is reflected in his concentration upon organizing a state which could be enlightened in its functioning despite the lack of enlightened citizens.

Spinoza strongly defends individual freedom and warns against the insecure foundations of a violent or oppressive government. His system strives to persuade by an appeal to self-interest on various levels, rather than force, and to benignly coerce, rather than oppress. A certain amount of authority must be exercised over the citizens if any semblance of a commonwealth can exist. The solution to this natural tension lies in philosophical moderation, which in turn is rewarded with continued survival (TP,V). In order to determine what constitutes moderation, or the extent to which non-assertion as a mode of being is advisable for either citizen or sovereign, their respective roles in the commonwealth first must be understood. The balance established between these two groups then can be exemplified in the democracy. This form of government was deemed the "most natural" by Spinoza due to its ability to harmoniously merge the two roles.

The ideal citizen in the Spinozistic commonwealth is an integral member of the body politic, either directly (in a democracy) or indirectly (in monarchies and aristocracies). It has been asserted that "the supreme ideal of all statecraft" for Spinoza consists in the perfection of the individual citizen.[98] This assertion seems to be true insofar as the perfect citizen is one and the same with the perfected or enlightened individual, the realization of which is to a large extent dependent upon the proper social and political conditions. Significantly, good citizenship is an acquired, not an innate, virtue: "men are not born fit for citizenship, but must be made so (PT,V,2).

The prime characteristic of the perfect citizen is obedience to the commonwealth, which flows spontaneously from the sense of shared interest appealed to in positive narcissism. Despite that common characteristic, underlying motives for obedience vary considerably, falling basically under the headings of the two types of citizens identified above, namely, those who are enlightened to the oneness of reality (either as a thing of reason or an intuitive experience), and those who are unenlightened. One need not comprehend the plan of Spinozistic reality to act in harmony with it. Being guided by reason, the enlightened citizen freely chooses to obey the common laws out of a desire for rational self-preservation, having determined that true self-interest is bound up with the interests of the state--"desires, in order that he may live more freely, to maintain the common rights of the State" (EIV,73, Demonst).

For those citizens who remain unenlightened, or in bondage to the passions, fear of punishment and/or hope of reward constitute the primary motivation for civil obedience. With his usual realistic outlook, Spinoza recognizes the fact that not all citizens will be able to live in accordance with their "own mind" within the commonwealth (PT,11,3). In many instances, the exercise of an indiscriminate freedom by the individual proves detrimental to the community as a whole. The method by which the state is to control the unenlightened citizens with their "common vices of peace" is indirect, that is, by a benign manipulation, so that they are "guided by those passions whence the republic has most advantage" (PT,X,6).

Although fear is in a superficial sense equally effective with reason for yielding concord in the commonwealth, it is a less desireable means of attaining obedience, being "without good faith" and lacking in mental power (EIV,Appr. 16). True obedience is not to be found merely in the superficial act of obeying, but rather has roots in "the mental state of the person obeying." The best dominion exerts an influence over the minds of its subjects (TP,XVII) beyond fear-induced reaction: "people should be kept in bounds by the hope of some greatly-desired good rather than through fear" (TP,V). Hence, use of the negative reinforcement tools of fear and force, characteristic of masculine assertiveness, prevents disobedience without actually promoting the will to obey. A dominion controlled by fear "will be rather free from vices, than possessed of virtue." Contrastingly, the feminine method is indirect and subtle--"men are so to be led, that they may think that they are not led, but living after their own mind, and according to their free decision". The parallel with the Taoist sage-sovereign's application of wu-wei is particularly strong here. Only slaves require tangible rewards for their virtuous actions (PT,X,8). For the free or enlightened individual, virtue/power is an end in itself.

Despite this division between the two classes of citizens in terms of perspective, Spinoza contends that political equality must prevail under the law of the commonwealth, most especially in the context of a democracy. Equality between citizens "is of the first necessity in a commonwealth" (PT,VII,20). This equality also is guaranteed by the conditions of reality, for the citizens are equal in impotence. In comparison with the power of the state, the power of each individual "is of no account" (PT,IX,4). Without such equality "the general liberty is lost" (PT,X,8).

The distinctive quality of the enlightened or reason-guided citizen is the desire to "convert" less fortunate fellow citizens to the most esteemed level of citizenship. Speaking of himself, Spinoza equated being "a good Republican" with desiring "the good of the Republic".[99] The good of the republic consists in none other than perfecting its citizenry, by means of which it too becomes perfected, or holds the potential for becoming a community of the blessed. In being charitable, the citizen attempts to keep the peace and promotes unity; "he does his duty, who helps everyone" (PT,111,10). Self-interest , as well as the common interest, is promoted by the endeavor to perfect others as citizens.

One further duty of the ideal citizen is intimately connected with the exercise of both freedom and reason--the right of free opinion and free expression of that opinion. An individual has a responsibility to work for the repeal of a law which is in fact "repugnant to sound reason", provided that this action proceeds by approved methods within the governmental structure. Spinoza would find no contradiction in the law stating that a protest march must be duly licensed. Spinoza contends that the liberty of citizens to voice their opinions and criticisms can not only be granted "without prejudice to the public peace, to loyalty and to the rights of rulers, but that it is even necessary for their preservation" (TP,XXX). The commonwealth cannot be expected to achieve or maintain a high standard of government in an intellectual vacuum.

Even this freedom of expression has its natural balancing force, however, namely discursive reason, whether imposed by the individual involved, in the case of enlightened, or by the state itself, with regard to the general multitude. The freedoms of thought and speech are not unrestricted, and can succeed and flourish only as "the ordered and self-regulated conduct of reasonable men acting in concert to achieve a common good."[100] The criteria for deciding who fits into this category have already been given in the discussion of the ethical ideal; those who do not live up to this criteria remain subject to the benign manipulations of the enlightened state structure.

The sovereign or sovereigns fulfill a role which is complementary to that of the citizen. The enlightened sovereign is a servant of the people, representing their interests alone through the exercise of the civil authority which has been bestowed by those citizens. Aware of the burdens and temptations posed by this authority, Spinoza considered it inadvisable to entrust that power to a single individual, this being "quite incompatible with the maintenance of liberty" (PT,VII, 29). Hence, personal interests are to be subordinated by the monarch. The duty of the sovereign consists of knowing the state and condition of the dominion thoroughly to determine where its true interests lie, and safeguarding the common welfare by acting in accordance with those interests (PT,VII,3).

More specifically, the sovereigns hold "supreme dominion", and thus are empowered to carry out the normal and necessary functions of a government. These powers include judging citizens, meting out punishments, interpreting laws, appointing judges, seeing to the administration and defense of the commonwealth, directing foreign policy, and imposing taxes (PT,IV,2). The three branches of governmental activity, the legislative, executive, and judicial, are encompassed here, although all are not necessarily under the control of a single individual. In a certain sense, the sovereign also is the source of divine precepts, the "means that God rules among men, and directs human affairs with justice and equity" (TP,XIX). Taking God as the Spinozistic equivalent of Nature, the sovereign is an embodiment of natural law and order within the human community. This is a task fit for a philosopher, although not necessarily restricted to philosophers.

But power and authority belong to the sovereign only insofar as the assent of the citizenry has been secured. Sovereigns must be ever mindful of the fact that their power is contingent upon the continued support of the masses, and that obedience follows only insofar as they are sovereign, that is, possessed of power: "sovereigns only possess this right of imposing their will, so long as they have the full power to enforce it" (TP,XVI). The doctrine of the divine right of kings is dismissed by Spinoza as fiction, for it is society alone that can bestow power upon the ruler (TP, XVII) (moreover, the impartiality of Substance forbids such interference in human affairs). Although it is assumed that sovereigns can never be accused of violating their own laws, being above the law, they can suffer from a decrease in real power. The more coercion is needed in the enforcement of the laws, the less sovereign right is held intact. Revolution is an ever-present option for the masses, as in Taoism.

In Spinoza's judgment, the greatest threat to a commonwealth comes from its own (seditious) citizens, and not from external foes (PT,VI,6). Given modern experiences with totalitarian rule, it is only natural that we should shudder at the prospect of a ruler who is deemed to be above the law. The masculine individual is hesitant to rely upon either the goodness of the sovereign or the power of the populace to resist an errant ruler, preferring the rule of laws. However, Spinoza assumes that the recognition of the citizens as the source of power serves as an effective check on the otherwise absolute authority of the sovereigns, balancing it against the potential power of the multitude. That sovereign is "most independent and most in possession of dominion when he most consults the general welfare of the multitude" (PT,VII,11).

Nor is absolute dominion required by the sovereign. In fact it is "very dangerous", to the citizen "very hateful", and "to the institutes of God and man alike opposed" (PT,VII,14). Instead, adhering to the dictates of positive narcissism, the sovereigns find it advisable to avoid "irrational commands", and promote their own interests "by consulting the public good and acting according to the dictates of reason (TP,XVI). The most successful sovereigns are thus enlightened individuals to the extent that they follow the practical guidance of reason with its intrinsic survival value. To keep the good faith of the citizens, the sovereign also must give evidence of leading a rational private life. (PT,VIII,47).

The limitations on the sovereign's exercise of absolute authority qua representative of the citizens and repository of the collective natural right have been outlined by Spinoza. While not entirely opposed to government intervention in the affairs of its citizens, neither is Spinoza in favor of totalitarianism, which attempts to control all phases of life. Like the philosopher, the commonwealth practices feminine receptivity by means of moderation, avoiding extremes of repression and license. This entails restricting intervention to those actions which affect the general welfare of the state without jeopardizing individual interests. Here too a delicate balance must be maintained in the original organization of the state. A state then would be justified in outlawing a group intent upon its own violent overthrow, but not justified in harassing a group which sought legal reform within the system, and hence offers the possibility of perfecting the commonwealth.

The standard of reality is applied in the political sphere, as in all other areas of Spinoza's philosophy. The limits of the commonwealth's authority extend as far as it reasonably expects that authority to be obeyed. Where neither rewards nor threats suffice to induce the desired behavior, the commonwealth's rights come to an end. Decrees which arouse indignation in the populace or are "abhorrent to human nature", e.g., those which entail matricide or self-torture, cannot be effectively legislated, and hence no attempt should be made to do so (PT,III,8 and 9). One can expect negative results to follow if this warning is ignored. The degree of tolerance incorporated in a civil code of law is proportionate to the degree of culture and morality of its citizens,[101] and the code can be modified to suit their changing needs. Tolerance is itself an indication that the state can afford to allow extensive freedom to its citizens, because they are worthy of its trust.

Three distinct types of decrees are deemed detrimental to the authority of the state and therefore are to be avoided-those which are inadvisable, or tend to weaken the state's authority and power; those which are unsafe, in that they pose a danger to the preservation of the state; and those which are impossible, or cannot be enforced practically.[102] Among the inadvisable decrees are those which overestimate the rationality of the population, assuming they will accept a code of conduct which is in their own best interests when that code is generally objectionable due to the incursion of the passions. In attempting to regulate *all* forms of conduct by law one is "more likely to arouse vices than to reform them. It is best to grant what cannot be abolished, even though it be in itself harmful" (cf. the Taoist view of law). In the category of uncontrollable vices Spinoza lists greed and envy (TP,XX), both of which continue beyond the effective power of law in all societies. Many types of "victimless" crimes are encompassed here as well, "crimes" an individual voluntarily perpetrates against the self or with a willing accomplice. A contemporary issue may serve as an example of this type of law-legalization of personal use of marijuana might well be agreed to by Spinoza as harmless to the commonwealth, or less harmful than futile laws against it, despite the negative effects it may have for the individual user.[103] The various factors would have to be weighed and balanced carefully.

The unsafe decrees include those whose enforcement would lead to rebellion among the citizens. Foremost among these, for Spinoza, are decrees against the freedom of speech. The state certainly may prohibit free speech, but only with detrimental effects. The resulting discontent among the most worthy segment of the population (namely, the intellectuals or philosophers) may well end in sedition (TP,Preface and XX). However, a distinction is observed by Spinoza, as noted above, between rationally considered opinions and mere seditious outbursts.

The state has a clear mandate to forbid sedition for reasons of self-preservation; any opinion which creates "bad" citizens cannot be sanctioned. The final test is the contribution to perfection.

Perhaps the most interesting of the ineffectual decrees are those judged impossible. Spinoza argues that the commonwealth has control only over the external behavior and actions of its citizens and can to no certain extent exert control over mental states. By trying to enforce impossible decrees, such as declaring what should be believed, it runs the risk of nurturing a nation of hypocrites, who conform outwardly, but rebel inwardly. Since these attempts at thought control are doomed to futility, the state merely exposes its own impotence in pressing them: "without such freedom [of opinion], piety cannot flourish nor public peace be secured" (TP,Preface). It would seem that today's "Moral Majority" has undertaken just such an impossible (and dangerous) task.

Given the historical circumstances of Spinoza's time, his criticism of attempts to control individual beliefs or opinions emerges as an attack on the mergence of religion with government and the enforcement of a set code of religious beliefs via state authority. In the centuries between Spinoza's era and our own, there has been a movement from religion as oppressor by means of the state to ideology as oppressor by that same means. A situation parallel to the one Spinoza had in mind now exists in totalitarian governments, which suppress free speech and avidly practice thought control using sophisticated propaganda techniques. The result, as predicted by Spinoza, is the alienation of intellectuals, transforming them into "dangerous" dissidents. The government "which attempts to control minds is accounted tyrannical, and it is considered an abuse of sovereignty and usurpation of the rights of subjects" (TP,XX). The abuse is no less evident when the devices of usurpation are made more subtle.

A similar case for impossibility can be made against the legislation of "morality", or rather, the attempt at such. The problems involved in enforcing the moral standards of one segment of a community with respect to the whole are obvious. Fornication, abortion, and homosexuality occur in states which forbid them as well as in those which ignore these acts. The problem of balance arises once more in determining the extent to which private behavior, deemed immoral by certain groups of citizens, constitutes a real hazard to the stability of the commonwealth, and whether the quality of life for the individual citizen is corrupted by such behavior. These questions must be answered within the context of a given society, by that society itself, keeping in mind Spinoza's realistic admission that "vice" can never be eliminated entirely where universal enlightenment does not prevail. The control of external behavior rather than the transformation of internal perspective amounts to a treatment of the symptom rather than the underlying disease.

The proper attitude for the citizen guided by reason in these controversies consists in not imposing one's personal views upon others and the open acceptance of their views (provided self-preservation, for the individual or the state, is not thereby placed in jeopardy). What Spinoza wants from a state is tolerance, whether with regard to religion or philosophy: "the best government will allow freedom of philosophical speculation no less than of religious belief" (TP,XX). The commonwealth is important primarily because it creates an environment conducive to the pursuit of truth. Spinoza himself personifies the appropriate attitude: "I let every man live according to his ideas. Let those who will, by all means die for their good, so long as I am allowed to live for the truth."[104]

Although the liberalism advocated by Spinoza may appear to be suspiciously masculine, in that it grants high priority to individual expression, it does so only as an interim means to an encompassing feminine end. Within the context of Spinoza's system, the freedoms of thought and speech perform a practical function, that of counteracting tyrannical, therefore uncommunal and unfeminine, rule. By balancing the government power between citizens and sovereigns, and providing an open forum in which governmental policies can be considered and criticized by all who are qualified, power is distributed throughout the community. Freedom is not a masculine end in itself, but a means to the higher feminine goal of a balanced society. As a philosopher of the feminine perspective, Spinoza's interests must lie in establishing the best commonwealth as an environment conducive to universal enlightenment/blessedness, not in securing the greatest possible freedom for the individual citizen (although he himself may have hoped for that). Free speech is instrumental in promothis feminine end, and free thought realistically cannot be suppressed, thus they both have a place in the Spinozistic society.

It is assumed by Spinoza, as in Taoism, that these conditions of balanced power will develop spontaneously, according to the order of Nature, once the proper sturucture is instilled in a society. This assumption is open to serious challenge by those uncommitted to the feminine perspective's view of reality, and thereby qualifies as one of the weaknesses of both feminine philosophies under examination. Although consistent within itself, a feminine system has difficulty assuring others of the necessity of its underlying tenets; final vindication is delayed until such time as the determined conditions have been fulfilled. If the universe is structured in the manner detailed by feminine metaphysics, then these social conditions will follow irrevocably. Metaphysical assumptions bear the overwhelming responsibility for validating socio-political theories. Similarly, enlightenment or blessedness eludes attempts to make it intellectually persuasive when the experiential knowledge of intuition is lacking.

The system of natural checks and balances between citizens and sovereign can be made operative in various forms of government, but is considered by Spinoza to function most effectively in a democratic organization. This form of government he deemed "the most natural and the most consonant with individual liberty" (TP,XVI). Unfortunately, Spinoza did not live long enough to complete his projected study of democracy, leaving us to speculate on his actual ideas based on his brief remarks. Citizenship in a democracy is determined by set legal criteria, entitling one to a share in the dominion. With its broad base of power, a democracy has a greater stake in peace (via positive narcissism) than in war, as advantageous to the majority of its citizens (PT,VII,5). Hence, the tranquillity and stability of such a commonwealth is assured. The citizens themselves must decide whether they should risk their peace and even their lives by declaring war, which would be done only under the gravest necessity. There one further advantage of a democratic form of government--"men's natural abilities are too dull to see through everything at once; but by consulting, listening, and debating, they grow more acute, and while they are trying all means, they at last discover those which they want, which all approve, but no one would have thought of in the first instance" (PT,IX,14). The result is a feminine government by consensus which resolves its own inner conflicts.

Spinoza does mention an alternative to democracy, namely, a government headed by those at a level above average humanity (TP,V). This reference bolsters our previous observations concerning the contingent elitism intrinsic to Spinoza's system of philosophy. Rule by an intellectual or enlightened elite can be expected to result in an efficiently run commonwealth, at least under optimum conditions. "If such were the nature of patricians, that they were free from all passion, and guided by mere zeal for public welfare in choosing their patrician colleagues, no dominion could be compared with aristocracy" (PT,XI,2). Moreover, intolerance is particularly prevalent in a democracy where citizens serve and are ruled by equals (TP,V), a problem which vanishes within the hierarchy imposed by an aristocracy.

A further complication arising from a democratic form of government, but avoided in an aristocracy, is related to the level of the average citizen: "such as persuade themselves, that the multitude or men distracted by politics can ever be induced to live according to the bare dictate of reason, must be dreaming of the poetic golden age, or of a stage-play" (PT,I,5). The existence of an elite is essential even in democracies; how else would the generally unenlightened citizens be able to determine where their true self-interest lies?

Nonetheless, the efficiency of an aristocracy seems to remain purely theoretical. The reality of life, which Spinoza so astutely surveys in all matters, must take account of the obvious deficiencies even among aristocrats, intellectual or otherwise. The negative remarks made in reference to the masses are applicable to all people, being founded on common human nature. Deceived "by power and refinement", we tend to neglect in the rich and noble the same vices which are glaringly evident in the poor (PT,VII,27). Political elitism, via an aristocracy, is contingent upon our being able to find a sufficient number of qualified, that is, reason-guided, individuals which would seem to be extremely limited in number. In any case, the very same checks and balances would apply as in a democracy, namely, positive narcissism. It is necessary to establish conditions in such a way that the senators identify their own profit with the maintenance of peace in the dominion (PT,VIII,31).

Monarchy is discounted as the least perfectable of the three possible forms of government envisioned by Spinoza. Despite the greater stability of a state under the domination of a single ruler, it amounts to slavery, and not peace (i.e., "a union or agreement of minds") (PT,VI,4). Furthermore, it is not possible for one person to rule alone, due to the necessity of delegating some of one's authority to others (PT,VI,5). Unfortunately, a monarch is a mere mortal, unable to sustain constant vigilance (PT,VIII,3). There is the added instability of the human character itself, if unbalanced by other opinions and other minds (PT,VII,1).

To be fully realistic, then, and taking account of the possible flaws in both monarchies and aristocracies, the Spinozist opts for a democratic form of government as best equipped to fulfill the needs of feminine philosophical speculation. Such an arrangement also is best suited for the maintenance of the delicate balance between the roles of individual citizen and sovereign, inasmuch as these roles are merged within a democracy. The system of natural checks and balances is very strong by reason of the large number of individuals involved, and, in addition, the greatest number of human resources are available to solve its problems.

Historical circumstances and his own experiences of contemporary aristocratic and monarchical governments undoubtably influenced Spinoza's conclusion that a democratic form of government would be best equipped to fulfill his conditions for a harmonious and efficient commonwealth. From the vantage point of the twentieth century, a socialist or communist society, in its purest form, appears to have even greater potential for realizing feminine goals. In theory, both socialism and communism adhere to the communal interest of the shared Self, incorporating as well as transcending narrow ego-self interests. At present such a governmental organization has yet to achieve concrete implementation. It is interesting to note that Marxist doctrine assumes an historical development from bourgeois capitalism (embodied in masculine liberal democracy) to interim socialism (with its feminine leanings) then into an altruistic communism, and ultimately, an anarchistic "withering away of the state" (the ideal of a feminine philosophy). In the final stage, as interpreted from the feminine perspective, each individual spontaneously acts from the recognition of participation in the shared Self, universal oneness, rejecting centralized authority, with its potential for totalitarianism, in favor of self-determining small communities (Taoism's plan).

To summarize the non-assertion mode of being, the system of checks and balances in the Spinozistic commonwealth arises naturally from conditions of power and is supported by the individual sense of self-interest. The citizen does not challenge the government (at least not seditiously) for its sovereign power far outweighs her/his own. Moreover, the commonwealth embodies our own best interests. The value of rational criticism remains a civic responsibility. On the other hand, sovereigns are careful not to alienate the citizens and thereby diminish their own power and authority. Thus, public self-interest is safeguarded. Furthermore, the sovereign must avoid those decrees which are unsafe, unadvisable, or impossible. From this it follows that free thought and free speech, the essentials of the philosophical quest communally expressed, remain unhindered and a fertile field for the personal cultivation of blessedness is opened to us.

c. The commonwealth in harmony with Nature. The final feminine mode of being to which the Spinozistic commonwealth conforms involves Nature, specifically, the intimate relationship, or spontaneous continuity, between natural law and order and civil law and order. The manner in which natural conditions are employed for the support of the state already has been demonstrated in terms of positive narcissism under the all-is-oneness mode of being, as well as in the system of natural checks and balances which recommend non-assertion, for both citizen and sovereign. The best state is the one most in harmony with Nature, by being collectively aware of Nature's laws and basing its functioning on those laws.

The ideal Spinozistic commonwealth itself functions as a single organism, acting by its own intrinsic nature and motivated by its own form of conatus. As a unified whole, acting by "one mind", the state carries on international relations, initially with the goal of avoiding disruptive wars and protecting its interests (which is determined in conjunction with the interests of all states). In its imitation of Substance, the commonwealth, if successful, is eternal, the foundation of unwavering social stability. The end result is perfect harmony with external reality, with God or Nature, and internal harmony among its citizens.

The unity essential for the success of the commonwealth also qualifies it as an organic whole. Spinoza's envisioned human societies have been described by Hampshire as "no more than highly complicated natural objects".[105] While its indirect source may be the human mind, the commonwealth ultimately derives from the one Substance, is a natural expression of our own human tendencies, the desire for survival, etc. The commonwealth is not the artificial creation of human intellect so much as it is a spontaneous expression of our relationship to Nature.

Like any other organism, the commonwealth is susceptible to disease. The spiritual, intellectual, and physical well-being of the state is to be maintained through the cultivation of "Moral Philosophy", "the Theory of Education", medical science, and technology (IU,5). These four elements contribute to a stable constitution in the state, just as their individual expressions (ethics, education, health care, and material progress) contribute to the citizen's over-all well-being. Spinoza was too practical to disregard the modern advances which could be instrumental to the happiness of the community.

This highly desired concord is attained in the commonwealth by the implementation of the dictates of reason, in contrast to the discord which is a consequence of being guided by the passions (reacting rather than acting) (PT,VIII,6). Adherence to discursive reason amounts to being faithful to human nature, which essence involves this second level knowledge. The commonwealth, composed of human individuals, is true to its nature qua human and gathers its members behind that one standard. Such "unity of mind" is possible only when the commonwealth adopts as its end what "sound reason teaches is the interest of all" (PT,lll,7). Intuition also seems to have a place. The commonwealth represents the individual citizen on a grand scale, and like the individual, is most successful when "guided by laws based on the highest possible understanding".[106]

The result is that the citizens of the commonwealth "together are to be considered a man in the state of nature" (PT,VII,22). This organism has a natural right to uphold its interests in the face of the rights of others, of other states taken as other organisms. Thus, the self-preservation or <u>conatus</u> essential to ethics is the foundation of international policy. No obligations exist to honor contracts or treaties with others if our true interest no longer lies in the support of said agreements (PT,111,13-15). Spinoza merely is reflecting the realities of international politics in his proposed doctrines without attempting to rationalize them away using moral platitudes. The fundamental difference in the Spinozistic commonwealth would be the assessment of its interests on a broader, and femininely-communal, scale. As the world is viewed from the feminine perspective of oneness, the threat of hostilities between any two nations becomes a matter of international concern. In a modern sense, for example, East-West detente is a concern of more than the United States and the Soviet Union, just as peace in the Middle East is a global affair.

If this indeed is the manner in which foreign policy has, is, and will be carried out, it is best to realize the truth and then attempt to deal with it. In the past, the breach of honor occasioned by the breaking of a treaty has led to war. If the world were to adopt Spinoza's attitudes, however, the violation of a treaty would be fully expected and would not be used as a pretense for open aggression. Under such conditions, one could well imagine that more time and effort would go into the writing of treaties and contracts so that they would be more flexible and less likely to be objectionable in the future. Perhaps they would include clauses which would allow the stipulations to change with changing circumstances. The interests of all parties concerned then would be safeguarded, leading to a correspondingly deeper commitment by all.

Positive narcissism prevails once more to insure that aggression and conquest do not follow from the pure pursuit of true self-interest by a commonwealth, the results that would be envisioned by an adherent of the masculine perspective. The true interests of a commonwealth lie in peaceful co-existence with its neighbors, rather than in war--"peace can never be bought too dear" (PT,VIII,31). Conflict is to be avoided at all costs, although in a case where the very existence of a state is in jeopardy, defensive warfare is fully justified (in full agreement with Taoism). If, as Spinoza assumes, knowledge is power, the knowledge of human nature and its communal interactions yields the power to structure societies in such a way as to avoid counterproductive hostilities.

The maintenance of peace is essential if the final criterion of a successful commonwealth is to be fulfilled, that it be eternal, just as Nature is eternal. The eternal commonwealth is one whose system is so perfectly arranged, adheres so well to the natural law and order, is so well balanced internally in its power, that it cannot be destroyed by any internal cause (wherein it is assumed the greatest potential dangers lie), but only some unforeseen, and unforeseeable, external turn of events. Durability derives from an attitude of self-contentment, as the commonwealth seeks to preserve its own status, once perfected, without attempting to infringe upon others. To accomplish this goal, peace must be preserved and war avoided (PT,VII,28). The goal of the state, indeed, is "nothing else but peace and security of life", where unity prevails along with obedience. This presupposes a government worthy of obedience, that acts in the interests of its citizens, and a citizenry enlightened to its own true interests, as represented by the state authority, in short, the perfection of humanity (reason). By means of this intermediate stage the anarchistic community of the blessed can be realized.

Being eternal, Spinoza's feminine commonwealth would have the advantage of being able to assess the interests of its citizens from a broad overview. Although Spinoza himself makes no mention of the topic, it seems safe to assume, with the help of hindsight, that revealed in such an encompassing overview would be ecological issues. The latter undoubtedly exert a long range effect upon the continued well-being, and the very survival, of any state, as is now admitted. Only a state which is convinced of its future would be willing to forego the pleasures and progress of the moment to safeguard that future. Furthermore, an ecology-conscious community remains in closer touch and harmony with Nature, is aware of the delicate balance in the natural order of things. As an organism, the commonwealth upholds its own interests by safeguarding its supportive environment. As in the case of the individual human being, the individual state cannot exist in isolation.

The element of eternality in a commonwealth has been criticized for creating a state too static to be taken seriously in the present, as well as being oblivious to history and the ongoing historical process. Hampshire disputes Spinoza's assumption that human needs do not change and, once taken care of, will pose no threats to harmonious living. Opposed to such a view is the modern idea of the continual development attendent upon historical change.[107] The classic opposition between masculine notions of progress and feminine notions of eternality emerge in this argument. Most interpreters too readily assume that the dispute already has been settled in favor of the masculine perspective, pointing to the claims of linear or dialectical progression in society and the crisis faced by nations which remain "undeveloped". Is success, then, simply to be measured by technological progress?

The feminine cyclical view of change, that is, flux, cannot be dismissed so easily. There seems to be no substantial change in the survival needs of a human individual; Spinoza's evaluations of human nature hold good even in today's "highly developed" society. Self-preservation, or conatus, continues to exert a decisive influence over human actions, despite the fact that the apparatus for securing our survival reflects the sophistication of the times. Intellectuals continue to demand freedom of thought and speech in order to pursue truth in whatever form, while the multitudes demand material incentives, although greater complexities are involved in achieving either goal. The mission of the Spinozistic commonwealth is to satisfy these needs at the appropriate level of knowledge and reality.

Our alienation from Nature, from reality, has advanced considerably even in the last three hundred years of modern times. "Civilization" retreats further and further into its own humanly-constructed shell of a world, replacing the simple and single 'is' with a host of unfilfilled 'oughts'. "Progress" at the price of alienation is unacceptable in the feminine perspective, and Spinoza is careful to trim the essentials of his commonwealth down to those things which insure peace and security. However, "progress" which aims at our true good, and is a means to that end rather than an end in itself, need not be sacrificed. Technology, medical research, science, all have their place in Spinoza's commonwealth insofar as they contribute to the common good. As products of second level discurcursive reason they are acceptable means to the ultimate end of intuitive knowledge, the experiential knowledge of reality. Spinoza might well observe that our present vision is distorted, leading us to assume that human progress has no other end. In fact it is a way-station in the search for perfection, first of a human and then of a universal sort.

That commonwealth is eternal which can accommodate itself to the flux of human conditions, without losing sight of the ultimate goal. It insures an environment of peace, harmony, and security in accordance with the natural laws and order, while leaving open the further option of achieving the final knowledge offered by philosophy, not only to know reality, via discursive reason (science), but to experience the oneness of reality through intuition. The average citizen of the successful commonwealth need not be a philosopher, but she or he has the opportunity to cultivate that aspect of human nature which is philosophical.

Undoubtedly, these opinions strike us as extremely naive, accustomed as we are to a masculine perspective on the universe. They will continue to be considered in that way until such time as the feminine perspective is taken seriously as an alternative means of viewing reality. Only then will Spinoza's commonwealth be seen to follow logically from his specifically feminine metaphysical, epistemological, and ethical assumptions. Even then, these extensions of his thought may be rejected. But if they are rejected, that rejection must encompass an entire system, and not merely be directed against certain awkwardly isolated elements which run counter to our ingrained assumptions. While the feminine perspective ultimately may fail to justify itself as a whole, its internal aspects can make sense when taken within the total context of thought, and cannot be adequately comprehended without that context.

The Spinozistic commonwealth thus maintains a vital link with Nature or reality. As itself a natural organism, the survival of the commonwealth is dependent upon a knowledge of Nature's laws as well as of its own nature, as representative of a community of human individuals. Its relations with other states are guided by discursive reason and the revelations of positive narcissism, all of which promote the avoidance of war and the fostering of international peace. Finally, the commonwealth may be said to be eternal, after the pattern of Nature, insofar as it fulfills the needs of its citizens on an encompassing scale in time and is able to sustain its internal equillibrium.

Chapter IV

CONCLUSIONS CONCERNING FEMININE PHILOSOPHY

Through the philosophical systems of the Tao Te Ching and of Spinoza, the diffuse feminine perspective, subsequently organized into a principle of being, has established itself as being capable of sustaining feminine philosophies. In perceiving reality from the feminine perspective, an individual draws assumptions concerning the feminine functioning of the universe, and consequently adopts a feminine attitude towards life, thereby establishing a feminine principle of being. This principle is in turn capable of being systematized as a feminine philosophy. Implementing feminine assumptions with regard to metaphysics (the Elementary and Transformative characters) and employing a feminine method of knowledge (intuition), a properly feminine code of ethics, expressed through feminine modes of being (inwardness, receptivity, materiality), has been set forth. The end result is a femininely-structured society which is communal, internally balanced, and in harmony with its natural environment.

In order to determine those specific elements which are held in common by feminine philosophies sharing the system of thought above-outlined, it is useful to bring together the insights gathered in our investigations of Taoism and Spinozism. The theoretical foundations of a feminine philosophy in terms of its metaphysics and epistemology rest upon certain bedrock feminine assumptions concerning the condition of reality, as reflected in the twofold manifestations of the feminine principle of being. Correspondingly, the praxis of a feminine philosophy, ethically and socio-politically, follows from the feminine modes of being. A philosophy can be designated feminine, in varying degrees, in accordance with the extent to which these elements are present in its system of thought.

There is a certain structure characteristic of the feminine universe as perceived by the adherent of the feminine perspective. Reality manifests itself under two forms, as determined by our changing points of view. We may relate either to its Elementary or Transformative character. The encompassing reality of Tao is defined in terms of its function, in much the same way as is Spinoza's Substance. In addition to its role as ground of being, the feminine reality represented by Tao/Substance is identified as truth, causal agent, life force, and sum of perfection. Its qualities or properties similarly are enumerated as infinitude, immanence, eternality, and immutability by both Taoism and Spinozism. The highest reality, as we human beings perceive it, must conform to these criteria.

Expressing the dual characters of the feminine principle of being, the Elementary and Transformative, are two metaphysical categories by which we approach reality. By means of these categories, feminine philosophers can relate to the absolute--from the focal point of the one to its manifested modes or from the individual mode to the one. In Taoism a distinction is made between Tao, both Nameless and Named, as the undifferentiated whole and the diversity of its Ten Thousand Things. Spinoza draws the line between Natura Naturans, naturing Nature consisting of Substance and its Attributes, and Natura Naturata, Nature which is natured in the various levels of modes.

The closed womb of the self-contained Elementary character, the impartial container, stands in contrast to the dynamic Transformative character of the "created" universe. The feminine element of positive narcissism in the absolute reality accounts for its "maternal" concern for things in the world as an extension of itself. The Elementary character operates by the feminine method of Eros/relatedness--Taoism's tz'u and Spinoza's double-edged intellectual love of God. The universe of diversified things functions under the guidance of the deterministic and non-human centered law and order of Nature. Universal flux occasions no disturbance in the unity of the whole in that it is merely a process of the interaction of complements (discussed as Yin/Yang and Spinoza's modes of Motion and Rest).

The metaphysical scheme offered by Spinoza is both better elaborated than that of Taoism and more systematic. The Spinozistic device of the divine Attributes successfully bridges the ontological gap between the one Substance and the plurality of modes. This gradated continuity is lacking between Tao and its Ten Thousand Things, leaving their precise relationship obscure. Thus, Spinoza is able to convey the encompassing wholeness of the universe, a prerequisite for a feminine philosophy, in a manner more comprehensible than that of Taoism. And yet the Attributes remain mere things of reason, constructions of the intellect which do not do justice to reality at its highest level.

The epistemology of a feminine philosophy grapples with the problems of how and to what extent we, as modes of the absolute reality (Tao/Substance), are able to attain knowledge of that reality. For both Taoism and Spinozism such knowledge culminates in an enlightened or blessed state of being, the direct intuitive experience of reality in the radical empiricism of the feminine perspective.

Within the feminine sphere of being knowledge is conceived of in a specific sense, with several levels posited to encompass the various methods of knowing and the corresponding objects of knowledge. In this way it is possible to understand feminine epistemology and to objectify the process of knowing. The feminine concept of knowledge incorporates the masculine method of discursive reason, while emphasizing feminine intuition. The latter is experiential in a radical sense, for the feminine individual is receptive to and identifies with the object of knowledge: knowledge at the highest level is participatory. The lowest level knowledge, that derived from sense data, is dismissed as inadequate by both Taoism and Spinozism. This also is the ultimate fate of discursive reason, with its human intellectual reconstructions of reality. However, Spinoza emphasizes the need to employ human reason as the "staircase" to intuition.

It is here that Spinoza's epistemological theories falter in not adhering strictly to the feminine perspective. Although his emphasis should be upon intuition, as the highest feminine level of knowledge and the culmination of both primal sense data and masculine discursive reason, Spinoza's interest tends to stray to the rational. In view of the masculine temperament of his times, Spinoza's hesitancy to advocate intuition is understandable, but nonetheless inappropriate for a feminine philosophy. He may, in fact, have been appealing to his contemporaries in this move. Unhindered by rational presuppositions, the Taoist freely espouses the intuitive method consistent with feminine thought.

Feminine knowledge of the highest type is ontological, a dynamic process by which the mode recognizes its mergence in the one reality. The subject/object distinction vanishes in Eros/relatedness. Feminine understanding acts from the immediacy of feminine intuition (chih or Spinoza's intellectual love of God) and the responsiveness of feminine consciousness (ming). It is the state of enlightenment or blessedness, Spinoza's "continuous, supreme, and unending happiness", which is the ultimate goal of a feminine philosophy, the epistemological means to harmony with the metaphysical reality. The relationship between knower and known parallels that between mother and infant. For Taoism a returning to the primal state of mergence in the one is a reversal of differentiation. In the same context, Spinoza speaks of "the light of Nature" which we as human beings all possess, a direct channel to God (the ground of being). The adherent of a feminine philosophy is able to know reality insofar as she or he is real, or shares in reality.

Ethics, for the adherent of the feminine perspective, presents the course of conduct by which we, as human individuals, attain the perfected life style requisite for enlightenment. The feminine mode of being--inwardness, receptivity, and materiality--serve as guides here, promoting the enlightenment path through the adoption of a certain code of behavior. The assumptions concerning reality held by the adherent of the feminine perspective result in a unique attitude toward life which is manifested through the three interrelated modes of being.

The inwardness mode of being indicates what feminine virtue, Taoism's Te and Spinoza's natural power, consists of, and enables us to perfect our specific nature in accordance with human virtue. The feminine urge towards wholeness leads us to seek an inner guide, in accordance with the microcosmic-macrocosmic principle of feminine reality. Turning within we realize the whole. The recognition of our personal nature as human beings and of our role in the universal context culminates in the recognition of a nature (Te) and role shared with all of humanity, and hence a sense of community. This last revelation engenders the feminine ethics of positive narcissism, which is enforced by the Eros/relatedness whereby our true interests are intimately bound up with interests of others. Fulfillment of self, in the sense of the true or shared Self, is contingent upon the fulfillment of others, and vice versa. The promise of immortality by means of the shared Self follows from this feminine code of ethics.

Receptivity as a mode of being is exemplified in the model of virtue/power, the Taoist sage or Spinoinozistic philospher (homo liber), who has experienced the enlightenment of the feminine state of reality and acts accordingly. Such an individual remains open or receptive to what is, to the determined conditions of existence, evaluating human potentials as well as limitations realistically. Included here is a willingness to yield in the face of an overwhelming force, to flow along the path of least (or no) resistance. This is the feminine option of non-assertion. The femininely ethical individual lives a life in imitation of reality (Tao/Substance), and is determined (as far as is humanly possible) by her or his nature, acting by the spontaneity of wu-wei or as a Spinozistically "free" entity. By this means, the disruptive desires or passions are overcome, having been exposed as counterproductive. The feminine sage/philosopher relates to others through Eros/relatedness, even though a certain contingent elitism is entailed by the state of being enlightened; that same enlightenment experience theoretically is accessible to all, but is not in fact enjoyed by all.

The final feminine mode of being involves the positive incorporation of the material aspect of our being for purposes of attaining the perfection essential to the enlightenment experience. The importance of Nature for both the feminine philosophies of Taoism and Spinozism is obvious. The body is a viable source of knowledge, provided that we approach the Taoist appearances or Spinozistic affects in their proper context within reality as a whole. The mind/body dualism common in masculine philosopies is denied, while the integration of all aspects of our existence is reasserted. Sensuality, and even sexuality, are to be found in the life of an enlightened individual, yielding positive benefits in the feminine perspective of reality.

In the realm of socio-political thought, feminine philosophies follow out their femininely realistic assessment of the human condition through the three modes of being, as applied to society in general, the Taoist community or Spinozistic commonwealth. Feminine ethics provides for the survival and perfection of the individual; socio-political thought provides for the survival and perfection of society. The mutually profitable structuring of human interrelationships is governed within the feminine political system, to culminate in the anarchy of positive narcissism which requires no state structure. Moreover, the community's relationship with other communities and with Nature, its supportive environment, are dictated by its feminine goal of harmony.

On this expanded scale, the inwardness mode of being emerges as the communal attitude of all-is-oneness. As Spinoza views this, the commonwealth is ruled "as if by a single mind", overcoming the disruptive state of Nature. Taoism differs in seeking to return society to its primal state, prior to our alienation from Nature. Both agree as to the support for the communal attitude in their respective societies, namely positive narcissism, appealing to the interests of the citizens at various levels so that they identify with a shared Self. In this way, the state provides the best possible environment for the expression, as well as the fostering, of human nature (Te or virtue).

The delicate balance of power shared by citizen and sovereign is maintained by virtue of the receptivity mode of being, recast in the form of non-assertion, Taoism's wu-wei. The feminine openness to reality results in a recognition of the natural limitations of human power, whether in the role of ruler or ruled. The Tao Te Ching concentrates its attention upon the figure of the sovereign, who by the practice of political wu-wei and imitation of Tao subtly influences and guides the people, identifying with their interests. Deeming a democratic form of government the best possible, Spinoza deals with the citizen who is simultaneously sovereign. Nonetheless, both the Tao Te Ching and Spinoza imply that anarchy would reign in a perfect society, where enlightenment was universal.

The fact that not all individuals have attained, or realistically can be expected to attain, that state of being necessitates a political structure. The value of their own systems lies in their fostering of the greatest possible non-interference on the part of the enlightened sovereign and the greatest possible freedom and self-determination for the individual citizen. Virtue/power filters down from the top. A doctrine of contingent elitism is demanded to bridge the gap between the ideal of universal enlightenment and the reality of certain unenlightened members of the community. The result is a state which functions "as if" it were enlightened by adhering to feminine assumptions.

Being optimistic about the possibility of achieving an enlightened anarchy consistent with the feminine perspective, the Taoist devotes most attention to the details of this non-state. Spinoza, on the other hand, is more concerned with outlining a practical alternative which can be implemented immediately, being pessimistic about the realization of the anarchistic ideal in the near future (if ever). He is careful to structure his commonwealth in such a way that the level upon which its various subjects are functioning does not hinder the state itself from being enlightened in its workings. Hence, Spinoza lays great stress upon the role of the rational individual who can be persuaded to act for the good of the commonwealth as a whole when this interest is linked firmly to self-interest.

Narrow egoism evolves into enlightened egoism, and thence into positive narcissism. Apparently, then, Spinoza's plan is to stimulate a gradual ascent from the bondage of the passions to the guidance of reason, and, ultimately, into the enjoyment of blessedness at the intuitive level. His underlying pessimism is most evident here. He assumes that the majority of the citizens have yet to negotiate the move from imagination to discursive reason, and expresses no positive hope for the establishment of a truly feminine anarchistic community. In any case, however, the philosopher can cultivate a society which will not hinder, and may even encourage, her or his work. The Taoist sage/sovereign, on the other hand, seems most optimistic about the possibility of consummating Taoist plans, if only we allow things to take their natural course (keeping bellies full and minds empty).

Similarly, the two philosophies vary with respect to their attitude towards the intuitive experience of enlightenment/blessedness. While Taoism emphasizes the enlightenment of the sage-sovereign or ethical model as the catalyst for producing an enlightened community, the Spinozistic philosopher tends to view society as a support for the attainment of blessedness, the final goal in Spinoza's plan. For the Taoist, enlightenment is indeed a personal end in itself, but likewise functions beyond to encompass the shared Self in universal enlightenment. More simply stated, Spinoza's sights are on individual enlightenment, to be stimulated when a proper environment is provided in the commonwealth; the Taoist, however, considers the community of the shared Self to have the greatest significance, within which the enlightened individual functions. Hence, the ego-centeredness of the masculine perspective continues to prevail in the Spinozistic system to some extent. It is a device for the persuasion of the general public. Nonetheless, in both cases the microcosmic-macrocosmic state of the universe in the feminine perspective insures that individual perfection promotes the perfection of the whole.

The community whose structure reflects a feminine outlook has the advantage of harmonizing with Nature and sharing in its power. Spinoza's commonwealth functions as a single organism under the laws of Nature. International diplomacy has the same goal of harmony, going beyond narrow national interests. The success of a society is reflected in its quality of eternality, whereby it imitates the ultimate reality (Tao or Substance) and maintains an internal equillibrium.

Thus, by systematizing the elements of the feminine principle of being, its manifestations and modes of being, a feminine philosophy offers a coherent and internally consistent approach to the universe. Building upon the foundations of metaphysical assumptions, primarily the oneness of reality, the tenets of feminine epistemology reveal the various levels from which that reality can be approached. The individual draws upon all levels of knowledge, but ultimately requires the highest, intuition, to achieve the experience of sharing in the absolute and encompassing reality. Practically implemented, these combined insights emerge as the feminine ethics of positive narcissism, motivated by our interest in the shared Self. Virtue is set forth as the power of our specific nature, and the ethical ideal resides in the enlightened sage or philosopher. Extended to the plane of society, these values are active in a feminine state which is communally-oriented, internally balanced, and in harmony with its natural environment.

The advantage of consulting both Taoism and Spinozism to systematize the feminine perspective as a philosophy lies in the movement from the Taoist's self-assured, but often obscured, poetic pronouncements to Spinoza's more tentative, but also more familiar, philosophical presentation. Although the Tao Te Ching offers a consistently feminine, or Yin, philosophy, its intelligibility for the modern reader cannot approach that of the Spinozistic works. By drawing upon the insights of these two sources it has been possible to provide an outline of feminine philosophy which is simultaneously complete and comprehensible.

The philosophical reworking of the feminine perspective also has exposed certain unanticipated elements as essential to the feminine outlook. Most significant among these has been the practical need for a doctrine of contingent elitism. Although enlightenment or blessedness is theoretically accessible to all, the fact of the unenlightened majority leads to the development of a unique form of elitism which aims at its own eradication (by promoting the conditions conducive to universal enlightenment). The realistic attitude of the feminine philosopher is illustrated in this doctrine, which subordinates theoretical speculations to the obvious conditions of the 'is'.

Also of note is the discussion of a distinctive human nature, with its appropriate virtue or power. Identified with reason in Spinoza's system, this power was revealed as a form of universal conatus. In human beings discursive reason outlines the course of survival, their true good, qua human. Taoism is equally concerned with our survival, but prefers to avoid the differentiation of reason, which last is not recognized as our Te. And yet there is a recognizable Tao of humanity, human Te.

An investigation of existing feminine philosophies likewise has served to emphasize the overriding feminine concern with harmony in all areas of thought. Harmony is sought, or re-established, between mind and body, individual and society, inner and outer, humanity and the universe, where in each case the adherent of the masculine perspective perceives an unavoidable competition. The firm link between feminine philosophy and life becomes clear in the natural flow of doctrines from metaphysics to epistemology, then into ethics and socio-political thought.

The same insights recur in each field and the same code of conduct is recommended by the feminine philosopher to promote the unifying goal of oneness with reality. If the universe is determined, as assumed in the feminine perspective, then we must practice feminine receptivity; if all things have a share in the one reality, then positive narcissism is both the most efficient and the most realistic attitude to adopt, etc. The individual, as person or community, seeks to imitate the spontaneity of Nature, to attain or participate in the free-flowing existence of reality. Our focus of attention is extended from the ego-self to the shared Self, from our narrow human interests to the interests of the universe as a whole, of which we are a functioning part. Our ends are achieved indirectly, subtly, not by masculine assertion or aggression, but by feminine receptivity, remaining open to existing conditions. The feminine individual works with, rather than against, natural processes, thereby gaining the strength of Nature. Feminine knowledge is the power to benignly manipulate the elements of our nature, or the elements of a society, to achieve the common goal of perfection. Here, as ever, the maternal archetype reigns supreme.

APPENDICES

I. Standard Interpretations of the Spinozistic System

The problems inherent in two standard interpretations of Spinozistic Substance, as indicated by E. H. Curley, illustrate the usefulness of a feminine option in philosophy. The consistency of Spinoza's thought has not been enhanced, but detracted from when approached by those who harbor masculine assumptions.

The first and most enduring of these interpretations is that espoused by Pierre Bayle and H. H. Joachim, among others, and assumes that Substance is to be taken in the Lockeian sense of a metaphysical substratum. The latter is then known only through its essential and dependent attributes or qualities. Although this understanding of substance concurs with that common during Spinoza's period, it can be criticized on several grounds. His own definition of Substance is much more restrictive. He viewed it as an entity simultaneously in itself and conceived through itself, rather than being conceived solely through its manifest qualities. These two stipulations of being in itself and conceived through itself do not necessarily coincide under a Cartesian view. Nor is it Spinozistically acceptable to grant Joachim's implication concerning the illusory character of everything except Substance as a whole.[1]

These are merely two possible objections to the Bayle-Joachim line of interpretation. Nonetheless, they serve to suggest the manifest problems of ascribing such a traditional view of substance to Spinoza. Hence, at the very least, Spinozistic Substance is something more than an imitation or extension of Cartesian substance. Its deeper significance must be sought in another context. As we have seen, the feminine principle is most accommodating in this respect.

The other major contender claiming to de-mystify Spinoza's concept of Substance in terms of Western philosophy is H. A. Wolfson. In his opinion Substance is a genus, the summum genus, following from the tradition of Aristotelian and Medieval thought. Such a view may be rejected on the basis of Spinoza's anti-Aristotelian stance: "The authority of Plato, Aristotle, and Socrates has not much weight with me."[2] Moreover, certain awkward details remain to be settled in the Wolfsonian interpretation, such as reconciling Aristotelian species and Spinozistic individuals, or determining whether Substance can be considered a summum genus in any real sense.[3]

Perhaps the most inescapable problem is that the traditional grounding of the Wolfsonian interpretation results in a godhead which is inconceivable. This stands in direct contradiction to Spinoza's numerous references to the knowability of God or Substance, e.g., "The human mind possesses an adequate knowledge of the eternal and infinite essence of God" (EII,47).[4] There must be some explanation for this explicability of Substance, an explanation of the manner in which mere modes are able to grasp the whole. Said explanation is provided within the Spinozistic system itself, with its detailing of metaphysics and epistemology, as has been shown in the course of our study.

Although the Bayle-Joachim and Wolfson interpretations are able to account for isolated elements of Spinoza's philosophy quite plausibly, neither appears to have fathomed the full scope of Spinozistic thought, the broad context of Spinoza's (feminine) Weltanschauung. Even if their respective analyses were logically impeccable, a grasp of the synthetic whole is wanting. Each of the interpreters insists upon emphasizing the similarities between Spinoza and other Western philosophers, thereby viewing Spinozism as a conscious continuation of some previous school of thought rather than as an originally-conceived system. Such a view is unsatisfying if we bear in mind Spinoza's independence of mind, his dedication to and reliance upon his own laborious philosophical investigations While the historical connections and influences are undeniably present in Spinozistic thought, they serve more as an impetus to further research than as the core of an expanded system. The depth of originality, the challenge which Spinoza's essentially feminine perspective poses for the entire tradition of Western thought, cannot be ignored. This has been the focus of the interpretation given above.

II. Individual Responsibility in a Deterministic Universe

The determinism of Spinoza's feminine universe

evokes numerous questions concerning the meaning of human freedom in the context of feminine ethics. Are all crimes to be pardoned based on the stance of rigorous determinism? Is moral responsibility an illusion? The answers to these and related problems lie in Spinoza's feminine notions of human freedom and human bondage, which are defined in terms of the purging of the passions and the development of discursive reason by human intellect. These issues belong to the sphere of human nature rather than to that of Substance.

God, the determiner of fate, is compared to a potter by Spinoza, molding each thing in accordance with a design appropriate to the nature of the material at hand.[5] Some vessels are ranked as works of art, others are merely common pieces with utilitarian value, and some are doomed to be imperfect specimens due to the inferior quality of their material. God makes no decisions as to the final product, but is guided by the potential, or lack thereof, in the "clay". Similarly, the potter cannot be accused of malice or favoritism when producing a variety of pots. The calm and "philosophical" attitude exhibited by Spinoza towards this situation sharply contrasts with the despair expressed by the outraged pots in Omar Khayyam's Rubaiyat, where the divine Potter is denounced vehemently.[6] This demonstrates Spinoza's feminine attitude of acceptance towards the impartiality of God.

In Spinoza's estimate, responsibility is not denied by the pottery analogy, but rather illustrated through it. Individuals are clay in the hands of God, shaped "from the same lump" to various ends, "some unto honour, others unto dishonour".[7] Our basic nature indeed is determined, and one cannot make a porcelain vase out of a chamber pot. However, even a chamber pot can distinguish itself by fulfilling its potential. In the same way our responsibility lies in attaining a full realization of our nature, exploiting it to its utmost, rather than wasting time and energy in the futile attempt to play a role for which we are not suited.

But what of the case of the "born" criminal, the individual whose potential appears to lie in criminality? Can such a person rightly claim that he or she was determined by God to murder, and therefore escape blame? The burden continues to remain on the individual, and one can be justly blamed for not controlling one's passions (as allowed by human intellect) or for not reforming the circumstances underlying the murderous act. Just as physically disabled individuals can learn to overcome, or at least cope with, their handicaps to lead a "normal" existence, the spiritually deformed can exert similar efforts to overcome their defects by rechanneling their energies and skills to function as contributing members of society. Positive narcissism brings the enlightened individual to the realization that criminal actions are contrary to our true self-interest, broadly conceived in the shared Self. In this sense, Spinoza's determinism is not absolute, but allows for adjustments on our part, again within certain determined ranges. The possibility that some individuals afflicted either in body or spirit may be beyond hope of rehabilitation, and hence would have to be ostracized or eliminated from the community, is not discussed by Spinoza.

As in the case of Substance's perfect freedom, human freedom lies in embracing necessity, consisting not "in free decision, but in free necessity". Spinoza rejects the contention that "fatalistic necessity" precludes "a firm and constant disposition", maintaining that unreflective necessity can be supplemented by knowledge whereby we are able to encompass the causes of our determination.[8] Only when we know our natural limitations can we make the most of our natural potential. Necessity and compulsion are not identical --e.g., it is necessary for a human being "to live, to love, etc.," but not at all compulsory that we carry out these necessities.[9] In other words, the nature of my being makes it necessary for me to be alive, or to experience love, at this moment in time, although the ever-present option of suicide, or of confronting the underlying causes of my emotion, eliminates any element of compulsion to either remain alive or in love. While we cannot change our circumstances in life or escape being "programmed" by both our individual nature and Nature as a whole, we at least can transform our attitude towards these circumstances, approach them at a new level of understanding. As Descartes puts it, "Conquer yourself rather than the world", or, in more feminine terms, learn to use the virtue/power you possess to work with reality.

Admittedly Spinoza's brand of freedom, a freedom which is essentially feminine in character, strikes one as alien to the more common egocentric notion of freedom espoused by the masculine perspective, and may even evoke denunciations as being slavish submission to fate. The word freedom itself conjures up images of individual defiance, as something to be won through our efforts. However, such images belong to the sphere of masculine thought alone, encountering the universe, and Nature in particular, as an opponent who taunts us with a challenge that cannot be ignored, a duel to the death (always the death of the individual).

In contemporary thought parallels might be drawn with B. F. Skinner's Behaviorism, which promises to take us <u>Beyond Freedom and Dignity</u>. Spinoza would clearly be opposed to this phrasing, although he may be sympathetic to some of Skinner's assumptions. Certainly both thinkers value reinforcement theory, particularly in its positive form, to benignly manipulate the masses while leaving them with a feeling of freedom. And yet there is a fundamental difference between Spinoza's system and Skinnerian behavior technology. Not only does Spinoza not dismiss freedom as an illusion, but moreover he assumes that each of us can be our own determiner, by virtue of our innate reason which grants us the knowledge/power of both our limitations and our potential. No outside controller, no <u>Walden Two</u> Frazier, is required for those at the second or third levels.

Feminine philosophy also transcends Skinner's homocentric perspective. The adherent of the feminine perspective, represented in Spinoza, seeks to understand the universe in order to harmonize with, not dominate, it, to become aware of the appropriate role for the human individual within the cooperative scheme of Nature. Harmony, not conquest, is the key element, as found throughout tenets of a feminine philosophy. For the feminine individual life is not a matter of ego against the world (Nature, other individuals, etc.), but of one's being a member of a single organism on which all depend for their survival (as the blood cells within the bloodstream). Freedom is made manifest within the natural boundaries of mutual existence. If we accept the metaphysical presuppositions of Spinoza's system, this cooperative attitude is seen as the only one feasible or even rational.

To introduce another analogy, we can compare life to a cosmic game of tennis. All of us are on the court, whether we will or no, and suicide is the only source of control over our exit. The game of life is ongoing, whether or not we choose to play it, and even our refusal to play has its impact. If we do choose to play, we can do so successfully only if we follow the rules and an understanding of the acceptable patterns of behavior. Once we understand these restrictions we can work to stay within their limitations and thus improve our "game" immensely. Even the net has its function, as do the various other barriers we encounter in life.

It follows that there can be no <u>absolute</u> freedom or free will at the human level of reality. Only God/Substance can escape being acted upon by externals. External forces, the manifestations of Substance's necessity, are continually imposing themselves upon us in the form of environmental factors, psychological traumas, other individuals, and so on. The will is "nothing but a thing of reason", not accountable as the actual cause of our volitions, which last are determined by and dependent upon some other cause in Nature.[10] In effect, even the desire for blessedness must be traced to universal determinism, as leading to a harmonization with Substance, or, more properly, within Substance's encompassing being. Through it all we retain our individual responsibility to work toward that goal of harmonization, by making the most of our individual capacities and contributing to the cosmic play.

NOTES

Chapter I: THE FEMININE/MASCULINE POLARITY

[1] Carl Gustav Jung, Two Essays on Analytical Psychology, trans. R. F. C. Hull (New York World Publishing Company, 1956), p. 206.

[2] Lou Andreas-Salomé, The Freud Journal of Lou Andreas-Salome, trans., intro. Stanley A. Leavy (New York: Basic Books, Inc., 1964), p. 144.

[3] Margaret Mead, Sex and Temperament in Three Primitive Societies (New York: William Morrow and Company, 1963).

[4] "If you want to know more about femininity, you must interrogate your own experience or turn to the poets, or else wait until science can give you more profound and more coherent information." Lecture 33 of "New Introductory Lectures on Psycho-Analysis" (1932), trans. W. J. H. Sprott and contained in The Major Works of Sigmund Freud, Vol. 54 of The Great Books of the Western World, ed. Robert Maynard Hutchins (Chicago: Encyclopedia Britannica, Inc., 1971), p. 864.

[5] Salomé, p. 60.

[6] Erich Neumann, The Great Mother: An Analysis of the Archetype, trans. Ralph Manheim (Princeton: Princeton University Press, 1972), p. 18.

[7] Ann Belford Ulanov, The Feminine in Jungian Psychology and in Christian Theology (Evanston, Ill.: Northwestern University Press, 1971), p. 154.

[8] Ulanov, p. 143.

[9] Richard Wilhelm in his rendering of The I Ching or Book of Changes, trans. from the Ger. Cary F. Baynes, 3rd ed. (Princeton, New Jersey: Princeton University Press, 1974), p. 10.

[10] Richard Wilhelm in his introduction to The I Ching, p. lvi.

[11] Wilhelm, in his commentary on Ta Chuan, 1,iv,2 and 3; pp. 294, 302.

[12] Wilhelm, commenting on Ta Chuan, 1,i,1;p. 282.

[13] Wilhelm, comment to Ta Chuan, 1,v,1;p. 297.

[14] Wilhelm, in his introduction, pp. 1-li.

[15] Wilhelm, in his introduction, pp. 1-li.

[16] Ta Chuan, 1,i.4, trans. Wilhelm, p. 285.

[17] Wilhelm's commentary to Ta Chuan, 1,i,4; p. 286, note 3.

[18] Wilhelm's commentary to the hexagram K'un, pp. 10-11.

[19] Wilhelm's commentary to K'un, pp. 13-14.

[20] Wilhelm's commentary to Ta Chuan, 1,i,6; p. 286.

[21] Wilhelm's commentary on K'un, p. 11.

[22] Commentary on the Decision for K'un, trans. Wilhelm, p. 386.

[23] Wilhelm's commentary to Shuo Kua, 11,3; p. 268.

[24] Commentary on K'un, trans. Wilhelm, p. 387.

[25] Shuo Kua, 111,11; trans. Wilhelm, pp. 277-79.

[26] Wilhelm's commentary to Ch'ien, pp. 7, 9.

[27] Wilhelm's commentary to Ch'ien, p. 6, note 7.

[28] Shuo Kua, 111,11,trans. Wilhelm, p. 275.

[29] Shuo Kua, 111,11,trans. Wilhelm, pp. 276-79.

[30] Jung, Two Essays, p. 200.

[31] Jung, Two Essays, p. 245.

[32] Ulanov, p. 269.

[33] Ta Chuan, 11,xii,2, trans. Wilhelm; p. 354.

[34] Wilhelm's commentary to Chun, p. 17.

[35] Ulanov, p. 140.

[36] Shulamith Firestone, The Dialectic of Sex: The Case for Feminist Revolution (New York: Bantam Books, 1970), p. 52.

[37] Experiments by M. C. H. Van Den Heuvel-Bastian, as noted by F. J. J. Buytendijk in Women: A Contemporary View, trans. Denis J. Barret (New York: Newman Press and Association Press, 1968), p. 302.

[38] Sigmund Freud, "New Introductory Lectures on Psycho-Analysis" (1932), Lecture 33, 'The Psychology of Women', trans. W. J. H. Sprott, included in The Major Works of Sigmund Freud, Vol. 54 of The Great Books of the Western World, ed. Robert Maynard Hutchins et al. (Chicago: Encyclopaedia Britannica, Inc., 1952, 19th rpt. 1971), p. 855.

[39] Buytendijk, p. 283.

[40] Buytendijk, quoting Steinbeck's Grapes of Wrath, p. 273, and Gaston Bachelard in The Poetics of Reverie: Childhood, Language, and the Cosmos, trans. Daniel russel (Boston: Beacon Press, 1960), p. 60.

[41] Ulanov, p. 175.

[42] Buytendijk, p. 50.

[43] Buytendijk, pp. 251, 358.

[44] Buytendijk, pp. 199-200, note 3.

[45] Buytendijk, p. 299.

[46] Friedrich Nietzsche, as quoted by Buytendijk, p. 262.

[47] Eva Firkel, Woman in the Modern World, trans. Hilda Graef (Chicago: fides Publishing Association, 1956), p. 93.

[48] Irma Kurtz, "Women Apart", from World Health, the UN World Health Organization, rpt. in the St. Louis Post-Dispatch, Fe. 24, 1975, Vol. 95, #54, p. 2B.

[49] Karen Horney, New Ways in Psychoanalysis (New York: W. W. Norton and Company, Inc., 1939), p. 110.

[50] Horney, pp. 111-13.

51 Horney, pp. 114-15.

52 Mead, pp. 310, 280-89.

53 Ulanov, p. 145.

54 Jung, Two Essays, p. 230.

55 Salomé, p. 68.

56 Buytendijk, p. 252.

57 Salomé, p. 188.

58 Ulanov, p. 42.

59 Ulanov, p. 42.

60 Buytendijk, in reference to Sartre, p. 29.

61 Jung, Two Essays, p. 220.

62 Marie Louise von Franz, "The Process of Individuation", in Jung's ed. Man and His Symbols (New York: Dell Publishing Company, Inc., 1973), p. 206.

63 Irene de Castillejo, Animus: Friend or Foe, property of The Kristine Mann Library, The Analytical Psychology Club of New York, pp. 5, 11. Quoted by Ulanov, pp. 336, 275.

64 Bachelard, pp. 68-69.

65 Neumann, p. 24.

66 Ulanov, p. 156.

67 Neumann, pp. 31, 33. It is interesting to note that both the Elementary and the Transformative characters hinge on the maternal associations of the feminine. For an excellent discussion of the consequences this has on the individual woman see Nancy Chodorow's The Reproduction of Mothering: Psychoanalysis and the Sociology of Gender (Berkeley: University of California Press, 1978).

68 Neumann, p. 29.

69 Buytendijk, p. 265.

70 Friedrich Nietzsche, Twilight of the Idols,

Aph. 5, part 10, as quoted by the author in Ecce Homo, trans. Anthony M. Ludovici; Vol. 17 of The Complete Works of Friedrich Nietzsche, ed. Oscar (New York: Russell and Russell, Inc., 1964), p. 73. Interestingly enough, there has been speculation that a woman, Lou Salomé, was the model and inspiration for Nietzsche's Zarathustra (see H. G. Peters' My sister, My Spouce: A Biography of Lou Andreas - Salomé (New York: w. W. Norton and Company, Inc., 1962), pp. 142ff.

[71] Esther M. Harding, Woman's Mysteries--Ancient and Modern: A Psychological Interpretation of the Feminine Principles as Portrayed in Myth, Story, and Dreams (New York: Bantam Books, Inc., 1971), p. 38. Cf. H. R. Hays' study, The Dangerous Sex: The Myth of Feminine Evil (New York: G. P. Putnam's Sons, 1964).

[72] Erich Fromm, The Art of Loving (New York: Harper and Row, 1956), p. 38.

[73] Buytendijk, pp. 270, 321.

[74] Firkel, p. 25, and Ashley Montagu, The Natural Superiority of Women (New York: MacMillan Company, 1954), p. 99.

[75] Montagu, p. 99.

[76] The poet Milosz, from Epistle to Sorge, quoted by Bachelard, p. 61.

[77] Simone de Beauvoir, as quoted by Firestone, plus the latter's views on the subject, p. 135.

[78] Jung, Mysterium Coiunctionis: An Inquiry into the Separation and synthesis of Psychic Opposites in Alchemy. trans. R. F. C. Hull. Bollingen Series XX, Vol. 14 of The Collected Works of C. G. Jung, ed. Herbert Read, et al., 2nd ed. (Princeton, New Jersey: Princeton University Press, 1970), pp. 179-80.

[79] Harding, 1935 ed., Women's Mysteries, p. 143, as quoted by Ulanov, p. 341.

[80] Quoted by Buytendijk from Les Idees et les ages (Paris: Gaillimard, 1927), p. 237; p. 353 in Buytendijk.

[81] Fromm, p. 50.

[82] Salomé, p. 117.

[83] Montagu, p. 145.

[84] Montagu, p. 192.

[85] Buytendijk, p. 354.

[86] Fromm, pp. 39, 41, 50.

[87] Salomé, p. 110.

[88] Salomé, pp. 60-61.

[89] Buytendijk, p. 352.

[90] Firestone, p. 72.

[91] Arthur Schopenhauer, "On Women", in *The Essays of Arthur Schopenhauer*, trans. T. Bailey Saunders (New York: A. L. Burt Company, n.d.), p. 435.

[92] Buytendijk, p. 143.

[93] Firkel, p. 22.

[94] Stanley A. Leavy in his introduction to Salome's book, p. 23.

[95] Similarly, in Plato's *Symposium*, Diotima tends that a soul (*anima*) can be pregnant with many things, including wisdom, virtue, justice, and temperance. In such cases the Elementary character shades imperceptibly into the Transformative, as will be seen.

[96] Ulanov, p. 61.

[97] Fromm, p. 42.

[98] Buytendijk, pp. 264-65.

[99] Ulanov, p. 185.

[100] Ulanov, p. 160.

[101] Bachelard, p. 89.

[102] Ulanov, p. 159.

[103] Ulanov, p. 170.

[104] Ulanov, p. 159.

[105] Carl Gustav Jung, "Woman in Europe", Civilization in Transition, Vol. X of The Collected Works, p. 123.

[106] Montagu, p. 100.

[107] Harding, Woman's Mysteries, p. 223, quoted by Ulanov, p. 340.

[108] Ulanov, p. 341.

[109] Salomé, p. 94.

[110] Leavy's introduction to Salome's work, p. 16.

[111] Ulanov, p. 333.

[112] Ulanov, p. 191.

[113] Ulanov, p. 176.

[114] Ulanov, p. 171.

[115] Erich Neumann, "on the Moon and Matriarchal Consciousness", Dynamic Aspects of the Psyche, trans. Hildegard Nagel (New York: The Analytical Psychology Club, 1956), p. 53, quoted by Ulanov, p. 169.

[116] Helene Deutsch, The Psychology of Women (New York: Grune and Stratten, 1944), I, pp. 136-37, as quoted by Montagu, p. 103.

[117] Salomé, p. 118.

[118] Montagu, p. 99. Cf. Harding, p. 224.

[119] Ulanov, p. 191.

[120] Leavy, in his introduction explaining Salomé's philosophy, p. 22.

[121] Ulanov, pp. 332-33.

[122] Montagu, p. 135.

[123] Buytendijk, p. 259.

[124] Montagu, pp. 104, 143.

125 Salomé, pp. 164-65.

126 Lou Andreas-Salomé, "Narzismus als Doppelrichtung", *Imago*, VII (1921), 361-86, trans. Stanley A. Leavy, *Psychoanalytic Quarterly*, XXXI (1962), 1-30, and included in his trans. of Salome's book, p. 203, note 94.

127 Harding, p. 10.

128 Jung, "Woman in Europe", p. 130, as quoted by Ulanov, p. 329.

129 Ulanov, p. 328.

130 Ulanov, p. 184.

131 E. C. Whitmont, *The Symbolic Quest* (New York: C. G. Jung Foundation, 1969), pp. 174-75, as quoted by Ulanov, p. 339.

132 Montagu, p. 192.

133 Montagu, p. 193.

134 Anonymous quote in Salomé, p. 118.

135 Leavy, discussing the philosophy of Salomé in his introduction, pp. 15-16.

136 Leavy, in his introduction to Salomé's book, p. 23.

137 Buytendijk, p. 172.

138 Leavy, discussing Salomé's philosophy, p. 22.

139 Karen Horney, *The Neurotic Personality of Our Time* (1937), as discussed in *New Ways in Psychoanalysis*, p. 248.

140 Buytendijk, p. 181.

141 Montagu, p. 140.

142 Montagu, p. 96.

143 Firkel, p. 23.

144 Buytendijk, p. 164.

145 Buytendijk, p. 297.

146 Montagu, pp. 89-94.

147 Bessie Bunzel and Louis Dublin, To Be or Not to Be (1933), as quoted by Montagu, p. 93.

148 Montagu, p. 98.

149 Experiments of H. A. Witkin, Sex Differences in Perception, cited by Buytendijk, p. 150.

150 Ulanov, p. 332.

151 Ulanov, p. 183.

152 Ulanov, pp. 172-73.

153 Ulanov, pp. 184-85.

154 Salomé, p. 118.

155 Salomé, p. 99.

156 Horney, p. 117. See also Hays.

157 Salomé, p. 125.

158 Salomé, p. 118.

159 Rilke's view discussed by Buytendijk, in addition to the latter's own view on the subject, pp. 64, 248.

160 Simon de Beauvoir, The Second Sex, quoted by Firestone, p. 73.

161 Plutarch, quoted by Harding from G. R. S. Mead's Thrice-Greatest Hermes (London: 1906) I, p. 333; p. 215 in Buytendijk.

162 Harding, pp. 35, 80.

163 Ulanov, p. 187.

164 Neumann, "On the Moon and Matriarchal Consciousness", p. 62, as cited by Ulanov, p. 172.

165 Bachelard, p. 66.

[166] Jung, Two Essays, p. 220.

[167] Buytendijk, p. 295.

[168] Sam Keen, "Transpersonal Psychology: The Cosmic Versus the Rational", Psychology Today (July, 1974), 58-61; also the source for the majority of the social distinctions regarding the Cosmic and the Rationalistic viewpoints.

[169] Suzuki's views as discussed by Van Over, p. xxi.

[170] Keen, p. 57.

[171] Nietzsche, Ecce Homo, p. 65.

[172] Wilhelm's commentary to Shuo Kua, III, 16, pp. 275-76.

[173] Salomé, p. 70.

Chapter II: THE YIN PHILOSOPHY OF THE TAO TE CHING

[1] Chang Chung-yuan, *Creativity and Taoism: A Study of Chinese Philosophy, Art and Poetry* (New York: Harper and Row, 1970), p. 205.

[2] *Ta Chuan*, V,vii, from Richard Wilhelm's trans. of *The I Ching or Book of Changes*, Bollingen Series 19 (Princeton: Princeton University Press, 1974), p. 300.

[3] Chang, p. 71.

[4] Chang, pp. 36, 40.

[5] Chang, p. 68.

[6] Noted by Lin Yutang in his trans., *The Wisdom of Laotse* (New York: Random House, Inc., 1948), note 30, p. 134.

[7] Huston Smith has listed three basic uses of Tao: as "the way of ultimate reality", "the way of the universe", and "the way man should order his life". *The Religions of Man* (New York: Harper Colophon Books, 1958), pp. 176-77. Given these three uses, my claims that a feminine philosophy is all-encompassing seems appropriate when applied to Tao.

[8] Chang Chung-yuan, introduction to *Tao: A New Way of Thinking: A Translation of the Tao Te Ching with an introduction and Commentaries* (New York: Harper and Row, 1975), pp. vii-viii.

[9] Paul Carus, *The Canon of Reason and Virtue: Being Lao-tze's Tao Teh King* (LaSalle, Illinois: The Open Court Publishing Company, 1964), p. 13.

[10] Arthur Waley, *The Way and Its Power: A Study of the Tao Tê Ching and Its Place in Chinese Thought* (New York: Grove Press, Inc., 1958), pp. 30-31.

[11] Chang, *Creativity and Taoism*, p. 33.

[12] Laurence Binyon, *The Spirit of Man in Asian Art*,

[13] Holmes Welch, The Parting of the Way: Lao Tzu and the Taoist Movement (Boston: Beacon Press, 1957), p. 57.

[14] Ta Chuan, V,ix, quoted in Wilhelm's trans. of the I Ching, p. 301.

[15] Henri Borel, in his interpretaion of "Wu Wei," trans. M. E. Reynolds, and included in Dwight Goddard's trans. Laotzu's Tao and Wu Wei (New York: Brentano's Publishers, 1919). p. 66.

[16] Wing-Tsit Chan, The Way of Lao Tzu: (Tao-te ching) (New York: Bobbs-Merrill Company, Inc., 1963), p. 23.

[17] Chang, Creativity and Taoism, p. 15.

[18] Chang, Creativity and Taoism, p. 183.

[19] Fung Yu-lan, A History of Chinese Philosophy: Vol. 1 The Period of the Philosophers (From the Beginning to Circa 100 B.C.), trans. Derk Bodde, 2nd Eng. ed. (Princeton: Princeton University Press, 1952), p. 178

[20] Fung, p. 187.

[21] Lin Yutang, not 4, p. 106.

[22] Chang, Creativity and Taoism, p. 67.

[23] Chang, Creativity and Taoism, pp. 21, 24.

[24] Chuang-Tzu, chap. 33, pp. 266-67, as quoted by Fung, pp. 178-79.

[25] Lin Yutang, note 28, p. 132.

[26] Chang, Creativity and Taoism, p. 66.

[27] Chang, Creativity and Taoism, pp. 68-69.

[28] Erich Neumann, The Great Mother: An Analysis of the Archetype, trans. Ralph Manheim, Bollingen Series 47 (Princeton: Princeton University Press, 1972), p. 47.

[29] Wing-Tsit Chan, p. 9

[30] Lin Yutang, note 8, p. 109.

[31] Carl G. Jung, foreword to Wilhelm's trans. of the I Ching, p. xxiii.

[32] Wing-Tsit Chan, p. 10.

[33] Lin Yutang, p. 15.

[34] Kuo Hsiang, discussed by Wing-Tsit Chan, p. 23.

[35] J. J. L. Duyvendak, Tao Te Ching: The Book of the Way and Its Virtue (London: John Murray, 1954), p. 10.

[36] Alan Watts, The Way of Zen (New York: Vintage Books, Random House, 1957), p. 5.

[37] Abraham Kaplan, The New World of Philosophy (New York: Vintage Books, Random House, 1961), p. 270.

[38] Ta Chuan, V, i, note 1 and V, ii, in Wilhelm's trans. of the I Ching, pp. 297-98.

[39] Chang, Creativity and Taoism, p. 146.

[40] Fung, p. 182.

[41] Carus, p. 14.

[42] Chang, Creativity and Taoism, p. 79.

[43] Chang, Creativity and Taoism, p. 78.

[44] Chang, Creativity and Taoism, p. 41.

[45] Chang, Tao, xiii.

[46] Raymond Van Over, ed. Chinese Mystics (New York: Harper and Row, 1973), p. xviii.

[47] Wing-Tsit Chan, p. 13.

[48] Chang, Creativity and Taoism, p. 80.

[49] Gaston Bachelard, The Poetics of Space: Childhood, Language, and the Cosmos, trans. Daniel Russell (Boston: Beacon Press, 1960), p. 92.

[50] Chang, Tao, xxv.

[51] D. C. Lau, in his intro. to his trans., Lao Tzu:

Tao Te Ching (Baltimore, Maryland: Penguin Books, 1963), p. 35.

[52] Fung, p. 189.

[53] Ludwig Wittgenstein, Tractatus Logico-Philosophicus, trans. D. F. Pears and B. F. McGuinness, 2nd ed. (London: Routledge and Kegan Paul, reprt. 1972), 7, p. 151.

[54] Chang, Creativity and Taoism, p. 47.

[55] Daisetz Teitaro Suzuki, "Reason and Intuition in Buddhist Philosophy," from The Japanese Mind, ed. Charles A. Moore (Honolulu: East-West Center Press 1967), p. 77.

[56] E. A. Burtt, "Intuition in Eastern and Western Philosophy," Philosophy East and West, 2, No. 4 (Jan., 1953), 283.

[57] Chang, Creativity and Taoism, pp. 81-82.

[58] Chang, Creativity and Taoism, p. 115.

[59] Fung, p. 189.

[60] Chang, Creativity and Taoism, pp. 114, 116.

[61] F. H. Bradley, as his views are discussed by Chang, p. 101.

[62] Chang, Creativity and Taoism, p. 41.

[63] Chang, Creativity and Taoism, p. 123.

[64] Chang, Creativity and Taoism, p. 106

[65] Chang, Creativity and Taoism, p. 220.

[66] Chang, Creativity and Taoism, p. 203ff.

[67] Chang, Creativity and Taoism, pp. 169, 171.

[68] Li P'o as quoted by Chang, Creativity and Taoism, p. 173; for more on this subject see chapter 5 in Chang's book, "Tranquillity Reflected in Chinese Poetry."

[69] Chang, Creativity and Taoism, p. 50

[70] Chang, Creativity and Taoism, p. 39.

[71] This fact was recognized even by the Neo-Confusian Wang Yang-ming (1472-1529), whose biography is quoted by Chang, Creativity and Taoism, p. 85: "Wang realized that what the Sage teaches us exists already, self-sufficient, within ourselves. What he formerly sought for through analytic principles was incorrect."

[72] Chuang Tzu's comment, from his chapter "The Great Supreme"; both are quoted by Chang, Creativity and Taoism, pp. 42-43.

[73] Chang, Creativity and Taoism, p. 87.

[74] Chang, Creativity and Taoism, p. 100.

[75] Suzuki, p. 79.

[76] Suzuki, p. 80.

[77] Chang, Creativity and Taoism, pp. 130-31.

[78] Ellen Marie Chen, "The meaning of te in the Tao Te Ching: An examination of the concept of nature in Chinese Taoism," Philosophy East and West, 23, No. 4 (Oct., 1973), 467.

[79] Chang, Creativity and Taoism, p. 112.

[80] Van Over, p. xii.

[81] Chang, Creativity and Taoism, p. 35.

[82] Chang, Tao, xiv, and Creativity and Taoism, p. 70.

[83] Laurence Binyon, The Spirit of Man in Asian Art, pp. 94, 99; as quoted by Chang, Creativity and Taoism, pp. 92, 94.

[84] Chang, Creativity and Taoism, pp. 173-74.

[85] Zen enlightenment poem, quoted by Chang, Creativity and Taoism, p. 195.

[86] Chang, Creativity and Taoism, notes 4-7, p. 127.

[87] Chang, Creativity and Taoism, p. 169.

[88] Chang, Creativity and Taoism, pp. 102-3, 120.

[89] Ancient character as derived by Kuo Mo-jo from Shang oracle bones and Chou bronzes, cited by Chen, 460.

[90] Chen, 462.

[91] Chen, 461.

[92] Chen, 461.

[93] Chen, 462.

[94] Chen, 457.

[95] Chen, 457.

[96] Duyvendak, p. 8.

[97] Wing-Tsit Chan, p. 11.

[98] Chen, 466.

[99] Chen, 458.

[100] Friedrich Nietzsche, The Genealogy of Morals, trans. Francis Golffing (Garden City, New York: Doubleday and Company, Inc., 1956), p. 178.

[101] Wilhelm's trans. of the I Ching, 6, p. 30.

[102] Chen, 457.

[103] Chen, 467.

[104] Carus, p. 15

[105] Chen, 464.

[106] In all fairness it must be admitted that the thought of Confucius himself (Analects), as well as many later Confucian and Neo-Confucian scholars (e.g., Wang Yang-ming) shows evidence of the feminine perspective. The feminine element is particularly strong in references to Tao and Te as natural forces. The primary Taoist objections to Confucian philosophy are its humanistic context, the stress placed on striving and accumulation, and the insistence that names be rectified rather than rejected. This state of affairs proves the point made in the first chapter that no philosophy is purely masculine or feminine, but a synthesis of the two. Hence, even the study of Confucian thought can benefit from an understanding of

the feminine principle.

[107] Chen, 464

[108] Lu Hui-ch'ing, as quoted by Chiao Hung, Lao-tzu, 1, chüan 5, p. 2, in Fung Yu-lan, p. 180.

[109] Chang, Creativity and Taoism, p. 57.

[110] Chen, 463.

[111] Chen, 468.

[112] Chang, Creativity and Taoism, pp. 40, 20.

[113] Jung, Mysterium Coniunctionis, p. 380.

[114] Chang, Creativity and Taoism, pp. 77, 81, 83.

[115] Lin Yutang's translation, p. 120.

[116] Lin Yutang's translation, p. 218.

[117] Lau, p. 40.

[118] Chang, Creativity and Taoism, p. 178.

[119] Suzuki, p. 94.

[120] Chuang Tzu, chapter 6; Nan-po Tzu-k'uei seeks advice from the aged but incredibly well-preserved Woman Crookback. Trans. Burton Watson, The Complete Works of Chuang Tzu (New York: Columbia University Press, 1968), p. 83 and also note 15.

[121] Chuang-tzu, chapter 33, as quoted by Fung, p. 173.

[122] Chang, Creativity and Taoism, p. 125.

[123] Chuang Tzu, chapter 6, a conversation between Nu-yü and Non-po Tzu-kuei, concerning the enlightened Po Liang-1; quoted by Chang, Creativity and Taoism, p. 119.

[124] Chang, Creativity and Taoism, pp. 213, 55.

[125] Jacques Maritain, 1952, (Spring) lectures at the National Gallery of Art in Washington D. C., as quoted and discussed by Chang, Creativity and Taoism, p. 8.

[126] Chuang Tzu, chapter 23, as quoted by Chang, Creativity and Taoism, p. 124.

[127] Chuang Tzu, chapter 22, a conversation between P'i-i, who is speaking here, and Nieh Ch'üeh. Burton trans., p. 237.

[128] Wing-Tsit Chan, p. 13.

[129] Chen, 462.

[130] Chang, Creativity and Taoism, pp. 131, 119, 113.

[131] Chan, p. 13.

[132] Chang, Creativity and Taoism, pp. 37-38.

[133] Wilhelm's commentary to the I Ching, 6, pp. 28-29.

[134] Chang, Creativity and Taoism, p. 172.

[135] Fung, p. 183.

[136] Chang, Creativity and Taoism, p. 90.

[137] Van Over, p. xiv.

[138] Correspondingly, the sage-philosopher of India is credited with a dramatic approach, rich in images and figures; Suzuki, pp. 80-81.

[139] Duyvendak, p. 19.

[140] Chan, p. 11.

[141] Chuang Tzu, "The Main Currents of Thought", prolegomena to Lin Yutang's translation, p. 24.

[142] Lin Yutang, note 9, p. 16.

[143] Jung, Mysterium Coniunctionis, p. 419.

[144] Lin Yutang, note 6, p. 27.

[145] Lin Yutang, note 2, p. 14.

[146] Lin Yutang, note 1, p. 153.

[147] Lau, p. 41.

148 Chan, p. 15.

149 Carus, pp. 16-17.

150 Chang, Creativity and Taoism, pp. 234, 236.

151 Tao-an, introduction ot Sutra on Breathing, as quoted by Chang, p. 133.

152 Duyvandak, p. 6.

153 Van Over, p. xix.

154 Borel, note 5, p. 115.

155 Kuo Hsiang, as quoted by Chang, Creativity and Taoism, p. 109.

156 Wilhelm's commentary to K'un, in the I Ching, p. 14.

157 Chang, Creativity and Taoism, p. 108.

158 Chen, 461.

159 Chen, 468.

160 Burtt, 284.

161 Wing-Tsit Chan, A Source Book in Chinese Philosophy (Princeton New Jersey: Princeton University Press, 1963), p. 429. the remark is made in a discussion of the Ch'an school of Buddhism, known for its strong parallels with Taoism.

162 Chang, Creativity and Taoism, p. 137.

163 For an indepth exploration of this topic see R. H. Van Gulik, Sexual Life in Ancient China: A Preliminary Survey of Chinese Sex and Society from ca. 1500 B. C. till 1644 A. D. (Leiden: E. J. Brill, 1961).

164 Chang, Creativity and Taoism, p. 67.

165 Chan, TTC, p. 10.

166 Wilhelm's commentary to the I Ching, 8, p. 37.

167 Fung Yu-lan, p. 187.

168 Literally, 'death'; Lin Yutang, note 6, p. 310.

[169] Fung Yu-lan, p. 190.

[170] Jung, Two Essays on Analytical Psychology, trans. R. F. C. Hull (New York: World Publishing Company, 1956), pp. 203, 205.

[171] Fung, p. 187.

[172] Lin Yutang, not 5 to chapter 58, p. 266.

[173] Fung, p. 186.

[174] Chen, 461.

[175] Fung, p. 190.

[176] Chen, 461-62.

[177] Wilhelm's commentary to Ta Chuan, 7, p. 287.

[178] Lin Yutang, citing also a variation from the Yü Yüeh text; note 18, p. 293.

[179] Lin Yutang, note 15, p. 167.

[180] Wilhelm's commentary to the I Ching, 4, p. 24.

[181] Fung, p. 186.

[182] Chen, 468, 469.

[183] Chang, Creativity and Taoism, pp. 110-11.

[184] Chang, Creativity and Taoism, p. 89.

[185] A. W. Whitehead, Adventures of Ideas, p. 369, as quoted by Chang, Creativity and Taoism, pp. 89, 106.

[186] Chen, 469.

Chapter III: SPINOZISM AS A FEMININE PHILOSOPHY

[1] Spinoza to William Van Blyenbergh, June 3, 1665; Letter XXVII, trans. A. Wolf in his edition The Correspondence of Spinoza (London: George Allen and Unwin Ltd.), p. 199.

[2] T. M. Forsyth, "Spinoza's Doctrine of God in Realtion to His Conception of Causality" from Studies in Spinoza: Critical and Interpretive Essays, ed. S. Paul Kashap (Berkeley, California: University of California Press, 1972), p. 6.

[3] Wolf's annotations to letter IX, p. 392.

[4] Spinoza to Oldenburg, November 20, 1665, letter XXXII; Wolf's ed.

[5] Quoted by Wolf in his commentary to the Short Treatise, p. 184.

[6] Spinoza to Jargis Jellis, June 2, 1674; letter L; Wolf's ed., pp. 269-70.

[7] Wolf's commentary to the Short Treatise, p. 198.

[8] Maimonides, Guide for the Perplexed, lviii, quoted by Wolf in his commentary to the Short Treatise, p. 198.

[9] Spinoza to Henry Oldenberg, November 20, 1665, letter XXXII, Wolf's ed., pp. 210-11.

[10] Spinoza to Oldenberg, November 20, 1665, letter XXXII, Wolf's ed., p. 211.

[11] H. H. Joachim, A Study of the Ethics of Spinoza (Oxford: 1901), p. 114.

[12] Spinoza to Hudde, April 19, 1666, letter XXXV; Wolf's ed., p. 220.

[13] Spinoza to Oldenberg, October, 1661, letter IV; Wolf's ed., p. 83.

[14] Hampshire, p. 71.

[15] Note 4, addition to the Dutch translation of 1664 of Thoughts on Metaphysics, 11,iv,5, p. 135.

[16] E. M. Curley, Spinoza's Metaphysics: An Essay in Interpretation (Cambridge, Mass.: Harvard University Press, 1969), p. 40.

[17] Spinoza to Oldenburg, November or December, 1675, letter LXXIII; Wolf's ed., p. 343.

[18] Spinoza to Oldenburg, November 20, 1665, letter XXXII; Wolf's ed., p. 210.

[19] Curley, p. 158.

[20] Spinoza to Oldenburg, November or December, 1675, letter LXXIII; Wolf's ed., p. 343.

[21] Spinoza to Meyer, April 20, 1663, letter XII; Wolf's ed., p. 118.

[22] Spinoza to Schuller, July 29, 1675, letter LXIV; Wolf's ed., p. 308.

[23] Spinoza to Meyer, April 20, 1663, letter XII; Wolf's ed., p. 117.

[24] Spinoza to Oldenburg, April, 1662, letter VI; Wolf's ed., p. 93.

[25] Hampshire, p. 70.

[26] H. F. Hallett, Creation, Emanation, and Salvation: A Spinozistic Study (The Hague: Martinus Nijhoff, 1962), p. 47.

[27] Wolf, commentary to Short Treatise, p. 187.

[28] Annotation to letter LXIV; Wolf, p. 462.

[29] Hampshire, pp. 56. 58.

[30] Wolf, annotation to letter IX, p. 392.

[31] Spinoza to Oldenburg, November 20, 1665, letter XXXII; Wolf's ed., p. 212.

[32] Spinoza to Oldenburg, October, 1661, letter IV; Wolf's ed., p. 83.

[33] Curley, p. 58.

[34] Bayle, p. 307, N.

[35] The question will naturally arise as to the metaphorical significance of the fourth and final quarter of the moon, when the sliver of light/truth occupies the position opposite to that of the first quarter. This full cycle cannot be accounted for in Spinoza's linear progression of knowledge. However, given the cyclical, returning, principle of Taoism, the fourth quarter may be interpreted as a mirror image of the first emergence of knowledge. This seems indicated in the parallels between the infant, who lives Tao unconsciously, and the enlightened sage, who has reverted to the state of Tao.

[36] Alasdair MacIntyre, "Spinoza", included in The Encyclopedia of Philosophy, ed. Paul Edwards (New York: Macmillan and Company and the Free Press, 1967), Vol. VII, p. 537.

[37] Curley has suggested that scientific developments in the seventeeth century, such as the telescope and microscope, in opening up new realms of perception, may have influenced Spinoza to consider the various points of view from which the world may be interpreted, specifically with regard to the Attributes; see p. 153.

[38] Spinoza to Blyenbergh, January 28, 1665, letter XXI; Wolf's ed., p. 173.

[39] Spinoza to Albert Burgh, December, 1675, letter LXXVI; Wolf's ed., p. 352.

[40] Spinoza to de Vries, March, 1663, letter X; Wolf's ed., p. 109.

[41] Spinoza to Boxel, September, 1674, letter LII; Wolf's ed., p. 272.

[42] MacIntyre, p. 537.

[43] Meyer's Preface to Principles of the Philosophy of Descartes, p. 8.

[44] Spinoza to Ehrenfried Walter Von Tschirnhaus, August 18, 1675, letter LXVI: Wolf's ed., p. 310.

[45] Hampshire, p. 93.

[46] MacIntyre, p. 537.

[47] Hampshire, pp. 89, 103.

[48] Albert G. A. Balz, "Spinozism", from *Dictionary of Philosophy*, ed. Dagobert D. Runes (Totowa, New Jersey: Littlefield, Adams and company, 1970), p. 299.

[49] Hampshire, p. 114.

[50] A similar opinion is upheld by Balz: it is "highly probable that Spinoza would have admitted the tentative character of at least some of the definitions, axioms, and postulates formulated by him . . . Just as he recognizes the role of hypothesis in science, in a similar way, he would recognize the tenative chracter of some metaphysical and theological elements." p. 299.

[51] Spinoza to Oldenburg, November 20, 1665, letter XXXII; see also letter XXX, September to October, 1665; Wolf's ed., pp. 205, 209.

[52] Spinoza to Boxel, October, 1674, letter LVI; Wolf's ed., p. 288.

[53] Spinoza to Boxel, October, 1674, letter LVI; Wolf's ed., p. 289.

[54] Note added to the 1664 Dutch translation of *Thoughts on Metaphysics*, 11,i,1 p. 127.

[55] Wolfson, p. 148.

[56] Hampshire, pp. 103-4.

[57] Spinoza to Oldenburg, November or December, 1675, letter LXXIII; Wolf's ed., p. 244.

[58] Spinoza to Tschirnhaus, January, 1675, letter LX; Wolf's ed., p. 300.

[59] Annotation to letter LXXVI; Wolf, p. 474.

[60] Spinoza to Oldenburg, commenting on Robert Boyle's book, *Certain Physiological Essays*, April 1662, letter VI; Wolf's ed., p. 93.

[61] Hampshire, p. 96.

[62] Every philosopher, Spinoza declares, knows the "truth of this Axiom, namely, that every definition, or clear and distinct idea, is true." Letter IV, to Oldenburg, October, 1661; Wolf's ed., p. 81. It is

useful to recall here that a level of truth corresponds to each of the three levels of knowledge, ranging from the creative "truths" of imagination to the absolute truth of reality as a whole.

[63] Spinoza to Schuller, July 29, 1675, letter LXIV; Wolf's ed., p. 307.

[64] Wolfson, p. 162.

[65] MacIntyre, p. 537.

[66] Wolf's commentary to the Short Treatise, p. 184.

[67] John A. Wheeler, a theoretical physicist at the University of Texas at Austin, discusses this situation in a recently published paper, Frontiers of Time (North-Holland). Of particular interest are his comments concerning the actual nature of the universe: "a self-excited circuit. As it expands, cools and develops, it gives rise to observer-participancy. Observer-participancy in turn gives what we call 'tangible reality' to the universe." This viewpoint shows a marked correspondence to feminine philosophy in general and Spinoza's Substance in particular. Furthermore, Wheeler's remarks about the lack of causality in the cosmos and the dynamic interaction of the observer with the object of observation are prefigured in the Chinese concept of synchronicity. The quotes from Wheeler and his text are taken from John P. Wiley jr.'s article "Phenomena, comment and notes," in Smithsonian, 12, No. 5 (Aug., 1981), pp. 24, 26.

Another physicist, Fritjof Capra, has devoted an entire book to the link between modern science and what we have termed feminine philosophy: The Tao of Physics: An Exploration of the Parallels Between Modern Physics and Eastern Mysticism (Berkeley: Shambhala, 1975). In short, we may venture to say that the feminine perspective is beginning to be taken more seriously in the realm of science as more suitable for and adept at portraying reality than masculine discursive reason.

[68] Spinoza to William Van Blyenbergh, January 28, 1665, letter XXL; Wolf's ed., p. 174.

[69] Spinoza to Blyenbergh, January 5, 1665, letter XIX; Wolf's ed., pp. 150-51.

[70] Spinoza to Blyenbergh, january 5, 1665, letter XIX; Wolf's ed., p. 147.

[71] Hallett, p. 45.

[72] Spinoza to Oldenburg, September, 1675, letter LXVIII; Wolf's ed., p. 335.

[73] Nor can we ignore the moral problems latant in Spinoza's views. If human beings are classified as human in terms of intellectual faculties, and only thereby entitled to respect as equals, what of those who attempt to exclude certain races or nationalities from the ranks of humanity? This is often done on the basis of intellectual deficiencies. Surely, such an exclusion would amount to a perfect rationalization for inhumane treatment of those "non-humans" classified along with the "brutes". This is merely one of the possible unintended extensions of Spinoza's doctrines when he strays from the feminine perspective.

[74] Spinoza to Boxel, October, 1674, letter LVI; Wolf's ed., p. 287.

[75] Wolf, in his commentary to Spinoza's Short Treatise, p. 232.

[76] Spinoza to Blyenbergh, March 13, 1665, letter XXIII; Wolf's ed., p. 192.

[77] Spinoza to Bouwmeester, June 10, 1666, letter XXVII; Wolf's ed., p. 288.

[78] Spinoza to Boxel, October, 1674, letter LVI; Wolf's ed., p. 288

[79] Spinoza to Schuller, October, 1674, letter LVIII; Wolf's ed., p. 295.

[80] Spinoza to Oldenburg, February 7, 1676, letter LXXVIII; Wolf's ed., p. 358.

[81] Spinoza to Jelles, March 25, 1667, letter XL; Wolf's ed., p. 234.

[82] Spinoza provides us with a description of the superstitious mind, in the person of Lambert de Velthuysen, critic of the Theologico-Political Treatise: "he finds nothing to please him in virtue itself and in understanding, but would rather live under the impulse of his feelings, if it were not for this single obstacle, that he fears punishment. Thus, he abstains from evil deeds and follows the divine commands as a slave, unwillingly, and with a vacil-

lating mind, and for this servitude he expects to be honoured by God with gifts, far pleasanter to him than the divine love itself, and more so in proportion as the good which he does is repugnant to him, and he does it unwillingly." (letter XLIII, to Jacob Ostens, February 17, 1671; Wolf's ed., p. 256).

[83] Spinoza to Ostens, February 17, 1671, letter XLIII; Wolf's ed., p. 255.

[84] Spinoza to Oldenburg, November 20, 1665, letter XXXII; Wolf's ed., p. 210.

[85] Hilail Gildin, "Spinoza and the Political Problem, in Spinoza: A Collection of Essays. ed. Marjorie Grene (Garden City, New York: Anchor Press, Doubleday, 1973), pp. 384f.

[86] Gildin, p. 377.

[87] Errol E. Harris, Salvation From Despair: A Reappraisal of Spinoza's Philosophy (The Hague: Martinus Nijhoff, 1973), p. 185.

[88] Gildin, p. 381.

[89] Spinoza asserts his variance from the Hobbesian view on this point: "I ever preserve the natural right intact so that the supreme Power in a State has no more right than is proportionate to the power by which it is superior to the subject". This he identifies with the situation existing within the state of Nature. Spinoza to Jelles, June 2, 1674; letter L Wolf's ed., p. 269.

[90] Spinoza to Oldenburg, November or December, 1675, letter LXXI; Wolf's ed., p. 343.

[91] Spinoza to Jelles, February 17, 1671, letter XLIV; Wolf's ed., p. 260.

[92] Hampshire, p. 183.

[93] Spinoza to Blyenburgh, January 28, 1665, letter XXI; Wolf's ed., p. 178.

[94] Hallett, p. 190.

[95] Hallett, p. 197.

[96] Spinoza to Ludovicus Meyer, August 3, 1663,

letter XV; Wolf's ed., p. 135.

[97] Hampshire, p. 189. Harris (p. 198) argues that interests must be balanced within the state itself and incentives provided for citizens and sovereigns alike. Hallett (pp. 195-96) contends that the state must maintain "a nice balance between the extent to which its civilizing functions are requisite by reason of the barbarity of its subjects, and the extent to which those subjects will tolerate the exercise of these functions".

[98] Wolf, in his introduction to the Short Treatise, p. xciv.

[99] A quote by Spinoza, reportedly uttered in response to the threats of a mob over his visit to the Prince of Conde; cited by Wolf, in his introduction to the Short Treatise, p. lxxxix.

[100] Harris, pp. 196-97.

[101] Hallett, pp. 195-96, note 5.

[102] Hallett, pp. 192-94.

[103] Given the intimate interrelationships in a feminine society, a possible problem here concerns the extent to which something judged detrimental to the individual citizen has consequences for the commonwealth, either directly or indirectly. It seems that Spinoza is adverse to the use of brute force to insure that people conform to social codes or to the sacrifice of the individual in the interests of the state. Such actions would be self-contradictory in any case, for the feminine state is merely a means to the end of blessedness, not an end in itself, as it is for the masculine perspective. As an acceptable feminine alternative, Spinoza prefers the force of example and persuasion. Both the Taoist and Confucius agree with him on this point.

[104] Letter XX to Oldenburg, September or October, 1665; Wolf's ed., p. 206.

[105] Hampshire, p. 196.

[106] Wolf, annotations to letter XXI, p. 409.

[107] Hampshire, p. 192.

APPENDICES

[1] E. M. Curley, Spinoza's Metaphysics: An Essay in Interpretation (Cambridge, Mass.: Harvard University Press, 1969), pp. 14-28.

[2] Spinoza to Hugo Boxel, October, 1674, letter LVI, Correspondence as ed. by Wolf, p. 290.

[3] Curley, pp. 28-31.

[4] Curley, pp. 35-36.

[5] Spinoza to Oldenburg, February 7, 1676, letter LXXVII; Wolf's ed., p. 357. A similar analogy is found in Paul's Letter to the Romans, 8:19.

[6] "O Thou who Man of base Earth didst make,
And ev'n with Paradise devise the Snake:
    For all the Sin the Face of Wretched Man
Is black with--Man's Forgiveness give--and take!"
The Rubaiyat of Omar Khayyam, trans. Edward FitzGerald (New York: Pyramid Books, 1967), pp. 89-97.

[7] Spinoza to Oldenburg, December, 1675, letter LXXV; Wolf's ed., p. 347.

[8] Spinoza to G. H. Schuller, October, 1674, letter LVIII; Wolf's ed., p. 295, 297.

[9] Spinoza to Boxel, October, 1674, letter LVI; Wolf's ed., p. 287.

[10] Spinoza to Oldenburg, September, 1661, letter 11; Wolf's ed., p. 77.

GLOSSARY

ALL-IS-ONE-NESS--A sense of identity with all beings as modes or expressions of a single reality; reflected in the assumption of a microcosmic-macrocosmic pattern in the universe. The INWARDNESS mode of being practiced on a communal scale.

BLESSEDNESS--For Spinoza the experience of salvation or freedom which consists of the INTELLECTUAL LOVE OF GOD.

CHING--Path of self-realization for the Taoist sage in imitation of Tao (RETURNING).

ELEMENTARY CHARACTER--One of the dual manifestations of the feminine principle of being, under which reality is conceived of as stable, encompassing, undifferentiated, impartial, originating source. Its symbol is the Great Mother archetype, the one in relation to its multitude of offspring.

EGO-SELF--The narrow personal sense of selfhood concerned with the "I" as a specific individual distinguished and in isolation from all other individuals (characteristic of the masculine perspective). Gives rise to competition.

EROS/RELATEDNESS--The method of the feminine perspective (corresponding to the role of LOGOS in the masculine perspective, which involves analysis). EROS proceeds by synthesis, drawing upon the similarities between its objects. Jung defines it as "capacity to relate". Loving as an activity of mergence with another being, as in the nondifferentiation of the ELEMENTARY CHARACTER. It culminates in the experience of the SHARED SELF and is symbolized in the mother-child relationship.

FEMININE CONSCIOUSNESS--Perception of reality through one's entire being, not restricted to intellect (as in the masculine perspective) nor exclusive of it. The consciousness which is instinctual and/or intuitive and reaches back to the root of the primal unconscious.

FEMININE UNDERSTANDING--Immediate intuitive form of comprehension attained by being personally involved in the "object" of knowledge. In fact, the distinction between knower and known disappears, as does that between object and subject. The feminine individual is extended to experience the other through the SHARED SELF.

INTELLECTUAL LOVE OF GOD--For Spinoza the love of intellect (as both rational and intuitive) which has God as its object. Also "part of the infinite love with which God loves Himself" (EV,36). (See INTUITION)

INWARDNESS--One of the three feminine modes of being, based on the metaphysical assumption that the inner is the outer or the individual is a microcosm of the universal macrocosm. A turning within to our individual resources or nature (TE) to reveal the condition of the external world. The end result is an urge towards wholeness, as inner-directedness is gradually extended from the EGO-SELF to the human community, and ultimately to all of Nature.

INTUITION--Third level knowledge which incorporates and transcends sense data and reason by being a direct experience of their insights. (See RADICAL EMPIRICISM).

LINK WITH NATURE--Communal expression of the MATERIALITY mode of being, emphasizing the need to harmonize with Nature. We prosper by working with, rather than against, the natural spontaneity of our being, and so must abstain from futile attempts to conquer Nature or bend it to our human will. We are Nature.

MANIFESTATION--The means by which a principle makes itself manifest to us, that is to say, the forms or categories of thought under which we perceive it to exist. The symbolic personifications (in terms of imagination) and/or fundamental assumptions and reconstructions (of reason) concerning the state of the universe. When systematized in a philosophy they yield its metaphysics and epistemology.

MATERIALITY-- The third of the feminine modes of being which recognizes the significance of the material aspect of our being, and the positive contributions of sensuality (including sexuality). The integration of our material being with our spiritual and intellectual being is indicated here.

MING--Sudden enlightenment in Taoism as brought on by intuitive insight or direct experience of Tao. (See RADICAL EMPIRICISM).

MODE OF BEING--A form of behavior which follows from the espousal of specific values, with those values themselves founded on the fundamental assumptions made about the state of reality (metaphysics). Each of these modes contributes to an over-all code of conduct in fulfilment of the assumptions, and each is also one facet of a single, unified attitude towards life. Ethics and Socio-Political philosophy emerge from the modes of being.

NON-ASSERTION--The RECEPTIVITY mode of being communally represented, by which the advantages of not attempting to impose our limited human value judgements upon events is recommended. This entails a code of non-interference in natural processes, Taoist WU-WEI. Through this approach we can supplement our own power with the power of Nature, and insure final success.

POSITIVE NARCISSISM--Following from the assumption of ALL-IS-ONE-NESS, concern for the self is both personally beneficial and universally necessary. The love of self involved here focusses on the encompassing SHARED SELF. The model is that of maternal love for the child as an extension of the self.

PRINCIPLE OF BEING--The assumptions and attitudes entailed when reality is approached from a specific perspective. A principle of being underlies the forms of thought and modes of behavior of its adherents. It is an unsystematic collection of values and qualities organized loosely around a set of fundamental assumptions.

RADICAL EMPIRICISM--An epistemological option which is radical in the sense of getting to the root of our being and being in general. It is empirical insofar as it demands a direct experience. Under the feminine perspective to understand the ultimate in the fullest sense we must experience its point of view--to know reality is to be reality. This is the foundation of feminine epistemology.

RECEPTIVITY--The feminine mode of being which requires an opennes to reality, a willingness to accept conditions as they exist and to work within our natural limitations(rather than futilely attempting

to surmount them, as in the masculine perspective).
Underlying the receptive or "yielding" attitude
is the metaphysical assumption of a life-affirming
determinism in Nature.

RETURNING--The action of TAO as it moves from differentiation back to primal oneness. Its symbols here
include the Mother, the Uncarved Block, the Valley
of the Eternal Female, the Infant, and the downward
action of water.

SHARED SELF--The selfhood which we share with other
beings by virtue of our status as members of a
universal community, both human and non-human,
founded on our mutual share in reality. (See POSITIVE
NARCISSISM).

TAO--In Taoism the "Way" as principle underlying
the universe and the source of reality in all its
forms.

TE--The Taoist term for individual nature. Human
TE reflects the Tao of humanity. (See/VIRTUE/POWER).

TRANSFORMATIVE CHARACTER--The dynamic manifestation
of the feminine principle of being which stimulates
the transformation or unfolding of our being. This
is the RETURNING movement from the second level
differentiation of reason to the unity of the one.
In the process we experience enlightenment (BLESSED-
NESS) which transcends while incorporating the primal
ELEMENTARY CHARACTER as well as masculine elements.

TZ'U--In Taoism love, compassion, or sympathy,
associated with mothers. (See EROS/RELATEDNESS).

VIRTUE/POWER--As in the Greek concept of Arete and
Taoist TE, virtue is considered in the feminine
perspective as an expression of our inherent power.
To be virtuous, thus, is to live in a manner appropriate to that nature, its limitations and potentials.

WU-WEI--The Taoist from of the NON-ASSERTION mode of

being, action by non-action.

LIST OF WORKS CONSULTED

Andreas-Salomé, Lou. The Freud Journal of Lou Salomé. Trans., intro., Stanely A. Leavy. New York: Basic Books, Inc., 1964.

Bachelard, Gaston. The Poetics of Reverie: Childhood, Language, and the Cosmos. Trans. Daniel Russell. Boston: Beacon Press, 1960.

Bayle, Pierre. Historical and Critical Dictionary: Selections. Trans., intro., nots Richard H. Popkin with Craig Brush. New York: Bobbs-Merrill Company, Inc., 1963.

Burtt, E. A. "Intuition in Eastern and Western Philosophy". Philosophy East and West, 2 (January, 1953), 283-91.

Butendijk, F. J. J. Woman: A Contemporary View. Trans., Denis J. Barrett. New York: Neuman Press and Association Press, 1968.

Carus, Paul. The Canon of Reason and Virtue; Being Lao-tze's Tao Teh King. La Salle, Illinios: Open Court Publishing Company, 1968.

Chan, Wing-tsit, comp., trans. A Source Book in Chinese Philosophy. Princeton, New Jersey: Princeton University Press, 1963.

Chan, Wing-tsit, trans. The Way of Lao Tzu: (Tao-te-ching). New York: Bobbs-Merrill Company, Inc., 1963.

Chang, Carsun. "Reason and Intuition in Chinese Philosophy". Philosophy East and West, 4 (1954-55), 99-112.

Chang Chung-yuan. Creativity and Taoism: A Study of Chinese Philosophy, Art, and Poetry. New York: Harper and Row, 1970.

Chang Chung-yuan. Tao: A New Way of Thinking: A Translation of the Tao Tê Ching with an Introduction and Commentaries. New York: Harper and Row,

1975.

Chen, Ellen Marie. "The meaning of *te* in the Tao Te Ching: An examination of the concept of nature in Chinese Taoism". Philosophy East and West, 23 (October, 1973), 457-70.

Chodorow, Nancy. The Reproduction of Mothering: Psychoanalysis and the Sociology of Gender. Berkeley: University of California Press, 1978.

Curley, E. M. Spinoza's Metaphysics: An Essay in Interpretation. Cambridge, Mass.: Harvard University Press, 1969.

Debon, Günther, trans., intro., notes. Tao-Te-King: Das Heilige Buch vom Weg und von der Tugend. Stuttgart: Philipp Reclam. 1967.

Dunner, Jospeh. Baruch Spinoza and Western Democracy: An Interpretation of His Philosophical, Religious, and Political Thought. New York: Philosophical Library, 1955.

Duyvendak, J. J. L., trans. Tao Te Ching: The Book of the Way and Its Virtue. London: John Murray, 1954.

Edwards, Paul, ed. The Encyclopedia of Philosophy. 8 vols. New York: Macmillan and Company and the Free Press, 1967.

Feng, Gia-fu, and English, Jane, trans. Tao Te Ching. New York: Vantage Books (Random House), 1972.

Firestone, Shulamith. The Dialectic of Sex: The Case for Feminist Revolution. New York: Bantam Books, 1970.

Firkel, Eva. Woman in the Modern World. Trans. Hilda G. Graf. Chicago: Fides Publishers, 1956.

Freud, Sigmund. "New Introductory Lectures on Psycho-Analysis" (1932). trans. W. J. H. Sprott. Great Books of the Western World, vol. 54, ed. Robert Maynard Hutchins. Chicago: Encyclopedia Britannica, Inc., 1971.

Fromm, Erich. The Art of Loving. Vol. 9 of World Perspectives, ed. Ruth Nanda Anshen. New York: Harper and Row, 1956.

Fung Yu-lan. A History of Chinese Philosophy: Volume 1 The Period of the Philosophers (From the Beginnings to Circa 100 B. C.). Princeton, New Jersey: Princeton University Press, 2nd Eng. ed., 1952.

Goddard, Dwight, trans. Laotzu's Tao and Wu Wei. Interpreted by Henri Borel; trans. M. E. Reynolds. New York: Brentano's Publishers, 1952.

Grene, Marjorie, ed. Spinoza: A Collection of Critical Essays. Garden City, New York: Anchor Press/Doubleday, 1973.

Hallett, H. J. Creation, Emanation, and Salvation: A Spinozistic Study. The Hague: Martinus Nijhoff, 1962.

Hampshire, Stuart. Spinoza. Baltimore, Maryland: Penguin Books, 1951, rev. 1962.

Harding, M. Esther. Woman's Mysteries: Ancient and Modern--A Psychological Interpretation of the Feminine Principle as Portrayed in Myth, Story and Dreams. New York: Bantam Books, Inc., 1971.

Harris, Errol E. Salvation from Despair: A Reappraisal of Spinoza's Philosophy. The International Archives of the History of Ideas, #59. The Hague: Martinus Nijhoff, 1973.

Hays, H. R. The Dangerous Sex: The Myth of Feminine Evil. New York: G. P. Putnam's Sons, 1964.

Horney, Karen. New Ways in Psychoanalysis. New York: W. W. Norton and Company, Inc., 1939.

James, Edwin O. The Cult of the Mother-Goddess: An Archaeological and Documentary Study. New York: Frederick A. Praeger, 1959.

Joachim, H. H. A Study of the Ethics of Spinoza. Oxford:1901.

Jung, Carl G., ed. intro., et al. Man and His Symbols. New York: Dell Publishing Company, Inc., 1973.

Jung, Carl G. Mysterium Coniunctionis: An Inquiry into the Separation and Synthesis of Psychic Opposites in Alchemy. Trans. R. F. C. Hull. Bollingen Series XX, The Collected Works of C. G. Jung, vol. 14, ed. Sir Herbert Read, et al. 2nd ed.

Princeton, New Jersey: Princeton University Press, 1970.

Jung, Carl G. *Two Essays on Analytical Psychology.* Trans. R. F. C. Hull. New York: Meridian Books, World Publishing Company, 1956.

Kant, Immanuel. *On History.* Ed. Lewis White Beck. Trans. Lewis White Beck, Robert E. Anchor, and Emil L. Fackenheim. New York: Bobbs-Merrill Company, Inc., 1963.

Kant, Immanuel. *On the Old Saw: That May be Right in Theory But It Won't Work in Practice.* Trans. E. B. Ashton. Philadelphia: University of Pennsylvania Press, 1974.

Kaplan, Abraham. *The New World of Philosophy.* New York: Vintage Books, Random House, 1961.

Kashap, S. Paul, ed. *Studies in Spinoza: Critical and Interpretive Essays.* Berkeley, Calif.: University of California Press, 1972.

Keen, Sam. "Transpersonal Psychology: The Cosmic Versus the Rational". *Psychology Today.* July, 1974, 58-61.

Kurtz, Irma. "Women Apart: From Birth, 'Different Is Not Equal' is Subtly Taught". *World Health,* Rpt. *St. Louis Post-Dispatch,* 24 February 1975, vol. 95, No. 54, p. 2B.

Lau, D. C., trans. *Lao Tzu: Tao Te Ching.* Baltimore, Maryland: Penguin Books, 1963.

Legge, James, trans. *I Ching: Book of Changes.* New York: Bantom Books, 1969.

Lin Yutang, trans., ed., intro., notes. *The Wisdom of Laotse.* New York: The Modern Library (Random House, Inc.), 1948.

Mead, Margaret. *Sex and Temperament in Three Primitive Societies.* New York: Wm. Morrow and Company, 1963.

Montagu, Ashley. *The Natural Superiority of Women.* New York: Macmillan Company, 1954.

Nakamura, Hajime. *Ways of Thinking of Eastern Peoples: India, China, Tibet, Japan.* Ed. Philip P. Wiener, rev. trans. Honolulu, Hawaii:

Neumann, Erich. *The Great Mother: An Analysis of the Archetype.* Trans. Ralph Manheim. Bollingen Series XLVII. Princeton, New Jersey: Princeton

University Press, 1972.

Nietzsche, Friedrich. Ecce Homo (Nietzsche's Autobiography). Trans. Anthony M. Ludovici. Vol. 17 of The Complete Works of Friedrich Nietzsche, ed. Oscar Levy. New York: Russell and russell, Inc., 1964.

Nietzsche, Friedrich. The Genealogy of Morals. Trans. Francis Golffing. Garden City, New York: Doubleday and Company, Inc., 1956.

Plato. The Republic. Trans., intro., notes Francis MacDonald Cornford. New York: Oxford University Press, 1965.

Schopenhauer, Arthur. The Essays of Arthur Schopenhauer. Trans. T. Bailey Saunders. New York: A. L. Burt Company, n. d.

Smith, Huston. The Religions of Man. New York: Harper Colophon Books, 1958.

Spinoza, Benedict de. The Chief Works of Benedict de Spinoza: A Theologico-Political treatise and A Political Treatise. Vol. 1. Trans., intro. R. H. M. Elwes. New York: Dover Publications, Inc., 1951.

Spinoza, Benedict de. Earlier Philosophical Writings: 'The Cartesian Principles' and 'Thoughts on Metaphysics'. Trans. Frank A. Hayes; intro. David Bidney. New York: Bobbs-Merrill Company, Inc., 1963.

Spinoza, Benedict de. Opera. 2 volumes. Ed. J. Van Vloten and J. P. N. Land. The Hague: Martinus Nijhoff, 1895.

Spinoza, Benedict de. Selections. Ed. John Wild. New York: Charles Scribner's Sons, 1958.

Spinoza, Benedict de. Spinoza's Short Treatise on God, Man, & His Well-Being. Trans., ed. A. Wolf. New York: Russell and Russell, Inc., 1963.

Suzuki, Daisetz Teitaro "Reason and Intuition in Buddhist Philosophy". The Japanese Mind: Essentials of Japanese Philosophy and Culture, ed. Charles A. Moore with Aldyth V. Morris. Honolulu, Hawaii: East-West Center Press and University of

Hawaii Press, 1967. pp. 66-109.

Ulanov, Ann Belford. The Feminine in Jungian Psychology and in Christian Theology. Evanston, Illinois: Northwestern University Press, 1971.

Van Gulik, R. H. Sexual Life in Ancient China: A Preliminary Survey of Chinese Sex and Society from ca. 1500 B. C. till 1644 A. D.. Leiden: E. J. Brill, 1961.

Van Over, Raymond, ed., intro. Chinese Mystics. New York: Harper and Row, 1973.

Waley, Arthur. The Way and Its Power: A Study of the Tao Te Ching and its Place in Chinese Thought. New York: Grove Press, Inc., 1958.

Watson, Burton. The Complete Works of Chuang Tzu. New York: Columbia University Press, 1968.

Watts, Alan. The Way of Zen. New York: Vintage Books, Random House, 1957.

Welch, Holmes. The Parting of the Way: Lao Tzu and the Taoist Movement. Boston, Mass.: Beacon Press, 1957.

Wiley, John P. jr. "Phenomena, comment and notes". Smithsonian, 12, No. 5 (August, 1981), 22-26.

Wilhelm, Richard, trans. The I Ching or Book of Changes. Eng. trans. Cary F. Baynes. Bollingen Series XIX. Princeton, New Jersey: Princeton University Press, 1974.

Wolf, A. The correspondence of Spinoza. London: George Allen and Unwin, Ltd., 1928.

Wolfson, Harry Austryn. The Philosophy of Spinoza: Unfolding the Latent Processes of His Reasoning. 2 vols. Cambrige, Mass.: Harvard University Press, 1934.

Wu, Joseph S. "Chinese Language and Chinese Thought". Philosophy East and West, 19 (October, 1969), 423-34.

INDEX

ABORTION, 258

Acceptance, Fem. (see Receptivity; Realism)

Activity, masc., 4, 6, 9, 14, 53, 71, 109, 112-113, 132

Adler, Alfred, 12

Affects, Spinozistic, 152, 189, 206, 210, 213, 215-23, 225, 226, 227, 228, 230, 273
benign manipulation of, 217-25, 234, 239-45, 247, 249-50, 252-53,
(see also Joy; Passions; Sorrow)

<u>Agape</u> (divine love), 22

Alain, 22

Alighieri (Dante), 21

All-is-one-ness, fem. mode of being of, 314
in fem. prin., 28, 29-32, 33, 36, 47
in Spinozism, 182, 192, 235-50, 262
in Taoism, 50, 86, 119, 120-25, 134

Altruism, xxii, 22, 261

Amazon, 10

Analysis (masc.), 9, 16, 35, 56, 71, 75, 80, 88, 94, 142, 148, 190 (see also Differentiation)

Anarchy, 120, 124, 132, 134, 236, 239, 242, 250, 261, 265, 274-75

Androgyny, 14

<u>Anima</u>, xvi, 14, 17-18, 25, 31, 38, 47, 51, 72

Animal nature (masc.), 10

Animism, 41

<u>Animus</u>, xvi, 14, 16

Anthropocentrism (masc.), 16, 38, 43

Apollo, xvi

Apollonian, 16
/Dionysian polarity, xvi, 40-45

Aphrodite (Goddess of love), 26

Aquinas, 41

Arabic philosophy, 149

Archetype, 8, 14, 39
fem., xiv, 18, 20, 23, 28, 38, 47, 116
Jungian, xv, 14, 53

<u>Arete</u> (virtue/power), 25, 96, 198
(See also Virtue)

325

Aristocracy, 133, 251, 260-61

Aristotle, xxi, 41, 280

Aristotelian thought, xiii, 34, 155, 279

Artificiality, masc. (see Homo-centric view)

Artist,
and fem. creativity, 25, 47
woman as, 24
woman as inspiration of (see Transformative char.)

Asceticism (masc.), 36, 231
fem. rejection of, 36, 214, 231, 232

Assertiveness,
(aggression) masc., xxii, 34, 43, 80, 108, 128, 190, 213, 235, 250, 252, 264, 278

Athena, 24

Attributes,
of Spinozistic Substance, 142-44, 146-47, 151, 152, 155, 157, 160, 162-64, 166, 170, 179, 181, 182, 190, 199, 226, 227, 270-71
of extension, 144, 146, 151, 153, 157-58, 160, 161-64, 175-177, 181, 186, 198, 229, 231
of Thought, 144, 146, 151, 153, 156-58, 159, 161-64, 174, 175-177, 181-82,
199, 209, 227, 229

"Auguries of Innocence", 73

Augustine, 41

BACHELARD, GASTON, xvi, 9, 18, 25, 38, 72

Balance of power, in society, 125, 130, 131, 134, 235, 241, 150-62, 269
312 (note 97)
in nature, 265, 267

Balz, Albert G.A.

Bayle, Pierre, 148, 150, 279-80

Beatrice, 25

Beck, Lewis White, xx

Begegung (meeting), 31

Behaviorism, 41, 283

Being, Tao as, 54-56, 58-59, 62, 66, 69, 76, 78, 100, 102, 115
(see also Yu)

Being-here-now, 9, 27, 40, 60, 81

Belief, Spinozistic, 171, 178, 181
(see also Discursive reason)

Belly, fem. center of being in, 10
in Taoism, 88, 118, 126-27, 275

Bernard, Saint, 44

Beyond Freedom and Dignity, 283

Bible, 156, 183, 227

Binyon, Laurence, 299 (note 83)

Biological approach to polarity, 7-11, 14, 46

Biological clocks, gender differences of, 9

Biological determinism, 7, 8, 12

Birth of Tragedy, xvi

Blake, William, 41, 73

Blessedness, Spinozistic, xxiv, 141, 145, 152-53, 162, 164, 173-74, 177, 180, 184-93, 196-98, 200, 201, 206-209, 215, 218, 219, 220, 222, 223, 224, 226, 227, 230, 232, 233-34, 236, 240-41, 242, 246, 248-50, 253, 258-59, 262, 271, 277, 284, 314

Body, gender differences of, xxi (note 13), 10-11
attitudes toward, 10, 36, 117
stature, 10
importance in fem. perspective, 31, 117, 129, 231-32, 246, 273

Body, as mode of Subst., 151, 154, 160, 162-64, 172, 185-86, 189, 191-92, 208, 214, 215, 216-18, 226, 227-33, 244, 273

Bondage, human, 37, 202-203, 210, 214, 217-18, 225, 251, 252, 281 (see also Passions)

Book of Changes (see I Ching)

Borel, Henri, 269 note 15)

Bourgeois capitalism, 261

Brave New World, 45

Buddha, 25

Buddhism, 44, 76, 78, 86, 111
(see also Ch'an; Zen)

Burtt, E. A., 116

Business (masc.), 29

Butendijk, F. J. J., xiv, 8, 20, 22, 23, 33

CAPRA, F., 309 (note 67)

Capital Punishment
in Spinoza, 282
in Taoism, 121, 124, 131

Carmen, 19

Cartesian school, 41, 142, 263, 165, 184, 227, 279

Carus, Paul, 55, 91

Cassirer, Ernst, 3

Catillejo, Irene de, 16

Causality (masc.), 65-66, 156-57
fem. denial of, 65, 158, 309 (note 67)
(see also Synchronicity)

Chan, Wing-Tsit, 72, 89,

327

117, 120

Ch'an Buddhism

Chance (see Synchronicity)

Chang Chung-yuan, 81, 94, 117

Ch'ang (Eternal Law), 64

Change (see Flux)

Chaos, masc. prob. with, 41, 43

Chauvinism, 39

Chên (the Arousing), 4, 6

Chen, Ellen Marie, 88

Ch'eng (sincerity), 71

Chi (system), 107

Ch'i (vital force), 68, 105

Chi Tsang, 76

Ch'ien (the Creative), 4, 53

Chih (intuition), 72, 75, 77, 87, 272

Childbirth, 25, 53
pain in, 33

Children, women as, 23, 42

Chinese culture, xv, 66, 78, 102, 116, 130, 135
language, xix, 58, 68
painting, 66, 78-79,
86, 95, 98-99, 116
poetry, 66, 79, 86, 95, 99, 116

Ching (quiescence), 78, 85, 97, 99, 100, 112, 119, 314

Chodorow, Nancy, 288 (note 67)

Chou period, 88

Christianity, 44, 210

Chronos (time) as masc., 9

Chuang Tzu, 71, 72, 76, 81, 99, 105, 134

Circe, 19

Citizenry, Spinoza's view of, 140, 194, 234-62, 267, 274
enlightened citizen, 235, 237, 242
ideal, 251-53
unenlightened citizen, 237, 239, 243, 250-51

Civilization, 29, 67, 105, 122, 123, 134, 266

Coleridge, 41

Collective unconscious, 13, 16, 51

Common sense knowl., 74, 77, 78, 102, 166, 172, 183, 189
(see also Levels of Knowl.)

Commonwealth, Spinozistic, 220, 224, 233-67, 273-74
(se also Enlightened community, Spinozistic)
probs. of, 244

Communism, 133, 261

Compassion
  in fem. prin., 22, 42, 60
  in Spinoza, 206
  in Taoism (see Tz'u)

Completion, fem. urge toward, 31, 47, 50, 53, 57, 68, 97

Compulsion, 214-15, 282
  (see Passions)

Conatus (striving), 43, 152, 182, 195-96, 199, 203-205, 209, 215, 234, 239, 249, 262, 264, 266, 277
  (see also Desire; Self-preservation)

Concreteness,
  in fem. prin., 24
  in Spinoza, 159, 164, 194, 228, 234
  in Taoism, 52, 56-57, 61, 74, 79, 85, 91, 108, 114-16, 118

Conflict, masc. value of, 42, 89, 101, 240, 260

Confucianism, 41, 66, 71, 75, 91

Confucius, 300-301, (note 107), 312 (note 103)

Conquest, masc. value of, xxii, 2, 92, 264, 283

Consciousness (masc.), 6, 13, 51, 53, 71-72, 78, 81, 88-89, 91, 96, 100, 122, 157
  cosmic, 99 (see Shared Self)
  (see also Fem. consc.)

Containment, fem. symbol of, 20, 24, 55, 151, 153
  (see also Womb)

Contentment, fem. value of,
  in Spinoza, 187, 211, 264
  in Taoism, 72-73, 101-102, 107, 122, 125-26, 132, 134, 135

Contingent elitism (see Elitism, Contingent)

Contrasexuality, xiv

Cosmic View, 40-45, 72
  Rationalistic polarity, 40-45, 47
  (see also Apollonian / Dionysian polarity)

Cow, fem. symbol of, 48, 99

Creation, creativity
  in art, xvi, 66, 95, 98
  in fem. prin., 31, 53
  in Spinozistic Subst., 147, 153-54, 161, 163, 201
  in Tao, 53-54, 63-64, 78-79, 82, 86, 119
  in women, 21, 24

Crime, criminal behavior,
  in Spinoza, 245, 255-57, 281-82
  in Taosim, 122-23, 128

Creative, the (Chien), 3-7, 21, 46, 53

Cultivation, masc. morality of, 75, 89, 91

329

Cultural approach to polarity, 7, 11-13, 46

Cultural conditioning of gender roles, xiv-xv, 1, 8

Curley, E. H., 278

Cyclical change, 2, 67-69, 76, 126, 136, 266

DARK AND LIGHT, IMAGERY OF, 3, 5, 54, 75, 78, 95, 98, 104, 106, 109, 113, 141, 166, 307 (note 35)

Darwin, 200

Death, 19, 45, 95-96, 100, 109, 121, 124, 127, 131, 161, 169, 207-208, 212, 220, 223, 230, 231, 243, 258, 283

Death wish, 42-43

de Beauvoir, Simon, 21, 37

Debauchery (masc.), 36

Definition, Spinozistic, 142-44, 171, 180-81, 184, 215, 278

Demiurge, Platonic, 24

Democracy, 127, 130, 133, 235, 251-52, 259-61, 274

Depth psychology, 36

Descartes, Rene, 41, 167, 182, 191, 282

Desire, 21, 45, 157

"blind", 219, 248
good, 171, 216, 231, 242
in Spinoza, 181, 197, 199, 204, 206, 211-12, 215, 218-19, 220, 223, 231, 241, 244, 251, 273
in Taoism, 73, 77, 95, 99-100, 103, 108, 111, 119, 122, 126, 127, 132
probs. of, 73, 77, 100-102, 111, 117, 119, 127

Destruction, 100, 164, 230, 231

Destructive, feminine, 19 (see Feminine, Negative)

Detente, 264

Determinism (fem.), 35, 54-55, 64-66, 93-94, 101, 105, 144, 147, 150, 156-57, 161, 173, 197, 203, 211, 213, 216, 218, 223, 225-27, 231, 237, 240, 270, 280-84

Deutsch, Helene, 27, 32, 81

Differentiation (masc.), 9, 17, 43, 51, 55-58, 64-65, 72, 74, 77, 86-88, 91, 94-96, 100-103, 115, 123, 132, 136, 145, 186, 194, 207, 277

Dionysian view, 19, 31, 33, 45, 47
(see also Apollonian/ Dionysian polarity)

Dionysos, xvi

Diotima, 290 (note 95)

Discursive reason (masc.), xxiii, 7, 16-17, 21, 40, 165, 186, 192, 195, 200, 271

as means to intuition,
46, 75, 170, 172, 175-76, 178-79, 187, 192, 195, 198, 233-246, 266-67
in Spinoza (second level knowl.), 138, 142, 146, 148, 155-56, 158, 165-68, 170-77, 180-82, 184-92, 194, 198-207, 212, 217, 219, 222, 224, 228, 233-35, 236, 243, 246, 247-48, 253, 263, 267
in Taoism, 50, 70-78, 80, 83, 88, 91, 126

Division of labor, social, 240

Doctrine of the Mean, 71

Don Juan, 21

Dualism, Mind/Body (see Mind/Body Dualism)

Duyvendak, J. J. L., 89

Dynamism,
gender differences of, 10-11
in Spinoza's levels of knowl., 164-92
(see also Transformative char.)

EARTH, 5, 28, 47, 52, 61, 67, 94, 106, 109, 125, 135, 237
(see also Mother Earth)

Eckhart, 41

Ecology, fem. value of, 43, 45, 120, 135-36, 265

Education,
in Spinoza, 232, 246, 263
in Taoism, 125 (see also 'Losing and Losing' Method)

Ego (masc.), 14, 16, 18, 34, 42, 94-95, 117, 205, 283

Ego-self (see Self, ego), 314

Egotism (masc.), xxii, 13-14, 21-22, 95, 152, 243
fem. rejection of, 97, 100, 127-28, 152, 190, 220, 243

Einfall (hunch), 27

Einfühlung (empathy), 27

Elementary character of the fem. prin., xxiv, 7, 17-24, 32, 47, 49, 51-62, 63, 67, 76, 78, 90, 126, 140, 141-42, 145-47, 151-53, 182, 192, 268, 269, 314
encompassing, 5, 151, 182
impartial, 18, 19, 153
maternal, 10
nondifferentiation, 18, 20, 51, 60, 62, 82, 152, 162
stability, static, 46, 68, 238

Elitism, contingent, 273-74, 277
in Spinoza, 210, 222-25, 235, 248-60
in Taoism, 104-105, 112

Emanation, xx, 64, 142, 154-55

Emerson, 41

Emotion (fem.), 2, 14, 20, 40, 43, 152, 210, 216, 218, 221, 225, 230
(see Affects)

Emotionalism, 30

Empiricism, 74, 227, 237
(see Radical empiricism)

Enlightenment, xviii, xxiv, 7, 44-45, 189, 220, 229, 233, 248, 251, 258, 270, 274
Taoist (ming), 50, 52, 59, 63-64, 66, 70-71, 73, 76-83, 86-87, 95, 97-100, 104-105, 110, 112, 119, 120, 125-26, 133, 135

Enlightened community, Spinozistic, 214, 220, 234-67, 258
Taoist, 50, 120, 133, 136

Enlightened egoism, 195, 204, 206, 218, 233, 249, 274

Epistemology, 15, 50, 51, 275
fem., 266 (see Radical empiricism; Intuition)
Spinozistic, 141, 148, 156, 164-93, 196, 198, 200, 207, 211, 217, 224, 233, 238, 267, 280
Taoist, 69-83, 85-86, 96, 101

Eriugena, Scotus, 57

Erkenntnis, 7 (see also Knowl. accumulated)

Eros/relatedness (fem. method), 2, 21-22, 25, 27-28, 31, 32, 41, 47, 68, 270, 272, 314
in Spinoza, 152, 171, 186, 189, 191, 213, 221, 225, 242
in Taoism, 54-56, 60, 62, 67-68, 78, 80, 82, 92, 100, 113
vs. Logos, 4, 6, 21

Eroticism, 19, 36

Esalen Institute, 41

Eternal law, 55, 56, 64, 74, 105 (see also Ch'ang)

Ethics, 237, 246, 271
fem., 15, 38, 243, 267, 268
Spinozistic, 141, 174, 177, 192-233, 240-41, 242, 245, 264, 267
Taoist, 51, 69, 78, 84-119, 132, 136

Ethics, xvii-xviii, 141-43, 165, 167-68, 178-81, 193, 196, 210, 215, 217, 222, 223, 244

Euclidean proof, 172

Eve, 36

Ewig-Weibliche, das (the Eternal Feminine), 21, 28, 32, 45

Existentialism, 16

Extension (see Attribute of Extension)

Experience, personal (see Radical empiricism)

FAME, 97, 106-107, 112,

196, 212, 232, 244

Family, role of, 39, 121, 123

Fan, 69 (see Reversion principle)

Fascism, 41

Faust, 28, 32

Fear reaction (fem.), 34-35 (see also Survival)

Feminine,
characters, manifestations, 7, 17-28, 38, 47, 49-50, 52-69 (see also Elementary; Transformative)
consciousness, 26, 81, 184, 189, 192, 272, 314
/masculine polarity, xiv, 2
modes of being, xiv, 15, 22, 28-38, 46, 109, 111, 120, 136, 141
negative aspect of, 19, 33, 45
perspective, xiii-xiv, xvi-xvii, xix, 3, 13, 15-17, 24, 26, 28-29, 39, 44-45, 48, 56, 85, 95, 112, 120, 127, 135, 136, 140, 146, 148, 149, 164, 166, 167, 188-89, 192, 198, 199, 203, 205, 208, 209, 226, 229, 231, 234, 237, 239, 243, 249-50, 258-59, 261, 264, 266-67, 269, 271
philosophy, xvii, xxiii, xxiv, 6, 13, 39, 40, 46, 48, 51-52, 54-56, 68, 83-84, 86, 93, 117, 141, 141, 149, 165, 194, 216, 231, 233, 261, 267, 269-71, 273, 276, 282
principle, xxiii, xxiv, 1, 3, 5, 6-8, 10-11, 13-19, 21, 23-24, 26, 28-33, 35-40, 45-54, 59-60, 63, 67-69, 72, 80, 82, 84-86, 111, 113, 116-117, 119, 129, 140-41, 146-47, 152-53, 172, 184, 192, 201, 232, 279
Understanding, 26-27, 79, 184, 268, 314
"weakness", xii-xxi, 23, 90, 101, 105, 109-10, 11, 113, 123, 135

Feminism, feminists, xiii-xiv, xx

Femme fatale, woman as, 19, 36

Firestone Shulamith, 23

Firkel, Eva, 11, 20

Flexibility (fem.), 21, 211, 213-14, 264

Flux, 54, 65, 67, 160, 162, 266-67, 269

Fornication, 258

Forsyth, T. M., 143

Frankenstein, Doctor, 230

Freedom, freewill, 241, 259
masc. concept of, 16, 281
of speech, 253, 256-57, 258-59, 262, 266
of thought, 253, 257-59, 262, 266
Spinozistic definition of, 155-56, 161, 168,

202, 210, 211, 214-19, 223, 235, 247-48, 250-51, 258, 280-84
Taoist sense of, 65, 98, 105-106, 134

Free individual, Spinozistic, (homo liber), 211-242, 232, 240, 242, 247-49, 252, 273 (see also Spinozistic philosopher)

Freud, Sigmund, 1, 7, 8, 12, 20, 34, 46

Freudian school, 7, 8, 11, 33, 41, 46

Friendship, value of, 221

Fromm, Eric, 22

Fu, 69 (see Returning action of Tao)

Fung Yu-lan, 52, 59, 102, 122

GAIA, 60

Garden of Eden, 42

Generosity (fem.), 22, 110, 218, 221

Geometrical method, 142, 143, 167, 228

Gestalt, 31, 146

Glance, gender differences of, 9

God, 25, 47, 57, 102
anthropomorphic (masc.), 33, 43, 66, 145, 151, 157, 181, fem., 44, 66
masc., 44
Spinozistic, 141, 143-44, 147-48, 151-53, 156-65, 167, 170-74, 178-82, 184, 186-87, 189, 191, 193, 199, 202-203, 207-209, 210-13, 217, 218, 220, 223, 225, 556, 227, 231-33, 246, 254-55, 263, 279-84 (see also Subst.)

Goethe, 21, 28

Golden Age of Society, 134, 237, 260

Good, the

Good and evil, knowl. of, 66, 90, 177-78, 203, 218, 245

Grace, fem. source of, 20

Great Mother archetype, 10, 17, 19, 20, 24-25, 60, 278

Great Round (Uroborus), 2, 3, 7, 18, 19, 82

Great Ultimate (T'ai Chi), 55

Guerilla warfare, 128

HALLETT, H. F., 199, 247

Hamlet, 237

Hampshire, Stuart, 179, 243, 250, 263, 265

Happiness, 165, 169-70, 194, 215
"continuous, supreme and unending", 179, 187, 193, 196, 204, 212, 215, 230, 272

Harding, Esther

Harmony, fem. value of, 2,

13, 18, 42, 57, 72,
85, 91, 98, 111, 147,
227, 244, 249, 272,
283
in self, 50, 85, 233
in society, 29, 50,
73, 106, 120-21, 123,
125,-35, 234, 249,
251, 261, 263
with Nature, xvii,
30, 35, 42, 45, 50,
55, 56, 64, 85, 97,
99, 105, 106, 111,
114, 120, 121, 125,
129, 134-36, 140,
156, 161, 192, 211,
224, 227, 233, 236,
262-67

Hays, H. R., 289 (note
71)

Heart, masc. center of
being in, 10, 88, 91
(see also Hsin)

Heaven, 52, 61, 67, 73,
78, 94, 105, 106,
108, 110, 121, 125,
130, 135, 237

Hegel, G. W. F., xx-xxi,
10, 41, 55

Hell, 16

Hobbes, 238-40, 243,
311 (note 89)

Holistic medicine, 29

Holy Spirit, 26

Homo-centric view
(masc.), 16, 38, 40,
43, 59, 71, 152, 157,
167, 179, 188, 195,
199, 204, 209, 216,
266
fem. rejection of
relativity, 55, 62,
66, 69, 73, 74-75, 77,
82, 99, 103, 110, 112-
13, 115-17, 122, 125,
129, 145, 149, 152, 158,
161, 162, 174, 175, 183,
184, 186, 187, 190, 194,
196, 198-201, 209, 216,
233, 237, 240, 246, 269,
283-84

Homo faber, 41

Homo liber, 211
(see Free individual)

Homo ludens, 42

Homosexuality, 258

Horney, Karen, 8, 12, 33,
46

Hsieh Ling-yun, 81

Hsin (heart), 88, 100, 126

Humanism, 51, 66, 71, 89-
91, 104-05, 113, 119,
156

Humanity, 2, 20, 24, 29,
31, 43, 70, 86, 89, 91,
92, 103, 108, 112, 123-
24, 136, 152, 158, 195,
200, 201-03, 206, 209,
221, 224, 226, 234, 247-
48, 260, 272
(see also Jen)
superiority of (Spinoza),
195, 201, 202, 215, 224,
310 (note 73)

Human nature, 11, 82, 91,
140
fem. view, 34, 42, 43,
65, 71, 89, 91, 93, 96,
115, 122, 133, 135, 159,
161, 179, 181-82, 185,
190, 193-209, 211-16,
220, 224, 226, 232-34,
236, 237-38, 240, 242,

244-46, 263, 266-67,
  masc. view, 41, 43,
  86, 91, 236

Human relationships,
  fem. value and
  concern with, 29-30,
  86, 93, 107, 122,
  125, 174, 195, 205-
  06, 208-09, 220, 221,
  225, 244

Huxley, 45

Hypocrisy, avoidance of,
  236, 257

I (RIGHTEOUSNESS), 92,
  123-24

I Ching (Book of
  changes), 3, 46, 47,
  65, 68, 71, 101

Idealism, fem.
  rejection of, 27-28,
  89

Ideas (Spinozistic),
  45-47, 158, 160, 163,
  171, 173-74, 178-79,
  181-83, 185, 198, 201,
  208, 217, 226, 227-28
  adequate, 163, 174,
  180, 182-84, 191
  inadequate, 171, 183,
  218
  true, 148, 158, 175,
  177, 180, 181-84, 220

Ideatum, 158, 163, 183,
  201, 227, 229, 230

Imagination, xvi, 40
  in Spinoza (first
  level knowl.), 149,
  157, 159, 166, 167-
  68, 170-72, 176, 181,
  188, 214, 234, 240,
  249

Imitation of reality/
  Nature, 40, 67, 69, 272,
  of Substance, 156, 210,
  214-16, 218, 225, 262,
  of Tao, 64, 67, 83, 87,
  95, 97-114, 116, 119,
  120, 128-31, 133

Immanence (fem.), 10
  (see also Wholeness)

Immortality, 271
  for Spinoza, 185, 188,
  207-09, 230-31
  for Taoism 95-96, 97,
  136
  personal, 96, 230
  universal, 96, 136, 154,
  231

Impartiality of reality,
  18, 19, 22, 25, 44, 48,
  62, 90, 105-06, 109,
  112, 129, 147, 151-53,
  225

Impotence, 155, 197, 204,
  218, 252, 257
  (see also Sorrow)

Improvement of the Under-
  standing, 170, 180, 196,
  213

Individualism (masc.),
  xxii, 6, 45

Infant ideal in Taoism,
  77, 82-83, 90, 99, 103,
  105, 112-13, 134

Infant-mother relationship,
  20, 22, 45, 60, 82, 205
  (see Positive Narcissism)

Inner and outer, xxiv, 2,
  30-31, 59, 72, 85-87,
  118, 136, 172, 173, 181,
  207, 243

Inner-directedness (fem.),

29-30, 47, 77, 82, 87, 110, 172, 190, 191, 196-97, 233

Innocence (see Simplicity)

Instinct, fem. value of, 7, 17, 26, 27, 30-31, 35, 37, 42-43, 47, 76, 81, 88, 90, 100, 114, 118, 119, 127, 204, 240

Integration (see Wholeness)

Intellect, 2, 14, 17, 29, 65, 71, 75, 79, 144, 146, 148, 152, 154-55, 158, 159, 161-62, 165-66, 173-75, 178-80, 182, 187, 189-92, 195, 198-99, 202, 217, 219, 226, 228, 229, 248

Intellectual love of God, (Amor Dei Intellectualis), 152-53, 168, 171, 187-90, 191-92, 197, 201, 207, 209, 215, 218, 225, 230, 233, 246, 269, 272, 315

International relations fem., 136-37, 236, 262, 264-65, 267, 275

Intuition (fem.), xxii, 7, 11, 17, 26, 27, 40, 43-47, 141, 268, 271, 315
in Spinoza (third level knowl.), 142, 145, 165-82, 184-92, 195, 197-204, 205-08, 216, 217, 219, 222, 233-34, 235-36, 238-39, 240, 243, 248-50, 251, 259, 263, 266-67
in Taoism, 74-83, 92, 95-96, 102, 111-12, (see also Chih)

Inwardness, fem. mode of being of, xvi, 314
in fem. prin., 28-32, 47, 268, 271
in Spinoza, 140, 192, 195-209, 217, 226, 233, 235
in Taoism, 50, 85-97, 110, 114, 119-20

'Is', fem., 15, 27, 54, 84, 172, 179, 182, 194, 240, 266
vs. masc. 'ought', 15, 35, 54, 158, 172, 237, 276

Isis, 37

Isolationism, fem. rejection of, 30, 68, 86, 120, 137, 206, 243, 265

JEN (HUMANITY), 66, 91, 92, 96, 119, 123, 125

Jesus Christ, 25

Jewish philosophy, 148

Joachim, H. H., 150, 279-80

Johnson, Samuel, 23

Joy and power, 169, 187, 189, 191, 205, 206, 215, 218, 219, 221, 223-24, 231-32
absolute, 215, 218
(see also Blessedness)

Judaism, xviii, 200-01

Judeo-Christian doctrines, xx, 16

Jung, Carl Gustav, 1, 6, 8, 13, 16, 18, 21, 31, 38, 41, 65, 94, 106, 122

Jungian thought, xvi, 17, 21, 53, 60

KAIROS (TIME) as fem., 9

Kali, 19, 60

K<u>lan</u> (the Abysmal), 4, 6

Kant, Immanuel, xx, 84, 177

Kaplan, Abraham,

Keen, Sam, 40-45, 47

K<u>ên</u> (keeping still), 4, 6

Khayyam, Omar, 280, 313, (note 6)

Knowledge, xxiv,
  accumulated, cumulative (masc.) 2, 7, 70, 72-73, 77, 97, 100, 123, 125-27
  fem., 27, 36, 75, 166
  "hearsay" (see Opinion; Imagination)
  object of, 76, 80, 173-74, 178, 182, 187,
  of essences, 170-71, 179, 181-83 (see also Intuition)
  of ignorance, 72-74, 103, 126, 127, 166, 195
  of reason (see Discursive reason)
  of sense data (see Sense data)
  Spinozistic, (of God) 141, 153, 157, 165, 170, 174, 177-78, 180-96, 199, 200, 203, 206-209, 212, 214, 218-20, 223-24, 226, 227-28, 231, 235, 237, 240, 246-47, 264, 267, 282-83
  Taoist, 62, 70, 77, 82-87, 93, 95, 96, 102, 107, 116, 118, 126, 127, 130

Knower/known distinction, 82-83, 174, 184, 186, 272

Krishna, 25

K'un (the Receptive), 4, 53, 55, 97

Kuo Hsiang, 114

Kuo Mo-jo, 89

Kurtz, Irma

Kwan-yin, 25

LANGUAGE (masc.)
  abstractness of, 17, 24, 74
  artificiality of, 17, 74, 93, 98, 123, 190
  in Spinoza, 147-49, 151-53, 166-67, 169-71, 190-200
  in Taoism, 52, 74-75, 93, 110, 114, 116, 149
  problems for fem. perspective, 38, 58, 77, 116, 148-49, 169-71
  suspicions and distrust of, 73-75, 110, 149, 167, 169
  Wittgenstein and, 73-74

Lao Tzu, xx, 6, 97, 123

Lau, 95

Law, divine of natural,
3, 30, 37, 55, 64,
65, 68, 84, 102, 154,
156, 158, 160-61,
164, 172, 173, 183,
198, 203, 205-206,
217, 223, 226, 227,
238, 245, 249, 262,
267
  of the conservation
  of matter/energy,
  164, 231
  human or civil, 16,
  30, 43, 126, 156,
  158, 220, 244, 245-
  46, 249, 252-53,
  262
  types to avoid, 131,
  256-57, 262

Law and order,
  in Nature, 42, 53,
  69, 147, 155, 158,
  183, 202, 203, 216,
  226, 236, 254, 259,
  264, 267
  in society, 24, 43,
  126, 244

Learning, Taoist (see
  'Losing and Losing'
  method)

Leavy, Stanley A.

Legge, James, xix

Levels of knowledge
  (means to knowl.),
  275
  in Spinoza, 140, 148,
  150, 155, 165-73,
  181, 188, 190-91,
  195, 199, 206, 234,
  240, 243, 247, 266
  in Taoism, 75-79,
  102-103

Levels of reality
  (varying perspectives)
  in Spinoza, 140, 146,
  148-57, 159, 161, 162,
  164-65, 185, 197, 227,
  240, 247, 266
  in Taoism, 54, 58, 59,
  63, 67, 84-86, 102,
  109, 125

Leviathan, 239

Li (the Clinging), 4, 5

Li (propriety), 92

Li P'o, 79

Liberalism, 258

Liberty (see Freedom)

Libido, xxii, 42

Life force
  in fem. principle, 18-
  19, 37, 48
  Substance, 144, 151
  Tao, 64, 88, 90-91, 96,
  98, 109, 114, 115, 118-
  19, 131

'Light of Nature', 158,
  183, 191, 199-200, 272
  (see also Discursive
  reason)

Lin Yutang, 66, 95, 99,
  115, 117-18

Linear progress (masc.),
  2, 41, 68, 76, 266

Link with Nature, fem.
  mode of being of, 314
  in fem. prin., 28, 35-
  38, 47
  in Spinoza, 192, 214,
  225-33, 315
  in Taoism, 50, 85, 114-
  20
  (see also Materiality)

Locke, 155, 278

Logic, 71, 142-44, 148, 150, 151-53, 155, 167, 172, 175, 178-81, 183, 184, 187, 190, 191, 203, 229, 230, 267
both/and (fem.), xxiii, 28
either/or (masc.), xxii, 28, 40, 240

Logos, 24, 37, 65, 70
masc. method, 7, 25, 56, 63, 65, 76, 93

Love, 43, 171, 232
as fem. method, 21, 42, 221, 222 (see also Eros/relatedness)
of God to humanity, 152-53, 187, 215, 225
maternal, 20, 22, 31, 47, 60, 123
object of, 153, 188, 206, 215, 217, 218, 219
"overevaluation" by women, 12
paternal, 22, 123
probs. for men, 21
(see also Intellectual love of God; Tz'u)

Lover-beloved, union of, 26, 187, 191, 215

'Losing and Losing' method, 71-72, 76, 88, 94, 97, 100, 111, 112, 125

Lu Hui-ch'ing, 93

Lunar Cycle and women, 37

Lust, 19

MACINTRYNE, ALASDAIR, 166

Maimonides, 148

"Mana-personality", 6

Manifestations of fem. prin., 17-28, 315
in Spinoza, 140-92
in Taoism, 51-83

Marcuse, 41

Maritain, Jacques, 98

Martineau, J., 147

Marxism, 41, 261

Masculine,
perspective, xiii, xvi, 8, 16, 28, 36, 44-46, 83, 109, 113, 115, 126-27, 138, 149, 157, 194, 198, 235, 237, 240, 243, 264, 266-67, 281
philosophy, xiii, xxii, xxiii, 55, 83, 84, 88, 125, 165, 273
principle, 1, 3, 7, 11, 14-18, 24, 29, 35, 42, 45-46, 56, 113

Masochism, 12, 28
in women, 12, 32-34
perversion of receptivity, 33-34, 47, 97

Materialism, matter (fem.), 24, 26, 47, 63, 68-69, 82, 85, 100, 116, 122, 140, 151, 159-61, 164, 198

Materiality, fem. mode of being of, 315
in fem. prin., 28, 35-38, 268, 272
in Spinoza, 147, 192, 225-33
in Taoism, 114-19, 130

(see also Link with Nature)

Maternal love (see Love, maternal)

Matriarchal society, 18, 26, 40-41

<u>Maya</u> (illusion), 14, 42, 150, 159

Mead, Margaret, xiii, 1, 8, 13, 46

Medicine, 136, 214, 246, 263, 266

Medieval phil, 149, 279

Men, 8-14, 16-17, 20-21, 36, 37

<u>Men</u>, (primal state), 126

Metaphysics, xxiv, 15, 51, 268
fem., 51, 84, 243, 259, 267
Spinozistic, 141-64, 167, 180, 182, 187, 190-93, 196, 200-201, 209-11, 216, 217, 224, 233, 238, 250, 267, 279-80, 283
Taoist, 51-69, 70, 77, 80, 82-83, 85-86, 91, 93, 96, 101, 105, 107, 109, 112, 115-16, 127, 132, 134, 136, 142

Meyer, Ludovicus

Microcosmic-macrocosmic view (fem.), xvi, 26
in fem. prin., 27, 30-31, 37, 271
in Spinoza, 155, 162, 172, 181, 195, 199, 203, 207, 209, 236, 243
in Taoism, 72, 77, 78, 80, 86-87, 135

Military strategy, Taoist, 128

Milosz, 21

Mind (masc.), 29, 63, 70, 75, 78, 87, 146, 148, 151, 156, 158, 160, 162-65, 167, 172, 174, 179, 182-85, 189, 191-92, 196, 198-99, 208, 210-11, 214, 216, 217-18, 224, 226, 227, 233

Mind/body dualism (masc.) 2, 26, 40-41, 114, 117-18, 162-63, 189, 192, 208, 227, 229, 273

<u>Ming</u> (enlightenment), 54, 59, 78, 87, 97, 117, 272, 315

Model, Tao as (see Imitation of Tao)

Moderation, Middle Path (fem.), 36, 69, 76, 100, 124, 130-31, 214, 231-33, 250-51, 255

Modes, Spinozistic, 141-42, 145, 147-78, 151-56, 170, 174, 180, 182-84, 186, 191, 202-203, 207-208, 210, 231, 234, 269, 179
finite, general, particular, 151, 153, 160-61, 166, 175, 177, 190, 191
infinite immediate, 147, 153, 160-61, 166, 175, 179, 190, (see also Motion and Rest; Understanding)
infinite mediate, 160,

162, 166, 175, 179, 190
of Extension, 147, 153, 160
of Thought, 153, 160

Modes of being, 46, 49, 268, 316
fem., 26-38 (see All-is-one-ness; Inwardness; Link with Nature; Materiality, Non-assertion; Receptivity)
masc., 46

Monarchy, 133, 251, 261

Monism, 41

Montagu, Ashley

Moon, 2, 37, 166

"Moral Majority", 257

Moral model (see Spinozistic philosoper; Taoist sage)

Morality, legislation of, 257-58

Mother, archetype of, 7, 23, 47
caring, 20, 21, 47, 62
containment, 20, 47, 62
link with children, 22-23, 30-31, 60
nurturing, 20, 22, 61

Mother Nature, 37, 40, 147

Motion and Rest, mode of, 147, 153, 160-61, 229, 269

Movement, gender differences in, 3-4, 8-9, 20, 111, 162, 175, 183

Multitude,
Spinoza's view of 201, 213-14, 220-25, 235, 289, 241-43, 245, 248-49, 253-55, 256, 260, 277
Taoism's view of, 73, 80, 100, 103-104, 106, 112, 115, 121, 125-27, 130-34

Muse, woman as, 17

Mystic Female, 79

Mysticism, mystics, 36, 42, 44, 77, 102, 118, 120, 136, 167

Mysterious power of the fem., 11, 37, 59, 79, 94, 99, 107, 186

Myths, 8, 21

NAPOLEON, 6

Narcissism, 13 22, 32, 47, 60 (see also Positive Narcissism)

Narcussus, 30

Natura Naturans (Nature naturing), 140, 145-53, 157, 162, 178, 226, 269

Natura Naturata (Nature natured), 140, 145-47, 153-61, 178, 226, 269

Naturalism, 64, 69, 114

Natural law (see Law, divine or natural)

Nature, xvi, xxii, 2, 3, 16, 18-19, 23-28, 30,

37, 38, 41, 45, 104, 272, 277
fem. view of, 30-33, 35, 42-43
imitation of, 40
in Spinoza, 140, 145-64, 177-78, 180, 183, 189, 191-92, 194, 196-98, 100, 202, 203, 210-11, 214, 216, 226, 227-28, 232-34, 236-37, 239, 244, 254, 259, 262-67, 283
in Taoism (tse-jan), 55, 64, 66-67, 69, 72, 79, 84-86, 88-89, 91, 93, 105, 110, 112, 114, 119, 125, 134-36

Nature, human (see Human nature)

Natural right, 236, 238-41, 244-45, 249, 255, 263-64

Necessity (see also Freedom, Spinozistic) 154, 156-59, 161, 168, 170, 180, 181, 183, 184, 189, 196, 202, 204, 206, 208, 211, 212-13, 215, 216-17, 219, 226, 228, 235, 240, 247, 259, 282, 284

Needham, Joseph, 89
Negative Theology, 149

Neo-Confucianism, 91

Neo-Platonism, 149

Neo-Taoism, 58, 67, 114

Neumann, Erich, 17-19, 24, 27, 63

Newtonian physics, 190

Nicholas of Cusa, 57

Nietzsche, Friedrich, xvi, 11, 33, 45, 90

Non-action, non-attachment (see Wu-wei)

Non-assertion, fem. mode of being of, 316
in fem. prin., 28, 32-35
in Spinoza, 140-213, 235, 250-62
in Taoism, 50, 85, 90, 107-108, 110, 113, 119-20, 125-34

Non-being, Tao as, 52, 55, 57-60, 62, 66, 67, 70, 76, 79, 87, 99-100, 102, 109-111, 113, 155 (see also Wu)

Nondifferentiation, fem. (see Wholeness)

Non-human beings, 201-202, 205

Non-interference, fem. value of,
in Spinoza, 239
in Taoism, 80, 111, 113, 115, 125-25, 127, 131, 133-34, 136

Non-possession, 62, 106-107, 113, 128, 132

Non-violence (see Violence, fem. rejection of)

Northrop, F. S. C., 96

Notions, Spinozistic, common, 183, 191 (see also Ideas, adequate)
Pure, 160

OBJECTIVITY, MASC.
MASC, VALUE OF, 29,
79, 83, 101

Oldenberg, 200

One, the; Oneness, xvi,
38, 42, 43, 52-53,
55-56, 62-63, 68-70,
74, 80, 86, 96, 106,
111-12, 114, 117,
141-42, 145, 147-48,
152-53, 155, 162,
180, 192-93, 201,
204, 207-208, 225,
233-34, 242, 249,
262, 264
and the many, 48, 51,
52, 57, 62, 93, 118,
142, 145, 148, 150-
64, 174, 183

'Ontological exper-
ience', 60, 78-80
(see also Ming)

Opinion (first level
knowl.), 76, 166,
170, 172, 181, 214
(see also Imagination
in Spinoza)

Opposites, interaction
of, 55, 64-65, 67-69,
98, 102-103, 107-108,
110, 112, 147, 172
(see also Yin/Yang
polarity)

Order,
fem. sense of, 39,
63-65, 67, 83, 98,
106, 114, 143, 158,
159, 227, 259
masc. sense of, 16,
41, 43, 179-80

Otherness (fem. as),
xxi-xxii, 8, 11, 35,
44, 51, 93, 149, 177,
180

'Ought' (masc.), 15, 27,
54, 84, 89, 172, 178-80,
182, 190, 194, 237, 240,
266 (see also 'Is' vs.
'Ought')

PALLAS ATHENA, 25

Pantheism, xviii, 57

Paradox in fem. perspec-
tive, xxiii, 13, 22, 27,
29, 53-54, 58, 70, 72,
82, 94, 100, 102-103,
108, 110, 112-13, 129-
30, 149, 155-56, 174,
177, 190, 202, 204-205,
246-47

"Participation" (partici-
pare) experience in
reality,
in fem. principle, 24,
27, 36, 38, 44, 47, 271
in Spinoza, 141, 151,
153-54, 164, 182, 184-
186, 189, 197, 201, 231,
233, 262 (see also Union
with God)
in Taoism, 51, 57, 76,
78, 80, 82-84, 87, 89,
93-94, 96-97, 133-34

Passions, 100, 116, 118
155, 170, 173-74, 178,
195, 202, 205, 214, 216-
21, 223, 225, 239-40,
242-43, 245, 249, 251-
52, 260, 263, 274, 281

Passivity, fem. Trait of,
2, 12, 15, 28, 34, 35,
54, 85, 97, 112-13 (see
also Receptivity)

Patriarchal society, 26,
40-41

Paul, Saint, xviii, 311
(Note 5)

Peace, fem. value of,
111, 117, 136, 194,
224, 266-67
  in society, 73, 131,
  135, 234, 241-42,
  244, 249, 267, 261,
  264, 265, 267
  of mind, 42, 169-70,
  178, 187, 191, 210,
  213, 215, 220, 234

Penis envy, 12

Perfection, xxiv, 45,
103, 144, 153, 158,
163, 168, 240, 266
  individual, 169-71,
  174-78, 181, 185-87,
  189-90, 192-209, 212,
  214, 117, 220, 222,
  226-29
  Social, 230, 231-32,
  234-35, 236, 241,
  255, 257, 265, 275

Perspective, change of,
59, 63, 66, 73, 80,
82, 94, 104, 124,
145-46, 149-51, 158-
59, 171, 177, 181,
188, 202, 203, 216,
232, 242, 266, 307
(note 37) (see also
Fem. perspective;
Masc. perspective)

Persona, 1, 14, 123,
145, 160, 208

Philo Judaeus of
Alexandria, 149

Philosophy, 1, 165,
169, 179, 183-84,
191-93, 198-200,
206-208, 211, 213,
126, 228, 258, 267
(see also Fem. phil.
Masc. phil.)

Physician (fem. and masc.) 29

Physics, 141, 190, 231,
309 (note 67)

Piety, 167, 200, 223, 257

Ping (weapons, soldiers),
129

Plato, xiii, 24, 26, 37,
41-42, 125, 169, 182,
230, 245, 279

Plotinus, 57

Plutarch, 37

Polarity, 1, 4, 6, 7, 31
  approaches to, 7-15, 46
  (see also Biological
  approach; Cultural
  approach; Symbolic
  approach)

Politicans, politics
(masc.), 29, 236-37, 250

Positive Narcissism, 316
  in fem. prin., 22, 30,
  43, 45, 269, 273
  in Spinoza, 147, 151-53,
  195, 203-06, 209-10, 212,
  218, 221, 225, 233-34,
  241, 243-45, 249-50,
  251, 255, 259, 261, 262,
  264, 267, 282
  in Taoism, 61, 83, 92,
  94-96, 119-20, 125, 129,
  134

Potential, individual (see
Te; Virtue/Power)

Power (fem.), 24-25, 50,
53, 61, 67-68, 78, 83,
85-86, 89-91, 93-94, 96,
105, 109-10, 113, 119,
121, 125, 130, 133-34,
140, 148, 159, 161, 168,
173, 178, 181, 185, 188-

89, 193, 195-209, 211, 215, 217-22, 226, 229, 231, 233, 236, 240, 244, 252, 254, 258, 262, 264, 283

Pragmatism
fem., 127, 298-99, 213, 225, 237, 263,
masc., 40, 237

Pregnancy,
physical, 25, 36, 48, 63
spiritual, 25, 48

Priestess, woman as, 17

Principle of being, xv, xvii, 3, 316
(see also Fem. prin.; Masc. prin.)

Principles of the Philosophy of Rene Descartes, 168, 249, 176

Process philosophy and Taoism, 68

Profit,
fem., 59-60, 106, 124, 204-05, 243, 261
masc., 59, 106, 243

Progress, masc. value of, 29, 41, 122

Protestant work ethic (masc.), 16

Psyche, 2, 13, 16, 21, 25, 31, 51

Psychoanalysis, 48

Psychology, 1

P'u (Uncarved Block), 54, 59-60, 62, 101, 122

Purdah, 12

Puritan morality, 16

QUIESCENCE (SEE CHING)

Radical Empiricism, 316
in fem. prin., 27, 270
in Spinoza, 142, 184-94, 216, 227, 234-35, 259, 266
in Taoism, 50, 75, 79, 80, 116

Rationalism, rationality (masc.), xxii, 16, 26, 40, 71, 75, 81, 88-89, 91-92, 96, 111, 153, 165-67, 187, 190, 199, 227, 222, 247, 257

Real self (see Shared self)

Realism (fem. acceptance of reality), 273, 275,
in fem. prin., 11, 15, 27, 28, 35, 42, 84
in Spinoza, 158, 194, 210-25, 227, 233, 236-37, 242-43, 248, 250, 255-58, 260-61
in Taoism, 66, 84, 89, 92, 98, 101, 106, 108, 119

Reason, 43, 70, 116, 140, 155, 158, 167-69, 171, 174, 181, 190, 200, 207-208, 233, 240, 245, 246, 251
guidance of in Spinoza, 142, 145, 165, 185, 187-88, 193-94, 201, 203, 205, 206, 212, 215-17, 219, 221-23, 234-35, 239, 242, 244, 245, 247-48, 260, 263
reconstructions of, 75, 78, 142, 144-46, 150-53,

155, 163, 164, 172-73, 177-78, 180, 182-84, 186-90, 200, 227, 228, 239, 242, 249, 308 (note 50)
Taoist probs. with, 65, 72, 102
(see also Discursive reason)

Receptive, the (see also K'un), 3-7, 21, 46, 47, 53, 97

Receptivity, fem. mode of being of, xxii, 2, 9, 28, 32-35, 272 - 73 277, 316-17
in fem. prin., 33, 36, 47, 268, 272
in Spinoza, 139, 192, 209-25, 233-35, 250
in Taoism, 50, 71, 80, 85, 90, 94, 97-114, 119, 120, 125, 133

Reconciliation with reality (see Wholeness)

Reinforcement theory, 222-23, 243, 245, 252, 283

Relatedness, 63
(see also Eros/relatedness)

Relativity of masc. values (see Homocentric view)

Religion, 42
fem., 38
Spinoza's view of, 152, 156, 168, 183, 200, 206, 216, 222, 223, 228, 257, 258, 310-11 (note 82)
(see also Taoist religion)

Republic, Plato's, 125, 245

Responsibility, individual, 42, 50, 126, 132-33, 220 253, 280-84

Rest, repose (fem.), 5, 9, 18, 64

Returning action of Tao (Fu), 64, 71-73, 77, 81, 86-87, 89-90, 93, 115, 124, 133, 317

Reversion principle (fan), 53, 55, 58, 65, 67, 68-69, 85, 91, 94, 96, 102-103, 107, 112, 124, 128, 131, 132, 134

Rilke, 37

Root, returning to, 58-60, 64, 77, 98-99, 109, 112, 115
(see also Returning action)

Rousseau, 134

Rubaiyat, 280

SACRED AND PROFANE, 44

Sage, 6, 65, 88
(see also Taoist sage)

Sage-sovereign (see Taoist sage-sovereign)

Salome, Lou-Andreas, 1, 2, 22, 30, 33, 36, 48

Salvation, 16, 26, 101, 117, 178, 200, 201, 207, 222, 226
(see also Blessedness)

Sartre, Jean-Paul

Savioress, woman as, 7

Scholasticism, 144

Schopenhauer, Arthur, xxi, 23, 37

Schumacher, E. F., 120

Science, scientist (masc.), 29, 41
  in Spinozistic system, 167, 171, 172, 175, 190, 200, 249, 266-67, 309 (note 67)

Seductress, woman as, 7, 19

Self, 10, 13, 31, 80-81, 95, 114, 117
  ego, narrow, 22, 25, 29, 43, 55, 72, 80, 94, 97, 99, 117, 120, 129, 203, 234, 261, 277, 314
  shared, extended communal, 21, 25, 27, 29, 30, 32, 34, 43, 45, 55, 72, 78, 80, 86, 93-95, 97-99, 117, 119-20, 124, 129, 134, 182, 195, 203, 205, 218, 221, 234, 243, 251, 261, 262, 272, 278, 282, 317

Self-interest, 43, 72, 86, 93, 96, 98, 120-21, 124, 129, 134, 151, 157, 158, 195-96, 198, 203-06, 218, 221, 231, 233-34, 235, 239, 241-42, 243, 247, 249-50, 254, 260, 262

Self-preservation, 43, 195, 198-99, 203-05, 211-12, 218, 220, 225, 239-40, 242, 244, 247, 252, 257-58, 264, 266

Self-sacrifice, 20-21, 129

Sense data/experience, 269
  in Spinoza, 159, 166, 170, 171-72, 175, 183, 187, 190-91, 195, 201, 226, 227-33
  in Taoism, 73, 75-79, 116-19

Sensuality, integration of in fem. prin., 21
  in Spinoza, 196, 214, 231-33, 273
  in Taoism, 86, 116, 118, 122

Sensuous philosopher, Spinozistic, 226, 231-33

Sex, xiv, xxiii, 32

Sexual intercourse, 36, 232
  in Taoist religion, 36, 118
  symbolism of, 20, 36, 118

Sexuality, fem. function of, xiv, 3, 13, 21, 36, 47, 48, 119, 273
  masc. prob. with, 36, 42

Shared self (see Self, shared)

Shelley, Mary Wollstonecraft, 230

Shen (self), 117

Simplicity, 59-60, 80, 99,

348

101, 103, 111, 113,
122, 123, 126-27, 136,
139, 164

Sin, woman as symbol of,
36

Skinner, B. F., 282

Slave of passion, 212,
214, 252
(see also Bondage,
human)

Small is Beautiful, 120

Smith, Huston, 295,
(note 7)

Social conditioning of
gender differences,
11ff.

Social Contract, 43,
134

Socialism, 133, 261

Socio-political
philosophy, xxiv
in fem. phil., 38-46,
268
in Spinoza, 141, 192-
94, 196, 206, 233-67
in Taoism, 51, 106,
112, 119-37

Socrates, 279

Solitude, life of,
in Spinoza, 206, 243-
44, 249
in Taoism, 19, 120

Son/lover archetype, 2

Sophia, fem. wisdom
archetype, 17, 26-27,
47, 79

Sorceress, woman as, 5

Sorrow and impotence, 73,
169, 205-06, 223
(see also Passions)

Soul, xvi, 16-17, 20, 31
(see also Anima;
Psyche)

Sovereign,
Spinozistic, 139, 194,
235, 241, 244, 250-62
limitations on, 245, 253-
58
Taoist, 88, 112, 126-35

Space and Time, 81

Spinoza, Benedict de, xvii-
xx, xxiv, 48, 138-267,
268
epistemology, 140-41,
148, 156, 164-92, 193,
194, 196, 198, 200, 207,
211, 217, 224, 233,
238, 280
ethics, 140-41, 163,
174, 177, 192-233, 240-
41, 242, 245, 264
metaphysics, 140-64,
167, 180, 182, 187, 190,
191-94, 196, 200-201,
209-11, 216-17, 224,
233, 238, 250, 259, 280,
283
modes of being, 192-267,
probs. of system, 140-
41, 148-50, 167-68, 173,
177, 184-85, 193, 198-
99, 208, 229-30, 246-49,
267
Socio-political philo-
sophy, 140-41, 192-94,
196, 206, 233-67

Spinozism (see Spinoza)

Spinozistic philosopher,
140, 167, 172, 179, 190,
209-26, 229-30, 231-34,
240, 242, 248-49, 267,
272-274

349

Spirituality (fem.), 36, 66, 82, 101

Spontaneity (fem.), 9, 42, 47, 54, 65, 67, 69, 71, 75, 79, 85, 87, 89, 91, 97, 111, 113-15, 118-19, 125, 128, 130, 135, 136, 159, 219, 225, 229, 250, 251, 259, 262

Stability, fem. value of, 18, 21, 263 (see also Substance; Tao)

State, function of, 311 (note 103)
as organism, 236, 262-63, 265, 267, 275
fef., 39
masc., 40, 45
Spinozistic, 240, 241, 244, 247-79, 265
Taoist, 120, 125, 127, 131-34

State of Nature, 134-35, 194, 235, 238-41, 263

Steinbeck, John, 9

Subject/object distinction, 36, 59-60, 79, 82, 178, 184, 186, 191,

Subjectivity (fem.), 16, 30, 79, 83, 98, 226

Sub species aeternitatis (under the form of eternity), 35, 40, 52, 63, 156, 172, 174, 185-86, 189, 191, 203, 208, 246

Substance/God, Spinozistic, 141-67, 170-74, 178, 181-82, 184-85, 90, 194, 198-99, 202, 207-209, 213, 215-18, 225, 226, 227-28, 232, 234, 236, 262-63, 268, 271, 279-82
encompassing, 141-45, 151, 163, 172, 180, 187
eternal, 143-45, 154, 183, 186, 188, 191, 202, 207-208, 215, 262
ground of being, 141-44, 151, 166, 182, 189, 191-92
immanent, 144-45, 151, 159, 182, 188
immutable, 144-45, 159-61, 188, 208
impartial, 151-53, 198. 210, 218, 240, 254, 281
indivisible (undifferentiated), 141-45, 148, 152, 155, 186-87, 231
infinite, 143-44, 146, 159, 163, 182-83, 202, 207
necessary existence, 141, 143-44, 148, 155
self-caused, 143-45, 226
sustaining source, 141, 145, 147, 154, 162
ultimate cause, 143-45, 147, 186

Suffering, fem. view, 33, 213
masc. view, 16, 33

Suicide, 283

Sun (the Gentle), 4, 5

Sung dynasty landscapes, 79

Super-ego, 42

Survival, 21, 109, 136, 203, 211, 251, 255, 277
personal, 34, 101, 195,

219, 234-35, 244, 250
social, 124, 136,
235, 250, 263, 265-
66, 267

Suzuki, 44, 74

Symbolic approach to
  polarity, 7, 13-15,
  46

Sympathy, 114, (see
  also Compassion;
  Tz'u)

Symposium, 26, 290
  (note 95)

Synchronicity, 43, 65,
  309 (note 67)

TA T'UNG (grand
  infusion), 82

T'ai Chi (the Great
  Ultimate), 59, 87

T'ai-yin (the Great
  Dark), 3

T'ai-yang (the Great
  Light), 3

Tantrism, 36

Tao, xx 49-137, 141,
  186, 219, 270-71, 317
  dynamic, 53-54
  encompassing, 55-57,
  73, 77, 80, 91, 93
  eternal, 56, 61
  immanent, 56, 57
  impartial, 66, 83, 90
  maternal source, 52,
  54, 57, 60-62, 68,
  91, 96, 103, 106
  Named (yu-ming), 52,
  54, 57, 61, 62-69,
  93, 269
  Nameless (wu-ming),
  52, 54-62, 68, 70,
  77, 93, 122, 141, 269
  of humanity (see Te),
  stable, unchanging, 53,
  54, 56, 67-68, 109

Tao-an, 111

Taoism, xix-xx, 6, 48-137,
  141, 142, 162, 182, 186,
  194, 233, 242, 259, 262,
  264, 269-77
  epistemology, 49, 69-83,
  85-86, 96, 101
  ethics, 49, 51, 54, 65,
  69, 78, 84-119, 132,
  134, 136
  metaphysics, 49, 51-69,
  70, 77, 80, 82-86, 91,
  93, 96, 101, 105, 107,
  109, 112, 115-16, 127,
  132, 134, 136, 142
  modes of being, 83-137
  probs. of system, 50, 83
  socio-political phil.,
  49, 51, 84, 106, 113,
  119-37

Taoist philosopher, 50,
  72, 102

Taoist religion, 96

Taoist sage, 54, 72, 74-
  81, 84-85, 87-88, 92-
  96, 126, 128, 272
  ideal of, 97-114, 119,
  121, 125, 135, 219

Taoist sage-sovereign, 84,
  88, 95, 109, 111, 120,
  125-36, 229-30, 239,
  252, 274

Taoist society, 119-37,
  272-73
  criteria of, 121-22, 133

Tao Te Ching, xix-xx,
  xxii, xxiv, 50-52, 84,
  87-89, 91, 96, 114-17,
  120, 133, 138, 141-42,

162, 268, 273, 275
imagery of, 17, 52,
82, 114, 118, 142
references to chapters, (1) 52, 59, 62,
74, 114, 117; (2) 66,
68, 101; (3) 87, 125;
(5) 66, 74; (6) 61;
(7) 61, 93; (8) 64,
106; (9) 107; (10)
75, 104, 105, 117;
(11) 57, 59; (12) 73,
87, 116, 117; (13)
116, 129; (14) 58;
(15) 100; (16) 64,
95, 97, 104, 114,
135; (17) 131; (18)
122; (19) 94, 123;
(20) 61, 73, 102;
(21) 62, 89; (22)
101, 105; (23) 67,
104; (24) 106-107;
(25) 61, 67, 113,
124; (26) 108; (27)
106; (28) 60, 69,
108, 112, 129; (29)
90, 99, 127; (30)
127; (31) 126; (32)
122, 129; (33) 72,
91, 94, 106; (34) 62,
106; (35) 135; (37)
110; (38) 90-91; (39)
61, 129; (40) 59, 69;
(41) 61, 101, 103;
(42) 53, 62, 64, 68,
107, 126; (43) 89,
109, 110; (44) 94;
(45) 102, 108; (46)
106; (47) 72, 78;
(48) 72, 96, 108,
111; (49) 105, 125;
(50) 95; (51) 90,
105; (52) 60-61, 62,
116; (53) 126; (54)
120; (55) 97, (56)
74, 98, 105; (57)
130, 131; (58) 105,
131; (59) 129; (60)
130; (61) 134; (63)
107, 111; (64) 99,
107, 114; (65) 73;
(66) 130; (67) 103, 109;
(68) 107; (69) 127; (70)
103; (71) 72; (73) 109;
(74) 120; (75) 130;
(76) 89, 108; (77) 150,
109; (78) 128; (79) 128;
(80) 121; (81) 72, 74,
105, 128

Te (virtue/power) 50, 65,
 67, 81, 82, 84-97, 104-
 105, 107, 109, 112, 114,
 115, 117-21, 124-26,
 132, 134, 136, 156, 198,
 272, 277

Technology, role of
 in masc. society, 41,
 266
 in Spinoza, 246, 263,
 266
 in Taoism, 122, 131

Teleology,
 fem. rejection of, 151-
 53, 167-78, 266
 masc. adherence to, 151,
 266

Temperament, social
 assignment of, 1, 11,
 18, 44 (see also Mead,
 Margaret)

Ten Thousand Things, 54,
 61, 64, 67-69, 83, 86,
 89, 91-93, 96, 99, 106,
 118, 270

Teresa of Avila, 36, 44

Theologian, Spinoza's view
 of, 167

Theologico-Political
 Treatise, 167-68, 200,
 222

Theology, 1, 39, 43, 143
 fem. (immanence), 44
 masc. (transcendent), 44
 Negative, 149

"Thing of reason', 150, 175-76, 178, 212, 223, 238, 240, 271, 284 (see also Reason, reconstructions of)

Thought (see Attribute of)

Thrasymachus, 95

Tiger/tigress, fem. image of 19, 90

Time, gender differences in, 9

Tolerance, fem. value of, xxii
in Spinoza, 256, 258
in Taoism, 105, 112

Totalitarianism, fem. rejection of, 239, 250, 254-55, 262
thought control, 257

Tranquillity, fem. value of,
in Spinozism, 210, 246, 259
in Taoism, 64, 97-102, 105, 109, 111, 119, 125-27, 132-33, 135-36

Transformative character, xxiv, 5, 7, 17-19, 24-28, 36, 47, 49, 51, 62-69, 76, 78, 90, 126, 140-42, 145-46, 153, 162, 184, 192, 235, 268, 269, 317
enlightenment, 18, 32
dynamism, 10, 18, 25, 46, 52-53, 59, 65, 67-68, 80
inspiration, 18, 47, 79
salvation, 18, 24, 26, 47
transcendent, 18, 25, 26, 54

Transpersonal psychology, 41

Trinity, Christian, 26

'True World', 45

Truth, 51, 55, 71, 74-76, 80, 82, 86, 102, 112, 115-16, 144, 159, 165-67, 169-70, 180-81, 183-84, 189, 191-92, 211-12, 214, 228, 241, 258, 266, 308-309 (note 62)

Tse (raw material), 106
tse-jan, 67, 114, 132

Tui (the Joyous) 4, 5

Tz'u (compassion, love), 54-55, 60, 62, 78, 82, 92, 110, 113, 317

UBERMENSCH, 90, 229

Ulanov, Ann Belford, 7, 15, 26, 31

Uncarved Block (P'u), 54, 59-60, 62, 78, 80, 90, 101, 113

Unconscious (fem.), 1, 6, 13, 16, 18, 20, 26-27, 51, 53-54, 78-79, 81, 83, 88-90, 94, 96-97, 99, 115, 118-19, 121-22, 124-25, 130, 157

Understanding, Spinozistic mode of, 153, 160, 162, 174, 182 (see also Attribute of Thought)

Union with God, 183, 186-87, 208, 220, 227, 246

Unity, fem. value of, 17, 30-31, 53, 54, 56-57, 82, 86, 96, 135, 146-54, 158, 160, 172-73, 178, 180, 182, 187, 190, 202, 253, 261-63, 265

Untermensch, 90, 230

Upanishads, 76

Uroborus (the Great Round), 2, 19, 24, 46, 61

Urvernunft (primal reason), 55

Utopia, 40, 45, 134, 136
  fem. criticism of, 237

VALLEY, FEM. SYMBOL OF, 78, 90, 104, 113

Van Over, Raymond, 57, 102

Vegetative nature (fem.), xxi (note 14), 10, 37, 90, 118

Venus idol, 10

Verbs reflecting gender differences, 15

Vessel, fem. symbol of, 20, 59 (see also Womb)

Violence, fem. rejection of, 35, 98, 125, 127-28, 133, 244

Virgin, archetype, 7, 10, 21

Virtue/power, xxiv, 317
  in Spinoza, 140, 178, 181-82, 194-211, 214-216, 219, 221-26, 231, 234-35, 238, 245, 250, 252, 272, 274, 282
  in Taoism, 50, 67, 84-86, 89-91, 93-94, 96, 99, 104-106, 109, 113, 119, 121, 124, 130, 134, 136 (see also Te)

WALDEN TWO, 282

Waley, Arthur, 56, 89, 117

Wang (cosmopolitan), 105

Warfare, avoidance of,
  in Spinoza, 262, 264-65, 267
  in Taoism, 128-33

Water, fem. symbol of, 5, 21, 63-64, 90, 94, 113, 116, 118, 120

Watson, Burton, 96

Watts, Alan, 68

Way, 55-57, 62, 68-70, 74, 99, 106, 110

"Weakness", fem. value of (see Fem. "weakness")

Wealth, 108, 196, 212, 232, 244

Weisheit (wisdom), 7 (see also Wisdom; Sophia)

Weltanschauung (world view), xxiii-xiv, xx, xiii-xxiv, 1, 3, 13, 16, 39, 44-46, 194, 280

Wen (ornament), 124

Western view of philosophy, xvii-xxi, 55-56, 65, 70, 74, 77, 84, 89, 114, 138, 142-43, 166, 169, 190, 194, 231-32, 279-80

Wheeler, John A., 309 (note 67)

Wholeness of fem. being, xviii, 29, 31, 35, 47, 49, 56, 57, 62, 64-65, 71, 77, 79, 81, 84-87, 92, 94-96, 99, 101, 110-111, 114, 117, 119-21, 123-24, 129, 135-36, 142, 145-47, 150, 153, 157, 174, 179, 184, 186, 189, 192-93, 195-96, 202-204, 206-209, 211, 216, 226, 27, 229-30, 232, 236, 238, 243, 262, 269, 272

Wilhelm, Richard, 4

Will, 37, 148, 154, 181, 193, 284

Wisdom (fem.), 2, 20, 26-28, 65, 72, 75, 79-80, 92, 103, 107, 126, 130, 167, 183-84, 188, 201, 211-12 (see also Sophia)

Wittgenstein, Ludwig, 73-74

Wolf, A., xviii, 149

Wolfson, H. A., 279-80

Womb, fem. symbol of, 5, 19-20, 48, 151
birth and rebirth, 25

closed (Elementary char.), 5, 18, 53-54, 63, 67, 69, 155

Wu (Nonbeing), 52, 58, 62, 76, 93, 110

Wu-chi (Ultimateless), 87

Wu-ming (Nameless), 52, 58 (see also Tao)

Wu-yu (negation of desire, 100

Wu-wei ("non-action"), 53-54, 59, 80, 85, 97, 110-11, 113-14, 119, 125, 128, 131-32, 134-36, 239, 252, 273-74, 317 (see also Non-assertion)

Yang, 3, 5, 21, 50, 68-69, 91, 130 (see also Yin/Yang polarity)

Yarrow sticks, 65

Yi Pu-liang, 96

Yielding (fem.), xxii, 3-6, 14, 85, 90, 101, 109, 113, 125, 128, 134, 202, 211, 221, 250

Yin, xx, 3, 5, 19, 21, 50, 59-60, 68-69, 85-86, 90-91, 97, 101, 109, 113-14, 130, 140, 233, 275

/Yang polarity, xvi, 3-7, 14, 38, 46, 49, 62, 67-68, 102, 118, 161, 269

Yu (Being), 52, 58, 64, 76, 93

Yu-ming (Named) Tao, 52

Zarathustra, 19, 90, 288-89 (note 70)

Zen, 44, 86-87
    koan, 79

ABOUT THE AUTHOR

Sandra A. Wawrytko, Ph. D., originally from Chicago, Illinois, received her undergraduate training at Knox College, graduating magna cum laude. Continuing her training in philosophy, she was awarded an M.A. and Ph. D. from Washington University in St. Louis, Missouri, where she held a graduate fellowship. At Washington University, she studied under such distinguished professors as Richard H. Popkin and Richard S. Rudner. Professor Wawrytko has delivered papers at several international conferences, including The Interamerican Congress of Philosophy, The Third World Congress, and The World Congress of Logotherapy, and has also been a speaker at a conference of the American Philosophical Association conference. A major portion of her research has focused on Chinese philosophy, including an article soon to appear in Philosophy East and West. Her work in progress includes a text and companion anthology on Chinese ethics. As a member of the Board of Advisors for The Institute of Logotherapy in Berkeley, California, Professor Wawrytko has worked closely with Dr. Viktor E. Frankl, of Vienna, Austria, founder of the Logotherapy movement. In her position as Director of The World Congress of Logotherapy, she is coordinating the 1982 conference to be held in Hartford, Connecticut. Among her most recent publications is the Analecta Frankliana, the collected papers of The 1980 World Congress of Logotherapy of which she is both editor and contributor. Her teaching experience includes positions at Washington University and the University of San Diego. Currently she is on the faculty of the department of philosophy at San Diego State University.